Constructing Rhetorical Education

Edited by Marie Secor and Davida Charney
Penn State University

SOUTHERN ILLINOIS UNIVERSITY PRESS
Carbondale and Edwardsville

Library of Congress Cataloging-in-Publication Data

Constructing rhetorical education / edited by Marie Secor and Davida
    Charney.
          p.   cm.
    "This book grew out of the 1988 Penn State Conference on Rhetoric
and Composition which honored the career of Professor Wilma R.
Ebbitt"—Pref.
    Includes bibliographical references and index.
    ISBN 0-8093-1764-8
    1. English language—Rhetoric—Study and teaching—Congresses.
I. Charney, Davida. II. Ebbitt, Wilma R. III. Penn State
Conference on Rhetoric and Composition (1988)
PE1404.C63375 1992
808'.0427—dc20
                                                    91-15153
                                                         CIP

The paper used in this publication meets the minimum requirements of
American National Standard for Information Sciences
–Permanence of Paper for Printed Library Materials, ANSI Z39.48-1984. ⊗

Frontispiece: Wilma R. Ebbitt
(Photograph by Greg Grieco)

Contents

Preface

This book offers an argument for what it takes to construct a complete rhetorical education. It espouses neither a single methodology of composition research (such as process description or ethnography) nor does it adopt a univocal ideological or pedagogical stance (such as expressivism or neo-classicism). Rather, the approach we take here is pragmatic and pluralistic. We assume that a rhetorical education, like all other rhetorical pursuits, is teleological; it pursues definite goals within specific cultural contexts. A rhetorical education is not limited to teaching freshman composition (or any specific writing course), and the contexts in which it occurs are not limited to classrooms. An effective rhetorical education certainly results in the growth of writing skills, but its larger goal is to foster a critical habit of mind.

A rhetorical education requires that all the inhabitants of a classroom understand the grounds of agreement (and disagreement) that underlie the discourse they examine and produce. Although, as teachers, our goal is to help students recognize rhetorical strategies at play in the discourse they read and incorporate them appropriately in what they write, we must also be aware of the rhetorical character of the classroom itself. The grounds of agreement on which we meet our students are influenced by the makeup of the individuals in the room—their ages, genders, cultural heritages, and so on. But the inhabitants of the classroom alone do not determine what goes on there; as we all know, action is also shaped and constrained by the larger institution, including such agents as university administrators and faculty in other disciplines. And, of course, the larger cultural and political milieu shapes the goals of educational institutions by defining what it means to be an educated citizen. These forces all impinge upon the writing classroom, but the education fostered there, if effective, does not simply reflect externally imposed goals and values. A rhetorical education is both socially constructed and socially constructing.

In his recent *College English* essay, Walter H. Beale makes exactly this point, noting that "every serious treatment of rhetoric is also by impli-cation—and sometimes by design—a work of cultural criticism" (October 1990, 626-640). His definition of rhetorical education envisions an appro-priate balance between the fulfillment of private and public goals. In his view,

> Rhetorical education is an attempt to shape a certain kind of character capa-ble of using language effectively to carry on the practical and moral busi-ness of a polity. It is based implicitly or explicitly on ideals of individual competence and political well-being. Its dual purposes are the cultivation of the individual and the success of a culture. This is why thoughtful treat-ments and programs of rhetoric are inevitably cultural projects: they are either celebrations of a particular character type and a particular ideal or—at their most engaging moments—attempts to change or rehabilitate both char-acter and culture (626).

This is a generous definition. It recognizes that a cultural critique simultaneously celebrates, censors, and builds on shared values. It emphasizes that rhetorical education reflects and influences the socio-political culture of contemporary America, the pedagogical culture of the classroom, and the culture of the workplace. Finally, a rhetorical educa-tion has consequences for individual students beyond what happens to them in college; it initiates intellectual activity that we hope will continue throughout their careers. Given such a definition, it is clear why we adopt a pluralistic approach; no single methodological or ideological perspec-tive on rhetoric and composition studies will suffice. We need input from many disciplines, including philosophy, psychology, history, sociology, and linguistics. We need to examine writing in all its aspects from the rough drafts of a struggling freshman to the preserved texts of the profes-sional orator.

This volume gathers together essays that illustrate these many aspects of rhetorical education. The shape of the book is like an hour-glass. It begins and ends with broad cultural concerns, narrowing in the middle to consider the processes of individual writers and readers. The first section, "How Culture Constructs Students and Teachers," considers how race and gender influence the attitudes teachers and students in writing classrooms adopt toward literacy. The second section, "How Institutions Construct the Writing Classroom," focuses on the culture of the college or university setting, exploring how writing programs adapt to specific institutional and disciplinary profiles. The next two sections, "How Writers Develop" and "How Writers Respond to the Needs of Readers," narrow the focus, examining the growth of rhetorical skill; these essays relate cognitive and social approaches to writing, showing how writers develop textual strategies that evoke and satisfy their readers' expectations. In the final two sections, the perspective broadens out again. Section V, "How Discourse Communities Construct Readers and Writers," considers the writing practices of academics and professionals in the workplace. Section VI, "How Affective Discourse Constructs Its Public," expands the notion of readership to the polity at large. The essays in this section show how orators and institutions use pathos to shape public opinion and action.

Rather than discussing the individual essays in detail here, we provide extended introductory notes at the head of each section. These notes explore the relationships among the essays and foreground the larger issues they raise for rhetorical education. In drawing these theoretical and pedagogical implications from an essay (or conjunctions of essays), we often extrapolate from the particular conclusions drawn by the authors to issues of broader concern. Individual authors may not agree with the larger points that we attempt to make. But we believe that this volume as a whole offers a consistent argument for pragmatism and pluralism.

One thing we have learned from putting this book together is that rhetorical education, as a form of cultural critique, necessarily encompasses a wide variety of classroom practices and research agendas. These practices and methodologies are polysemous; that is, any political or social ideology can be advanced by many different practices, and any given practice can serve different ideologies. This realization is somewhat counterintuitive, for our first impulse may be to assume that our teaching practices and our ideologies are isomorphic. For example, we may assume that classroom governance ought to recapitulate the dynamic of the ideal social and political condition. But the relationship between teachers and students may not—and perhaps even should not—parallel that between government and governed. Outside the classroom, teachers and students are equal citizens, but inside, teachers exercise their legitimate authority and expertise. Still, we have to be vigilant that our classroom practices do not undermine the political and cultural goals that we intend them to support. Nor should we dismiss useful practices just because they have previously been used to advance agendas other than our own.

This book grew out of the 1988 Penn State Conference on Rhetoric and Composition, which honored the career of Professor Wilma R. Ebbitt and her fourteen productive and influential years with the English Department at Penn State. Many of the essays included here were written by Professor Ebbitt's former students and current admirers. The concept of rhetorical education advanced here is one that she has embodied in practice and promoted in exhortation throughout her career. Professor Ebbitt is the consummate classroom teacher as evidenced by numerous awards from colleagues and the testimonials of generations of undergraduate and graduate students. In her continually evolving textbooks, she has drawn not only on her own matchless intuition as a writer and editor but also on every species of research. There is probably no research paradigm that she has dismissed as irrelevant, nor any that she has accepted uncritically. She has also had a continuing impact on the development of composition as a discipline, beginning in the early days of the Conference on College Composition and Communication. Although Wilma has always eschewed public notice, we shamelessly disregard her natural modesty in dedicating this book to her.

M.S. and D.C.

Acknowledgments

We are grateful to all the people who helped us produce this book. In particular, John Harwood encouraged us to undertake the project and offered sustaining technical advice and wry observations on the nature of computers. Linda Ferreira-Buckley helped us get started and find the shape of the book. Rosa Eberly copy edited, and along with Keith Diehl, designed and produced the volume, building on the groundwork laid by Robert Snyder. Kim Witherite kept our correspondence in order and typed cheerfully. We received generous financial support from David Palermo, Associate Dean for Research in the College of Liberal Arts, and from Christopher Clausen and Robert Secor as successive Heads of the English Department. We are also grateful to Lester Faigley, who read portions of the book in manuscript. Kenney Withers supported the project with much enthusiasm and made the editorial process seem simple. Finally, we thank all the authors represented here for submitting such good essays in the first place and for responding so thoughtfully and conscientiously to suggestions for revision.

Notes on Contributors

VALERIE M. BALESTER, Assistant Professor of English at Texas A & M University, received a Ph.D. in Rhetoric from the University of Texas at Austin. She earned her M.A. in English at Penn State University, where she took her first rhetoric course from Wilma Ebbitt. Reading Mina Shaughnessy's *Errors and Expectations* with Dr. Ebbitt and teaching basic writers from Pennsylvania's inner cities sparked her interest in Black English Vernacular speakers as Standard English writers.

KATHERINE BORLAND is a graduate student in English at Indiana University in Bloomington.

KATHLEEN S. BRANDT is Instructor of English Composition at the University of Colorado at Colorado Springs. Her special research interests include audience adaptation analysis, protocol analysis, intellectual development, and collaborative learning. She has published articles in *Research in the Teaching of English* (with Janice Hays and Kathryn Chantry) and in *The Arizona Bulletin,* and she is coauthor of a chapter in *A Sense of Audience in Written Communication.*

JOANN CAMPBELL decided to pursue rhetoric and composition after taking a course taught by Wilma Ebbitt. She is currently Assistant Professor of

English at Indiana University and is completing a manuscript on Gertrude Buck's feminist rhetoric and her teaching community.

DAVIDA CHARNEY is Assistant Professor of English at Penn State University. Her research focuses on document design, reading and writing processes, and the rhetoric of science. Her work has appeared in *Research in the Teaching of English, Memory and Cognition, Human Computer Interaction, Cognition and Instruction, The Journal of Business and Technical Communication*, and several collections of essays.

ANURADHA DINGWANEY teaches Anglophone literatures of the third world at Oberlin College. She has published essays on Salman Rushdie, cross-cultural pedagogy, and British Romanticism. She now is writing an essay on C. L. R. James as part of a book-length study of Anglophone immigrant writers whose works can be viewed as enactments of resistance.

DIANE DOWDEY is Assistant Professor of English at Sam Houston State University and participates in its writing across the university program. She is the author of *The Researching Reader: Source-Based Writings Across the Disciplines* and articles on the rhetoric of science. Her doctorate is from the University of Wisconsin.

JEANNE FAHNESTOCK is Associate Professor of English at the University of Maryland, where she directs the Professional Writing Program. Author of many essays on coherence, argument, and scientific rhetoric, she is also co-author of *A Rhetoric of Argument* and *Readings in Argument*. She and Marie Secor are working on *A Rhetoric of Style*.

JANICE N. HAYS is Associate Professor of English at the University of Colorado at Colorado Springs, where she also directs the Center for Excellence in Writing Across the Curriculum. She conducts research on writing and intellectual development and, more recently, on writing, intellectual development, and stylistic substructures linked to gender and race. Recent articles appear in *A Sense of Audience in Written Communication* (Duane Roen and Gesa Kirsch, editors) and forthcoming work in a collection on women's issues in rhetoric and composition.

ALETHA HENDRICKSON teaches in the Professional Writing Program at the University of Maryland. She has published several articles on writing, including a chapter on the rhetoric of CPA's in *Worlds of Writing*. She has also presented papers on professional *topoi*, modern rhetorical theory, and eighteenth-century accounting theory at CCCC, the Penn State Conference, and the Carolinas Symposium on British Studies. She is currently working on studies of the special *topoi* of accountancy and the rhetoric of intimidation.

ANNE J. HERRINGTON is Associate Professor of English and Director of the Writing Program at the University of Massachusetts at Amherst. With Charles Moran, she is editing a collection to be published by MLA, *Writing, Teaching, and Learning in the Disciplines*.

V. MELISSA HOLLAND is Senior Psychologist at the U.S. Army Research Institute in Alexandria, Virginia, where she studies the cognitive bases of foreign language learning and designs computer tools to teach languages. She has also conducted research on how to use technology to teach job skills and basic literacy to adults. Formerly at the American Institutes for Research (AIR), she investigated the writing and comprehension of technical text for AIR's Document Design Center.

STEVEN B. KATZ is Assistant Professor of English at North Carolina State University, where he teaches scientific and technical communication, rhetoric, and poetry writing. He has published both articles and poems that explore or enact the relationship among rhetoric, science, technology, and literature. He is currently working on a book on reader-response criticism, sophistic rhetoric, and the new physics.

ELIZABETH A. MCCORD teaches professional writing and journalism and law in the Department of English at the University of Cincinnati. Before returning to the classroom five years ago, she was a practicing attorney, specializing in employment relations and general litigation. She has published and presented papers examining diverse aspects of social rhetoric, including legal liability and gender differences in professional writing. She is currently studying the relationship between the power of judicial law and rhetoric.

LAWRENCE NEEDHAM is a Research Associate at Oberlin College. He is interested in the historiography of rhetoric and has published on the rhetoric(s) of British Romanticism. Currently, he is writing articles on Shelley and Landor examining the impact of empire-building and imperialist ideology on the production and reception of texts written in 1797-1832.

LOUISE WETHERBEE PHELPS is professor of Writing and English at Syracuse University, where she directs the Writing Program. She is author of *Composition as a Human Science: Contributions to the Self-Understanding of a Discipline* (Oxford, 1988) and has published articles and book chapters on diverse conceptual issues in composition theory, rhetoric, and teaching practice. She is currently completing, with Janet Emig, an edited volume of essays on feminism in composition and rhetoric.

MARY ROSNER is currently Director of Composition at the University of Louisville, where she teaches graduate courses in the rhetoric of science, the rhetoric of technical discourse, and the teaching of composition as well as undergraduate courses in business, technical, and professional writing, and freshman composition. She has published on Victorian literature, history of rhetoric, and technical writing.

CARMEN B. SCHMERSAHL is Associate Professor of Writing and Director of the Freshman Seminar at Mount Saint Mary's College, Emmitsburg, Maryland, where she tutors in the Writing Center, teaches advanced writing electives and the freshman seminar, and trains other freshman seminar faculty from across the college. In July 1991 she will become Associate Dean of the College. She has published and delivered papers on writing pedagogy and "The Mount's" core curriculum and freshman year program.

MARIE SECOR is Associate Professor of English at Penn State University. Her best-known work is on the theory of argumentation, though her research interests range from history of rhetoric to stylistics. Her research has appeared in *CCC, Written Communication, Pre/Text, Philosophy and Rhetoric*, and many other journals and collections; she is also coauthor, with Jeanne Fahnestock, of two books on argument, *A Rhetoric of Argument* and *Readings in Argument*. In 1990 she was named the Penn State Alumni Teaching Fellow, an honor previously held by Wilma Ebbitt.

CYNTHIA L. SELFE is Associate Professor of Composition and Communication at Michigan Technological University, where she serves as Assistant Head of the Humanities Department. With Art Young and Toby Fulwiler, she has participated in and written about MTU's writing-across-the-curriculum program in book chapters and journal articles. She has conducted numerous writing-across-the-curriculum workshops at the secondary and college levels, often focusing on computers as effective tools for supporting writing-across-the-curriculum efforts.

BARBARA M. SITKO, Assistant Professor of English and Director of the Avery Microcomputer Lab at Washington State University, received her Ph.D. from Carnegie Mellon University. An affiliate of the Center for the Study of Writing at Carnegie Mellon, her research focuses on writers' revising processes and on developing models of writing instruction based on cognitive process research. Her other interests include writing with computers and instructional uses of computers.

BYRON L. STAY is Associate Professor of Writing at Mount St. Mary's College in Emmitsburg, Maryland, and Director of the Writing and Communications Program. When he is not teaching argumentative writing or descriptive and narrative writing, he works in and manages the college Writing Center. He has published articles in the *Writing Center Journal*, the *Journal of Teaching Writing*, and the *Maryland English Journal*.

EVANGELINE MARLOS VARONIS is a Lecturer in the English Department of the University of Akron. She has published articles in the areas of discourse analysis, second language acquisition, and sociolinguistics. Her research interests include the negotiation of meaning between interlocutors and among author, reader, and text.

JEFFREY WALKER is Associate Professor of English at Penn State University. He is the author of *Bardic Ethos and the American Epic Poem: Whitman, Pound, Crane, Williams, Olson*, and of *Investigating Arguments: Readings for College Writing*, a rhetoric/reader focused on critical reading and argumentation, as well as articles on rhetoric and poetic discourse.

I

How Culture Constructs
Students and Teachers

In his recent critique of some overly facile applications of social and cognitive theories to composition pedagogy, Mike Rose notes that "social and political hierarchies end up encoded in sweeping cognitive dichotomies" (*CCC* 39 Oct. 1988, p. 268). The dichotomies that Rose discusses include field dependence vs. independence, left brain vs. right brain dominance, and orality vs. literacy. Within their psychological and anthropological contexts, these terms are generally used descriptively rather than diagnostically and may provide a set of useful distinctions. Rose points out, however, that when educators extract these terms and apply them to individuals "in a way that is meant to be value-free . . ., given our culture they are anything but neutral." One side of the dichotomy is taken as a sign of maturity, education, and intellectual sophistication, while the other is deprecated as a developmentally immature or culturally primitive stage, to be overcome by education. As Rose argues, these dichotomies have frequently been reductively misapplied to student writers, especially those in marginalized groups, resulting in profound social and political confusions.

The essays in this section examine the political and social implications of two powerful dichotomies that have come to shape the writing classroom: orality vs. literacy and feminist vs. traditional pedagogy. The familiar historical research on orality and literacy has entered composition studies in conjunction with the current resurgence of interest in promoting literacy, whether cultural or just plain. But the application of this research to writing pedagogy may carry along some subtle biases. The bias can go either way: toward preserving the authenticity of the oral voice or, more commonly, toward promoting an individual's progress along the scale of cognitive development from oral (read: illiterate) to literate—or, by extension, from nonstandard to standard English. Thus, those who invoke these terms sometimes privilege the oral voice as the more authentic and expressive, or, if they appeal to a cognitive developmental model, they deprecate the oral voice as a sign of inadequate education, or worse, arrested cognitive development. It is even possible to do both at once—romanticizing the oral voice as more authentic while somewhat reluctantly pushing students to write in the vapid but more politically and socially acceptable idiom of standard English.

A similar but less familiar dynamic comes into play in the call for a feminist pedagogy. In contrast to the orality/literacy debate, the feminist/traditionalist discussion is explicitly value-laden. Feminists want to empower marginalized women writers. More generally, they want to decenter the writing classroom, transforming it from a hierarchy dominated by traditional (usually male) authority into a more supportive and democratic environment. The feminist classroom thus liberates both men and women.

One of the means by which some feminists have attempted to achieve these goals is by rejecting agonistic discourse and encouraging self-expression. The reasoning goes something like this: as long as men have held power, the discourse of power has been agonistic; therefore, if women are to gain power, then they must use a different form of discourse, or else women are once again accommodating to male structures. One problem with this line of reasoning, however, is that it binds power and gender inextricably together and then conflates both with certain forms of discourse. In doing so, it assumes an essential cognitive, cultural, and political bipolarity between men and women. Women are assumed to have their own special kind of discourse antithetical to agonistic argument; therefore, the feminist classroom promotes expressive discourse. Although there are historical and cultural grounds for linking expressivist discourse and feminist ideology, we believe that such associations are accidental rather than essential. The linkage falsely implies that women are cognitively incapable of speaking effectively in the full range of discourse registers. While the focus on expressive discourse is intended to build women's confidence in their ability to speak and write, it may actually undermine their willingness and ability to engage in effective social, political, and professional discourse.

Those who see the purpose of writing programs as preserving or releasing the "authentic" voice of either women or minorities may thus be obscuring the complexity both of cultures and of individuals by assuming that women and minorities are univocal, expressing themselves authentically in only one register. Furthermore, a predominant focus on expressive discourse may actually deprive women and minorities of the resources of coalition and the means of building political power by effective argument. Rather than empowering the marginalized, such a pedagogy may actually reinforce inequitable social and political conditions.

On the other hand, those who see the purpose of writing programs as enabling students to acquire the literate discourse of power manifested in the use of standard English in the traditional genres of the academy and the professions may ascribe too much social, political, and intellectual authority to a single register. These educators often see themselves as promoting social and political equity by empowering marginalized students to join specialized discourse communities although their position has frequently been criticized for an uncritical acceptance of existing power structures. Once again, however, both sides tend to conflate discourse forms with particular power structures. We live in a society that mixes oral and literate modes, formal and informal registers, all of which can be authoritative in different rhetorical situations. In the writing classroom, we teach students the modes and registers they are least familiar with; not already knowing these modes is not a sign of arrested cognitive development, nor is acquiring them a route to political quietism.

Of the essays in this section, two are concerned with feminism and two with the orality/literacy debate. All four essays raise questions about the impact of social and cultural forces in the writing classroom. As a group, the essays remind us that in our concern to promote social and cultural equity, we must take care that our classroom practices and assumptions about our students' abilities do not unwittingly undermine it.

The first two essays concern feminism. Anuradha Dingwaney and Lawrence Needham critique the predominant form in which feminism has been applied to teaching composition, as reflected in the recently published volume, *Teaching Writing*. Their analysis suggests that while the goals of such feminist writing teachers are to foster equity and empower students, some of their practices actually undermine these goals, limiting women's self-concepts and providing practice in forms of expressive writing that are ill-suited to promoting either social change or attainment of individual goals. Dingwaney and Needham end by outlining alternative practices more appropriate to the feminist agenda. In particular, they advocate classroom practices promoting coalition between varied interests rather than forcing consensus.

JoAnn Campbell examines documentary evidence and published material to provide a historical account of Gertrude Buck's influential tenure in the English Department at Vassar at the beginning of the twentieth century. Campbell's research demonstrates that feminists like Buck considered expressive personal discourse as neither essentially feminine nor as useful for promoting social and political change. While rejecting sophistic rhetoric as self-indulgent and unconducive to social change, Buck embraced a kind of non-agonistic but also anti-expressive discourse in which both parties learn from the exchange. In other words, Buck's career and philosophy suggest that one can have a feminist pedagogy that is not expressivist. Although Dingwaney and Needham's notion of coalition may be more agonistic than Buck would have liked, Buck might well have sympathized with their rejection of individual expressivism and their search for a feminist pedagogy that promotes social change.

The two remaining essays in this section concern the orality/literacy debate. Katherine Borland focuses on anthropological research in order to extend Rose's critique. Rose argues that even if we accept the historical account of the social and cultural development of various societies from orality to literacy, we cannot assume that this model is recapitulated in the lives of the individual adolescents we find in our classrooms. Borland goes even further; she challenges the very notion that the historical and cultural development from orality to literacy entails a development to a superior cognitive or intellectual state. She also challenges the assumption that literacy in itself enhances a society's mode of thinking and that people in oral cultures are incapable of complex reasoning. Her analysis points to some serious flaws in the reasoning of three influential participants in the orality/literacy debate—Jack Goody, Ian Watt, and Walter Ong. This study helps refocus our attention on the question of what can appropriately or easily be accomplished in oral and written modes rather than on inferences about the speaker's or writer's mental abilities.

Valerie Balester examines the orality/literacy question from the perspective of African-American students themselves. She argues that the problems these students face in writing classrooms are not so much due to differences between standard English and Black English Vernacular

(BEV), but rather to the complex and ambivalent attitudes towards BEV held by the students (and their teachers). As historical background to her case studies, Balester examines the cultural sources of African-American students' attitudes toward BEV, in particular the traditional uses of "talking sweet" or "talking bad." Then, through interviews with students, she illustrates the range and complexity of students' attitudes towards their language(s). African-American students are not univocal: for some students in some situations, BEV is the most effective voice; others feel uncomfortable using BEV even with their peers. Balester's research supports Rose's and Borland's contentions that our students are not in any simple sense members of an "oral" culture.

One final point. The essays in this section vary greatly in methodology. Two offer theoretical critiques of the literature: Borland's of the anthropological foundations of the orality/literacy debate and Dingwaney and Needham's of recent applications of feminism to the writing classroom. Each theoretical critique is paired with a contextual examination. Balester talks and listens to black students as they explore their complex attitudes toward their own language. Campbell conducts documentary historical research to discover how a particular group of women designed a writing curriculum and how institutional constraints affected their project. The point is that our notions of educational policy must be informed by and tested against a variety of methodologies. We need both theory and history, both philosophy and empirical observation.

❦ 1

Feminist Theory and Practice in the Writing Classroom: A Critique and a Prospectus

Anuradha Dingwaney
Lawrence Needham

Feminist critiques of canons and disciplinary practices have challenged orthodoxies at the university and departmental level as women and men alike have argued for alternative subject matter and pedagogies in the classroom. Feminist theory and criticism have been especially prominent in English studies and current in English departments; it is not surprising, then, that feminist approaches to teaching composition have been advanced during the past decade or so, often by those same individuals whose scholarship is devoted to recuperating and reassessing writing by women. *Teaching Writing: Pedagogy, Gender, and Equity*, edited by Cynthia L. Caywood and Gillian R. Overing, is one of the latest and fullest contributions to an inquiry into the relationship between feminism and composition theory and practice. A collection of twenty essays representing a geographical and professional cross section of writers (mostly women), *Teaching Writing* attempts to articulate a new philosophic approach to teaching composition and a radical, innovative pedagogy, both of which are intended to foster equity in the classroom. Though emphasizing different aspects of composition study and differing in the details of their analyses and recommendations, these essays display remarkable affinities attributable to a shared indebtedness to mainstream Anglo-American feminism.[1] Collectively, they represent a major direction in the application of feminist thought to composition study.

In this paper, we critique *Teaching Writing* and, based on our analysis, offer a prospectus for work on feminism and composition. In conducting our critique, we will ask two questions: 1) Do the feminist approaches to writing outlined in *Teaching Writing* constitute radical pedagogies, as claimed? 2) More importantly, do these approaches foster equity in the classroom and empower students, again, as maintained by the contributors? At this time our answer to both questions is a qualified no, though we will demonstrate that their approaches offer much of merit. Basing our conclusion on an analysis of key terms and root metaphors, we will argue that the feminist pedagogies advanced in *Teaching Writing* are, in fact, rooted in quite traditional (neo)-Romantic assumptions about language, the self, and knowledge which pose difficulties for the genuinely liberatory classroom. In brief, by essentializing the difference between men and women and by valorizing the private voice (feminine) over the public voice (masculine), Anglo-American feminist theories and practices have constituted a separate sphere of activity—a writing classroom of one's own—that, while enabling the development of a strong ego and identity, insulate and ultimately disempower writers. Our critique is motivated by a belief that pedagogies based on feminist thought do offer the possibility of innovative new practices in the writing classroom and consequently are too important to be ignored—or uncritically accepted.

We have chosen to examine the essays in *Teaching Writing* because they represent the predominant approach to feminist writing instruction in America today. They also focus specifically on the relationship of feminism to composition study,[2] unlike many essays on the broader subject of women and writing, and therefore offer a sharp picture of what feminism offers today and may bring tomorrow to the writing class. As relevant, however, we will discuss other essays as they reflect the tendencies and directions outlined in *Teaching Writing*.

The common goal of the contributors to *Teaching Writing*—a goal, we would add, shared by most feminist writing instructors—is to invest writers, particularly women, with a sense of ownership of their language, of confidence in their authority, and, ultimately, control of their lives. Historically, women have been a "muted group," denied the right to speak their experience in their own words, permitted to speak only through the borrowed language of a self-alienating masculinist discourse. In the view of these writers, the traditional writing class and the current-traditional paradigm of writing it fosters reproduce the conditions that historically have silenced and disempowered women.[3] To feminist writing instructors, then, falls the enormous task not only of changing students' attitudes and practices of writing but also of restructuring the classroom environment in ways that enable students to discover their voice and speak the truth of their experience.

To accomplish these goals, the feminist writing class 1) exposes the limiting, coercive, potentially destructive power of sexist language and masculinist discourse; 2) introduces examples of writing by women, not so much as to provide models for composition (as would the current-traditional classroom) as to offer encouragement, inspiration, and the promise of success to the woman writing as Woman; 3) creates a safe, trusting, writing class that, compared to the traditional class, is "less hierarchical and authoritarian," is "student-centered rather than subject-centered or teacher-centered," and is one in which the "teacher no longer has the Truth," but the "student has the truth as she makes the writing her own" (Frey 97).

The liberatory practices of the feminist writing class have the salutary effect of investing students with confidence, motivating them to write, and giving them a sense of ownership of their language and lives. What shortcomings, if any, are inherent in the methods and goals outlined by the authors of *Teaching Writing?*

To answer this question, we must first identify the theoretical foundations of feminist writing pedagogy implied in their formulations about the feminist writing class. Consider, for example, the stated goals of the new writing class: it aims at fostering the student's "inner voice," of encouraging her "individual quest for self-definition" (Caywood and Overing xiii; xvi). The student is asked to look through "the image in the mirror society has created" in order to find "the genuine self behind the mask" (Frey 102), or the authentic person. How is the student to achieve the condition of authenticity? By eschewing models, heuristics, and discourse conventions for a "private process of discovery" (Caywood and Overing) of a "center," or core self,[4] which, when tapped, releases energies expressed powerfully in the student's "individual voice" (Caywood and Overing xiv) or authentic female voice ("Verena's" voice in Stanger

32). Clearly expressed here are the major tenets of a (neo)-Romantic or expressionistic theory of rhetoric as outlined by James Berlin, C. H. Knoblauch, and others.[5]

Like other systems and theories of rhetoric, expressionistic theories of composition have their virtues and shortcomings. On the one hand, by recognizing the power of the individual human voice "to organize experience according to personal needs" and by acknowledging the "creative potential of all students," expressionistic or (neo)-Romantic rhetoric "liberalizes and humanizes" the writing classroom (Knoblauch 132). In an American context, it is a powerful perspective, capable of galvanizing student and teacher alike since it forwards such liberal and familiar values as "self-determination," "freedom of speech," and "individualism." It also holds that each person, pursuing a personal truth or private vision, is capable of transforming society, though the source and, very often, the locus of change remains the individual.

At the same time, Knoblauch observes that, by "privileg[ing] imaginative consciousness apart from any explicitly social shaping of its character," expressionistic rhetoric often fails to acknowledge the very real material and social constraints that act on individuals (133). Raising and liberating one's consciousness through the transformation of the symbolic is achieved by downplaying social and material realities, which, if not denied, "are considered significant only insofar as they serve the needs of the individual" (Berlin, "Rhetoric and Ideology" 484). This tendency is especially evident in confessional modes of discourse which underpinned consciousness-raising efforts of the sixties and which are a marked feature of the feminist classroom today. Pursuing a line of thought by Michel Foucault, Biddy Martin observes that the urge to confess, so much a part of the American character, represents in part a desire to discover a more perfect self, to speak an authentic truth; at the same time, it also represents "a refusal to account for the position from which we speak, to ground ourselves materially and historically" (15) and, as such, constitutes a rejection of the political. The truth, lodged in the inviolate heart, demands only to surface, and the truth will set one free.

At their extremes, expressionistic theories of rhetoric encourage trust in the omnipotence of thought and the unconditioned individual consciousness. These "Romantic" tendencies entail potentially damaging consequences for students who "eventually blunt their energies struggling against institutional realities whose power they have not fully enough come to terms with" (Knoblauch 134). Recognizable in all this, and perhaps really expected, is the situation of the Romantic writer whose initial enthusiasm turns to melancholy, whose "fanaticism" for ideas sours to dis-illusionment, accompanied by a sense of powerlessness and anomie. Paradoxically, the rhetoric most associated with preventing blockage and freeing up the writer can create other conditions for blocking, not the least of which is placing the burden of responsibility on the individual for societal change. Finally, it is this emphasis on the individual and individu-al response that places yet another limit on political engagement in the feminist writing classroom.

An effective measure to counteract these tendencies would be to interject a social dimension into language production through writing groups of some sort. Most feminist writing instructors have done so, insisting that collaborative learning and writing, which support coopera-tion and the free exchange of ideas, distinguish the feminist writing class-room from the competitive, hierarchical, and masculinist traditional class-room.[6] All models of collaborative writing are not alike, however (nor are all those from a feminist perspective equal, we would argue). The version most often described or suggested for the feminist classroom does not so much transcend the limitations of expressionistic rhetoric as re-inforce them.

Consider, for example, the collaborative model recounted at length by Carol Stanger in *Teaching Writing* (31-44). In her account, a student (Marie) is writing a paper on abortion and wonders whether or not a par-ticular proposition "fits" her paper. She solicits the help of her classmates, who, to answer her question, determine that they first must identify the thesis of her paper. This, in turn, requires that they paraphrase each para-graph for comprehension. Groups convene, members iron out differences in reaching consensus, or, in rare instances, agree to disagree. The class then discusses written group responses, attempting to achieve a new, class-wide consensus, while Marie draws on the discussion to improve her writing.

Despite its social orientation in group work, the model described identifies the individual subject as the primary source and locus of mean-ing, whose experiences and thoughts are privileged and conceived as anterior to interaction with the group. Asked to express herself in her own language, the writer in this collaborative model turns to the group for support; the group responds with encouragement and guidance, all the while working to help the writer achieve her goals and intentions.

The group, then, acts as a support system, perhaps on the model of support groups for consciousness-raising during the sixties.

Such groups are important, especially for individuals asked to step outside conventional formulations of their lives and experiences. They provide a much-needed community. At the same time, they reinforce a belief in the primacy of the individual and her personal vision. The group's work is secondary, subsidiary; in most cases, group members are asked to help a writer realize her agenda, at best to identify instances of false consciousness or obstacles that stand in the way of her quest for self-definition. Though the individual may certainly be influenced by group members, she is under no compulsion to negotiate meaning with them, merely to be truthful to the truth of her own experience. This is certainly much different from collaborative work where the group establishes its agenda and negotiates a language to achieve its ends. Within the group, of course, members must negotiate a language to respond to her task; there is, however, little at stake and little to negotiate since the writers have already subordinated their interests to the writer's and their language to hers—or to the language of the writing classroom (the group, for example, is looking for a *thesis*). In short, the collaborative work envisioned for the feminist classroom reinforces the tendencies of expressionistic rhetoric to valorize the individual, personal, and private. Its effects may be all the more insidious since group response may suggest that one's personal vision is publicly authorized in the absence of any basis for public acceptance or rejection. This especially is a real danger in the feminist writing classroom which strives to be a "peaceable classroom,"[7] a writing environment free of strife, where members are asked to be supportive and, if critical, nonjudgmental and nonevaluative. The goal or end result of the "peaceable classroom" is neither competition nor conflict but cooperation and consensus, producing at its best what one writer on feminism and collaborative writing calls "an oceanic feeling" of oneness, of the "transcendence of one's individuality" (Stanger 40) as members of a group become a collectivity.

At this juncture an intriguing question presents itself: is the struggle for individual identity and self-expression compatible with a desire for consensus and "an oceanic feeling" which transcends or merges the individual into the collective? If not—if, in fact, the two goals are contradictory—how in practice or theory are they reconciled? In practice they are reconciled by subordinating the work of the group to the work of the writer. The writer sets the agenda and the group follows it, participating as fully as possible to help the writer achieve her intentions. In theory they are reconciled on the assumption that, despite personal differences and idiosyncrasies, women share something in common that transcends difference and bonds them: an essential, unchanging, homogeneous feminine nature.

The essentializing tendencies of the feminist writing classroom are usually betrayed in statements that the individual female subject should write as a woman or read as a woman in response to experiences lived as a woman. The category "woman" in these cases is taken to identify an irreducible, immutable, objective set of attributes making up the female subject after ethnic, racial, national, and class characteristics have been bracketed. As a self-conscious political strategy, essentializing women and their attributes is to some extent necessary to create the identification and solidarity necessary for social action. As an unexamined belief taken as objective truth, essentializing women and their qualities poses difficulties for feminist theory and the feminist writing class.

First, essentializing women is ultimately a reduction that threatens the play and space of difference which many feminists argue is crucial to the success of the feminist enterprise. It also replicates the objectification and reduction of women by men who discovered "woman's nature" as a means of social control. The danger for the writing class is that the "female voice" will drown out the disparate voices of diverse women articulating their own lived experiences and the heteroglossia of individual women whose histories are the site of many often contradictory crosscurrents. The danger is particularly acute since, as we have seen, students are directed by the pedagogical imperative to achieve a consensus and solidarity of purpose.

The problem often is reflected in the tendency of women "to tell the same story" when reflecting upon their experiences despite their different histories. This story usually recounts a history of victimization and oppression, followed by a struggle for liberation and, ultimately, success. (In the writing classroom, the story typically recounts the history of the female subject as writer, who—oppressed by male discourse, denied a language, and silenced—struggles successfully to achieve a personal voice, usually after reading the successful struggles of other women writers.) The difficulty arises when the story is purported or assumed to be universal, reflecting a woman's experiences or options, when in fact the story recounts the experiences and options of women from a particular milieu.

For women outside that social and cultural milieu, the story itself may become an obstacle to liberation and success. For all women, the story also may represent a limit if accepted uncritically. Adelaide Morris, reviewing *The Road Retaken: Women Reenter the Academy*, points to both problems in observing that the contributors to the volume reiterate the same experiences in the same way, articulating "the liberal feminist paradigm" of "identity and oppression," the "bourgeois tale of struggle and success," "the humanist notion of a coherent, bounded self and a white, heterosexual norm." She concludes that the narratives maintain the status quo and "provide little purchase for radical change" (469-70).

Similar difficulties arise when the attributes and characteristics of women are objectified and uncritically accepted as "true" of women, regardless of race, class, or historical circumstance—for example, claims that women are relational, nurturant, caring, feeling, intuitive, noncompetitive, nonauthoritarian. These qualities represent the flip or positive side of attributions that traditionally have demeaned and devalued women— women as dependent, emotional, irrational, passive—and consequently serve as correctives to negative stereotypical thinking. At the same time, these terms constitute limits to thinking about women and their options, which in certain cases may restrict a woman's choices and be detrimental to her development. A strong case can be made for the argument that characterizing women as egalitarian and nonauthoritarian has inhibited women from exercising legitimate authority in the classroom while pursuing a feminist agenda. How else to explain classroom practices that contradict or ignore some of the best feminist insights into the relation of language and power? For example, most feminist classrooms embrace the principle that each student has the right to speak her mind and be heard while at the same time recognizing that not every student has had equal opportunities to do so. Yet many feminist instructors, it would seem, hesitate to intervene in order to correct inequities and inequalities. They assume instead a model of pluralism where the sheer fact of participation is deemed enough to assure that all viewpoints will be articulated and considered and that the production and reception of discourse will be equitable. For example, when group activities are planned for the classroom, it is assumed that equal distribution of members—two women, two men; two blacks, two whites—and non-interference by the instructor will lead to a fair and equitable consensus. One instructor, for example, divides her class into groups of five or six members; each group "has a mixture of sexes, ethnic and racial groups, and personalities." Although she admits that one would expect male language to dominate in this setup, she offers the sanguine hope that "the new social structure of the peer learning group, the lack of a patriarchal presence 'teaching,' and the presence of strong and vocal women in the group can combine to give women's language the power to surface and replace men's language" (Stanger 39, 42).[8]

What is ignored in this view is the history of training and force of habit that reinforce the traditional behaviors grounding the asymmetrical distribution of power. Men will continue to choose the topics and lead the discussions, women to defer and follow, unless the instructor actively intervenes and structures reading and discussion activities. Conspicuously absent in feminist theories of writing, especially those that encourage collaborative work, is any consideration of the collateral arts of reading, speaking, and listening as well as any discussion of how texts are read, processed, and disseminated by women and men or how they might be or should be.[9] Silence on these matters, we believe, is not only a consequence of an expressivist paradigm that privileges the act of writing and authorship but also the result of a desire by women to be nonauthoritarian, to avoid dictating to their students or imposing on them interpretive schemata or models of interaction that would repeat the coercive practices of the traditional classroom and would betray a reliance on hierarchical and patriarchical modes of thinking.

In the context of the feminist writing class, the attribute or characteristic that has been essentialized most often and calls for the closest scrutiny is the idea of a "women's language" or "women's style." Historically, men have contrasted women's language or talk to men's language, finding women's language to be inferior to normative male discourse. During the seventies, Robin Lakoff and others studied the speech of men and women to determine whether differences really existed between the sexes and found that men and women do speak differently, that men tend to be direct and assertive while women tend to be indirect and inconclusive, displaying what she called "the rules of politeness"[10]—tag questions, vague intensifiers, and qualifiers. More recent studies have confirmed these findings, though some have found the differences not so pronounced or difficult to interpret or nonexistent.[11] Of course it cannot be assumed that differences observed in speech hold for writing as well; empirical support to date has been scant and inconclusive, in our opinion—especially concerning grammatical and syntactical features—and many studies are questionable in design and execution. This is not to say that "women's language" does not exist, only that the evidence does not support a conclusion either way. It is indisputable that historically women have favored and cultivated (or have been forced to cultivate) certain genres and forms (the letter, memoir, diary, confession, autobiography) and certain patterns of organization. It is less clear that these forms and patterns are marked for gender; these features also characterize the "ghettoized" literature of the oppressed, disenfranchised, and powerless— female or male. (A parallel argument obtains for "experimental" writing by women; its features are also present in writing by men intent on challenging traditional norms and conventions.)

At this point it is reasonably safe to conclude that women's language does exist, though many of its features have not been demonstrated to be significant statistically or otherwise; some have been, others undoubtedly will. Perhaps the more interesting question is: are these differences biologically or historically given or do they derive from some third alternative, say, the psychosexual development of the individual in the process of socialization? The answer to this question has profound implications for the writing classroom. It weighs heavily, for example, on any consideration of agency: what are the writer's choices, or what is the possibility of choice under each brand of "determinism"? It is our view that biological and psychosexual explanations diminish agency and that historical explanations allow for greater agency, though this might not be a good enough reason in itself to embrace historical explanations were the evidence to support the contrary. Such is not the case, however, and we side with those who are suspicious of explanations tending to gender-type language and/or thought in a rigid, exclusive, and permanent way.

Gender-typing in this way is a marked feature of the feminist writing classroom. Male discourse, we are told, is direct, linear, logical, hierarchical, impersonal, and abstract and reflects a desire to master subject matter and audiences. Female discourse is indirect, excursive, intuitive, open-ended, personal and concrete and reflects a desire to explore subject matter for personal significances as well as to engage audiences and solicit their participation.[12] It may be argued, of course, that the reduction originated with men, that characterizing "women's writing" in this fashion merely reflects an attempt to valorize traits traditionally used to denigrate women; that is, "circular" and "digressive" become "excursive"; "nonlogical" becomes "intuitive"; "uncommitted" or "weak" becomes "open-ended." Such a reassessment is valuable and recognizes the very real truth that stereotypes have currency; if people trade in stereotypes, why not valorize the traits or qualities supporting them? At the same time, reevaluating does not mean redefining, and accepting the terms as given may mean unwittingly assenting to unacceptable limits.

Such limits are reached, we believe, when "women's writing" focuses on private, personal, or exploratory writing to the exclusion of kinds of writing said to betray a masculine bias. Writing in the Disciplines, for example, is considered inherently suspect and ultimately is ignored because it cannot disguise the male idea of mastery inherent in the notion of discipline itself. (It is no surprise, then, that *Teaching Writing* advocates Writing to Learn Across the Curriculum instead.) Argumentative writing, because it is seen to barely mask violence and the will to dominate, is rejected, or assumes the specific yet limiting shapes of an essentially "non-impositional" kind of argument (Osborn 115-117, 124-129).[13] We have in mind here Rogerian argument, though it is interesting to observe that the argument against argument often assumes an adversarial stance and betrays such specifically "male" attributes as oppositional thinking and the will to win; that is, in practice, feminist writers recognize that traditional argument has its uses given particular times, places, and circumstances and is accessible to women, though in theory, the idea of adjusting discourse to context and purpose is hard to square with a conception of an essentialized, decontextualized "men's language" and "women's language" characterized by a restricted and rigid list of attributes. Overlooking or interdicting such forms of discourse is to yield too much of the field. At the very least we would argue for the need to understand conventional forms, if only to allow for the possibility of subverting or transcending them.

Prospectus

We hope we have demonstrated that, despite drawing on innovative methods of instruction such as peer editing and group writing, the feminist pedagogies advanced in *Teaching Writing* and other essays on the subject are rooted in quite traditional (neo)-Romantic assumptions about language, the self, and knowledge: language is a transparent medium for reproducing an irreducible core self that is the source of knowledge. These assumptions, in turn, limit the possibilities for empowerment and change. Building on our analysis, we now would like to suggest some alternative ways that feminists in the writing class might empower women.

First, we believe that feminists must extend their critique of language in the classroom to include not only masculinist discourse but feminist discourse as well. One of the great strengths of feminist instruction has been its insistence that saying is a mode of seeing, that language does not represent reality but rather in some fashion constitutes it. It has relentlessly and rightfully shown how masculinist discourse, wittingly and unwittingly, disseminates sexism and establishes the terms by which we come to know its object: women.

Our analysis suggests that feminist writing teachers should also critique the terms they use to represent women and writing by women. How do such terms enable and/or limit women writers? Empower or disable them?

Such a critique, founded on the assumption that language is an instrument of power, would necessarily reflect on the ideological biases of discursive formations. It would raise the following important questions, among others: "What is it possible/impossible to speak of in this discourse? What subject-positions and versions of sociality are inscribed in it? What meaning and contests for meaning does it display? Most importantly, what and whose interest does it serve?" (Morgan 456). It would take as its object what Marilyn Cooper calls the "ecology of writing," a term she coined to convey her understanding that "writing is an activity through which a person is continually engaged with a variety of socially constituted systems" (367).

An ecology of writing "encompasses much more than the individual writer and her immediate context" (368); it is the nexus of all the contexts and interrelated systems a writer engages in and inevitably alters. An ecology of writing includes among other things a historical dimension, and we believe that any critique of language in the feminist classroom must view its object as a historically specific social formation subject to change. Linguistic resources and options too often are accepted or rejected according to whether or not they are "female" forms, and these determinations are based on precedent—on what women have traditionally written—or on some transhistorical criteria.

The critique we envision assumes that language is a social practice grounded in changing material and historical realities. Language can be viewed differently, of course—as a transparent vehicle of expression or as a play of differences. In fact, the essays we have considered reflect three different ways of understanding language—what Bob Morgan has called three "dreams of language" (449)—sometimes within the same essay. The question is which "dream" or theory is most enabling for women and best suited to advance the agenda of the feminist writing class. We believe that in the future any feminist approach to composition must seriously engage this question. Up to this point, the question largely has been ignored, though the answer to it is important if not vital. As Morgan reminds us, a theory of language "always projects an implicit model of social relations," and to adopt a theory of language is to define a social space and possible interactions within it (449).

For our part, the view that language is a historically specific formation reflecting social orientations is a promising one. Its historicist orientation allows for change and limited agency on the part of women. Its sociological orientation provides a basis for understanding how the personal is the political, for it argues that language is a property of groups and that knowledge is negotiated through shared discourses and validated by language communities. From the start, then, any utterance, however personal, participates in the linguistic life of larger communities and communicates shared attitudes, values, and beliefs.

The question of how the personal is or becomes the political—perhaps the central question for feminist writing teachers—is related to another important question: how are women to bridge the gap between private expression and public voice? From the beginning, this has been a concern for feminists in the writing classroom.[14] Planning group work and collaborative activities has been one response, as we have seen, for it allows women to articulate their feelings and ideas—perhaps for the first time—in a mutually supportive social setting. Yet group work as typically constituted in the feminist writing classroom provides no real basis for public acceptance or rejection of ideas and no solid foundation for political action since it valorizes individual responses to material and historical realities.

Our analysis points to the need for a greater variety of group activities in the writing classroom. For example, collaborative writing, on the model described in "'Strangers No More,'" might be encouraged (see Fiore and Elasser). In this account, collaborative writing is described as a collective response to a shared problem rather than a group response to questions formulated beforehand by an individual with rights to her own language. The group establishes its priorities, sets its agenda, and negotiates a language to achieve its ends.

In addition to group writing on a collaborative model, group writing on a model of coalition might usefully be adopted for the feminist writing class. The idea of coalition has been advanced forcefully by Chandra Talpade Mohanty, who expands on the work of Bernice Reagon. Coalition is built on a recognition of differences within political struggles and political subjects and counterposes an "illusion of community based on isolation and the freezing of difference" (39). It is a useful idea to incorporate into group writing activities since it prevents collective activity from obscuring the recognition that women are the sites of many, often contradictory, cross-currents and possess different identifications and allegiances—that is, they reflect interests that are attached not only to gender but to race, class, age, and sexuality as well.[15]

Coalition also provides a basis for collective work by members of mixed groups. Though the authors of feminist approaches to composition often assert that their methods and activities, designed for the all-women classroom, can be adapted for a larger, mixed population of men and women, they provide no theoretical foundation to justify their contention. Coalition, on the other hand, though foregrounding differences to prevent the assimilation of one party by another, also recognizes that men and women have shared interests and identifications that can serve at a given historical moment as a basis for collective effort.

Finally, our analysis points to a need for feminist writing instructors to actively and authoritatively intervene in the writing class to further their agenda, specifically their goal of fostering equity in the classroom. Particular attention should be given to how oral and written discourses are received, processed, and disseminated among class members, for, as Knoblauch observes, it is naive to assume that speaking entails being heard (135). Does the reception and discussion of texts subvert or reinforce traditional behaviors supporting an asymmetrical distribution of power? If they reinforce traditional behaviors, what correctives are available to the writing teacher? To answer these questions what is called for, in particular, is an interdisciplinary approach to language study, drawing valuable insights from speech and reading on how women and men interact and process texts—or how they might or should, from a feminist perspective. ❦

NOTES

[1] Anglo-American feminism is usually contrasted with French femi-

nism. Unlike French feminism, it grounds its critique of patriarchal practices and the condition of women in the experience of women rather than in language and is seen to be practical and commonsensical rather than theoretical and hypothetical. All the essays we consider are squarely in the Anglo-American tradition, though to varying degrees, and in lumping them together and considering generalized tendencies, we no doubt sacrifice, in some instances, their subtlety and complexity. For example, a few draw on the insights of French feminism within certain limits and with certain reservations. See, for example, Pamela J. Annas ("Silences" 7-10) and Stanger (32-33). We concentrate on essays in the Anglo-American tradition because in terms of numbers and influence they represent the predominant approach to the study of feminism and composition. For a rare example of the implications of French feminism for the writing classroom, see Clara Juncker's "Writing (with) Cixous."

The essays we consider might be organized in other useful ways, of course. To the extent that they posit a sphere of difference for women, a separate women's culture, they can be said to participate in cultural feminism; to the extent that they argue for equity based on equal participation, they can be said to participate in liberal feminism (see Josephine Donovan, *Feminist Theory* for more on these labels). In *Feminist Criticism and Social Change*, Judith Newton and Deborah Rosenfelt postulate a "soft" division between those who concentrate on language as the site of political activity and transformation, and those who, in addition to focusing on the symbolic and the power of ideas, concentrate on the material and historical conditions of women and on avenues and sites of change other than language. They define themselves as "materialist-feminists" and represent an often overlooked perspective with which we have much sympathy.

2 There are, of course, innumerable books and essays on the subject of women and writing. For example, there are works on women writers, women as professional writers, women and opportunities in print, women and language, and women and poetics. *Teaching Writing* is the only book we know of devoted exclusively to feminism, composition, and the writing classroom. A useful collection of essays that, in part, is devoted to the subject of women's writing and the composition class can be found in *College English* 40 (1979).

3 Robert Mielke explicitly refers to current-traditional rhetoric and identifies some of its features—it is hierarchical, teacher-directed, agonistic, "emphasizing an ethic of competition for the grade, and, finally, prod-

uct-oriented" (172-73). Since *Teaching Writing* is the response to a call for papers on the relation of "revisionist writing theory" to feminism, almost all the essays are concerned with pointing out the shortcomings of "traditional" approaches. See, for example, Olivia Frey (95-97) and Wendy Goulston (24).

4 "Core Self" is the term Morgan uses in "Three Dreams of Language" to characterize what (neo-)Romantics conceive to be the essential, irreducible center of each human being. For the idea that women should write from such a center, see Annas ("Style as Politics" 371) and Goulston (22).

5 For a fuller discussion of expressionism and expressionistic rhetoric, see Berlin's essays, "Rhetoric and Ideology in the Writing Class" (484-487) and "Contemporary Composition: The Major Pedagogical Theories" (771-773), and his book, *Rhetoric and Reality* (43-46, 73-81, 159-165). See also Knoblauch (131-134).

6 According to most of the authors of *Teaching Writing*, in addition to being student-directed through collaborative work, the feminist writing class is also process-oriented. For the relationship between feminism and collaborative learning, see especially Stanger's "The Sexual Politics of the One-To-One Classroom and Collaborative Learning."

7 Mary Rose O'Reilley develops the notion of a "peaceable classroom" at length in "The Peaceable Classroom." Frey and Rebecca Faery explicitly refer to her essay; most of the other authors in *Teaching Writing* are concerned that the feminist writing instructor create a "nurturant" space for students.

8 Other essays on collaborative learning do not talk about the specifics of group makeup or interaction. In the absence of any detailed discussion, it might be assumed that they also depend on strong women, the dynamics of peer learning, and the lack of an authoritative presence to assure that all parties participate and are heard.

9 Barbara Cambridge's recent study (1987) on interactional differences between the genders in the writing classroom is the only exception of which we are aware.

10 Refer to Lakoff's *Language and Women's Place,* particularly pages 51-83, for an extended discussion of the "rules of politeness."

11 Over the past 10 years, Cheris Kramerae consistently has made this point. In "Perspectives on Language and Communication," coauthored with Barrie Thorne and Nancy Henley, she also remarks that "it is

notable how few expected sex differences have been firmly substantiated by empirical studies" (640). She also notes that research in linguistics has tended to emphasize findings of differences between the sexes rather than findings of no difference. A cursory look at the comprehensive bibliographies on language and gender in *Language and Sex* and *Language, Gender, and Society* bears out her observations. Her main point is that, regardless of the status of *real* differences, perceived differences do exist with important consequences.

[12] For an extended discussion of the differences between male and female discourse, see especially Thomas Farrell's "The Female and Male Modes of Rhetoric" and Pamela Annas's "Style as Politics." The essays in *Teaching Writing* usually reproduce part of the extended list of differences we mention.

[13] There are other reasons for rejecting this argument as well. Women are trained to be passive and nonconfrontational and run the risk of being labeled negatively should they assert themselves. See Sheila Ortiz Taylor's "Women in a Double-Bind: Hazards of the Argumentative Edge."

[14] In 1979 Margaret Pigott recognized the need for women to move from personal writing to a more general kind of writing. Eight years later in *Teaching Writing*, Goulston recounts her "public writing dilemma" (22). Refer also to the work of Pamela Annas, who addresses this dilemma by exploring the possibilities of a "blend of anecdote and abstraction" (Caywood and Overing xv).

[15] Coalition also points to the productive uses of conflict. For such uses refer to Greg Myers (168-69) and Wayne Pounds (55-56). Pounds makes the interesting observation that conflict is not only necessary for change but for personal growth as well.

WORKS CITED

Annas, Pamela J. "Silences: Feminist Language Research and the Teaching of Writing." *Teaching Writing: Pedagogy, Gender, and Equity.* Eds. Cynthia L. Caywood and Gillian R. Overing. Albany: State U of New York P, 1987. 3-17.

———. "Style as Politics: A Feminist Approach to the Teaching of Writing." *College English* 47 (1985): 360-371.

Berlin, James A. "Contemporary Composition: The Major Pedagogical Theories." *College English* 44 (1982): 765-777.

———. "Rhetoric and Ideology in the Writing Class." *College English* 50 (1988): 477-494.

———. *Rhetoric and Reality: Writing Instruction in American Colleges, 1900-1985.* Carbondale: Southern Illinois UP, 1987.

Cambridge, Barbara L. "Equal Opportunity Writing Classroom: Accommodating Interactional Differences Between Genders in the Writing Classroom." *The Writing Instructor* (1987): 30-39.

Caywood, Cynthia L., and Gillian R. Overing, eds. *Teaching Writing: Pedagogy, Gender, and Equity.* Albany: State U of New York P, 1987.

———. Introduction. *Teaching Writing: Pedagogy, Gender, and Equity.* Albany: State U of New York P, 1987. xi-xvi.

Cooper, Marilyn M. "The Ecology of Writing." *College English* 48 (1986): 364-375.

Donovan, Josephine. *Feminist Theory: The Intellectual Traditions of American Feminism.* New York: Ungar, 1985.

Faery, Rebecca B. "Women and Writing Across the Curriculum: Learning and Liberation." *Teaching Writing: Pedagogy, Gender, and Equity.* Eds. Cynthia L. Caywood and Gillian R. Overing. Albany: State U of New York P, 1987. 201-212.

Farrell, Thomas J. "The Female and Male Modes of Rhetoric." *College English* 40 (1979): 909-921.

Fiore, Kyle, and Nan Elasser. "'Strangers No More': A Liberatory Literacy Curriculum." *College English* 44 (1982): 115-127.

Frey, Olivia. "Equity and Peace in the New Writing Class." *Teaching Writing: Pedagogy, Gender, and Equity.* Eds. Cynthia L. Caywood and

Gillian R. Overing. Albany: State U of New York P, 1987. 93-105.

Goulston, Wendy. "Women Writing." *Teaching Writing: Pedagogy, Gender, and Equity.* Eds. Cynthia L. Caywood and Gillian R. Overing. Albany: State U of New York P, 1987. 19-29.

Henley, Nancy, and Barrie Thorne, eds. *Language and Sex: Difference and Dominance.* Rowley MA: Newberry, 1975.

Henley, Nancy, Cheris Kramarae, and Barrie Thorne. *Language, Gender, and Society.* Rowley MA: Newberry, 1983.

——. "Perspectives on Language and Communication." *Signs* 3 (1978): 638-651.

Juncker, Clara. "Writing (with) Cixous." *College English* 50 (1988): 424-436.

Knoblauch, C. H. "Rhetorical Constructions: Dialogue and Commitment." *College English* 50 (1988): 125-140.

Lakoff, Robin. *Language and Woman's Place.* New York: Harper Colophon, 1975.

Martin, Biddy. "Feminism, Criticism, and Foucault." *New German Critique* 27 (1982): 3-30.

Mielke, Robert. "Revisionist Theory on Moral Development and its Impact upon Pedagogical and Departmental Practice." *Teaching Writing: Pedagogy, Gender, and Equity.* Eds. Cynthia L. Caywood and Gillian R. Overing. Albany: State U of New York P, 1987. 171-178.

Mohanty, Chandra Talpade. "Feminist Encounters: Locating the Politics of Experience." *Copyright* 1 (1987): 30-44.

Morgan, Bob. "Three Dreams of Language' Or, No Longer Immured in the Bastille of the Humanist Word." *College English* 49 (1987): 449-458.

Morris, Adelaide. "Locutions and Locations: More Feminist Theory and Practice, 1985." *College English* 49 (1987): 465-475.

Myers, Greg. "Reality, Consensus, and Reform in the Rhetoric of Composition Teaching." *College English* 48 (1986): 154-173.

Newton, Judith, and Deborah Rosenfelt. *Feminist Criticism and Social Change: Sex, Class and Race in Literature and Culture.* New York: Methuen, 1985.

O'Reilley, Mary Rose. "The Peaceable Classroom." *College English* 46 (1984): 103-112.

Osborn, Susan. "Rhetorical Strategies of Women Student Writers." *Praxis* (1987): 113-133.

Pigott, Margaret B. "Sexist Roadblocks in Inventing, Focusing, and Writing." *College English* 40 (1979): 922-927.

Pounds, Wayne. "The Context of No Context: A Burkean Critique of Rogerian Argument." *Rhetoric Society Quarterly* 17 (1987): 45-58.

Stanger, Carol. "The Sexual Politics of the One-to-One Tutorial Approach and Collaborative Learning." Eds. Cynthia L. Caywood and Gillian R. Overing. Albany: State U of New York P, 1987. 31-44.

Taylor, Sheila Ortiz. "Women in a Double-Bind: Hazards of the Argumentative Edge." *College Composition and Communication* 29 (1978): 385-389.

❦ 2

Women's Work, Worthy Work: Composition Instruction at Vassar College, 1897-1922

JoAnn Campbell

Introduction

At the memorial service for Gertrude Buck, professor of English at Vassar College from 1897 to 1922, her colleague and coauthor Elisabeth Woodbridge Morris recalled that Buck's "classes were really and truly led—led and not pushed, led and not dragged—led by the gradual release in each participant of her own best powers, to her own best achievement" ("Addresses at the Memorial Meeting" 9). I find it significant that Morris notes it is the participants and their best powers that ultimately led the class, for this participatory emphasis is an important factor in Buck's theoretical and pedagogical writings, and it was an organizing principle of the community in which she worked, the English department at Vassar. Although Buck's theories of language and pedagogical innovations have come to the attention of historians of writing instruction (see Berlin, Mulderig, Burke), it is her role within the community of women in English—her role as a teacher—that best reflects her beliefs about the nature of language and the importance of rhetoric. Buck had an early interest in psychology and thus an interdisciplinary approach to rhetorical studies.

Most scholars have commented on Buck's innovations, labeling her ahead of her time, a precursor, an original thinker. This view of history, sometimes called "the great man" approach, imbues individuals with qualities that set them apart and sees them as changing the course of history: If only we'd listened to Gertrude Buck, how different would have been our history.

Without diminishing Buck's importance to composition history, I want to argue that the heart of her work—her emphasis on cooperation among individuals for a social good and the important role of rhetoric toward that goal—is best understood in the context of the community that supported and informed her theories. In retrospect, it seems that Buck was at the forefront of current theory in psychology, education, and composition. However, by placing her in isolation as a figure to be admired, we only add her to the other "great men," and the result of such an approach is to overlook the other communities of women quietly working throughout the country, women who have not yet come to the notice of scholars because they did not follow a model of individual achievement.

In her 1916 book *The Social Criticism of Literature*, Buck argues that literature is "not alone a creature, but also a creator of the society it serves" (60), and she calls upon literary critics to teach by taking up their "one priceless possession—a vitalized, *democratized* conception of literature" (31). Such an approach to literature is not surprising when one examines the community of women working in the English department at Vassar during Buck's career. While these women faced institutional challenges similar to those many composition teachers face today—large class sizes, heavy teaching loads, limited office space, low pay—Vassar's English department organized itself democratically, sharing power, rewards, and resources, and constructed a pedagogy rooted in cooperation.

Importance of Vassar

Discussion of the curriculum at women's colleges has not been included in many histories of writing instruction (see for example Halloran, Berlin, Connors). While I cannot comment in detail on the curriculum of the other women's colleges in the east, the English program at this first endowed women's college seems to have differed.

The women of Vassar's English faculty were in some ways typical of educated women's communities at the turn of the century: they were part of the first or second generation of women to attend college. Buck graduated from the University of Michigan with a PhD in rhetoric in 1898, and Laura Wylie, department chair from 1896 to 1922, earned her BA from Vassar in 1877 and her PhD from Yale in 1894. Wylie was, in fact, the first woman to earn the advanced degree from Yale. Other department members held advanced degrees from Cornell, Columbia, Barnard, Wellesley, Bryn Mawr, Mount Holyoke, Michigan and other schools. The majority of the women in the department remained unmarried, as did most women earning PhDs between 1877 and 1924 (Harris 101), and the community supported all kinds of needs—professional, pedagogical, creative, and social.

Such relationships were certainly not unique to Vassar. However, the close connection in theory and in practice between literature and writing classes at Vassar drew comments. After a 1922 writing conference for teachers from Smith, Wellesley, Vassar, and Mount Holyoke, the chair reported that "Vassar differs from the other colleges in placing more emphasis on the essential unity of the two kinds of 'English,' critical reading and creative composition, and hence in not separating into two departments the teaching of literature and composition" (1922 "Report of the Department of English"). This curricular distinction reflects the organization of the department, which was in fact cooperative. Moreover, the personal relationship between Buck and Wylie is credited for the smooth integration of rhetoric and literature. As a colleague, Katherine Warren, recalls, "the completeness of their cooperation made the growth of an integral relation between their courses in literature and in writing a natural process, and formed a nucleus for similar relations in the department as a whole" ("Retirement" 2). The equality of rhetoric and literature was stressed as Wylie advocated Buck's promotion to associate professor: "the next professorship created in the department should represent the rhetorical side of English, which maintains in all our courses a relation with the literature at once co-equal and complementary" (1899-1900 "Report of the Department of English"). In her annual report of 1909, Wylie urged "that Professor Buck's salary be made equal to that of the head of the department" because "Miss Buck does her full share" of administrative work, "relieving me entirely of a great deal of it." Elsewhere English departments were battling out the supremacy of rhetoric or literature, but at Vassar the English department harmoniously combined three branches of language study: history of the language, rhetoric, and literature. In the same request for equivalent salary, Wylie comments on the healthy consequences of hers and Buck's relationship.

Indeed, if we did not work together in entire harmony, it would probably be necessary either for me to do considerably less teaching, or to divide the department, as has been unfortunately done in many places, into the departments of English or Rhetoric, and of Literature. The present union of the two subjects in a single department has many advantages of economy and efficiency, and it seems unfortunate that in order to preserve these, one of the people concerned should suffer serious and permanent financial loss.

This close relationship between literature and writing was an unusual configuration for English departments at the turn of the century. Albert Kitzhaber, who studied writing instruction in male and coeducational colleges after 1850, writes that "when no miraculous results had been immediately forthcoming from daily themes, rhetoric as an academic subject had lost status; in the new century no one seemed to care much what was done in the composition course" (145). In many departments literary criticism replaced rhetoric, which had become "a much narrowed and more pedestrian subject that was wholly identified with teaching young people how to write in such a manner as to avoid social censure" (Kitzhaber 153). Buck no doubt had brought with her from Michigan Fred Newton Scott's philosophy that "rhetoric as a discipline [was] closely related to literary criticism; in fact, for him there was no sharp dividing line between the two subjects: they interpenetrated" (Kitzhaber 153). This view, along with Wylie's interest in writing instruction, created a unique first-year English course that formed the core of the department's offerings.

Vassar's Students

Student populations are not incidental to teaching strategies and theories. As an all-women college, Vassar had a unique opportunity to address feminist issues, to challenge the traditional hierarchy of subjects, and to create models of interaction different from the male colleges.

Barbara Solomon's study of women collegians at the turn of the century indicates that because the very wealthy educated their daughters at home and the poor could not afford a college education for their daughters, it was the expanding middle class who sent their daughters east to school. Given Vassar's $500 annual tuition, the student's family income had to be above the national average, especially when student annual budgets at the Seven Sisters ranged from $350 to $1,200 per year in addition to tuition (Solomon 71). "At a time when the average income for a U.S. family of four increased from $680 in 1869 to $830 in 1890, the average annual income of the families of these college graduates was $2,042 . . . [yet] more than 34 percent of the women surveyed were from families whose annual incomes were below $1,200" (Solomon 65). Vassar was a predominantly white institution, as were most of the women's colleges. Anna Julia Cooper, a black educator who graduated with an MA from Oberlin in 1887, "estimated that in 1891 there were thirty black college women in the United States" (Solomon 76). Clearly, then, this student population is by no means representative of women in the country, for although women comprised 39.6 percent of the college-aged population in 1910, college women represented only 3.8 percent of the 18- to 21-year-old female population in the United States (Solomon 63-4).

Obstacles to Good Teaching

The actual work of college teaching took up a great deal of teachers' time. Wylie described the workload of freshman instructors:

> Each of the freshman teachers gives, during each semester, about three hundred interviews, varying in length from ten minutes to an hour. She receives nearer two thousand than fifteen hundred papers during the semester (1915 Letter to MacCracken).

The specific conditions under which instructors worked included heavy teaching loads and large class sizes. Wylie recalls the situation during her first year, 1894, when she "taught four sections of freshmen averaging forty-five students each, and two classes in argumentation . . . averaging sixty each." Vassar still operated with assistants who did not lead classes but critiqued written work. Wylie concludes that "[u]nder such conditions good teaching was . . . manifestly impossible" (1915 "Report of the Department of English"). During Buck's first semester at Vassar, 1897-98, she taught four sections of the required argumentation class, one section of advanced composition/description, a section of freshman English, and an independent study graduate course. The second semester found her with the same schedule plus a section of advanced argumentation and oral debate. She continued with seven courses each semester until 1902, when she was promoted to associate professor and her teaching load dropped to only four courses each semester. In addition to teaching, Buck's duties included directing the freshman English program, maintaining relations with secondary schools, organizing department lectures, and serving on various university and national committees, such as NCTE's committee to revise grammatical terminology.

In her continuing effort to reduce class sizes and teaching loads and to hire more faculty, Wylie went to great lengths to gather statistics and present her argument to the college administration in a scientific way. Compared to other departments, for example, the number of students per teacher in English was 148.7; it was 39.4 in zoology and 100.5 in Greek. While the English conference of the Association of College and Preparatory Schools in the Middle States and Maryland had met and concluded that composition sections should be limited to 15 students each, Vassar's courses still exceeded 25. Vassar College President James Taylor's handwritten comment on this report—"Very satisfactory, I should think"—indicates one reason why the situation did not rapidly change (1914 "Report of the Department of English").

The problem of understaffing impeded cooperation between the English department and the college administration, yet it perhaps contributed to the unity of the department. In 1906 Wylie appealed to President Taylor for "a more efficient and a fuller corps of teachers" because, she said, we are "all overworked this year and while overstraining ourselves are getting relatively unsatisfactory results because of the conditions of our teaching." Despite this plea, the following year Buck taught two sections of narration, a course in poetics, and a section of advanced composition in the fall, for a total of 145 students; during the spring semester she taught 136 students in two sections of description, a class in advanced composition, and a course in literary criticism.

Having too few teachers for the climbing enrollment meant the Vassar English department could not offer the advanced or elective courses they had so carefully created. Wylie polled comparable colleges in the East. Her reports are interspersed with tables of figures indicating that for the number of students Vassar enrolled (972 in 1905-06), they offered rather few courses (9 1/2). By comparison, Bryn Mawr, which also had eleven instructors, enrolled 441 students, and was able to offer 18 courses. The course load did not let up although class size stabilized around 25-30 students per writing course. Again in 1920 Wylie wrote to President MacCracken that "nothing but dire necessity can excuse the allowing of an English teacher to carry more than nine hours, with two or three types of subjects, for many consecutive years. . . . [W]e would do better to sacrifice some of the quality and progressiveness of our work than continue to exact so much from our teachers" (1920 Letter to MacCracken).

The dedication of these teachers under such conditions exacted a toll. For example, the 1909-10 report of publications notes that "Professor

Buck has this year been so far from strong that it has been impossible for her to do any work outside of her regular college teaching" (9). In a request for some time off to expand the Vassar Dramatic Workshop into the Poughkeepsie Community Theatre, Buck commented that she must render the service

> at whatever sacrifice to me personally. But my energies are not limitless. And I shall be able to serve the college and the community longer if I may be allowed to apply three hours of college time to this work, instead of adding it to a full-time schedule plus at least one-third of a full-time schedule given to the Workshop productions that must be continued for the first semester (1920 Letter to MacCracken).

Unfortunately, the request was denied. Buck fell ill the following year and died in January 1922 at the age of 52.

Compounding the problems of large classes and heavy teaching loads was a continuing lack of office space. While Buck and Wylie lived in a house in town, not all the teachers could afford to. Wylie repeatedly asked for more space for her instructors because it was "inadequate" to have "but a single room in which to sleep, study, and carry on one's business and one's social life" (1915 "Report of the Department of English"). In addition to the tremendous number of students each teacher met with individually, entire classes met in Wylie's and Buck's offices: "small one-windowed offices in Rockefeller Hall, each of which could comfortably and hygienically accommodate no more than four or five students at a time." But occasional assignments called for students to view paintings and write about them, and at such times the offices were "packed almost every hour with twenty-five to thirty girls—as many as can gain a bare standing place—who emerge from the foul air and the pushing crowd physically exhausted—and it need not be said incapable of any intelligent or vigorous writing" (1900 "Report of the Department of English"). Requests for more offices, however, like requests for more faculty or for an increase in Buck's pay to the level of the chair's were refused year after year. Such small financial requests as a $6.85 bill for mimeographing work or a plea for a typewriter were also denied. As Wylie tried to hire qualified women, she grew impatient with the board's reluctance to grant competitive salaries; she cautioned them about a new nomination: "We cannot afford to lose her for $100, as we have several times done in similar cases" (1906 "Report of the Department of English").

Financial difficulties at women's institutions stemmed in part from fewer alumni gifts. In a comparison of four men's and four women's colleges in 1910, Sykes found the ratio of gifts ran 21 to 1 in favor of the men's colleges (Woody 188). Salaries for professors were lower at women's institutions, yet tuition was almost twice as much as at men's schools (Woody 189).

Financial difficulties and priorities delayed faculty promotions. Despite Wylie's repeated praise of her faculty members and requests for financial recognition of their contributions, many were not rewarded. After years of denied requests, Wylie wrote a special letter to President MacCracken stating the case of a few faculty women who needed "special consideration." Her request is worth quoting at length because it reveals the sexual discrimination in operation for so many women granted the new opportunity of college teaching.

> Associate Professors Fiske and Peebles, with Miss Warren in a closely parallel situation, form a group that at present seems to need special consideration. These women are all in their late forties, have taught at Vassar for twelve years or more, and have qualities of scholarship, teaching ability and personality that make them vital forces in our community. But though these women are at a time in their lives when they should be holding positions of utmost power and influence, they have reached only secondary positions, with small immediate outlook for promotion. Besides their slight professional advancement—apparently inevitable in the case of women teachers—they are now pressed upon very heavily by limitations of poverty. They are unable to look forward to a year of refreshment through study or travel; they have no freedom for travel or study in vacations; they often are unable to attend meetings which would bring them into contact with other professional workers; and they are forced to give far more time and thought to the mere mechanics of living than is compatible with the best intellectual and social life. (1920 Letter to MacCracken).

Despite this plea, Miss Fiske and Miss Peebles remained at the associate professor rank, and Miss Warren at instructor through 1922, the last year of records I studied. Wylie adds that her and Buck's situations were not very different. They too had "been compelled to cut our travel and attendance at meetings of professional societies, to change and to a degree limit the hospitality of our home, and to spend time and thought on making ends meet that is a serious drain on vitality."

The Women's Community

In contrast to, or perhaps because of, these institutional restrictions to the most productive teaching and scholarly life, the English department formed a supportive network. James Berlin has recognized Buck as "the most important" promoter of a democratic rhetoric of public discourse. Numerous department reports and personal accounts contribute to a picture of a democratically run English department. Wylie argued that it is "only through this joint organization of their common work that the members of any department can act effectively toward the development of a coherent educational policy" (1921 "Report of the Department of English"). It is probably not surprising that this department, which was literally cooperative, would stress a collective approach to its governance and teaching. Weekly department meetings, which helped "to further that spirit of sympathetic cooperation without which the highest efficiency is impossible," were devoted to their professional interests—reading original scholarship or sharing important books (1899-1900 "Report of the Department of English"). There were separate meetings for coordinating the various sections of courses and dealing with day-to-day details because "an understanding of our common ends seemed necessary to the best teaching" (1899-1900 "Report of the Department of English"). Wylie often described a new teacher in terms of her contribution to the whole department and her ability to cooperate. For example, Miss Adams proved "herself an excellent teacher, at once originative and faithful, and [she] possesses much executive power which she uses at all times for the common good" (1899-1900 "Report of the Department of English").

Meetings were not just for professional purposes, however. To nurture the creative side of their writing, the department formed a Journal Club, at whose meetings they read to one another their own short stories, novels, poems, and plays. To create stronger ties with the community outside the college, Buck formed a club with the town teachers of English to discuss the conditions and methods of teaching. More politically active was the Women's City and County Club of Poughkeepsie, which Buck helped form and Wylie presided over for ten years.

These community activities were informed by a distinct educational and administrative philosophy. In her last departmental report, Wylie explicitly refers to the "co-operative or democratic organization of the department" as the "second article of our educational creed." (The first article was that English is primarily an art and should be taught as such.) According to Wylie, what set the English faculty apart was that rather than conducting their work "perfunctorily, or with a view of the interests of the individuals conducting it," the Vassar members "work disinterestedly and intelligently for the common good, and through this intelligent co-operation make the ideas on which we act effective in the various spheres to which they are applied." Wylie specifically described the method of decision making in her democratic department:

> Matters affecting the interests of the whole group have in every case been made subjects for joint discussion, and whenever it was practicable have been jointly determined. Smaller units acting together in any capacity have invariably made the organization of their common task a definite part of their work. The sharing by all teachers in departmental activities has always been considered part of each teacher's work, for which provision was made and which she was bound to render as a part of her service to the college. (1921 "Report of the Department of English")

Freshman English

Such an explicit goal of a democratic process of governance is reflected in the curriculum as well. Attention to the individual's powers of expression was the first step in the student's active participation in the class direction. Buck and Wylie had changed the emphasis of English studies from correctness, propriety, elocution, and the production of elegant manuscript to increasing "the student's powers both of expression and of appreciation" (1910 "Report of the Department of English"). Writing instruction was described before Wylie's arrival as "a few set essays each year, often entirely unconnected with any course of study and latterly in a 'daily theme' course without definite content"—what is now referred to as a "current-traditional" approach to composition. Buck, however, approached writing as a process, and she believed that "the products or results of an active process can be rightly understood and strongly seized upon by the human mind only in connection with that process" ("Make-Believe Grammar" 31).

The first-year writing course was designed to give students a broad exposure to language, as the subject of two of Buck's lectures to the class indicate: "The Social Function of Language" and the "Functional Study of English" (1915 "Report of the Department of English"). With the publication of Buck and Woodbridge's text, *A Course in Expository Writing*, the freshman course gained uniformity, and new teacher training took less time (1900 "Report of the Department of English"). Most likely the textbook was based on the material Buck had developed in the two years she taught the course before the book's publication. Buck firmly believed that theory followed practice, and as "the normal writing act comes to be clearly distinguished from the artificial process of manufacturing a composition, the scientific study of the normal writing act becomes for the first time possible." With this scientific study of the actual writing process, she felt "a pure theory of rhetoric, following, not preceding, intelligent practice in composition, will go far to set the theory and the practice of writing in their proper relations to each other throughout the educational field" ("What does 'Rhetoric' Mean?" 200). Such an approach was radically different from the prescriptivist tack of Genung or Hill, whose textbooks were widely used at male institutions (Wozniak).

To better understand the relationship of this course to high-school courses, Wylie and Buck constructed a questionnaire and sent it to 127 schools that prepared students for Vassar. On the basis of the responses, the department planned to issue a bulletin to the schools, "which may serve at least to prevent some misdirected effort and to give us students with less to unlearn" (1900 "Report of the Department of English"). A decade later, the department had included a section, "Recommendations for the Preparation of Students," in the college catalogue, and the language sounds as if Buck had written it. A discussion of training in writing notes that "In order that the student be incited to a genuine rather than a merely perfunctory act of communication, it is necessary that she recognize in every case some real purpose and specific occasion for her writing" (1919-20 Catalogue 30). For this purpose, familiar forms of writing such as letters, narration, and description should be used. With a particular purpose in mind, the student should be able to "criticise her own work on the basis of its success or failure in reaching the end proposed" (31).

With eight different teachers in charge of the first-year course, Buck's text provided a unifying curriculum. In addition, all classes read some texts in common. For the 1910-11 school year, the texts were Huxley's *Piece of Chalk*, Carlyle's *Heroes and Hero Worship*, Emerson's *American Scholar*, Newman's *Literature*, Arnold's *Sweetness and Light*, *Beowulf*, Pater's *Essay on Style*, and Stevenson's or Lamb's *Essays* (1911 "Report of the Department of English"). But this unified approach eventually changed, and in 1919 Wylie reported that "there is no single essay read by every section," with the result that "the classes not only cover substantially the same ground but are much more interested in the reading when it is more varied and better adapted to their individual needs" (1919 "Report of the Department of English").

In addition to class discussions of the literature, students had individual and group interviews, on average three each semester for 25 minutes apiece. Consequently teachers of English 1 spent "an average of three hours a week in reading the themes of each section, three and one-half hours in interviews with each, and three hours in class-work" (1911 "Report of the Department of English"). Buck noted that the amount of time in interviews was almost doubled because "preparation for their interviews takes about the same length of time as do the interviews themselves" (1904 "Report of the Department of English"). In other courses lectures were "only given when absolutely necessary to supplement the results attained by the students alone," and in the freshman course they were never given at all. Quizzes were eliminated because they were considered "incompatible with free discussion" (1907-08 "Report of the Department of English"). Students from the freshman course contributed to a publication, *The Sampler*, established in 1917, which offered them a real audience for their writing.

Evidence of the cooperative nature of the classroom comes from student testimony. At Wylie's retirement, one former student recalled that "she never set girls competing with one another, but she did stimulate them to compete with themselves" ("The Middle Years" 105). Interestingly, this cooperative attitude was encouraged by the college, which until 1915 maintained a policy of withholding grades until graduation in an attempt "to avoid the competitiveness of male institutions" (Solomon 96).

Conclusion

To me, the most important elements of Buck's work are an underlying theme of cooperation in the construction as well as the use of language and her continuing focus on community, which she argued is ultimately more important than the individual. In "The Foundations of English Grammar Teaching," Buck argued that "the conceptions of the function of language as essentially social and of the structure of language as essentially organic should manifest themselves consistently throughout the teaching of English grammar" (487).

The dialectic between individual and community is established in Buck's discussion of two competing theories of rhetoric: one she calls Platonic, the other sophistic. In a 1900 article, "The Present Status of Rhetorical Theory," Buck examined the ends of discourse for both these categories. For the sophists, the speaker's goal was persuasion, and although attention was given to the hearer, it was only "in order simply that he may the more completely be subjugated to the speaker's will" (84). Plato's rhetoric, on the other hand, was in the service of truth, so that both speaker and hearer were elevated by the communication.

Buck discussed the social function of "real communication" using the romantic language of vitality to describe true communication between the speaker's mind and the hearer's. She even provided diagrams to contrast the flow of rhetoric from speaker to hearer as a straight line in Platonic dialogue and as skewed in sophistic, for the real conclusion of the speaker may not be what she or he is conveying to the hearer. This tension between the two parties in sophistic dialogue affects the nature of community for Buck, and she calls that one-sided communication antisocial, "discourse for the sake of the speaker." These ends are antisocial, for "instead of levelling conditions between the two parties to the act, as we are told is the tendency in all true social functioning, discourse renders these conditions more unequal than they were before it took place" ("The Present Status of Rhetorical Theory" 85). For the sophists the only measure of the success of a discourse was whether or not the speaker attained her end, whereas in Platonic discourse, truth, or the social good, was the goal from which both speaker and hearer benefitted.

Buck calls the individualistic emphasis of sophistic discourse antisocial because it pits the speaker against the hearer, where "the speaker wins and the hearer loses continually. Discourse is purely predatory—a primitive aggression of the strong upon the weak. The art of rhetoric is the art of war" ("The Present Status of Rhetorical Theory" 85). This war motif is carried throughout the essay; just as in "primitive warfare the stronger of two tribal organizations subdues and eventually enslaves the weaker, so in discourse the initial advantage of the speaker returns to him with usury" (85). This language may reflect the larger argument in which Buck participated—that in favor of women's suffrage. Equality is a theme running throughout her work. Her comment on the nature of uneven discourse brings attention to sheer brute strength winning out. The use of "usury" indicates further her sentiments not only about sophistic discourse but also about any situation of social injustice.

Buck argued that in Platonic discourse "the speaker has certain obligations, not perhaps directly to the hearer, but to the absolute truth of which he is but the mouthpiece, to the entire order of things which nowadays we are wont to call society" ("The Present Status of Rhetorical Theory" 86). This obligation to society is essential to the health of the social organism, and Buck faults "the sophistic account of discourse, [which] makes it a process essentially individualistic, and thus socially irresponsible" (85). Although Buck admitted "we are not now-a-days on such joyfully intimate terms with the absolute truth as was Plato," her analysis of the rhetorical theory of her day was a hopeful one. She saw a return to the Platonic view in allowing students to choose their own subjects and create a real communication: "Both the Platonic and the modern theory of discourse make it not an individualistic and isolated process for the advantage of the speaker alone, but a real communication between speaker and hearer, to the equal advantage of both, and thus a real function of the social organism" ("The Present Status of Rhetorical Theory" 86). Implications for the teacher included leveling the relationships in the classroom as well as granting students their voices and power through improved writing.

Buck's argument for a more social view of rhetoric sounds much like Sally Miller Gearhart's call for the "womanization of rhetoric." Arguing that "any intent to persuade is an act of violence" (195), Gearhart proposes a notion of communication as co-creating "an atmosphere in which people or things, if and only if they have the internal basis for change, may change themselves" (198). Buck also revealed this distrust of persuasion and interpreted rhetoric epistemically as a truer form of communication whereby both speaker and hearer learn something. I believe she could argue so eloquently for this form of rhetoric because that was what she lived in her daily life. Being part of a democratic community which put its energies into cooperating and working for a common good, Buck was able to model the kind of pedagogy we call for so often today. Rather than rely on their institution to create such an environment, the women in the Vassar College English department took responsibility for their governance. Without a matching institutional structure, however, the changes Buck and Wylie advocated ended with them. Today, writing teachers have called for institutional changes to create better working environments (the Wyoming Resolution is one such example), recognizing that unless our own working and living environments are intensely democratic, the effectiveness of our own rhetoric will be diminished.

The kinds of innovations Buck brought to the field of composition might not have been possible had she worked in a different context. This is not to say that arguments for a cooperative rhetoric and for a harmonious relationship between literature and writing instruction could come only from a women's college. Rather than make such an essentialist statement, I prefer to believe that a rhetoric that goes beyond persuasion to co-creation can come from any environment where one experiences being valued, where one's voice is heard and one's vote counts, every day for each decision. Only in a democratic environment can teachers begin to facilitate a democratic classroom, one in which all students feel empowered to speak, in which all voices are heard, and all subjects get named. That may be the worthiest work we can do. 🐝

WORKS CITED

"Addresses at the Memorial Meeting." *The Vassar Miscellany Monthly* (Feb. 1923): 1-47.

Berlin, James A. *Writing Instruction in Nineteenth-Century American Colleges.* Carbondale IL: Southern Illinois UP, 1984.

Buck, Gertrude. "The Foundations of English Grammar Teaching." *Elementary School Teacher* 3 (1903): 480-497.

———. Letter to Henry Noble MacCracken, 7 Jan. 1916, ts. Special Collections, Vassar College Library.

———. Letter to Henry Noble MacCracken, 3 June 1920, ts. Special Collections, Vassar College Library.

———. "Make-Believe Grammar." *School Review* 17 (1909): 21-33.

———. "The Present Status of Rhetorical Theory." *Modern Language Notes* 15 (1900): 167-174.

———. *The Social Criticism of Literature.* New Haven: Yale UP, 1916.

———. "What does 'Rhetoric' Mean?" *Educational Review* (Sept.1901): 197-200.

——— and Elisabeth Woodbridge. *A Course in Expository Writing.* New York: Holt, 1900.

Burke, Rebecca J. "Gertrude Buck's Rhetorical Theory." *Occasional Papers in Composition History and Theory.* Ed. Donald C. Stewart. Kansas State U, 1978: 1-26.

Connors, Robert. "Mechanical Correctness as a Focus in Composition Instruction." *College Composition and Communication* 36 (1985): 61-72.

Gearhart, Sally Miller. "The Womanization of Rhetoric." *Women's Studies International Quarterly* 2 (1979): 195-202.

Halloran, S. Michael. "Rhetoric in the American College Curriculum: The Decline of Public Discourse." *Pre/Text* 3 (1982): 245-269.

Harris, Barbara. *Beyond Her Sphere, Women and the Professions in American History.* Westport: Greenwood, 1978.

Kitzhaber, Albert R. *Rhetoric in American Colleges, 1850-1900.* Diss. U Washington, 1953.

"Laura Johnson Wylie." *Vassar Quarterly* 17 (1932)

Morris, Elisabeth Woodridge. "The Middle Years." *Vassar Quarterly* 17 (1932): 102-105.

Mulderig, Gerald. "Gertrude Buck's Rhetorical Theory and Modern Composition Teaching." *Rhetoric Society Quarterly* 14 (1984): 96-104.

Reed, Amy L. "Opening Address." *Vassar Miscellany Monthly* 9 (1923): 1-2.

——. "Report of the Department of English." 1922. Special Collections, Vassar College.

Solomon, Barbara Miller. *In the Company of Educated Women.* New Haven: Yale UP, 1985.

Vassar College Catalogue, 1910-1911, Special Collections, Vassar College Library.

Vassar College Catalogue, 1919-1920, Special Collections, Vassar College Library.

Warren, Katherine. "The Retirement of Miss Wylie." *Vassar Quarterly* 10 (1924): 1-6.

Woody, Thomas. *A History of Women's Education in the United States*, 2 vols. New York: The Science P, 1929.

Wozniak, John. *English Composition in Eastern Colleges, 1850-1940.* Washington: UP of America, 1978.

Wylie, Laura Johnson. Letter to Henry Noble MacCracken. 17 Jan. 1920, ts. Special Collections, Vassar College Library.

——. Letter to Henry Noble MacCracken. 20 Jan. 1915, ts. Special Collections, Vassar College Library.

——. "Report of the Department of English." 1900, ts. Special Collections, Vassar College Library.

——. "Report of the Department of English." 1904, ts. Special Collections, Vassar College Library.

——. "Report of the Department of English." 1905, ts. Special Collections, Vassar College Library.

——. "Report of the Department of English." 1906, ts. Special Collections, Vassar College Library.

——. "Report of the Department of English." 1909, ts. Special Collections, Vassar College Library.

——. "Report of the Department of English." 1910, ts. Special Collections, Vassar College Library.

——. "Report of the Department of English." 1911, ts. Special Collections, Vassar College Library.

——. "Report of the Department of English." 1912, ts. Special Collections, Vassar College Library.

——. "Report of the Department of English." 1913, ts. Special Collections, Vassar College Library.

——. "Report of the Department of English." 1914, ts. Special Collections, Vassar College Library.

——. "Report of the Department of English." 1915, ts. Special Collections, Vassar College Library.

——. "Report of the Department of English." 1916, ts. Special Collections, Vassar College Library.

——. "Report of the Department of English." 1919, ts. Special Collections, Vassar College Library.

——. "Report of the Department of English." 1921, ts. Special Collections, Vassar College Library.

❦ 3

Spoken to Written Language: Thoughts on the Evolution of Consciousness

Katherine Borland

As highly literate students and teachers in the university system, we naturally think of literacy as a good thing, but we rarely examine the basis for this assumption. One powerful current assumption is that literacy constitutes a "state of grace"; that is, instruction in reading and writing develops the individual mind and enhances its capacity for critical thinking.[1] Many of us know this to be true of ourselves as scholars. As proficient writers, we often use writing to discover what we think about a subject. Whether we can extend this notion to the not yet proficient writer, however, remains open to question. For our students, the act of writing things down may prove more a hindrance than an aid to lucid expression.

Nevertheless, we often describe what we do in the composition classroom as teaching students not only to write but to think clearly. This seems an admirable goal. But what, in fact, is the relation between thinking and writing? Recently, Mike Rose has identified a tendency in American education to seek explanations for poor school performance in theories of cognitive difference. One such theory, the orality-literacy theory, views the development of a writing system in a given culture as a neces-

43

sary precondition for the exercise of certain higher-level mental activities. It is this theory that I would like to examine critically here, for if we are to achieve our dual goal in the composition classroom, we must be clear about the relation among speaking, writing, and critical thinking.

Rose has already pointed out a major problem of applicability in the orality-literacy theory (268, 287). Much of the research on differences in cognitive style has focused on ancient and modern peoples who have no experience of literacy. To view the thought processes of such primary oral groups as somehow analogous to those of imperfectly literate inner-city American students (who may participate in a vibrant oral culture but who are at the same time firmly located in a literate culture) is dangerously misleading.[2]

But other problems intrinsic to the theory also warrant examination. Most generally, the theory may lead to three assumptions that will affect how we perceive our role as teachers. First, the theory implies that nonliterate individuals and groups are mentally deficient with respect to their literate neighbors. Second, it implies that the mere teaching of literacy will effect a transformation in mental processes. Third, and most important, it implies that oral habits of thinking act as a kind of negative interference to the acquisition of literacy.

On the cultural level, as well, we must question our motives for positing differences in modes of thought between literate and nonliterate, "progressive" and "traditional," "rationally based" and "mythically based" societies. Several orality-literacy theorists embrace the notion of cognitive evolution in which the pinnacle of achievement is most often identified as modern Western scientific empiricism (Havelock; Goody and Watt; Goody, *Domestication*; Ong, *Orality and Literacy*). Although it certainly seems evident that this mode of thought has led to an unprecedented ability to manipulate and transform elements of the natural world, the conclusion that nonliterate societies that do not demonstrate this control over nature represent a prior stage in a unilinear intellectual evolution is more open to question.

Indeed, considering the present state of world affairs in which the proponents of the modern Western world view are exercising more and more global domination in the realms of politics, economics, and communication, we must recognize that identifiable differences may well be used to justify existing relations of dominance and subordination between societies. Nevertheless, having recognized the problematic nature of such scholarship, one may argue that the exploration of differences in societies' modes of thought is important because it allows us to better understand our own systems of understanding by contrasting them with those of others.[3]

What, then, is the basis for the argument that the development of a writing system changes or, more radically, enhances a society's mode of thinking? Scholars who argue this position (Havelock; Goody and Watt; Goody, *Domestication*; Ong, *Orality and Literacy*) assume that the way in which people symbolize thought affects what they are able to think; in other words, language systems determine the ways in which we conceptualize the world. Since speech and writing are demonstrably distinct systems for symbolizing language, they constitute instruments of communication with different potentials. Spoken language, for instance, is a more powerful communicative instrument than writing in face-to-face interactions because it allows for the transmission of meaning on a number of different semiotic levels simultaneously (gesture, tone, verbalization, speaker-listener interaction).

Writing, on the other hand, allows for indirect communication between subjects removed in time or space, communication that is not compromised by the variability inherent in the oral transmission process and that presumably encodes a message that is in a way independent of the original context in which, or for which, it was produced.[4] While speech can be viewed as natural to human beings because it is present in all societies, writing has been developed in only some societies and usually necessitates special instruction in its use. Therefore, a language with a writing system is considered a more powerful communication tool than one without a writing system simply because writing constitutes an additional communicative means (Stubbs).

The claim that writing actually transforms mental processes, however, is more difficult to accept because determining the relation between thought and language (speech or writing) is always problematic. Even if we agree that we can communicate our thoughts only through language, it does not necessarily follow that we can think only what we can express in language. Language, rather than containing or expressing whole thoughts, may instead convey only a partial reflection of an idea that indexes a larger context of associations in the hearer or reader. Thus, while we can make hypotheses about thought processes by referring to their products in language, we cannot justifiably reduce thought to its expression in language.

Furthermore, when encoding thought into speech or writing, one must follow the conventions specific to each of these communication media. Thus the language products of speech and writing will appear formally different. These conventional differences in expression cannot, however, be used as proof for differences in elemental thought processes without careful investigation since they may reflect a secondary encoding process rather than a primary thinking process. Finally, communication forms can be understood to differ according to their predominant discourse aims. For instance, a reconstruction of a past event for the purposes of settling a legal dispute will differ from a reconstruction of the same event for dramatic or poetic purposes. Thus, when comparing spoken or written discourse modes in order to speculate about differences in modes of thought, we must be careful to compare like materials (Hutchins).

Having stated these initial difficulties in the development of any theory that seeks to link the medium of communication with the content and form of thought, I would like to move to an examination of the general theories proposed by Jack Goody, Ian Watt, and Walter Ong that attribute intellectual development to the invention of a writing system. These scholars accept as self-evident the dichotomy of "traditional" and "progressive" societies' modes of thought propounded by nineteenth-century social theorists. There is, Goody claims in *The Domestication of the Savage Mind*, a recognizable difference between societies whose tradition is based on a mythical understanding of the universe and those that embrace a historical and scientific world view, and intellectual history displays a unilateral movement from the first to the second.

Goody is dissatisfied, however, not only with nineteenth-century explanations that appeal to innate differences in the mentalities of different culture groups, but also with the continuation of this "ethnocentric binarism" in modern structuralist theories of mythical as opposed to rational thought, epitomized in the work of Lévi-Strauss (*Domestication* 5-9). In order to explain what they see as the emergence of rational from mythical thinking and account for the possibility of cross-cultural communication between these two types of cultures, Goody and Watt turn instead to a consideration of the effects of changing technologies of communication on the human mind. Their argument for a fundamental difference in thought based on the existence or absence of a writing system proceeds on two levels.

First, they identify a difference between the oral and the literate modes of transmitting a society's "accumulated cultural capital"—its tradition. While a literate society can store knowledge in writing, an oral society must rely entirely on human memory. Since memory in this case is functioning socially, there is a tendency for all that is not socially significant to be forgotten. This leads to a homeostatic organization of the cultural tradition in which what is retained from the past is always brought into line with the needs of the present. Moreover, since knowledge is being conveyed directly through individuals in face-to-face encounters, it is much more deeply socialized in oral societies.[5]

In a literate society, the proliferation of written texts, which are relatively invulnerable to the homeostatic adjustments operating on oral materials, provokes an awareness of the differences between past and present as well as of variant accounts of the tradition. Out of this confrontation, Goody and Watt argue, members of the literate society develop a critical consciousness that leads to a search for methods of determining the validity of any account. Thus is born a sense of the historical dimension of existence and of the problematic nature of truth. Furthermore, alphabetic writing allows for the description in writing of the very process of interaction in speech and for the description and preservation of individual rather than socially reified thought. In this way writing expands the consultable record of human thought ("Consequences" 48-49).

The second level of Goody and Watt's argument rests on the nature of the written language itself and "the fact that writing establishes a different relationship between the word and its referent, a relationship that is more general and abstract and less closely connected with the particularities of person, place, and time than obtains in oral communication" ("Consequences" 44). In other words, writing allows for a standard or "fixed" definition of words quite apart from their various uses in changing contexts. For this reason, agreement about definitions in terms becomes a significant intellectual activity in literate societies, an activity that leads to the development of taxonomies and to formal logic.

Specifically, Goody and Watt consider this tendency toward abstract analytic and logical thinking a result of the development of alphabetic writing, a writing system that in its simplicity, and its efficiency, its minimization of the ambiguity of symbolic depiction offers significant advantages over other, more complicated and pictorially based writing systems. The abstract formalization of verbal statements in writing makes possible the dissection of indivisible wholes on the semantic level into their constituent parts. This activity forms a model for similar operations on the level of statements or claims that result in the discovery and description of syllogistic reasoning. Indeed, Goody and Watt see syllogistic reasoning as a kind of thought essentially tied to writing, since it involves the inspection of a series of objectified statements and a determination of their formal relations to one another—something that is more difficult to accomplish when statements are embedded in an undifferentiated flow of speech ("Consequences" 53).

Admitting to the speculative nature of their conclusions about the effects of writing on thinking, Goody and Watt offer as support for their assertions the correspondence between the rise of historical inquiry, notions of objective knowledge and syllogistic reasoning, and the invention and diffusion of alphabetic writing in Greece.[6] In her article "Implications of Literacy in Traditional China and India," however, Kathleen Gaugh objects to the Western bias in Goody and Watt's early work and their identification of the Greek invention of the alphabet as the fundamental cause for all subsequent developments in modern scientific knowledge. She points out that both India and China exhibited similar periods of widespread literacy with some different results. Both civilizations developed schools of logic and scientific reasoning after the introduction of writing. On the one hand, these developments support Goody and Watt's notion that literacy encourages sequential and syllogistic thinking; on the other, however, they challenge their notion that logical thinking is tied specifically to alphabetic literacy. (India developed a syllabic and China an ideographic writing system.)

Furthermore, while both civilizations developed concepts of historical time, both continued to recognize a larger cyclical conception of universal time. The otherworldly orientation of the literate group in India prevented the growth of a skeptical attitude towards the oral tradition. In China, however, a Confucianist orientation towards correct behavior and social responsibility in this world led to a great historiographic tradition. Finally, Gaugh points out that both societies exhibited advances in certain scientific fields—India in medicine and surgery, China in the natural sciences—that far outstripped contemporaneous achievements in the Western world.[7] Gaugh concludes that literacy seems to constitute an enabling factor leading to the large-scale organization, critical accumulation, storage, and retrieval of knowledge; the systematic use of logic; the pursuit of science; and the elaboration of the arts. Yet, she argues, the particular uses to which this invention is put will be determined by the ideological orientation of a given culture, its social structure, and its perceived needs.

Responding to Gaugh's modification of his theory, Goody qualifies his notions of the transformative power of widespread literacy, emphasizing that the development of a writing system constitutes a necessary but not a sufficient cause for the development of the modern rational-historical consciousness ("Introduction"). Thus he posits an intermediary category between his two poles (literate and nonliterate societies) and labels it societies with "restricted literacies." This formulation continues to assume an evolutionary development in thought that is tied to fully exploiting the potential of the writing system for constructing objective bodies of knowledge and abstract modes of reasoning. The notion, however, that nonliterate societies lack the ability to perform certain "higher" or more abstract intellectual operations remains problematic. Goody himself points out that Malinowski identified instances of empirical reasoning among Trobriand Islanders, but he continues to insist that "any changes in the system of human communication must have great implications for its content" (*Domestication* 9).

It is thus important to note that scholars involved in the ethnographic study of nonliterate societies are more cautious than the orality-literacy theorists about attributing differences in thinking to literate and nonliterate cultures.[8] They point out that the original characterizations of nonliterate or "traditional" thinking, which were simultaneously labeled "concrete" (as opposed to abstract) and "abstract" (vague, less precise), were made by armchair theorizers and have been proven unfounded by careful studies in ethnographic semantics. Furthermore, the earlier discussions of "primitive" or "traditional" thought failed to distinguish between the content of thought expressed in language—or belief—and its form—or the way in which people thought about their beliefs (Colby and Cole 65-67).

Another problem with studies that attempt to define an oral-literate polarity in thinking is the tendency to make comparisons based on unlike rhetorical materials. In "Reasoning in Trobriand Discourse," Edwin Hutchins presents a clear example of this confusion in reviewing Lee's argument that the nonliterate Trobriand Islanders' mode of reasoning differs fundamentally from that of Western peoples. Working from Malinowski's field notes, Lee characterized Trobrianders' thinking as irrational, concrete, and dominated by right-hemispheric (affective/integrative) functions. Yet Hutchins points out that in the absence of tape recording instruments, these field notes focused on the most easily transcribable units of discourse—memorized myths and magical formulas—two metaphoric and cryptic discourse forms that strikingly lack extended explanations or arguments.

When Hutchins examined the discourse involved in settling land disputes, however, he found that the Trobrianders employ language that demonstrates an ability to treat concrete instances as members of abstract classes of events, a comprehension of the causal and temporal relations between abstract event classes, and an ability to determine the truth values of hypothetical concepts by recognizing their logical relations to other concepts whose truth values have already been established. Hutchins concludes from his own findings that, by assuming logical inquiry arises only after the development of writing, Lee and Goody have confused the technology required for a description of the rules for syllogistic reasoning with that required for the performance of syllogistic reasoning. Indeed, he points out that inference is necessary for any form of planning and thus is likely to be a universal mode of thought.

James Fernandez used Scribner and Cole's protocols for eliciting data on logical thought processes among the Fang peoples of Western equatorial Africa. He found that these subjects' responses to the syllogisms presented to them were indeed logical if one accepted their additions to, or denials of, the syllogisms posited; but his subjects did not proceed according to the Western school's conventions of problem solving in which the syllogism is understood to be internally coherent and self-contained. Fernandez then looked at an indigenous problem-solving task, the riddle, and found that this puzzle is aimed at edification—"the cognitive construction by suggestion of a larger integration of things." He concludes that in this culture's orientation, the analysis of wholes into parts is not as significant or valuable as the periodic construction or reconstruction of a sense of the whole through metaphoric and metonymic associations of elements that are presented on the surface as distinct and unconnected.

Goody and Watt's second hypothesis—that writing is necessary for the development of grammar, the formal description of language—has been questioned by scholars like William Bright and Gary Gossen, who identify orally transmitted systems of language description in the cultures of ancient India and of the Chamula Indians of Mexico. Bright considers it reasonable to assume that the celebrated grammar of Panini, which not only described but standardized Sanskrit, was composed and initially transmitted before the development of writing in India (273-4).

Gossen, reporting on field research, describes a highly elaborated categorization of language among the Chamula that, if not a grammar of words, attends to various formal and stylistic aspects of speech in order to distinguish rhetorical modes. He also points out that Chamula children acquire adult verbal competence both through linguistic play and through instruction. Thus, although the components of spoken language may be identified and described in a variety of ways cross-culturally, an attention to and description of language do not seem dependent upon the development of a writing system. If notions of grammar do not depend on written language, then Goody and Watt's argument for the necessity of writing to the development of formal logic is weakened, for they view this development as a consequence of the attention to the relationships between words enforced by grammatical systems.

Given the evidence for the existence of both logical reasoning activities and nonlogical forms of edification in nonliterate societies, it seems more reasonable to posit a variety of thinking processes—adapted to specific contexts of use in nonliterate societies—than to assume *a priori* that without a writing system, a culture's mental capacities are restricted. Indeed, a better model for understanding differences in modes of thought across cultures might be to consider each culture as providing its members with a repertoire of thinking procedures that are applied toward the effective understanding and management of recurrent and unfamiliar situations. One might then view the social structure and ideology as providing a particular orientation towards the world that would privilege certain modes of thought over others and result in the development of identifiably different cognitive styles.

Turning to Ong's additional claims for a fundamental difference between the capacities of societies with and without literacy for artistic expression, one finds a similar confounding of the materials being compared. Ong's concern is to avoid logocentric thinking in our approach to oral or verbal art, a literate bias that he finds epitomized in the term "oral literature."[9] Building on Goody and Watt's description of the limits that human memory place on the development of tradition, Ong describes an evolution in consciousness viewed through a development in art forms from collective to individual expressions; from episodic and repeated to tightly plotted and singular presentations; and from a focus on action, on agon and the concrete world, to a focus on interior psychological realities.

Much of Ong's model for the differences between oral and written expression is based on a prior awareness of their different modes of composition. Making use of Parry and Lord's investigation of the composing process of early twentieth-century illiterate Yugoslav epic singers, Ong asserts the necessity of distinguishing between works arising out of an oral milieu and those developing from an internalization of the writing process. He rightly points out that scholars long accustomed to associating great art exclusively with written traditions can commit grievous errors in interpreting orally based works.

Parry and Lord discovered that epic singers did not rely on verbatim repetition of a traditionally fixed text in their performances. Instead, they constructed a story in performance by relying on a vast number of traditional formulas and themes that constituted prepackaged units of discourse. In this way, each performance became a unique realization of a recognizable traditional story. The stitching together of traditional materials was effected not only by the creative capacities of the individual singer but also by the situational context of the narrative event, including such things as audience reaction, time limitations, and competitions between performers.

Parry and Lord's study constituted an important contribution to oral-literary scholarship, for it offered an ethnographically grounded explanation of how lengthy and intricate verse narrative might be "spontaneously" composed without the assistance of written texts. It proved that performers did not rely on rote memorization, as literate scholars assumed would be necessary for a nonliterate tradition.

Generalizing from this data, Ong postulates that all verbal art conforms to this model of oral composition. He conveniently brackets contrary evidence from the ethnographic study of other cultural traditions for the existence of verbal art forms that do, in fact, exhibit a high degree of verbatim repetition achieved through rote memorization of an entire text (e.g., Sherzer). Nor does he consider the practice, common to a number of nonliterate cultures, in which a poet separates himself or herself physically from the community, sometimes for days, in order to commune with his or her muse and compose before performance (Finnegan, "Literacy"). Instead of allowing that different cultural traditions and indeed different genres within a single tradition allow for different compositional methods, Ong insists on the primacy of the oral-formulaic method since it provides such a striking contrast to literate modes of artistic creation and transmission. I would argue that a better model for understanding the nature of verbal as opposed to literary artistic expression would be to recognize a continuum of compositional methods that range from the production or reproduction of relatively fixed to relatively improvisational "texts" in performance. At the very least, the notion that book traditions are all fixity while oral traditions are all variability should be discarded.

Parry and Lord's findings were enthusiastically received by scholars concerned with the interpretation of classical and medieval epics because they viewed Yugoslav epic singers as the last in a dying breed, a group whose conservation of an oral composing tradition provided a sort of looking-glass back into the past before the rise of literacy and written methods of composition (*Singer* 129). Folklorists, however, have recently questioned the demise of the oral composing process and have looked to other groups of oral performers in literate and nonliterate societies to gather corroborating evidence for Parry and Lord's theory.

Bruce Rosenberg, for instance, studied the performances of American folk preachers and found that they employed the oral-formulaic method in constructing their sermons. However, in "Oral Sermons and Oral Narrative" Rosenberg modifies Parry and Lord's notion of the traditional formula, pointing out that definitions of what syntactic units constitute a traditional formula vary in their and other scholars' work. He suggests that formulas be considered not as a separate body of verbal resources given by tradition (a sort of second-level lexicon) but instead as part of the total verbal resources existing in a language. Thus the oral composer's skill might be more aptly described as a special sensitivity to the poetic qualities of language and an ear for metrical and rhythmic speech. This modification of our understanding of the formula allows for greater recognition of an individual performer's creativity and inventiveness.

Indeed, the notion that artists working in an oral tradition act as mouthpieces for a collectively created body of knowledge and expression is founded as much on oral artists' claims to traditionality (claims that Ong himself proves are open to question) as on early collectors' patronizing assumptions about the conservative and uninventive nature of their informants. Throughout the nineteenth century many folklore collectors assumed that the identity of the performer was peripheral to an understanding of his or her art. Therefore, the names of raconteurs and their comments on or interpretations of their own art were seldom appended to collections of traditional tales, legends, and other genres of verbal art. More recent scholarship attending to these features has demonstrated that particular performers often have widespread reputations extending beyond their own communities; stories are often considered the particular property of an individual storyteller; and oral performers are quite eloquent about their reasons for selecting, organizing, and presenting identifiably traditional materials to a particular audience in a particular way.[10]

Ong bases his notion of the limitations on individual expression posed by an oral tradition on the fact that verbal art is always presented to an audience in performance. If the audience judges the performance negatively, its adoption into oral tradition is unlikely. In other words, in order to be successful, the artist must please the immediate audience; otherwise, the artist's work is not admitted into the traditional repertoire and is lost. In contrast, a written text does not depend on immediate audience approval for its survival; it may lie quiescent for long periods only to be revived at a later date by a newly appreciative audience. Yet this argument assumes a kind of fixity for the written message that is open to question. Does a revived text read in a new context constitute the same text written by an author in an entirely different context?

Moreover, is it possible that, within a culture, written or oral texts can emerge which do not constitute a cultural expression, which are, in fact, so alien to the culture that they are rejected after a single performance or reading? These questions raise the important issue of determining where meaning resides in an act of communication, written or oral. They point to the necessity of investigating not only how audience censorship works to shape or constrict the oral tradition but also how, in a written tradition, forgotten works are revived for present uses.[11]

Two final claims made by Ong for the differences between oral and written literary traditions must be examined. First, Ong asserts that the social character of oral transmission prevents the performer from distancing himself from his subject in the way that the literary artist can. However, an examination of the techniques employed in oral performances demonstrates that, while distancing presents a problem in verbal art since the performance always occurs in face-to-face interactions, it is not an insuperable problem. In "Literacy versus Non-Literacy: The Great Divide," Ruth Finnegan points to the use of masks in cultural performances throughout the world and to the popularity of animal tales in African tribal societies as only two of the ways that oral artists achieve psychological distance both from their subjects and from their audiences. Indeed, traditional verbal art forms can be used specifically to achieve a sense of distance, as Barbara Kirshenblatt-Gimblett has shown in her study of a Canadian Jewish woman's use of a Yiddish proverb to settle a family dispute. This woman explained that she used the proverb in order to admonish her brother by example without referring to his shortcomings specifically.

Finally, Ong claims that the oral tradition does not allow for psychological depth, introspection, or the conveyance of individual emotion but must rely on concrete description, action, and stereotyped characters. In response, one need only point out that Ong's characterization is based on the investigation of a limited number of genres, most notably the epic and proverb. Again, Finnegan points out that an examination of African lyric easily throws into question the assertion that oral performers are unable to express deep psychological insights or evoke complex patterns of emotion.

On another level, Ong's characterization of verbal art as limited to the depiction of the outsides of things fails to take into account the multiple semiotic channels employed in an oral performance. When one compares simply the verbal components of oral and written literatures, one is necessarily drawn to attribute much greater verbal elaboration, expressiveness, and coloring to the written forms. This kind of comparison, however, ignores the subtle nuances, ironies, and additions of psychological depth that voice quality, facial expression, intonation, and gesture (to name only a few performance dimensions) contribute to the experience of the whole. Instead of attributing limitations to the expressiveness of oral traditions, it might be more fruitful to examine the ways in which written works, restricted in their expression to the construction of mute words on the page, develop techniques to include expressive dimensions in the text that are given in oral performance. It seems clear that each medium operates under different constraints, but the supposition that writing actually expands in significant ways an individual artist's or a culture's expressive power is yet to be proved.

Ong asserts that the formulaic qualities of oral tradition indicate that people in oral traditions are restricted to formulaic thinking (*Orality* 33-36). This assertion is untenable not only because we know that not all verbal art is composed formulaically but also because in many cultures highly formulaic, densely packed verbal art forms are presented in performance along with more elaborated explications of their meaning. Joel Sherzer, for instance, describes the nightly chanting of myths among the Kuna Indians of San Blas as a kind of simultaneous translation process. The chief, using an archaic language, chants the myth while a second interpreter repeats it line by line in a more modern but still highly formalized idiom. Gossen describes the native taxonomy of Chamula speech forms and notes that knowledge encoded in myths is transmitted in a number of more elaborated, less metaphorically dense speech registers. He advises those scholars interested in understanding myths to examine them in relation to other discourse modes in a given society. Finally, Sandra Dolby-Stahl looks at the differences between the oral and written styles of prose narratives composed by an American storyteller and finds significant differences associated with the medium of expression. She demonstrates that a storyteller versed in the use of oral formulas is quite capable of expressing himself in writing without resorting to those formulas.

Taken together, these studies strongly challenge Goody, Watt, and Ong's assumptions of a basic deficiency in the conceptual and expressive powers of oral with respect to literate cultures. Determining the cross-cultural differences in thought and expression clearly represents an important field for further research. However, it seems unwarranted to construct a unilinear evolutionary model for intellectual development in which literate cultures are understood to have progressed to a higher level of human consciousness. Such a model can distort our appreciation of varieties of modes of thought and expression. As Gaugh has pointed out with respect to Western and non-Western literate cultures, the ideology of a culture group, its articulation of its perceived needs, and the value it places on certain kinds of knowledge seem the most important factors in subsequent developments of cognitive and expressive style. Cross-cultural studies of the differences between these styles may in fact reveal to us Westerners new areas of knowledge and expressiveness that we, limited by our own perspective, have ignored or failed to elaborate.

How does all this relate to our work in the classroom? First, I think it is important to point out that when we construct a notion of ourselves as educators, we often uncritically adopt some of the premises about literacy that form the basis for Goody, Watt, and Ong's arguments. Oral and literate modes of communication are different; therefore, we see them as oppositional polarities. In this way we are led to an erroneous understanding of orality as that which is not literate. Stubbs, for instance, distinguishes the conventions of writing from those of speech in order to emphasize that writing conventions and purposes are not obvious to people, specifically children, for whose needs and experiences literacy is not essential. To illustrate this difference he asserts that spoken language has to be listened to and interpreted linearly at the same speed and in the same sequence in which it is presented. In contrast, written texts allow the reader to skim, reread, backtrack, and jump forward in order to comprehend the message of a text. Thus, students who read a text straight through, according to Stubbs, are adopting an oral communication strategy with regard to the text that fails to exploit the full potential of the written format.

What Stubbs ignores in this description is that conversational speech provides the same kind of flexibility under certain conditions that he attributes to reading. An auditor may interrupt a speaker at any point and request him or her to repeat, clarify, summarize, or move on to the next point. Less obviously, the listener may selectively attend or ignore aspects of the oral presentation. Or a listener may directly dispute a speaker's argument, bringing to bear his or her own knowledge of the subject under discussion. All these critical activities depend not on the communicative medium but on the auditor's or reader's conception of the power relations operating between himself or herself and the text. If the speaker or author is regarded as an unquestionable authority, it is not likely that the auditor or reader will interrupt the unidirectional flow of information.

Another implication is that critical thinking and engagement seem less a consequence of the development of a particular kind of reading skill than a particular kind of communication skill generally. And this skill rests on a sense of self in the educational setting as powerful and active rather than powerless and passive. Being literate in our society is a sign that one is a communicatively powerful person compared to nonliterates, but this power is socially assigned to the literate person rather than acquired only through the process of learning to read and write.

Goody and Watt emphasize the importance of writing for the accumulation of knowledge and the subsequent development of a critical, historical mode of thought. We also tend to think of wide reading as an activity that contributes to an individual's critical understanding. However, the assumption that written traditions allow for the formation of an objective body of knowledge is itself a curious and highly problematic notion. It ignores the obvious fact that while books are in one sense decontextualized discourse, they must be recontextualized in order to convey meaning. Moreover, communication—written or oral—involves interpretation by a recipient, and that interpretation will be influenced by the perceived usefulness of the message to the recipient. The search for a kind of Knowledge or Truth that is not mediated by contexts of use seems to me as problematic in literate traditions as literate scholars have claimed it is in oral cultures.

Similarly, the argument that writing allows for the expression of knowledge through the growth of a consultable historical and intellectual tradition ignores the fact that schooling and scholarly institutions in literate cultures continually select out from the record those cultural items that speak to their present needs, just as oral traditions do. Canons are formed that purport to reflect the most significant or most beautiful products of our culture, and we are trained to appreciate them rather than to choose for ourselves from the wealth of our written tradition what items constitute the best or the most personally useful formulations of knowledge. Thus learning to read, write, and study our cultural tradition does not necessarily produce critical thinking. Indeed, for many groups in our society whose needs and interests do not correspond to those of the dominant group, to resist such learning activities constitutes a critical act.

These factors are important to consider for all of us who intend to teach reading and writing skills in a complex modern society where what one reads and writes is as important to gaining admission as a knowledgeable member in the culture as whether one reads and writes at all. I think it is evident from the preceding discussion that literacy is neither essential nor sufficient to the development of critical thinking and personal expression. Nor is the teaching of skills a value-free endeavor, for the practice of reading and writing is inseparable from what one reads and writes about. Thus, we must recognize that as scholars and teachers, we are ourselves arbiters of culture since we construct or transmit canons and teach cultural values in the classroom. We must realize as well that while our students come to us perhaps deficient in some kinds of learning they hold a wealth of knowledge and expressive capacities that have value in their own communicative spheres. Tapping that knowledge in the literacy classroom is a challenge that we may approach in a variety of ways. While literacy is of course essential for our students, we can no longer assume that reading and writing are good in themselves, that literacy constitutes a "state of grace." Instead, we must consider what we are teaching to whom and for what purpose, and we must ask ourselves what uses our students might make of the cultural tradition we offer them. ❧

NOTES

[1] For a description of the "state of grace" metaphor, see Scribner.

[2] Here one thinks of Ong's assertion that a young black student who arrived in class and insisted on participating in discussion without referring to the written text being examined behaved according to the dictates

of his primary oral culture and therefore misunderstood the literate nature of the classroom exercise ("Literacy and Orality" 124).

3 This is Horton and Finnegan's argument in their introduction to *Modes of Thought*. However, the important differences seem to reside more in belief, or what is considered socially valuable knowledge, than in processes of thought. For example, Finnegan points out that the reverence for exact replication of words appears to be a value embraced most strongly by print cultures ("Literacy versus Non-Literacy" 140).

4 See Stubbs on Popper's theory of World Three Knowledge (103-5).

5 Goody and Watt recognize that, in practice, nonfunctional survivals of formerly culturally significant material are retained in oral traditions, and that such instruments as mnemonics operate in opposition to the homeostatic process to stabilize the traditional record. Nevertheless, they argue that these elements are not comparable to the annals of literate societies, which enforce a much stronger recognition of the distinction between past and present realities (31-34).

6 These correspondences are derived from Havelock's reconstruction of ancient Greek historical, intellectual, and chirographic developments that are themselves speculative and subject to debate. See Adkins for counterarguments to Havelock's reconstruction.

7 Gaugh sees the Indian development of zero in mathematics and the subsequent Western application of mathematics to experimental science as a fundamental cause for the relatively recent distinction between supernatural, or mythical, and natural-scientific modes of thought.

8 For a bibliographic essay on recent anthropological studies of the relationship between writing and speaking, see Chafe and Tannen.

9 See Finnegan's introduction to her *Oral Literature in Africa* for a defense of this term.

10 See Degh (165-86) and Delargy for a detailed description of the folktale performer in his or her community. For examples of modern folktale collections sensitive to the role of the individual performer, see the Folktales of the World Series.

11 My own interest in these issues tends toward a consideration of how received knowledge about the past is employed in order to legitimize or question existing power relations in society. Victor Turner discusses these issues in oral cultures, while C.L.R. James's history of Haiti, *The Black Jacobins*, provides a wonderful illustration of how in a literate

culture the reinterpretation of history may function to empower a currently oppressed group. Much feminist research in history, literature, and folklore attempts a similar revaluing of the actions and products of a previously ignored group. See Herrnstein Smith for a discussion of this process
with respect to literary scholarship.

WORKS CITED

Adkins, Arthur W. H. "Orality and Philosophy." *Language and Thought in
    Early Greek Philosophy*. Ed. Kevin Robb. LaSalle IL: Monist Library of
    Philosophy, 1893.

Bright, William. "Literature: Written and Oral." *Analyzing Discourse: Text
    and Talk*. Ed. Deborah Tannen. Washington: Georgetown UP, 1982.
    271-83.

Chafe, Wallace, and Deborah Tannen. "The Relation Between Written and
    Spoken Language." *Annual Review of Anthropology* 16 (1987): 383-
    407.

Colby, Benjamin, and Michael Cole. "Culture, Memory and Narrative."
    *Modes of Thought: Essays in Thinking in Western and Non-Western
    Societies*. Eds. Robin Horton and Ruth Finnegan. London: Faber,
    1973. 63-91.

Degh, Linda. *Folktales and Society: Storytelling in a Hungarian Peasant
    Community*. Bloomington: Indiana UP, 1969.

Delargy, James H. *The Gaelic Storyteller*. London: G. Cumberlege, 1947.

Dolby-Stahl, Sandra. "Style in Oral and Written Language." *Southern Folk-
    lore Quarterly* 43 (1979): 39-62.

Fernandez, James. "Edification by Puzzlement." *Persuasions and Perfor-
    mances*. Bloomington: Indiana UP, 1986. 172-87.

Finnegan, Ruth. "Literacy versus Non-literacy: The Great Divide?" *Modes
    of Thought*. Eds. Robin Horton and Ruth Finnegan. London: Faber,
    1973. 112-44.

——. *Oral Literature in Africa*. Oxford: Clarendon, 1970.

Gaugh, Kathleen. "Implications of Literacy in Traditional China and India."

Literacy in Traditional Societies. Ed. Jack Goody. London: Cambridge UP, 1968. 69-85.

Goody, Jack. *The Domestication of the Savage Mind.* London: Cambridge UP, 1977.

——, and Ian Watt. "The Consequences of Literacy." *Literacy in Traditional Societies.* Ed. Jack Goody. London: Cambridge UP, 1968. 27-68.

——. Introduction. *Literacy in Traditional Societies.* London: Cambridge UP, 1968.

Gossen, Gary. "Chamula Genres of Verbal Behavior." *Verbal Art as Performance.* Ed. Richard Bauman. Prospect Heights IL: Waveland, 1977. 81-115.

Havelock, Eric. *Origins of Western Literacy.* Toronto: Ontario Institute for Studies in Education, 1976.

Horton, Robin, and Ruth Finnegan. Introduction. *Modes of Thought.* London: Faber, 1973. 13-62.

Hutchins, Edwin. "Reasoning in Trobriand Discourse." *Language, Culture and Cognition.* Ed. Ronald W. Casson. New York: Macmillan, 1981. 481-89.

James, C. L. R. T*he Black Jacobins: Toussaint L'Ouverture and the San Domingo Revolution.* London: Allison and Busby, 1980 (1938).

Kirshenblatt-Gimblett, Barbara. "A Parable in Context: A Social-Interactional Analysis of Storytelling Performance." *Folklore Performance and Communication.* Eds. Dan Ben Amos and Kenneth S. Goldstein. The Hague: Mouton, 1975. 105-30.

Lord, Albert B. *The Singer of Tales.* Cambridge: Harvard UP, 1960.

Ong, Walter. *Orality and Literacy: The Technologizing of the Word.* New York: Methuen, 1986.

——. "Literacy and Orality in Our Times." *Journal of Communications* 3 (1980): 197-216.

Rose, Mike. "Narrowing the Mind and Page: Remedial Writers and Cognitive Reductionism." *College Composition and Communication* 39 (1988): 267-302.

Rosenberg, Bruce. "Oral Sermons and Oral Narrative." *Folklore Performance and Communication.* Eds. Dan Ben Amos and Kenneth Goldstein. The Hague: Mouton, 1975. 75-101.

Scribner, Sylvia. "Literacy in Three Metaphors." *Literacy in the American Schools: Learning to Read and Write.* Ed. Nancy Stein. Chicago: U Chicago P, 1984. 7-23.

Sherzer, Joel. "Cuna Ikala: Literature in San Blas." *Verbal Art as Performance.* Ed. Richard Bauman. Prospect Heights IL: Waveland, 1977. 133-50.

Smith, Barbara Herrnstein. "Contingencies of Value." *Critical Inquiry* 10 (1983): 1-35.

Stubbs, Michael. *Language and Literacy: The Sociolinguistics of Reading and Writing.* London: Routledge, 1980.

Turner, Victor. "Social Dramas in Brazilian Umbanda: The Dialectics of Meaning." *The Anthropology of Performance.* New York: PAJ, 1986. 33-71.

❦ 4

A Reexamination of Attitudes Towards Black English Vernacular

Valerie M. Balester

In the best of all possible worlds, teachers of writing would be able to approach all students in the same way. Such is the desire behind the advice Paul A. Ramsey offers graduate teaching assistants: "The real problem [is] not how to teach black dialect speakers to write, but how to teach any student to write. The basics of writing . . . are not racial." Certainly his words ring true. There is no doubt that race *per se* is not an important factor in developing language skills. However, dialect *is*. Ramsey's words belie the fact that his graduate seminar is entitled "The Teaching of Writing to Speakers of Dialect." The course title, if not the professor, acknowledges that we cannot approach all students of writing in the same way. Why does Ramsey downplay dialect differences? One reason might be his discovery that actual grammatical, lexical, and phonological differences between the Black English Vernacular (BEV) of many students and the Standard American English (SAE) of the classroom are slight in comparison to their similarities. Most students should be able to adjust comfortably to speaking and writing SAE. Yet too many African-American students apparently perform below their capabilities on standard tests of language skills, and too many drop out of high school and college. To understand the problem, we must look to more than simple dialect differences. Language attitudes toward both BEV and SAE are a highly influential and little-studied factor affecting the performance of the BEV dialect-speaking student. The language arts education of most BEV speakers will not significantly improve until we have explored and acknowledged our society's complex attitudes toward language.

Differences Between BEV and SAE

Although it is a simple matter to recognize by ear the combination of features that constitute BEV, precise description of it is difficult, particularly because it shares with other nonstandard dialects of English many such features as negative concord—as in "Nothing can't happen." It is also important to remember that BEV is not a written dialect, while SAE is both written and spoken. William Labov has shown that BEV is quite similar to SAE in its grammar, lexicon, and phonology; this similarity, along with widespread ignorance of their true differences, makes detecting the shift from BEV to SAE subtle and difficult for most teachers (*A Study*, Vol II). Linguists now agree that BEV is not, strictly speaking, a different language from SAE and that the differences that do exist are not substantial enough to affect abstract thinking or the ability to form concepts. Labov hypothesizes that most of the difficulties of communication between members of different discourse communities probably stem from social factors, for example, from language attitudes or from ignorance of the proper community-based conventions for language use.

Besides grammatical, lexical, and phonological differences, there are functional and rhetorical differences between BEV and SAE. Study of these differences is just beginning, and very little solid evidence about them has been amassed. For example, textual cohesion (Tannen) and the arrangement and development of a topic (Erickson; Michaels and Collins) have been studied, and researchers have found that these rhetorical strategies appear to be tied to culture or dialect. As for functional differences, Roger D. Abrahams ("Black Talking") contends that the existence of special terms for particular speech events in the black community argues for their uniqueness: "the range, the intensity, the proliferation of terms, and the importance of such events are, on the whole, quite different from the configuration of communicative systems found elsewhere" (241). Examples of the functions he notes include "signifying" ("aggressive, witty performance talk") and "running it down" ("informational" talk with a "content focus"). In "Inventing the University," David Bartholomae provides a framework for understanding the importance of functional and rhetorical differences for a student of writing. He points out that all students entering the university are learning the discourse conventions of a new community and that learning to write is in part learning to join in the voices of this community. In a school setting, BEV speakers may be acting according to conventions appropriate to speech events which are unfamiliar to those in the mainstream academic community.

Miscommunication may be a major source of some negative attitudes toward BEV or SAE. However, differences that stem from grammar, lexicon, phonology, function, or rhetorical patterns have regularly been overcome, either by bidialectal speakers or by willing listeners. Many differences would probably go unnoticed if attitudes were neutral. "Nothing can't happen" is readily translated into SAE as "Nothing can happen." But because of attitudes, this statement conveys much more than its linguistic content. For example, it may convey something about the speaker's social status or level of education or about the degree of familiarity between the speaker and the listener.

Perhaps the subjective reality of BEV is more important to the lives of its speakers than objective descriptions of its structure or conventions. Labov devotes an NCTE publication to the question "Is nonstandard English illogical?"—reflecting the fact that although actual differences may be small, perceived differences are great (*The Study of Nonstandard English*). From the earliest exposure to so-called good English—or SAE— in school, the BEV speaker learns to adjust not only to SAE forms and discourse conventions but also to the attitudes of SAE speakers, particularly of teachers, toward BEV and SAE. Numerous factors influence how successfully they accommodate to school language, including, from a linguistic standpoint, degree of exposure to SAE and attitudes toward SAE—in other words, how the learner feels about SAE and about learning it. Likewise, learners' attitudes toward BEV must have an influence, although for lack of solid evidence we can only speculate on what it is.

Research does show that we frequently base opinions of individuals or groups on speech styles. Bruce Fraser extended an experiment conducted by G. R. Tucker and W. E. Lambert aimed at determining how one group judges another based solely on voice recordings. He investigated whether judgment of a speaker's race correlates with overall evaluation of the speaker by measuring evaluation of nine traits: intelligence, friendliness, level of education, speech, trustworthiness, ambition, talent, determination, and honesty. Results supported his hypothesis that judgment of a speaker's race does affect evaluation of character: "The simple fact is that people will judge differently on the basis of certain cues—in this case speech alone—because of their experience and certain, albeit inaccurate, stereotypes" (35). Another study by C. R. Seligman, Tucker, and Lambert of teachers' responses to students' speech styles indicated that teachers' assessments of students' intelligence and personal characteristics were affected, though not solely determined by, students' speech styles. Even physical appearance was found to have a significant effect on judgments. More recently, Beverly Kerr-Mattox surveyed 132 students in graduate education classes who were former or current teachers and 244 undergraduate education majors, all at Texas A & M University. Among her respondents were six African-Americans, twenty-four Hispanics, and eight Asian-Americans. They listened to tapes of middle-school children of different ethnic backgrounds and were asked to decide what occupation would best suit the speakers. The respondents for the most part designated occupations such as factory worker or cashier for the BEV speakers. While Kerr-Mattox's survey is somewhat limited in scope, it points to a problem in image for BEV speakers that stems from negative attitudes toward BEV.

All of these studies suggest that as BEV speakers learn to read or write, they may get negative messages about their abilities because of the image they create in teachers' minds when they speak. Their problems are probably compounded if, as emerging bidialectals, their writing exhibits unmistakable BEV features or if in reading aloud they translate the SAE of their schoolbooks back into BEV. Although we can only speculate on the effects of such a negative image, it is obvious that it stereotypes students and probable that it creates obstacles to learning. It almost certainly creates conflicts in identity, and for many BEV speakers it affects self-esteem.

The study of language attitudes is complicated by a number of factors. For one thing, informants may express attitudes that reflect only part of the story. It is not uncommon for BEV speakers to express mainstream attitudes toward SAE (as "proper" English) or negative attitudes toward BEV. However, actual attitudes are seldom so simple, and in the presence of the right researcher different attitudes could well emerge. In this regard Labov mentions covert prestige, whereby certain positive traits are associated with the minority dialect (*Sociolinguistic Patterns* 310-14). Thus the statement "Nothing can't happen" may convey to a BEV speaker a sense of solidarity or familiarity in some contexts. Another complicating factor, a related one, is that attitude is tied to situational context. In some contexts

BEV might be perceived as appropriate and therefore viewed positively, while in other contexts it might be perceived as inappropriate and therefore viewed negatively. A third complicating factor is that attitude cannot be clearly correlated with any one element such as race or social role (as, for example, student or teacher) or even economic class, in spite of the fact that we tend to stereotype as if such correlations could be made. I said above that "Nothing can't happen" may convey information about the speaker's social status or level of education. The reader may have assumed the statement reflects a lower-class status or a lack of education, but this assumption could easily prove erroneous. An upper-class and well-educated BEV speaker may very well have positive associations with BEV and feel comfortable using it in particular contexts, mostly in casual and familiar intercourse with other BEV speakers. Geneva Smitherman-Donaldson uses BEV in academic discourse. As she writes in "White English in Blackface, or Who Do i Be?," "The only percentage in writing a paper with WE [White English] spelling, punctuation, and usage is in maybe eliciting a positive *attitudinal* response from a prescriptivist, middle-class-aspirant-teacher. Dig on the fact that sheer 'correctness' does not a good writer make" [italics preserved from original] (308).

The stylistic effects of language attitudes make them of special interest to language arts teachers. Speakers and writers who are aware of their audience's attitudes toward particular speech styles can shape their discourse to enhance their ethos. BEV features can be employed consciously in speech or writing as a stylistic option by the rhetor who has some sense of individual and community-based attitudes towards the dialect. Similarly, BEV used unconsciously might affect ethos in unanticipated ways. One who judges that her audience rates BEV negatively for all uses, for example, would try to avoid BEV in a formal situation where a "respectable" ethos would be desired. And someone aware that his audience associates BEV with a lack of education would avoid using it when trying to project an educated ethos. Conversely, a speaker who knows that her audience associates BEV with friendliness or sincerity may employ it to create good will.

While attitudes must always be determined for individuals in particular contexts to be truly meaningful, we do have some information about attitudes toward BEV not widely known by language arts educators. Most of this information, gathered by linguists and anthropologists, concerns the African-American community's attitudes toward BEV. An understanding of this background illuminates individuals' attitudes, as I will show by presenting both the relevant background and a number of case studies of African-American college student writers.

Talking Sweet, Talking Proper, Talking Bad

Abrahams has investigated folk culture within the African-American community. Basing his studies on Anglophone Creoles in coastal South America, Central America, the Caribbean, and the southern United States, he has discovered similar attitudes toward language among these groups. He finds two predominant attitudes toward speech in African-American communities, one related to the African traditions of elaborate oratory, the other to everyday talk (*Afro-American Folktales* 10-11). The former is associated with church, school, women, home life, and propriety. It is the so-called "proper" or "sweet talk" used by the preacher, the intellectual, and the lady, and it often involves hypercorrect forms. "Sweet talk" in this sense is not restricted to romantic persuasion, although this is a common use of the term. According to Abrahams:

> This talking sweet is widely observable as the prestige form of serious speech in Afro-American communities throughout the New World. Speaking in this manner elevates the status of the speakers as they address themselves to the important subject of how to endure with dignity and respect. Being able to master such speech is to startle the audience members into attention and provide them with a sense of the possibility of a different kind of mastery—a dominion over their lives and their souls. (*Afro-American Folktales* 11)

As Abrahams points out, sweet talk is associated with good manners and may be used to address older women who command respect.

The African roots of sweet talk are suggested by J. L. Dillard (who uses the term "fancy talk"): "the use of intentionally glittering and sesquepedelian words and phrases, and . . . disregard for dictionary precision . . . can be documented from many African-American sources" (246-47). Abrahams has noted that the oratorical tradition which seems an integral component of sweet talk is so strong in many African-American cultures that formal training in it is institutionalized. For example, on St. Vincent young men and women are often privately trained by a respected master speaker to perform in the "tea meeting," where rhetors compete with one another and also with a purposely difficult audience ("Training of the Man of Words"). The rhetors excel in talking sweet, which is associated with the standard language, as opposed to broad Creole, and also with behaving well and being sensible (17). The speeches at the tea meeting rein-force, as Abrahams puts it, "household values," specifically, rites of pas-sage such as weddings and baptisms that "are strongly associated with the maintenance of the family and household system" (18). In judging the speakers, value is placed on "mental and verbal agility" (27) and on "high speaking," meaning "not only to ascend the heights of rhetorical inven-tiveness but to speak long and copiously" (25). Handling the audience by keeping its interest and preventing it from heckling are measures of suc-cess. The best rhetors employ elaborate diction to "confuse" (i.e., amaze) the audience and gain "that special kind of active receptiveness character-istic of Afro-American performances" (27).

Perhaps the best way to get the flavor of sweet talk is by example. The following is from a tea-meeting speech by an advanced student of the art:

> Mr. Chairman, judges, ladies and gentlemen, I feel totally ineducate to expi-ate upon a question so momentously to ourselves. It would be happy and necessary for Africa and the East, for I will be able to express myself before thee. And it is with privilege, hearing my name being called, I stand before you on this rostrum. Chairmen, ladies, and gentlemen, the grandeur of this meeting fills my mind with joy and remitting felicity and, like Alexander the Great when he having manifest his vicinity at Alexandria and thus explain in the language Athenian, *careto claret primus disjecta membera* of the fes-tivity. (24)

Dillard gives two basic characteristics of sweet talk, both displayed here: first, "flashy vocabulary, often beyond appropriateness to the subject under discussion from the point of view of the speaker of Standard English" and second, "'poetic' diction, or 'highly seasoned' talk" (249). Dillard's description reinforces my point that attitude is context-depen-dent. The judgment of the audience for this display of "high talking" will be colored by their cultural values. A different audience, one that knew nothing of the tea meeting, would certainly hear the example just quoted very differently from how the rhetor intended. And the rhetor may be judged by such an ignorant audience as being herself ignorant or comical, of "misusing" or "murdering" the "King's English."

Although tea meetings are far removed from the everyday experi-ence of African-American students in the United States, it would be a mis-take to dismiss them as foreign to their cultural background. Tea meetings reflect a general attitude in African-American culture toward the power and poetry of oratorical language, and they show us that African-American traditions offer ways to use language quite different from European traditions. Sweet talk as it exists in the tea meetings is only one version of a wider phenomenon in the oral African-American tradition.

The connection between sweet talk and Standard English (whether British or American) is noted by Dillard (251) as well as by Abrahams. But this association is not absolute. Another way to understand the connection between Standard English and sweet talk is to consider how sweet talkers regard the standard. We cannot assume that they regard it in the same light as the majority in the dominant culture. In fact, as sweet talkers demonstrate, they have alternate ways of using Standard English, ways the dominant culture does not appreciate or understand: "fancy talkers," Dillard explains, "have never been bound by schoolmarmish injunctions to use the plain word where it will do, to avoid words with which one is not entirely familiar, etc." (247). Thus, although sweet talk is indeed associated with propriety and "proper" English, it also has a certain subversive dimension in relation to the standard language of the dominant culture. In short, sweet talk is a variety of Standard English, sharing many of its stylistic features but differing in other features and in function.

The other style Abrahams reports, "talking bad" (or talking country, broad, patois, or broken), is primarily associated with the street corner, the good-time world of men, and nonstandard dialects. It is a more private or individual way of speaking—private, at least, in being apart from the dominant culture as well as from school and church. For many BEV speakers, talking bad has many positive connotations; in Labov's terms, it carries covert prestige. It may also carry negative associations, especially for those who aspire to upward mobility and who see their membership in the vernacular culture as a handicap. For example, in St. Vincent talking bad is also called talking nonsense or playing the fool and is associated with rudeness ("Training of the Man of Words" 17).

Just as talking sweet serves a function at the tea meetings of St. Vincent, talking bad serves a function in the culture, primarily as the language of subversion. While talking sweet reinforces domestic values, talking bad undermines and challenges them: "There are certain ceremonial occasions (like carnivals and wakes), in which it is regarded as appropriate and encouraged" (17). Not only does talking bad undermine domestic values; it celebrates the counter-values of licentious performances (18). For example, in the tea meetings designated members of the audience, called "pit boys," try to confuse the orators with rudeness ("Training of the Man of Words" 20).

Talking sweet and talking bad undoubtedly carry more negative associations than positive ones. Indeed, both styles have been parodied and lampooned by African-Americans and whites alike. Dillard and Abrahams tell of African-American gatherings where blacks are portrayed by ignorant whites as imitating their masters' eloquence or aspiring to their facility with English. The minstrel show is perhaps the best-known example: "the white reaction was commonly one of amused derision, seeing the effort as simply one more bungled African attempt to imitate white cultural practices.... [O]ratorical forms were mimicked in hypercorrect and ultracorrupted fashion in the 'fancy talk' speeches" (*Afro-American Folktales* 12). Such ridicule of a culture's discourse conventions often has remarkable endurance.

When ridicule comes from a dominant culture, those whose language is under fire may find themselves in conflict: by talking sweet or bad they run the risk of assuming an ethos that is read by the dominant culture according to negative stereotypes. But by avoiding their culture's sanctioned ways with words, they may become alienated from their background. Thus they must sharply separate their uses of language according to audience, just as they must separate their use of BEV dialect features. To err by using BEV dialect or discourse conventions with the wrong audience could cause them to lose face. Their dilemma is eased by the fact that BEV and SAE are limited to very different domains; but especially for those who have little contact with SAE or little ability as bidialectals, the problem can intensify in situations where language use is less rigidly prescribed.

Evidence from Case Studies

My case studies consider the crucial role of attitudes toward BEV in self-presentation. The data was collected over a three-month period for a larger study of the relationship between students' spoken and written discourse. I began by recruiting Max and Shanique, both of whom were 17-year-old freshmen at the University of Texas at Austin when the research began (all the subjects picked their own pseudonyms). Max and Shanique agreed to help me in my study of "Black English," a term we used in lieu of BEV, by acting as both subjects and interviewers. Max recruited three men friends, Thomas, Polo, and Spike. Shanique recruited two women friends, Laurie and Divinity, and Divinity recruited Dinese. By examining their writing and speaking to them, as well as from self-reports and the reports of Max and Shanique, I could discern that all the subjects were highly competent bidialectals. Their writing showed no evidence of the sorts of errors typically associated with dialect interference.

However, in spite of their facility with SAE, their ability to speak BEV was an integral part of the way they presented themselves—their ethos—in both spoken and written discourse. Moreover, my own attitudes toward BEV affected my interpretation of each student's ethos. I saw them as BEV speakers, as subjects in my study, and as students from an alien culture, much as they may have seen me as a teacher who either misunderstood or did not respect the way they speak in their most comfortable, intimate moments.

I collected both spoken and written data. For the spoken data, I interviewed the students on topics ranging from their views on hazing and minority recruitment and retention at the university to stories about their lives. I was attempting to elicit both expository and narrative discourse. In addition, Max interviewed the men and Shanique, the women. They were instructed to converse as naturally as possible on any topics. All interviews took place in my office with a tape recorder in full view. For the written data, I asked each subject to compose a personal letter, on real stationery, to be sent to a friend after I photocopied it. In addition, I asked them to write expository and narrative essays. They had 60 to 75 minutes to compose an in-class essay that I considered of first-draft quality.

Subjects' Attitudes Toward BEV

In the preliminary collection of biographical information, I asked all the subjects to respond in writing to the following request: "I am interested in your opinion of Black English. I would appreciate any comments you have on the subject." Their responses, along with comments made about this topic during their conversations and in their essays, reveal a complex range of attitudes toward BEV.

Max shows some cultural relativism in his response, and he shies away from value judgments about either BEV or SAE although his writing and interviews demonstrate that he feels a keen interest in this issue. Max generally maintains an objective stance in all his discussions of BEV, but it is also clear that he often views it in a positive light:

I feel there is really no set language in America, especially pending on the environment one has grown up in. I believe that there are only different variations in which one is able to communicate with different breeds and cultures of people. Black or white English therefore placing a person in a very opinionated area.[1]

Although his last comment is difficult to decipher, I suspect that he simply means that discussions of BEV or SAE are controversial.

Polo's response reveals a decided attitude that BEV is "uneducated" and that SAE is "proper," even though he wishes to express understanding for blacks' use of BEV:

I not quite sure what Black English is defined as. I do realize that most uneducated blacks speak what is defined to be slang terms but most people put blacks down for speaking this way, and I don't think it's truly our fault because we had to learn a new language and in the course of learning English either we weren't taught well or we had to improvise or put words in because of lack of knowledge of the "proper" English.

Polo is on the defensive; while he displays sophisticated knowledge of language issues (note how he puts "proper" in quotes), he seems bent on making the point that blacks can speak as "properly" as anyone.

Thomas, who flatly states during interviews that BEV is a "joke" and who actually claims to have learned it as a second dialect because of peer pressure, simply states: "I think [BEV] allows for less structured communication." Spike, who displays little inclination in his interviews to use BEV, does not answer the question.

Shanique, like Spike, chooses not to answer this question; however, unlike Spike, she freely uses BEV in speaking to me and does not express negative attitudes toward it in her interviews. Dinese expresses what seems to be a more ambiguous view than the others; yet, like Polo, she is usually defensive: "A lot of people associate ungrammatical English with 'Black English,' but even with my father's family (from country Mississippi) we had to speak with correct structure. Nevertheless, it still sounds 'Black.'" I would characterize her position as similar to Polo's; like him, she asserts that African-Americans can speak just as "properly" as anyone, even when they may be considered "hick." At the same time, she implies that there is nothing wrong with sounding "Black," that BEV is a matter of pronunciation and maybe lexicon, but not structure (i.e., grammar).

Divinity's answer is cryptic although, again because of interviews, I believe she means it to be primarily positive: "The English spoken by

Blacks is beyond description." My belief is supported by the fact that in some of her short stories, which she invited me to read, she makes extensive creative use of BEV in dialogue. Laurie answered with the most positive comment of all: "I feel that Black English is a distinctive English. I've been accustomed to speaking Black English all my life and it's become a part of me." She shows quite a bit of sophistication here in that she reserves value judgment but feels comfortable in associating herself with BEV. She certainly does not seem to share Polo's concern that BEV is the language of the uneducated.

In these responses, then, we see a complex range of attitudes: BEV is a sign of ignorance, or a joke, or simply the way blacks talk, or just as good as SAE, or essentially the same as SAE except for phonology and lexicon. Like SAE, it is seen as having both "correct" and "incorrect" forms. BEV is "indescribable" but distinctive, different, a mode of self-expression or a special dialect of a culture. The subjects' opinions of BEV differ and even show quite a bit of ambivalence, yet I believe it is safe to say that none of them, simply by virtue of participation in this study, is indifferent to it. They are all aware that it contributes, sometimes positively and at other times negatively, to their ethos.

Although I expected to get information on language attitudes only from the biographical data sheets, I actually learned a great deal more from the interviews and essays, especially Max's because he is so concerned with the topic of "Black English." A paragraph from his expository essay on Black English, a topic he chose to write on, provides an example:

> The black world has been shuned for many deep scared years. Forced to remain silent and forced to exist with out an education for the greater part of their lives, Blacks have had to create their own median of communication. Whether it be through song, music, dance, weeping, church, or family unity and love, Blacks have managed to escape their silent punishment and have created their own way of expressing themselves to each other. Because Blacks were stolen from their native land, Africa, their native culture, their native tongue, and their native people, their exist an excuse for the ignorance they possessed and have not yet grown out of to the unfamiliarity of the [word missing] with language and customs.

We can see from this excerpt that Max does indeed display ambivalence: he attaches prestige to BEV, yet he also associates it with a lack of education and with injustice to blacks. While BEV may be the language of the ignorant, it is black, the unique language of a people, with a poetry of its own, a medium of solidarity and identity.

Talking sweet, talking proper, talking bad—some of these folk terms and the language attitudes that go with them are expressed by all the men in the study. On the whole, the men discuss Black English more frequently than the women, so it is to their tapes I will turn for most of my examples. The men tend to take every opportunity to discuss language, to turn attention to it. Apparently they are quite aware of language as a component of their ethos as African-Americans.

While none of them uses the term sweet talk, they do distinguish between different ways of speaking well—correctly, fluently, intelligently. Max's interview with Polo shows that they certainly believe one can create a positive ethos by speaking well. Max says admiringly of Thomas that he displayed an "intellectual air" when he first attended Bible study: he "spoke real well, and people were impressed." All the subjects use the term "proper" to describe grammatically correct SAE, while "intellectual" seems to convey not only correctness but something beyond, something that creates that "intellectual air" and that uses the "big" words characteristic of sweet talk. Anyone with a certain level of education can talk "proper," but it takes real wit to talk "intellectual."

Polo uses the term "big words," which he seems to associate with intellectual speech; big words are a hallmark of sweet talk. In my interview with him, he explicitly connects the use of big words and sounding intellectual:

> My school's half white, half black, therefore I was exposed to, you know, speaking more Standard English . . . and . . . I was ALSO put in a situation where I had to watch . . . because, you know, I was in many academic contests. But most blacks that, you know, they just in the neighborhood and . . . they're not necessarily academically ORiented, so they don't see any need to be tryna to, to say all that BIG words, as they call it, you know, [changes voice] "Don't be sayin' all those BIG words."

As Polo indicates, talking intellectual is an achievement that sets one apart from the average. Notice that his comment shows that he correlates talking intellectual with SAE. One cannot talk intellectual in BEV, although talking SAE does not in itself constitute talking intellectual. He also indicates that big words are an important feature of talking intellectual.

Polo frequently uses the terms "talking intellectual" and "proper." His comments show remarkable sophistication and attention to language:

> See ACTually, I've learned that in order to succeed in this world there's a certain way you hafta TALK, in certain situations I must talk in that manner. That's why I decided I was not gonna use double negatives and things, AIN'T and things like that. It wasn't because I . . . didn't LIKE the way I was speaking. It was because I realized that if I DID talk that way I would . . . be looked down upon or have lesser intelligence.

At first glance he seems to be saying that BEV grammar is acceptable but different. He recognizes the social handicap of using it in the wrong situations. However, his attitude is ambivalent. He goes on to argue that "poor, uneducated whites" and "poor, uneducated blacks" speak the same way: "As far as using AIN'T and improper language, that's universal." Thus, we see his attitude change. Now, like Max, he calls BEV grammar "improper." He takes pains to relate this improper grammar to economic class rather than to race. Middle-class blacks usually talk "proper" unless they are in conversation with their lower-class counterparts because, like Polo himself, "Mostly intellectual blacks just realize that they need to speak proper if they want to succeed." In other words, they learn not a new dialect (SAE) but the "right way" to talk, the way school teaches. At the same time he uses "proper" to designate correct grammar, Polo shows sensitivity to the situational nature of language: "I think because some blacks when they're speaking Black English they use improper English. They use AIN'T and stuff and then that just makes the whole thing sound bad to some people." In this comment he seems to avoid condemning the way lower-class people speak (with, as he puts it, double negatives and "ain't"). Still, he expresses clearly his sense that such language leaves a taint for some people, presumably educated and upper-class people. To summarize, Polo seems sometimes to mean correct English by the term "proper," that is, SAE used without regard to the situation, and at other times to mean SAE used in appropriate settings for particular purposes. He may be struggling to make sense of his conflicting negative and positive attitudes toward BEV.

In another instance, making a distinction between "talking intellectual" and "talking proper," Polo demonstrates the same ambivalent attitude toward BEV:

> Polo: You can talk PROPER and then you can talk intellectual. . . . Now I could talk to my black friends I'm saying, well, you know, using all these

BIG words, you know, intellectually oriented, "This IRKED me," and such and such, but I don't talk like that cause that takes an EFFORT, not a effort but when you talk intellectually you're using the thought process in what you're saying . . . so that everything can, uh, be cohesive . . . but, when, you know, when I talk to my black friends I don't use, I don't use AIN'T and I do NOT use double negatives, so I, I try not to, you know, I know I do . . . but I try not to. And my CLOSE black friends are the ones I . . . correct them . . . it's like, "Man," . . . they say . . . "Hey, you got to REALIZE that you gonna have to learn to speak Standard English," and . . . now they appreciate it. . . . But it's hard for 'em . . . like most times they'll . . . say, "Man, I'm not gonna do nothing today." And I say, "I'm doing WHAT?" And I say, well, I repeat, I say, "You're not going to do NOTHIN'?" and, you know, then they see how it sounds . . . and once someone, you hear someone else say something that you pick it up quick. . . . And . . . when I say that, you know, "I'm not going to do ANYthing" and . . . I speak like that where, wherever I'm at. It's just that, I don't . . .

Interviewer: Is that so you can get the practice or because you just think that's the right way to talk?

Polo: I don't necessarily think it's the right way to talk, you know, a CERTAIN right way to talk. I just believe that that's the way it's most accepted.

In spite of the fact that Polo does not believe that BEV is inherently wrong, he is clearly, and rightly, convinced that it is an unacceptable way to speak because socially (not linguistically) it is a handicap. His use of the term "improper" also suggests that he feels that in some senses it is indeed the wrong way to talk.

Polo's ambivalence reflects the dilemma of the BEV speaker who has been educated in the tradition that recognizes only one correct English, the formal standard, often in its written variety. He cannot totally reject BEV, the language he had to train himself to avoid, because it is also the language of his neighborhood and of many of his friends. And although his writing and, when he speaks, his diction display few hints of his first dialect, his accent makes it clear that he is a BEV speaker; if he should slip into a BEV feature, as when he says "a effort" above, many listeners will be quick to relegate him to the class of the uneducated. He is well aware of this danger, and he takes pains to avoid it, but he is not willing to condemn himself or BEV completely. His dilemma is reflected again in the subjects' distinction between "bad" English (i.e., ungrammatical and lacking prestige) and BEV. They take pains to associate BEV exclusively with slang. In other words, they define BEV solely in terms of lexicon. BEV grammatical and phonological forms are considered "bad" grammar. Bad grammar is a constant because the rules of grammar, learned in school as correct English, never change. In order to salvage BEV from being considered bad, then, it is necessary for them to define it as slang. Slang is good—it is colorful, homey, and familiar, and it promotes solidarity and a sense of identity.

Max describes a friend of his who talks bad although he does not explicitly use that term:

> I know a young lady who, I mean, she'll just talk and everything's backwards and mixed up, who attends this university, and, you know, I find myself, "Oh? Well you mean such and such and such".... And then, it's "Well, didn't I say that?" You know, but it's backwards, "She be IS" and just SLIPS ... because she's so used to, uh, speakin' a certain way that it becomes habit and, uh, you don't really notice what you're doing.

He betrays his prejudice against BEV grammar when he imitates it by saying "she be is," which hardly resembles any legitimate BEV form.

In talking to Thomas, Max indicates by the following comment that while BEV is not the correct medium for "intellectual" talk, it is the medium to create a sense of familiarity and solidarity:

> And I found that even in talking, you talking to me, you know, sometimes, you know, we can get BLACK with each other, but then we can talk intellectual, also. But because a the menTALity of us being black, I find that you know, you find yourself MORE, or MOST of the time, relating to me in black dialect.

Ironically, in this semi-formal situation at least, Max and Thomas speak very little BEV. It is possible that in a situation that was truly informal they would speak more of it, but given Thomas's very low opinion of BEV and the fact that both of them are in an environment where fluency in SAE is far more valued, it is unlikely.

They do point out that BEV is valued among certain African-American campus groups as a way to show solidarity, a fact which is quite annoying to Thomas, who claims he had to learn BEV as a second dialect in order to get along with his African-American peers. He believes Black English is a "joke" in which he must participate in order to speak informally with other African-Americans. His opinion of Black English is low indeed: "I don't feel it's really a language," he told me. He sees African-Americans as speaking either Black English, which is incorrect, or SAE, the language of the educated. He does not recognize that they might legitimately shift between dialects to accommodate the situation. He seems to see such shifts as insincere. As he tells Max:

> Not every person who is BLACK can actually go intellectually and SPEAK with a Standard English that is, really is, the King's English and PROPER and all that, and actually USE the words that constitute proper English. And phrases and all THAT kinda thing. There not that many blacks here who are, you know, below average but . . . there are a FEW, and . . . it seems like even a lot of the intellectual ones that I've met like to go to BLACK English as compared to Standard English when communicating with other blacks. And it's HARD. Because I don't always wanna do that. I don't LIKE to at all. But it's just I'm being kinda force fed the idea because I'm mingling with blacks, and . . . if I come off where there's FIFTY people speaking BLACK English and I'm tryna speak STANDARD English that, you know, is naturally just gonna be a lot of misunderstanding about what I'm tryna do to them and what I'm tryna not to be and I just don't wanna . . . FIGHT it anymore.

Thomas is frustrated by the fact that to show solidarity with other African-Americans and to show black identity he must speak a dialect he looks down upon. He seems so intent upon creating an intellectual ethos that he cannot accept the other men's limited definition of BEV as slang. For Thomas, even slang is improper.

In his interviews, Thomas expends a great deal of energy on the question of identity, relating it consistently to the use of BEV versus the use of SAE. He provides a good example of a student struggling with the identity problem spawned by negative attitudes toward BEV. He himself holds negative attitudes toward it, and he reports that his mother does. As a result, he strives to speak and write only SAE, and he succeeds well although there are traces of sweet talking excesses in his written prose. However, he is caught in a bind. While his SAE may please his teachers, it sometimes alienates him from his African-American peers.

Spike has an attitude toward BEV similar to, though not as strong as Thomas's in that he sees it as something of a joke. Max reminds him: "Now you yourself, from, ah growin' up with me, you know, you never really spoke, uh, a lotta slang. And when we'd be kiddin' around you'd always laugh about it, you know." In his interview with me he at first expresses confusion over how BEV is to be defined, and he seems somewhat unwilling to admit that it exists at all. As our conversation illustrates, he has for many years been completely bidialectal, and since he moved from an all black to a much more mixed high school his use of BEV has diminished:

> Interviewer: Do you notice yourself switching [between SAE and BEV] any?
> Spike: Um, I guess, I guess that happened pretty much when I was in Middle School . . . . Cause I guess I was under a lotta pressure then, I know I was under pressure cause when I played basketball it was DEFINITELY all black there . . . and, uh, that wouldn't a went over too well, so I, now that I think back I guess, yeah [laughs].

The pressure he refers to is pressure to speak BEV in order to show his solidarity with his group of friends. Notice how he confines his admission of speaking BEV in middle school to an acceptable domain, the basketball court, where young African-American men typically use a great deal of slang. Unlike Thomas, Spike seems to accept Max's definition of BEV as slang as an acceptable compromise. In semi-formal conversation with Max, who grew up in the same neighborhood as he did, he sometimes lapses into a style that uses some BEV forms, primarily BEV slang. Thus he somewhat relieves the pressure of conflicting attitudes toward BEV. He usually speaks and writes in SAE, but he will use BEV, mostly its lexicon, in situations where he feels the need to draw on its covert prestige.

For BEV speakers like Polo, Max, Shanique, Divinity, and Laurie, the pressure to resolve conflicting attitudes seems to result in a generally positive attitude toward BEV. They may have a substantial stake in reconciling the conflict because all display a few distinctive BEV phonological and grammatical features in speaking—not many, but enough to identify their knowledge of the dialect. They tend to use BEV comfortably in situations that would normally call for its use, and they show respect for BEV slang as a legitimate dialect with functions closely related to identity and group solidarity. On the other hand, their formal schooling and probably their general social attitudes have left them with the erroneous belief that BEV grammar and phonology (which generally is very difficult, often impossible, to change) are wrong, improper, and incorrect and signs of the ignorance that results from poverty and oppression. They do not acknowledge that the social and economic isolation of African-Americans has simply ensured the survival of their unique dialect.

Speakers like Thomas, Spike, and Dinese seem on the surface to have adjusted more readily to conflicting attitudes toward BEV. Their SAE is quite polished, and they show no trace of the accent associated with

BEV. Underneath the surface, however, there may well be great conflicts. For Thomas, at least, this appears to be the case. He feels as if he is forced to denigrate his language in order to be accepted into African-American culture. His unrelentingly negative view of BEV pushes him farther away from resolution. He is indeed a successful student, yet his success seems to have resulted in conflict. I cannot deduce from this limited study what the effects of Thomas's negative attitudes toward BEV may be. There are no immediately apparent effects on his writing, but I can hardly conclude from that fact that negative views of BEV are harmless.

As far as writing is concerned, all the subjects are highly competent in producing written SAE and none displays dialect interference on the level of grammar, syntax, or phonology. Max provides an interesting example of the controlled and limited view of BEV as slang. His letter to a friend is laced with slang expressions and seems particularly aimed at showing me his agility with BEV, that is, as slang used within his peer group, in keeping with his role as my research assistant and as a subject for this study. However, Max's general avoidance of BEV in writing indicates, I believe, that he wishes to be taken seriously as an intelligent student and black man. At the same time that Max avoids BEV in writing, he relies heavily on complicated and often hypercorrect diction. I have elsewhere hypothesized that his writing style is influenced by sweet talk because he associates it with formal, intellectual discourse (Balester). Unfortunately, Max is unaware of the negative effects of using hypercorrect sweet talk in academic prose. Polo and Thomas display the same tendency toward sweet talk in writing although the other subjects do not.

Shanique's case illustrates a different set of problems that may arise from negative attitudes toward BEV. She uses BEV freely in speaking, employing not only its lexicon but also much of its grammar. She seems unconcerned with the negative stereotypes that the men so carefully avoid, though she can hardly be unaware of them. Furthermore, Shanique's strong sense of identity leads her to be less self-conscious about her speech than some other nonstandard speakers; thus she does not attend to it closely and lapses more easily and more naturally into casual style. I explain her use of BEV by relating it to the concept of covert prestige: she attaches to BEV certain positive attributes such as friendliness, toughness, and independence. Rather than show me she is capable and intelligent by speaking SAE, she shows her confidence by not monitoring her speech and by being herself.

Her writing, however, studiously avoids BEV features. It is quite correct and fairly typical in many ways of the writing of any student, just as Ramsey suggests it will be. However, when I compared Shanique's spoken and written narratives, I was struck by the lack of life and color in the written version, the loss of humor and realistic detail. Much of the success of her first version was the result of her skillful use of BEV to create an ethos as a tough, independent, and witty narrator and to make her characters come alive with realistic dialogue. In my analysis elsewhere of her prose, I hypothesize that her perception that BEV should be avoided in school writing has deprived her of a valuable stylistic tool (Balester).

Conclusion

What are the effects of negative attitudes towards BEV on students' learning of language? The question cannot yet be answered on the basis of solid evidence. However, it can be answered by appealing to common sense. A society that expresses extremely negative attitudes toward BEV through schools, churches, homes, major media, and other transmitters of social values is expressing racism. Racism fosters low self-esteem, alienation from the home and community culture—a crisis of identity. Often it fosters alienation from the dominant culture. If, on the other hand, extremely positive attitudes are expressed in an attempt to negate the effects of racism, if covert prestige is stressed without regard to the social reality of language prejudice, students will be put at risk. Simply calling for more positive and open attitudes toward BEV is inadequate. We may never reform social attitudes toward BEV on a large scale. The success of *Students' Right to Their Own Language* has not been overwhelming, although it was based on the best of linguistic science. Therefore we must encourage students to approach dialect as a situationally governed stylistic tool and school them in its appropriate use. Otherwise, they are at the mercy of prejudices, their own and ours.

Although we cannot pinpoint all the effects or calculate all the risks of negative attitudes toward BEV, we can be sure there are some. While we can applaud students who, like those in this study, have overcome the odds and thrived despite negative attitudes toward BEV (much less toward African-Americans), we must remember that others have withered. Perhaps what we need most at this moment, besides a good dose of basic linguistic training for language arts teachers at all levels including college, is more thorough research. We know little about the attitudes of teachers, parents, politicians, and other powerful groups toward SAE, BEV, or other minority dialects. Evidence from the popular press suggests that their attitudes are generally intolerant, inflexible, and misinformed, yet this evidence is inadequate and suspect. We must also gather more extensive evidence of the attitudes of students themselves. And perhaps most important of all, we must begin to examine the effects of negative attitudes on speaking, reading, writing, and thinking. Such research, if it is widely disseminated, may be an important step toward lasting social change. ❧

NOTES

[1] All comments are reported exactly as they were spoken or written. The following symbols have been used in the transcripts of the taped interviews:

? = upward rise in intonation

XX = unintelligible

[ ] = nonverbal actions such as laughter or pointing or verbal actions such as descriptions of tone of voice

CAPITALS = extra stress and/or increased loudness

Italics = reduced loudness

WORKS CITED

Abrahams, Roger D. *Deep Down in the Jungle: Negro Narrative Folklore from the Streets of Philadelphia.* 1st rev. ed. Chicago: Aldine, 1970.

——. *Positively Black.* Englewood Cliffs: Prentice-Hall, 1970.

——. "The Training of the Man of Words in Talking Sweet." *Language in Society* 1 (1972): 15-29.

——. "Black Talking on the Streets." *Explorations in the Ethnography of Speaking.* Eds. Richard Bauman and Joel Sherzer. London: Cambridge UP, 1974. 240-62.

——. *Talking Black.* Rowley MA: Newbury, 1976.

——, ed. *Afro-American Folktales: Stories from Black Traditions in the New World.* New York: Pantheon, 1985.

Bartholomae, David. "Inventing the University." *When a Writer Can't*

Write: Studies in Writer's Block and Other Composing Problems. Ed. Mike Rose. New York: Guilford, 1985.

Balester, Valerie. "The Social Construction of Ethos: A Study of the Spoken and Written Discourse of Two Black College Students." Diss. The University of Texas at Austin, 1988.

Dillard, J. L. *Black English: Its History and Usage in the United States.* New York: Random House, 1972.

Erickson, Frederick. "Rhetoric, Anecdote, and Rhapsody: Coherence Strategies in a Conversation Among Black American Adolescents." Tannen 81-154.

Fraser, Bruce. "Some 'Unexpected' Reactions to Various American-English Dialects." *Language Attitudes: Current Trends and Prospects.* Eds. Roger W. Shuey and Ralph W. Fasold. Washington: Georgetown UP, 1973. 28-40.

Kerr-Mattox, Beverly. "Language Attitudes of Teachers and Prospective Teachers Toward Black and White Speakers." Masters Thesis. Texas A & M University, 1989.

Labov, William, Paul Cohen, Clarence Robins, and John Lewis. *A Study of the Nonstandard English of Negro and Puerto Rican Speakers in New York City.* Report on Co-operative Research Project 3288. Vols. I and II. New York: Columbia U, 1968.

Labov, William. *The Social Stratification of English in New York City.* Washington: Center for Applied Linguistics, 1966.

——. *The Study of Nonstandard English.* Champaign: NCTE, 1970.

——. *Sociolinguistic Patterns.* Philadelphia: U Pennsylvania P, 1973.

Michaels, Sarah, and James Collins. "Oral Discourse Styles: Classroom Interaction and the Acquisition of Literacy." Tannen 219-44.

Ramsey, Paul A. "Teaching the Teachers to Teach Black-Dialect Writers." *Tapping Potential: English and Language for the Black Learner.* Ed. Charlotte K. Brooks. Urbana: NCTE, 1981.

Seligman, C. R., G. R. Tucker, and W. E. Lambert. "The Effects of Speech Style and Other Attributes on Teachers' Attitudes Towards Pupils." *Language In Society* 1 (1972): 131-42.

Smitherman-Donaldson, Geneva. "White English in Blackface, or Who Do i Be?" *Exploring Language*. Ed. Gary Goshgarian. 4th. ed. Boston: Little Brown, 1986.

Students' Right to Their Own Language. *College Composition and Communication* 25 (1974). Special Issue.

Tannen, Deborah, ed. *Cohesion in Spoken and Written Discourse*. Norwood NJ: Ablex, 1984.

——. "Spoken and Written Narrative in English and Greek." Tannen 21-44.

Tucker, G. R. and W. E. Lambert. "White and Negro Listeners' Reactions to Various American-English Dialects." *Social Forces* 47 (1969): 464-68.

II

How Institutions Construct
the Writing Classroom

What is the purpose of writing instruction? Though many people address this question as if it could have one definitive answer, the purpose of writing instruction really cannot be considered independently of the institution in which it occurs. The essays in this section raise the issue of how institutional resources and goals influence the very definition of writing instruction. All four essays assume that the primary purpose of writing instruction is the individual development of the student, but they differ significantly in their notions about the nature or goal of that growth— whether it is acculturation into a professional discourse community or personal intellectual engagement. Accordingly, these essays consider the purpose of writing instruction from two different kinds of perspectives: from that of a large research university as opposed to that of a small liberal arts college and from that which examines an institution's entire undergraduate curriculum as opposed to one that focuses on an individual classroom.

In her essay, Louise Phelps describes the writing program at Syracuse University, which treats learning to write as a cumulative developmental process from the freshman to the senior year. The writing program consists of a sequence of four studio writing courses that are highly integrated both with each other and with courses across the undergraduate curriculum. The progression of studios leads students through a series of "basic skills," a term which Phelps attempts in her essay to reclaim from those who have denigrated it. The role of the writing class in this context is to support the entire academic mission of the university; in that sense, the skills that the students practice in the studios are indeed basic.

Phelps's goal, to acculturate students into an academic and professional discourse community, is similar to Anne Herrington's concern. She examines how students learn to write by adopting the stance and discourse strategies of a specific academic discipline. Her institutional perspective, however, while still that of a research university, is slightly different. Phelps looks outward from a writing program to the institution as a whole, trying to define what the program can do to achieve the goals of the university. For her, the primary responsibility for writing instruction rests with the teachers in her program, although there is much interchange with faculty in other disciplines. In contrast, Herrington works within an institution in which advanced writing instruction is perceived as a component of the students' disciplinary education. Herrington inhabits one particular classroom—an anthropology class—and examines how writing is used there to acculturate students to the discourse community of practicing anthropologists. This class operates on two basic assumptions: that studying anthropology means learning how anthropologists write and that students should imitate that discourse at some level by taking on the role of novice anthropologists.

Although Herrington does not present this particular anthropology class as an ideal, the teacher's commitment to writing, her awareness, and her sophistication make this class an impressive representative of this form of writing in the disciplines. The important point, however, is neither the typicality of the class nor the structure of the writing program. The point, rather, is that Phelps and Herrington are operating within institutions that support this kind of developmental approach—recognizing that writing skills develop both over the course of a semester and over the four-year undergraduate curriculum. The goal of writing instruction at both the University of Massachusetts and Syracuse University is to have students become familiar with the writing and assumptions of academic or professional communities and begin to enter them. The fact that these programs have developed at research-oriented institutions is not accidental.

In contrast, Carmen Schmersahl and Byron Stay write from the perspective of a small liberal arts college. In examining how individual faculty members outside of English use writing to facilitate learning, they describe very different institutional assumptions. From this perspective, the goal seems less to initiate students into professional and academic discourse communities than to use writing to promote learning and personal intellectual growth. The classroom itself, then, constitutes a school discourse community made up of generally educated people who can investigate critically and ask intelligent, disinterested questions about the work of a discipline as well as relate that work to their own beliefs and actions. The role of writing in such a classroom is exploratory, the writing assignments providing the occasion for students to engage in this kind of intellectual growth rather than to imitate the forms of writing used by expert practitioners in their fields.

Schmersahl and Stay point out that the faculty at their institution often have a distant relationship to the writing in their own disciplines. The faculty in the various disciplines at Mount Saint Mary's see the purpose of writing as making the disciplinary material relevant to students in a personal intellectual way, not as preprofessional training. They believe that it is possible to learn about (and even teach) a discipline without trying to contribute to the conversation in that discipline's discourse community. The extent to which a writing across the curriculum program depends on the faculty's relationship to their own discipline has not often been recognized in our literature. Nor do we often hear from the small liberal arts college.

Cynthia Selfe's essay reminds us that fostering personal intellectual growth and engagement in learning need not be sacrificed at research-oriented institutions. Like Schmersahl and Stay, Selfe is interested in the way students can use writing to make knowledge personal and to engage in thoughtful intellectual exchange with teachers and peers. She is particularly concerned about those students who have too often been silent in traditional classrooms. She describes how computer networks—specifically a bulletin board with pseudonymous contributions—can be used to create a sense of community and personal involvement. Such a bulletin board may relieve students of classroom pressures to formulate quick responses, to compete with other students for the teacher's attention and approval, and to express controversial opinions in public. She observed that her students—even normally reticent ones—used the network to relate classroom topics to their own educational and personal experiences, expressing views that might not otherwise have surfaced in class discussion or formal papers. While Selfe's report is of a preliminary study, the benefits of this kind of technology seem promising and might apply to many kinds of institutions.

The essays in this section take account of the particular institutional circumstances in which writing instruction occurs. As such, they reflect an essential characteristic of rhetoric itself. Rhetoric is the art of developing arguments appropriate to particular contexts; it always attends to the *kairos*, the time and place, the occasion of the discourse. While each rhetorical situation is unique, rhetoric is still governed by principles. If we are to make our research and our pedagogy consistent with the principles of our discipline, we must recognize that writing instruction itself is just as situated as any other rhetorical act.

These essays suggest that the profound disagreements in our profession about the purpose of writing instruction may be rooted, at least in part, in differences among institutions. What follows from these essays, however, may not be simple acceptance of whatever institutional constraints and differences exist. Just as a rhetor uses discourse both to respond to and to reconstitute the rhetorical situation, so too must educators use rhetoric to improve and even redefine the institutional contexts in which rhetorical education occurs. Institutions may need as much educating as students.

❦ 5

Composing One's Self in a Discipline: Students' and Teachers' Negotiations

Anne J. Herrington

One of the important characteristics of composition scholarship is that it focuses directly on issues of teaching. Similarly, one of the more important effects of the interest in Writing Across the Curriculum over the past 15 years has been to broaden that focus to include not only our writing classes, but also our literature classes, as well as the classes of our colleagues in such other disciplines as history, engineering, and physics. In collaborative working sessions with these colleagues and in our research, we have been reexamining a number of questions central to our teaching. Some of those questions move us from focusing on direct applications of particular teaching approaches to examining more basic matters of the nature of teaching and learning in our classes. The assumption is that understanding more about students' experiences as they try to do the writing we ask of them will guide us in our teaching.

That assumption guides the research I will report on in this essay. The primary questions I will address are these: What is entailed for students in learning to write for courses in particular disciplines? What is our role as teachers in this learning? I will offer some initial answers to these questions on the basis of an ethnographic study of writing, teaching, and learning in one classroom context, a writing-intensive, upper-division course in anthropology. The primary claim I will advance is that for students in this course, learning to write entailed something more than learning conventions of texts. It also meant learning to present themselves as professionals. That may seem obvious; however, what it entails is, I believe, not so obvious. Specifically, it entailed for these students defining both their personal identity in relation to a professional audience and their relation to knowledge: the ideas they would formulate and put forth as claims to knowledge. While that may seem like a claim applicable to a specialized course, I believe it applies more broadly: whether we are teaching a course for majors or a general education course, our students fashion ways to present themselves and their ideas as they study and write for us, and we contribute to that composing process. It behooves us, then, to step back to consider what is entailed in that process.

Clifford Geertz offers a useful metaphor for viewing the challenge this learning entails for our students when he terms academic communities "intellectual villages" (157). To enter the village, students are trying to learn not only its ways of speaking but also its ways of thinking so that those ways become their own, so that they can feel that they are speaking in their own voices and making their own knowledge claims in ways effective within the community. For many, that means finding a way to bridge what seem like two extremes: at the one extreme, the personal—whatever personal way of speaking they bring to the village and their personal approach to whatever they are studying; and at the other extreme, the professional—what seems to them the distanced, impersonal, and confident voice and approach to knowledge of the village.

In this essay, to illustrate what is entailed for some students who attempt to bridge these extremes, I document the experiences of two students in one course as they try to enter the "intellectual village" of anthropology. The students themselves represent extremes; one is an able and confident writer and student of anthropology, the other lacks confidence as a writer, and, as her professor said, her "anthropological understanding is about as limited as anybody's in the class." I selected them because, despite these differences, both face the challenge of bridging the personal and professional in terms of the roles they project and their approaches to knowledge. While their specific experiences may differ from others, the issues they are struggling with and the dynamics of their interactions with their teachers are representative of others in the Writing in Anthropology class. Reading their experiences should provide a point of reference for reflecting on the experiences of students in our own classes and our inter-actions with them.

To document their efforts, I will trace their experiences working through drafts of specific assignments, including their exchanges with the teacher as they worked on the drafts. I will focus on the language they use in their writings, looking at that language in the larger context of their perceptions of what they are trying to do and their teacher's response to that language. My aim in this approach is to illuminate what I think we too often gloss over when we read students' writings: that the language they use is often a cue to fundamental issues of their perception of the role they are to project and their approach to knowledge. If we attend to those cues, we can learn more about what is entailed for our students in trying to write in our courses and, I believe, be more responsive as we work with individual students.

Background on the Course and the Study

First, a bit of background on the course, Writing in Anthropology. It is a one-semester writing-intensive course required of all anthropology majors at my university to complete their Junior Year Writing Requirement.[1] The semester that I followed the course, its thematic focus was "food and cul-ture." I chose the course in part because of its aims. As the teacher of the course, Professor Sylvia Forman, explained these aims to students in the syllabus, they were "to help you employ writing and research skills to better understand anthropology; and to help you improve your ability to write effectively and comfortably, both generally and in an anthropologi-cal context." While this primary focus on writing may make the course seem unique, such "writing-intensive" courses are characteristic of a pro-gram model of "writing across the curriculum" in place at other schools (e.g., University of Michigan and Bucknell University). Further, as I have claimed earlier, even when courses are not formally designated as "writ-ing-intensive," students face similar challenges if they are asked to write for those courses (Herrington, "Writing"; McCarthy).

I chose the course for two other reasons. First, I had reason to believe it was successful and well taught. I based that judgment on stu-dent evaluations from two previous times the course was offered as well as the program evaluation of the University Writing Committee. Second, peer review was central to the course. (See Herrington and Cadman,

"Peer Review and Revision" for a discussion of the role of peer review in the course.)

Forman is an experienced teacher who had designed the course and taught it four times, served on the University Writing Committee, and received a Distinguished Teaching Award.[2] She was assisted by a teaching assistant (TA), a PhD student in anthropology whom I will refer to using the pseudonym Jim. His only prior teaching experience was as a discussion leader in a large lecture course. As he explained in an interview, he had had no prior experience responding to writing as a teacher, other than "grading" short answer essays. He volunteered to be a TA for this course because he was interested in writing and wanted, as he said, "to see if I could do anything to get people to write better." Twenty-six students were in the course.

Both the assignments and the procedures of the course followed from its goals. The key components of the procedure included multiple drafts of all four papers, peer review and teacher review of drafts, and deferred grading—that is, no grades were given until the end of the semester, at which point a grade was given on the final draft of each paper in students' portfolios. In the syllabus, Forman explained the deferred grading by saying that "we do not want to discourage you when you are truly trying to improve your understanding and skills—even if, at the moment your efforts are not producing optimal results."

The assignments were clearly linked to the goal of learning to write "in an anthropological context." The first three were to be written as if for a professional journal, such as *The American Anthropologist* or *Food and Foodways*: a book review, a descriptive field report, and a journal research article.[3] Obviously, for these three writings, students were to attempt to present themselves as members of the village—as professional anthropologists speaking to other anthropologists.

For the study, I used multiple sources of information and multiple methods of obtaining it. I attended nearly every class, taking field notes and participating to a limited degree; collected all course documents; surveyed all students in the course about their perceptions of their strengths and weaknesses as writers, the writing assignments, and specific teaching approaches; analyzed drafts and final versions of the four major writings and peer critiques completed by nine students; conducted two audio-taped hour-long interviews with these nine students, including discourse-based interviews focusing on revision changes; and conducted two audiotaped hour-long interviews with the professor and her teaching assistant. Deborah Cadman, my research assistant, helped to organize and interpret the interviews and cross-check my field notes. For the case studies, we worked independently to interpret the multiple sources of information and then met to corroborate our findings.

I turn now to the cases of Sally and Kate. In discussing Sally, I will focus on her experience with the second assignment, the descriptive field report; in discussing Kate, I will comment briefly on the field report and then focus on the third assignment, the journal research article. It happens that Jim, the teaching assistant, responded to all of these writings. In reporting on each case, I will explain his manner of response and how it varied in particular instances. In the concluding section, I will draw some inferences for teaching on the basis of these variations.

Case Studies

Sally

Sally was a first-semester senior in the department's honors program and had taken seven courses prior to this one. She was also confident of her writing ability. In a questionnaire completed at the beginning of the study, she said, "I am a good creative and analytical writer. I can express myself well on paper." Her freshman English teachers and teachers for this course shared this assessment.

Although she had few difficulties with the first assignment, she struggled with the second, the descriptive field report. Students were instructed by the assignment sheet "to conduct a brief field study of some aspect of food and culture with local people." Sally chose to interview foreign graduate students living in a university residence area about their adjustments to American eating habits.

Sally made few revisions from her first to second draft. The second draft (Figure 1) was reviewed by Jim, the TA, who had also responded to Sally's first assignment, the book review. In response to this second draft, he wrote: "In general, it's a sound paper. Your method is set out well, and the description and conclusion read nicely. . . . This paper lacks the crisp tone of your book review. Just because it is for a journal doesn't mean you have to assume an 'academic air.' The complex constructions, use of forms of 'to be' and some wordiness really detract. Try to be more direct and active." Here, Jim responds to the persona Sally projects, implicitly inviting her to project a less formal, less distanced "academic

---

Figure 1. *Sally's Descriptive Field Report: Second Draft*

Introduction [excerpt]

. . .This report is based on exploring the question of how foreign students perceive the differences between American eating habits and those of their own cultures and what the consequences are of having to live and eat here.

Conclusion

It seems clear that to many foreign visitors to this country Americans suffer from a profound lack of appreciation of the esthetic and sensual pleasure that eating can involve. To a majority of the informants the concepts of fast food, junk food and improper eating habits (i.e., overeating, strict dieting or eating just for the sake of filling one's stomach) are distinctly American.... Few of the informants had any physical complaints in relation to their adjustments to eating in the U.S., aside from an occasional stomach upset. It was my impression that the major difficulty suffered was a psychological/emotional sense of loss.

It must be pointed out that at least some of this sense of loss was certainly due to the complete change in environment and to the fact that most students, in general, are not able to eat as well and as elaborately as they do when living with their families. However, these factors do not fully account for the dissatisfaction most of the informants feel with American foodways. Clearly there is a great deal of importance in the esthetic aspects of eating, illustrated by the nature of the complaints expressed by the informants. I would argue that the main source of dissatisfaction experienced by foreign students eating among Americans is based not on the types of food or the nutritional value contained within but instead on the 'enjoyability factor' of American eating in general.

---

air." Note that although he made these more global comments, he did not make changes in the text itself (e.g., did not recast sentences or replace words with alternatives).

The difference Jim sensed between this writing and Sally's book review was consistent with Sally's intentions. She said in an interview that she thought this second paper was to be more distanced and formal: "I assumed that I had to have this kind of detached tone, because of what I read—the report I read, you know—it was my assumption that the kind of writing you would do for a journal would have to have that quality of detached—like, you know, that false image of objectivity." (In Figure 1, I have underlined some of the language that, to me, conveys this effect.)

The report she refers to is a journal article the professor had given the students as an example, one in which the author used somewhat formalized language. From what Sally said in her interview, it seems that this article misled her in this respect.

After getting the draft back, Sally talked with Jim. She told him how she thought she was supposed to sound. She explained to me, "When I told Jim that he said, 'No, no, no. Writing in Anthropology is definitely shifting away from that, we don't encourage that.—So, I'm psyched." She also said, "I didn't present myself as a presence in this paper as strong as I could have." One reason she didn't, I think, was that she was also implicitly trying to sound "impressive," "conclusive," and "in control"; she did not want to admit to problems she had had with the field study, and she had had a number of them.

As she told Jim and indicated in her interview with me, doing her second paper was a frustrating experience. She had a good deal of difficulty finding a focusing question, and in her interviews felt she hadn't asked the right questions. As she explained to me just before she wrote her third draft, "[I felt] very insecure about my method, so what I'm gonna do when I rewrite is . . . include a section about my insecurity about method . . . so that I don't have to try to justify this and make this sound impressive when I don't even think it really is. You know, I didn't impress myself. That's the point."

Sally followed this plan in her revision. (See Figure 2.) The changes she made are significant because they include not just changes of "tone" and persona but also substantive changes. Most obviously, as the excerpt from the introduction and the new first paragraph of the conclusion show, she clarified her focus: instead of focusing on how foreign students adjust, she focuses on their opinions of American eating habits. Further, she tries to be less "pompous" in her language—her word to describe the tone of her second draft—and to be more honest about what she really found. For example, in the conclusion, she drops language like "it seems clear that," "it must be pointed out," "informants," and "I would argue that." Finally, she adds a final paragraph assessing her own research experience and her needs as a learner.

In response to this draft, Jim wrote: "the prose is much cleaned up. The tone less haughty, the conclusion improved. The final para. seems more like a note than part of the conclusion.—What does 'high degree of health per capita' mean?" For him, the problem remained one of tone and, implicitly, persona. As he explained to me, "I think she was very dis-

---

Figure 2. *Sally's Descriptive Field Report: Third Draft*

Introduction [excerpt]

. . .This report focuses on the question of how foreign students perceive the differences between American eating habits and those of their own cultures and **what their opinions are concerning these differences.**

Conclusion

I emerged from these interviews with a new perspective on my own culture's foodways. Although I hold my own opinions about the nutritional quality of the typically American diet, I had not even considered the esthetic elements of eating when preparing this study. To many foreign students, Americans suffer from a profound lack of appreciation for the esthetic and sensual pleasure associated with eating.

To a majority of those **interviewed**, the concepts of fast food, junk food and improper eating habits (i.e., ...

Although some of foreign students' dissatisfaction is probably due to the complete change in environment and the less elaborate eating habits they have as students, this does not fully account for their sense of loss. The fact that almost **every person interviewed** criticized Americans for their lack of appreciation of the 'enjoyability factor' of eating indicates that this aspect of eating is at least as important to them as feeding their bodies as well. **In a country known for it's abundance and high degree of health per capita, it may come as a surpize to some Americans to know that they are considered deprived by foreign students in their foodways.**

I would like to note that this paper does not represent what I consider a conclusive study. Although I do think that the trends which emerged in the interviews are valid representations of the impressions of foreign students, the design of the study itself was lacking in clarity and focus. This realization did not, unfortunately, occur until the study was underway and thus, it was impossible to correct. The exercise was a valuable one for me in revealing the importance of the preparatory steps involved in conducting field study research. I would benefit from more experience with defining topics, designing surveys and choosing representative populations before I take on another project like this.

Note: Bold print indicates changes from the previous draft.

Figure 3. *Sally's Descriptive Field Report: Fourth Draft*

Conclusion

This paper does not represent what I consider a conclusive study. Although I do think that the trends which emerged in the interviews are valid representations of the impressions of foreign students, the design of the study itself was lacking in clarity and focus. This realization did not, unfortunately, occur until the study was underway and thus, it was impossible to correct. **It was a valuable exercise in that it made some of my own cultural biases more apparent. For example, I had assumed that the questions about how well Americans eat would be interpreted in a health sense. This was in complete accordance with the opinion expressed by foreign students that Americans are more concerned with the nutritional aspect of food than the enjoyable.**

I emerged from these interviews with a new perspective on my own culture's foodways. Although I hold my own opinions about the nutritional quality of the typically American diet **(if there is such a thing)**, I had not even considered the esthetic elements of eating when preparing this study. **Ironically, this turned out to be the major complaint about American foodways that foreign students expressed.**

To a majority of those interviewed, the concepts of fast food, junk food and. . . . In a country known for its abundance and the relatively **high degree of good health** enjoyed by its population, it may come as a surprise to some Americans to find out that they are considered by foreign students to be deprived in their foodways.

Note: Bold print indicates changes from the previous draft.

---

appointed with the interviews she did. That may have ruined the tone of the paper." In explaining why he thought the final paragraph would be better as a note, he said "I don't think it's a really strong ending to be second-guessing yourself. I think there's a place for this kind of stuff, but I don't think it's here."

When I asked Forman about this passage in a follow-up interview, she agreed: "It is too apologetic on the one hand, but also it just doesn't have to do with the study. The fact that she could benefit from more experience—this has nothing to do with the study at all." In Forman's view, Sally perceived the paper as "a communication between herself and the instructor," focusing on her own learning experiences instead of the research project and its possible limitations.

The third draft was returned in mid-October. Sally wrote her fourth and final draft in early December. (See Figure 3.) In this draft, she responded in her own way to Jim's comment about the final paragraph of self-assessment. Instead of making it a note, however, she moved it to the beginning of the conclusion section. More significantly, she changed the focus from an assessment of herself, the learner, to an assessment of what she, the researcher, learned. Note also that she opened by focusing on the "paper," instead of "I." Further, the final sentences of the paragraph focus not on what she still needs to learn about research but on what her research experience says about American cultural biases. I asked her if she thought it was important to have this note in the paper. She said yes: "That's really important to know that the researcher's not happy with this. [Note she says "researcher."] Here I am making all these statements. If I were really confident about it, that'd be one thing. But I want them to know that I didn't think the study itself was good, and it could have been done better. So whatever is read should be read knowing that." I asked if she thought this kind of observation would lessen her credibility. She said "No . . . I mean, I'd rather know if I was reading something that the person didn't feel confident about."

When I showed this version to Forman, she agreed: "It's certainly less apologetic. And it better represents a kind of reflection on the work as opposed to a concern with I failed or something like that. 'Even though it's not conclusive . . . here's what you get out of it; here's what you can do with it.' It's built in a kind of analytic fashion into what she was trying to say in the conclusion. . . . It's a nice example of an anthropological style of a sequence."

By this draft, Sally had moved closer to presenting *herself* as a professional. Note that Sally seemed to figure out this "anthropological style" on her own. I suspect that other students might need more explanation than Jim's comment ("seems more like a note")—explanation of the sort Forman provided in her interviews with me. Still, for Sally, writing each draft as she was guided by Jim and encouraged to speak in a less distanced tone gave her an occasion for experimenting with different ways of presenting herself to arrive at the synthesis she achieved in the fourth draft. In the second draft, she projects a more impersonal, protected, and confident persona—the one she thinks the village expects. What her experience shows is that the "impersonal" face of the second draft represented a literal detachment from herself. More significantly, in projecting this impersonal, confident face, she was also effacing the major claim she wished to make on the basis of her field work.

In the third draft, she projects the other extreme, the personal, unguarded face of the student focusing on her personal learning experience. It is in this draft, though, that she expresses what she felt were the more important "findings" from her research: foreign students' impressions of our eating habits and our cultural myopia. In the fourth draft, Sally accomplishes a synthesis: she still makes the claim that is important to her but in a way that focuses on the subject, not the self as learner, and does not undermine her claims with too many apologies. In short, she has taken a big step toward writing her way in, bridging the gap between the perceived distanced ways of the academic village and herself where she feels she is speaking in her own voice and making her own claims.

Kate

Now Sally may seem like a rather neat, easy case: she's bright and a quite independent learner. The second student, Kate, provides a useful contrast: she was a less successful student and a more passive learner. Still, she faced the same challenge of needing to compose a place for herself between the two extremes. She was a first-semester junior who had taken only three anthropology courses prior to this one, and she was not an honors student in anthropology. Not only had she taken fewer anthropology courses than Sally, she seemed less able to accomplish the basic analytical work required by the course assignments. Also unlike Sally, at the beginning of the semester she didn't feel confident of herself as a writer. When I pressed her to identify some aspect of writing she was most confident about, she said "writing a mechanically correct paper and organizing it well." She said she was least confident about "getting my first, basic ideas down on paper." So, in terms of her competence as both a student of anthropology and a writer, she was, as Forman commented after working with Sally on her book review, "as limited as anybody in the class." After working with her on her second and third writings, Jim agreed. While for Sally the issue was to fashion a persona and a way to *present* some of the major claims she wanted to make, for Kate the issue was additionally a more basic one of *formulating* those interpretive claims in the first place and then presenting them.

These difficulties were evident in her book review and in the descriptive field report. Kate's field report was "A Study of Food and Social Attitudes in the Dining Commons." The draft she submitted to Jim for his review illustrates her difficulties with interpretation (Figure 4). It contained a fair amount of detail and quotations from her informants but very little interpretation of that information. Commenting on this draft, Jim focused on these problems, writing the following overall comment: "The quotes work well to support your points though at times I think you need to interject yourself in the discussion. Quotes should embellish, not make your points." Next to the final paragraph he wrote, "Bring in your findings. Your conclusion should be more than a restatement of your intro." Interestingly, in his comments he linked interpretation with inserting oneself. Kate apparently understood his comment; when I asked her what Jim meant by "interject yourself," she said "to analyze my information. Sometimes, I don't even think to do it." Her revision suggests that her difficulty may be more than just remembering to do it: she adds just two sentences (underlined in Figure 4) that add some, but very little interpretation.

Her drafts for the field report also show that she was conscious to some degree of trying to project an impersonal, confident persona. That is evident, for instance, in the assertive persona evoked in the first sentence of the final paragraph with the phrases "I must conclude" and "in fact." In addition, from the second to the third draft, in another section, she changed "the methodology I used" to "the methodology used." She did that on her own initiative. When I asked her about this change, she said, "I probably just thought it would sound less—maybe more professional or something. I don't know." Also, following the advice of her peer reviewer, she changed a "would" to "is." When I asked her about this change, she said, "because I think it was in the peer critique. You're not supposed to use 'would'. 'Would' doesn't sound as confident as 'is.'" These comments indicate she had some sense of trying to project an impersonal, confident air. (Jim did not comment on her persona at all, perhaps deciding it more important to focus on matters of precision and clarity. In his overall comments he advised, "Use similar verb tenses in sentences. Watch the use of 'it.' Make sure you are clear about what 'it' or 'that' refers to." In her revision, Kate found and altered sentences to which this advice pertained.)

Having finished the second paper, Kate was feeling somewhat more confident—at least of her ability to handle the subject matter as she worked through successive drafts of a paper.

The third writing was the journal research article, explained in the

Figure 4. *Kate's Descriptive Field Report: Second and Third Drafts*

Second Draft

4th paragraph [excerpt]

. . .The people who eat in Basics [a dining commons serving only a vegetarian menu] tend to be more "food aware" than those from other dining commons. They choose to eat in a place that offers a restricted menu of no red meat. In Hampshire dining commons, I got derogatory reactions for the most part, to my questions about food including this one from a female freshman "it's mostly gross, but sometimes it's okay."

Final paragraph

From these findings I must conclude that there are in fact differences perceived regarding both food values and social values among people who eat in the dining commons. The dining commons were created out of necessity: University residents need to eat. Where students eat may be a matter of convenience, but it is also a matter of choice, a choice which is partly based on and results in some of the perceptions and ideas that are reflected in my research.

Third Draft

4th paragraph [excerpt]

. . .The people who eat in Basics [a dining commons serving only a vegetarian menu] tend to be more "food aware" than those from other dining commons. They choose to eat in a place that offers a restricted menu of no red meat. **Food preference is not so much an issue in Hampshire D.C., people tend not to like what they are eating.** In Hampshire dining commons, I got derogatory reactions for the most part, to my questions about food including this one from a female freshman "it's mostly gross, but sometimes it's okay."

Conclusion:

From my research I found the Basics D.C. is more health orientated, laid back place, and attracts that kind of person. Hampshire is a more social place, concerned more with fashion then with food. From these findings I must conclude that there are in fact differences perceived regarding both food values and social values among people who eat in the dining commons. The dining commons were created out of necessity: University residents need to eat. Where students eat may be a matter of convenience, but it is also a matter of choice, a choice which is partly based on and results in some of the perceptions and ideas that are reflected in my research.

Note: Bold print indicates additions made to the text.

assignment as "the type generally published in a scholarly journal, to an audience of professionals and researchers." In the assignment, Forman stressed that since it was the "closest to the typical 'term paper,'" they were to "be especially careful NOT to fall into typical 'student' writing habits: don't write it for the teachers, don't rely on the tone or format of the 'term paper'. . . . Rather, be analytic, thorough, systematic, and professional." When I asked Kate what this advice meant, she said she wasn't sure although she did perceive this writing to be "different because I was much more serious about this because I wanted it to be done the way I wanted it. You know, you usually write it the way the teacher wants it, whatever, but I did it the way I wanted to do it." Interestingly, this is the first writing where Kate inserted herself as more of a presence. Still, she followed "the teacher" a great deal as well.

This assignment was the most difficult for Kate, right from the start—formulating a research question. Both in the printed assignment and in class discussions, Forman stressed that the research question for this writing was to be a "why-question" (instead of a "what-question" as with the descriptive field report) or a question of the relationship between x and y. One generic question type she illustrated in class was "how does a certain change in x affect health and nutrition for a given group?"

As Kate explained to me, initially she didn't know what she wanted to write on, other than "cultures that were isolated." The way she found her focus reflects her more passive approach in class. She mentioned her general interest to both Forman and the TA. As she explained, "then Jim and Sylvia mentioned Eskimos and restrictions on their hunting. I just did it. I really have no interest in Eskimos. Well, I do now." So she got her topic from them. However, as this comment implies, she became personally interested in the plight of the Eskimos as she did the research. (That may explain her statement that "I wanted it done the way I wanted it.") She formulated the specific research question to fit the frame Forman had presented in class: "What effect do legal constraints on marine mammal hunting have on Eskimo nutrition?"

In preparing her first draft, Kate had a number of difficulties, including finding information, organizing it, and interpreting it. These difficulties were evident throughout the first draft, including in the introduction and conclusion (Figure 5). Although her final sentence in the introduction states her research question, she does not keep focused in the full draft on this relationship. Instead, it describes the various mammals that Eski-

---

Figure 5. *Kate's Journal Research Article: First Draft*

Eskimo Nutritional Adaptations

Introduction [excerpt]

The conservation and protection of whales and other marine mammals such as seals and walrus was recently legalized under the marine mammal protection act of 1972. Included with it, along with ongoing debate, was an exemption for aboriginal and subsistence whaling, but this was not a definate status. . . . The 1984/85 annual report on the Marine Mammal Protection Act of 1972, called for a seperate management between commercial and subsistence whaling, placing quotas and limitations of whaling for subsistance purposes. This, along with state and federal controls on whaling has caused changes in Eskimo society. The U.S. government is prohibiting some of its native citizens from an activity that is intrinsic to their culture. I want to find out what effect legal constraints on marine mammal hunting have on Eskimo nutrition.

Conclusion

The questions of what adaptations the Eskimo has to make on his life because of legal restrictions stems from a bigger question: the question of human rights versus animal rights. The Eskimos see whaling and other such hunting as their unalienable human right, and if it is disrupted thier entire cultural matrix, and their health endangered. Why then, should the government have the right to place protective bans on people who have been living off the sea and it mammals for thousands of years.

---

mos hunt and their nutritional values, with a brief section on nutrition and alternative sources of nutrition.

The conclusion also shows that her interest has shifted to a quite different issue: an ethical one of "rights." Here, she seems clearly to be interjecting more of herself, at least her emotional response to the Eskimos' situation. It is evident in her claim that the issue is one of "human rights vs. animal rights," as well as in the rhetorical question she poses "Why should the U. S. government be allowed to restrict a societies nutritional means and in some cases, put people's health in danger?"

Her peer reviewer focused on the limited interpretation, writing questions and suggestions in the margins where she felt Kate needed to make the link between the hunting restrictions and Eskimo health. For instance, by one passage she wrote, "Elaborate this point by describing the importance of mammal hunting for the survival of the Eskimos." The peer reviewer made similar comments about the introduction and conclusion, trying to get Kate to foreground the effect on Eskimo nutrition:

> It may be an alternative to start the Introduction stating the status quo—i.e., the debate—and proceed with how this is going to affect the Eskimos and especially their diet and nutrition.
>
> The overall structure is good but the conclusion is a bit too concise. Maybe you can summarize the inadequacies of the different alternatives. Also, you may like to expand your pt. of human rights vs. animal rights. Most of all a summary of how the new legislation will affect the Eskimo nutrition will be helpful for the readers.

She did not question the new issue raised in the conclusion about rights. In fact, she suggested that Kate expand that point.

Note that her reviewer made no changes in Kate's text itself, and Kate on her own decided *how* to respond to the reviewer's advice. For instance, as Figure 6 shows, in the introduction she adds a statement about the effect on the Eskimo economy and "food source opportunities." She also inserts a statement about the rights issue, noting that the effect on nutrition and health is a "somewhat serious side-effect." In the conclusion, she alters the first sentence to make a more direct statement of the effect of the new legislation on the Eskimos. She also inserts more information to elaborate her general claims. Finally, in the last sentence, she reasserts the rights issue ("does not seem fair"). That final sentence also illustrates the dual voice evident throughout her draft: the everyday, plain speaking voice of "does not seem fair" and the formal, more distanced voice of "viable options" and "said alternatives."

While she made these sorts of paragraph-specific changes in substance, she made no global changes, and her reviewer did not suggest she do so. She responded only to the specific suggestions of her reviewer. Still, this exchange illustrates that Kate can decide on her own how to implement advice.

Kate's second draft was reviewed by two graduate students, Jim and another graduate student who was to give it a blind review as if she were a reviewer for *American Anthropologist*. Both reviewers were supportive: they encouraged Kate, and in their overall comments they gave her useful advice about reorganizing the paper and limiting her focus. Kate also had a conference with Jim in which he gave her specific advice on sections to

Figure 6. *Kate's Journal Research Article: Second Draft*

Eskimo Nutritional Adaptations

Introduction [excerpt]

The Marine Mammal Protection Act of 1972 resulted in legislation designed for the conservation and protection of whales and other marine animals. Included in it was an exemption for aboriginal and subsistence whaling. . . . The 1984/85 annual report on the management between commercial and subsistence whaling, placing quotas and limitations on whaling for subsistance purposes. **This limits the Eskimo economy and the Eskimos food source opportunities.** By placing these quotas on Eskimos, the U.S. government is prohibiting some of its native citizens from an activity that is intrinsic to their culture and personal survival. **This is a human rights vs. an animal rights issue, with a somewhat serious side-effect being Eskimo nutrition and health.** I want to find out what effect legal constraints on marine mammal hunting have on Eskimo nutrition.

Conclusion

Legal constraints on marine mammal hunting force Eskimos to adapt their subsistance practices to fit proposed quotas. This stems from a bigger question. That of human rights vs. animal rights. The government is proposing and questioning legislature each year that deals with this issue. **If the whale population goes up for a year bans will be lifted, but if the population goes down, bans will return. These actions seriously effect the stability of Eskimo life.** Why should the government have the right to restrict a societies nutritional means and in some cases, put people's health in danger. **Seperate management between commercial hunting is a viable option to protect Eskimo traditions, but forcing unacceptable food alternatives on them does not seem fair, especially when said alternatives effect Eskimo health.**

Note: Bold print indicates additions or changes from the previous draft.

omit and a way to reorganize. As Jim explained, "I had to kind of just really help her with her organization and say 'okay, what is it you want to say? Cut this out, put this in.' She wants somebody to narrow that field a little bit and say, 'Well, why don't you try out. . . .' And then she'll say, 'Well, that's what I thought. . . .'" The result of the conference was that Kate had a more workable overall focus given the research information she had: "the effects on legal constraints on whale hunting [not all mammals] on Eskimo culture, economics, and health [not just nutrition]." As Jim's comment suggests, he was aware of Kate's desire to have others make decisions for her. It also shows him trying to balance being more nondirective ("What is it you want to say?") with being more directive ("Cut this out, put this in.")

Both Jim and the *AA* reviewer were quite directive in their comments throughout the draft regarding what they seemed to perceive as superficial matters of style. They replaced words, recast some sentences, and lined out others. This editing approach differed from Jim's approach to both Sally's and Kate's field report drafts, where he made global comments or posed questions. As the following examples show, the language in this draft was a cue to more substantial issues of personal role and interpretive stance. By making the changes for Kate, the reviewers missed chances to help Kate understand conventions of academic discourse in anthropology and decide for herself how she would present herself and what issues she would focus on.

The final draft (Figure 7) shows how Kate responded to them. In the introduction, in the first excerpted sentence, the *AA* reviewer had crossed out "personal" and replaced it with "physical." Kate accepted this change. She dropped the next sentence on her own. The *AA* reviewer also substituted "investigate" for "want to find out." Kate carried out this change also. When I asked her why, she told me "I don't know. It's more professional I guess. Because that's what that person wrote and I usually do whatever they say." The word was given to her, and she passively accepted the change.

In the "Background" section, Jim crossed out Kate's first two sentences, which read as follows:

> In order to locate information on modern Eskimo problems I consulted journals, and for general information, I used van Steensals book. In my research I found much information on whaling history and hunting techniques, which was interesting, but not relevent to Eskimo nutrition.

He replaced them with the following alternative, which he wrote in the margin:

> Much literature on contemporary Eskimo populations focuses on whaling history and hunting techniques, but not on health, economic, or cultural problems.

Here he made a change without explaining that it is just a convention of

---

Figure 7. *Kate's Journal Research Article: Third Draft*

The Effects of Whaling Restrictions on Native Alaskan Eskimos

Introduction (final two sentences)

. . .By placing these quotas on Eskimos, the government has prohibited some of its native citizens from an activity that is intrinsic to their cultural and **physical** survival. * In this article, I **investigate** the effects of legal constraints in whale hunting to Eskimo culture, economics, and health.

Conclusion

    Legal constraints on marine mammal hunting force Eskimos to adapt their subsistence whaling practices to fit proposed quotas. This stems from a bigger question: that of human vs. animal rights. The government is proposing and questioning legislature each year that deals with this issue. If the whale population goes up for a year, bans will be lifted, but if the population goes down, bans will return. These actions seriously effect the stability of Eskimo life. * Seperate management of subsistence hunting from that of commercial hunting is a viable option to protect Eskimo traditions, and insure economic self sufficiency. But forcing unacceptable alternatives on the Eskimo such as commercial foods, and urban jobs, does not appear to be **adequate** and obviously does not preserve an important American cultural tradition.

Note: Bold print indicates changes from previous draft. Asterisks indicate deletions of sentences.

---

academic research to focus on the "literature" itself instead of the researcher's activities. In an interview, Jim indicated that his reason for making the change was that "she doesn't need to tell us that she went to the library. . . . They're meant to sound like professionals not like college students." The point is that Kate didn't know the conventions of "professionals."

    In the conclusion, the graduate reviewer recast the final sentence, again giving Kate the words. Most significantly, she changed "fair" to "adequate." Kate wrote in the change. When I asked Kate about this change, she didn't even pick up on it, choosing to comment instead on the end of the sentence, saying, "This draft is the one about the three things. . . . I couldn't just say health, because it wasn't just health anymore." The change is important because it implicitly shifts the basic issue from one of rights ("fair") to one of practical consequences (whether an action is "adequate"). Neither Kate nor, I infer, the *AA* reviewer seemed to realize this.

Jim crossed out the rhetorical question on the issue of fairness. Again, Kate followed Jim's direction. When I asked her about this change, she just said, "I just didn't want it in there . . . because I didn't really talk about it that much." Still, in her final draft, written at the end of the semester, Kate inserted the sentence "The Eskimos should not be punished." This sentence suggests she did want something like that in there— her personal feeling that the restrictions were unfair. In the previous draft, both the word "fair" and the rhetorical question were cues to Kate's personal view of the matter. By changing both instead of posing a question in the margin or talking with Kate about her view and their interpretation of her comments, the reviewers missed a chance to discuss with Kate what they perceived to be appropriate and help her work out a way to present *her* interpretive claim.

Kate's drafts of this third writing suggest that she had only just begun her entry into the village. Instead of effacing herself and standing silent as she did in her first writings, she was beginning to try to speak her own interpretation and include some of her own language, even though her view and voice were still not integrated into a professional way of speaking and interpreting. Interestingly, this move came when writing about an issue that she became personally interested in. Still, Kate seems to have taken an important first step and gained confidence in herself as a writer. As she said in her final interview with me, "I can organize my papers better because I know now to write down my thoughts. I can get my point across more clearly than before, and I am more confident about it." Recall that in her initial interview she said she was least confident of getting down her ideas.

Closing Reflections on Teaching

In "Some Needed Research on Writing," Mina Shaughnessy argued that one of the challenges students face when they enter college is learning the conventions of academic writing, including the accepted stance to project to one's audience (319-320). (See also Bizzell "Cognition" and "Ethos"; Maimon.) Shaughnessy observed that most of us learned through "such a long subtle process of socialization that we cannot remember how it happened" (317); consequently, to understand the challenges our students face, we need to study their experiences and reflect on our own.

The experiences of Sally and Kate offer one glimpse of what that socialization process entails for students. Their experiences also underscore a point that we too often neglect in our teaching, a point of connection between their experience and ours: to learn to participate in a new village—whether anthropology or composition studies—requires, as Michael Polanyi claims, an act of "personal assimilation" (61) to internalize those ways of speaking and thinking as our own. For this personal assimilation to occur, we need repeated occasions to try out those ways of thinking and speaking for ourselves, trying to speak our piece to accomplish specific ends in specific forums in our intellectual villages.

Three more specific implications for teaching follow from that general statement. I offer them on the basis of my observations of the students in the anthropology course and other courses I have studied as well as from my own experience learning to enter various intellectual villages.

1) Our work should begin with an appreciation of the *personal* challenge our students face in trying to enter our disciplines and classrooms. Kate and Sally illustrate a common problem: they perceive our intellectual villages as quite distinct from themselves—impersonal in terms of their relation to their audience and their relation to knowledge. That distanced image is evident in Sally's second draft of the descriptive field report and Kate's field report. The first step for many is literally to insert themselves as we see Sally doing in her third draft of the field report and Kate in her journal research article. I believe it is only when we insert—instead of effacing—ourselves that we can hope to *assimilate* the village's ways instead of using them as external tools or *accommodating* ourselves to them.

In "Discourse in the Novel," Mikhail Bakhtin introduces two terms that help conceptualize this personal challenge: "authoritative discourse" and "internally persuasive discourse." "Authoritative discourse" is that language we take on from other authorities and never really make our own. It remains distanced from us. "Internally persuasive discourse" is that language we internalize and interweave with our own language to use for our own purposes (342-346). It seems to me that this is what we and our students are trying to do when we learn to speak and think in a new intellectual village. We are trying to take on some of the language and ways of speaking of the village and make them our own. In order to internalize and make those ways our own, we have to insert ourselves by trying to use the language and ways of thinking to give voice to our own claims. I hypothesize that we, like Kate and Sally, are more likely to move from "authoritative discourse" and thinking to "internally persuasive discourse" and thinking when we have a personal investment in what we are writing and a personal claim we want to get across.

2) Frequent, purposeful writing and revising can be valuable means of developing our own identity and way of thinking in a new community. It seems particularly important to understand the purpose of revising in this way. Too often, revision is viewed as serving only the purpose of improving features of "writing," e.g., organization, development, grammar. Viewed in this way, there seems to be insufficient reason outside writing courses to ask students to write multiple drafts and take the time to review their drafts. If, however, revision is viewed as providing occasions to work out one's interpretation and fashion and refashion one's way of presenting one's self, then there is good reason to incorporate it into any course. As Sally commented in her final interview with me, "I think what I learned [from doing drafts] ... is that you get a much clearer idea of what you're trying to say in each paper. Because with each draft, you think about it more. Everybody told me that's why you write drafts. I just didn't do it."

3) When we respond to students' drafts, we should provide guidance but resist taking over the process for them. We might pose questions and make suggestions, but we should leave the task of actually revising to our students so they have occasion to "think about it more." Such an approach encourages them to be more active in learning: reflecting on their work, deciding how to act, and then carrying out that action. Jim's responses to Sally seemed to accomplish this aim, though more explanation of the reason for advised changes seems desirable. Probably, we are more likely to take such an approach with active learners like Sally. It seems equally important—perhaps more so—to resist taking over for more passive students like Kate, even though the results may be less dramatic and less obvious in the short run. As her exchanges with Jim for the field report and with her peer for the journal article illustrate, Sally can decide on her own how to implement revision suggestions although, granted, to a limited degree. Making the revisions for her, as Jim and the *AA* reviewer did with some sections of the journal article, only perpetuates her passivity and her dependence on others. While their actions were well intentioned, both reviewers, by giving Kate their words, missed a chance to help Kate integrate her personal reactions with the interpretive approach of anthropologists. As a consequence, Kate put in the changes

she had been given without understanding why and without being encouraged, as Sally was, to compose herself and her own position.

I cannot say whether the challenges Kate and Sally face are exactly the same for students in other disciplines, although my studies of students in chemical engineering and literature courses give me some reason to believe they would be similar ("Teaching," "Writing"). If one of our aims as teachers is to help our students succeed in our professional communities, or just the community we create for their undergraduate education, it seems important for us to understand more about what is entailed for them and how we might assist their learning. As Shaughnessy has advocated, we need to become students of our students' writing and of our own and the conventions we accept. If we do so, I believe we will be better able to talk with students about the choices available to them and about our reasons for advising certain actions (e.g., "seems more like a note") and less likely to make a substantive change unwittingly (e.g., "fair" to "adequate").

As teachers, we need to make room for students to compose themselves into the village, to learn to use the conventions to make their own claims. In this course, writing multiple drafts was one means of achieving that aim, as a way for Sally, Kate, and others literally to begin to write their ways into anthropology. Our role is to recognize the personal challenge entailed in this endeavor, to be sensitive to cues to their efforts in their language, and to encourage them to reflect for themselves and experiment with how they will present themselves and their claims. ❧

ACKNOWLEDGMENTS

I would like to thank Deborah Cadman, my research assistant, for her careful and insightful work throughout this study. I am particularly grateful to Professor Sylvia Forman, University of Massachusetts at Amherst, and her students for allowing me to join them for a semester and taking the time to assist me.

NOTES

[1]This requirement is the second part of their University Writing Requirement. The first part is satisfied by completing College Writing, the first-year writing course offered through the English Department. Students must also complete a Junior Year writing course offered through their academic major and designed to focus on writing in that academic discipline and/or related professions.

[2]Forman is also a co-author of an essay on the Junior Year Writing Program at the University of Massachusetts (1990).

[3]For the fourth and final assignment, they were to use the same material as for the research article to write a popular media article for a magazine such as *Natural History* or *Smithsonian*.

WORKS CITED

Bakhtin, Mikhail. "Discourse in the Novel." *The Dialogic Imagination.* Trans. Caryl Emerson and Michael Holquist. Austin: U Texas P, 1981.

Bizzell, Patricia. "Cognition, Convention, and Certainty: What We Need to Know about Writing." *PRE/TEXT* 3 (1982): 213-243.

———. "The Ethos of Academic Writing." *College Composition and Communication* 29 (1978): 351-355.

Geertz, Clifford. *Local Knowledge: Further Essays in Interpretive Anthropology.* New York: Basic, 1983.

Forman, Sylvia, et al. "The Junior Year Writing Program at the University of Massachusetts at Amherst." *Programs that Work: Models and Methods for Writing across the Disciplines.* Eds. Toby Fulwiler and Art Young. Portsmouth, NH: Boynton/Cook, 1990.

Herrington, Anne. "Teaching, Writing, and Learning: A Naturalistic Study of Writing in an Undergraduate Literature Course." *Advances in Writing Research, Vol. 2.* Ed. David Jolliffe. Norwood, NJ, 1988: 133-166.

———. "Writing in Academic Settings: A Study of the Contexts for Writing in Two College Chemical Engineering Courses." *Research in the Teaching of English*, 19 (1985): 331-361.

———, and Deborah Cadman. "Peer Review and Revising: Assuming Authority for One's Own Learning While Working with Others." Paper presented at the Conference on College Composition and Communication, Seattle WA, March 1989.

Maimon, Elaine. "Maps and Genres: Exploring Connections in the Arts and Sciences." *Composition & Literature: Bridging the Gap.* Ed. Winifred Bryan Horner. Chicago: U Chicago P, 1983: 110-125.

McCarthy, Lucille. "A Stranger in Strange Lands: A College Student Writing Across the Curriculum." *Research in the Teaching of English*, 21 (1987): 233-265.

Polanyi, Michael. *Personal Knowledge: Towards a Post-Critical Philosophy.* Corrected ed. Chicago: U Chicago P, 1962.

Shaughnessy, Mina. "Some Needed Research on Writing." *College Composition and Communication* 28 (1977): 317-320.

❦ 6

When "Basic Skills" Are Really Basic and Really Skills

Louise Wetherbee Phelps

A Heretical Proposal

For composition teachers, the term "basic skills" leaves a bitter taste on the tongue. They associate it with a tendency for colleagues to blame them because students "can't write an English sentence" and to insist that writing teachers give exclusive attention to ensuring minimal literacy. For many critics, it is a code term for all the failures of American schooling to teach standards: in the case of writing, the failure of early education to instill the rules of grammar, spelling, punctuation, sentence structure, logic, and clear expression. By implication, writing is nothing but the absence of error and the mastery of conventions and formulas.

Besides thinking this view conceptually flawed, composition teachers resist it as demeaning to themselves and to their students. Talk of basic skills is too often the occasion for dismissing writing (at the college level) as a nonintellectual, remedial subject, claiming that writing teachers need no special expertise, and moralistically condemning students as illiterate. In a recent, mean-spirited expression of this attitude in *The Chronicle of Higher Education*, David Lawton declares:

> I think most of us could agree that an acceptable standard of good writing
> is the ability to produce an intellectually mature essay that is grammatically

116

and stylistically correct and that proceeds logically from a premise supported by example and argument to a conclusion. Given the lack of acceptable
results from freshman writing courses according to that definition, it seems
to me that the continuation of such courses at the college level is an essentially spurious activity and could be classified as a racket. . . . If writing is a
discipline, then those who teach it should be required to meet certain standards. Since there is obviously no such requirement, judging from most of
the instructors, teaching composition is simply a job for people of varying
competence that has no place in higher education. No other country in the
world . . . offers pre-puberty training and preparation at the college level.
(B1)

(Notice that Lawton has quietly made composition teachers responsible
for the alleged intellectual immaturity of their students!)

Understandably, this academic fundamentalism with its message of
disrespect for the teaching of writing, even more than the limitations of
the concept itself, has led professionals in composition to vehemently
oppose the notion of basic skills. But they have not made much headway
outside the field. I have a heretical proposal. Let us set aside defensive
responses, reclaim the concepts "basic" and "skilled" from those who
have debased them, and put them to our own intellectual and rhetorical
purposes. That is the case I will argue in this essay.

On a theoretical level, we have learned in composition that terminological choices always have their costs. That point became clear when the
conceptual starting point of the field, the distinction between process and
product, reached its limits and became an unproductive dichotomy
(Phelps, *Composition as a Human Science* 132-36, 160-62). A theorist,
therefore, must ask what realities are deflected, what questions selected
out, when we submit to the pejoration of "basic skills." First, take basic.
By condemning this term for trivializing writing, we make it harder to
take seriously the root idea that some aspects of writing are more fundamental than others in a number of possible senses: important, prerequisite, developmentally earlier, or underlying to surface features. Second, by
giving up "skill," we lose a fertile metaphor as a source of suggestive
associations and comparisons from the domains of sports, crafts, fine arts,
and labor. The semantic fields associated with these domains encourage
researchers to study in writing such topics as technique, consciousness,
effort, expertise, self-control, tacit knowledge, and attention, among others. We could learn from the way thinkers in psychology and philosophy
(e.g., Bruner and Polanyi) have productively used analogies connecting

symbolization with tool use and visual perception to characterize language as a skill extending the mind (cf. Emig, "Hand, Eye, Brain").

These considerations are abstract and speculative, but it is a concrete problem that leads me to write this essay, as is usually the case with matters of conceptualizing and naming. In the process of constructing a curriculum for a new writing program, teachers at Syracuse University find themselves faced with new problems generated by the special circumstances and goals of this project. As Susanne Langer points out, the fundamental needs in such situations are for flexible, negotiable concepts, and one source of such concepts is reinterpreting and revitalizing existing terms. In our case, writing teachers need ways to study and respond to students' work over *time* and across multiple, simultaneous *contexts* of language use within their students' educational experiences. It is in this context that we have reexamined the notion of "basic skills."

Here is the background. Syracuse University has undertaken to build a developmentally sophisticated, multi-stage writing program that connects writing to research and learning at all levels of a university education. It is my responsibility as director to design and implement this program in collaboration with a teaching community comprising a small, growing group of full-time faculty in composition and rhetoric (currently six) and around 135 writing teachers, of whom 50 are teaching assistants (largely M.A. students in English programs) and the rest are professional writing instructors employed part-time.

The core of the new program is a sequence of writing studios (freshman, sophomore, junior-senior, and graduate) that are conceived as comprehensively situated within a broader academic experience for each student. This situatedness means, first, that studios must literally form a writing *curriculum*, ordering themselves in relation to students' literacy and intellectual development over *time*. Further, it means that studios must actively attempt to acknowledge, exploit, reflect on, and forge *two-way links* between their own content and students' concurrent intellectual work and writing within the university experience, in part through new forms of instruction and cooperative projects engaging faculty in other disciplines. On this axis, studios may be seen not only as situated by the academic context but as situating students' writing within and among their other courses. (See Phelps, "Developmental Challenges" for an interpretation of these axes of succession and simultaneity as forming a heuristic for curricular planning.)

Beginning with four existing courses, we planned to transform them progressively into a spiral curriculum of writing studios with a common design, recurring themes, and sequential relationships (Phelps, "The Spiral Curriculum"). In 1987 the program introduced the redesigned lower division courses, Studio 1 ("Writing to Learn") and Studio 2 ("Writing as Rhetoric"), followed in 1989 by Studio 3 ("Advanced Studies in Writing") and Studio 4 ("Professional and Technical Writing"). The first two courses are taken by almost all students in 12 undergraduate colleges, and one of the upper division courses is required of many students in preprofessional curricula. We have also developed gradually a network of reciprocal relations, collaborative ventures, and reflective conversations connecting the Writing Program with an increasingly coherent set of projects at Syracuse to renew and support undergraduate teaching. A functional unit of the program, called "Writing Resources," coordinates diverse projects still in pilot form for linking studios to students' other academic experiences, courses, and curricula.

The Writing Program at Syracuse is a complex enterprise, still in its early stages of development yet already innovative in many dimensions—from its course designs centered on topics of inquiry to its mobile corps of writing consultants, co-teaching practices, in-house publications, orientation and mentoring programs, and teacher research. It is not my purpose to provide a detailed description and rationale of its curriculum and structures (represented dynamically in numerous program documents, some of which are collected in Briggs and Faivre). Rather, I have introduced the Syracuse Writing Program here as a practical context in which it became historically and situationally useful to redefine and reappropriate the concept of "basic skills" for composition teachers. My focus hereafter will be on studios in their earliest stages of conception as a site for this practical theorizing.

It is a defining feature of the program that it makes teachers the central designers and thinkers about curriculum, no matter what their background or experience. At the beginning, teachers invented their course plans in response to theory texts (curriculum proposals, official course descriptions, and commentary) that laid out principles, hypotheses, and speculations about the possible relations of studios within a spiral curriculum. As time went on, teachers tested these documents against their own interpretive texts (syllabi, reflections on teaching, articles in the program journal) and talk (in coordinating group meetings, graduate classes, hallways and lounge), along with new readings from composition and rhetorical theory. These various practical and reflective sources came hermeneutically to discipline one another, to constantly reinterpret, revise, and generate new teaching plans (Phelps, "Practical Wisdom").

Perhaps the most dramatic influence on such curricular thinking in this early stage was the teachers' novel experience of encountering students in successive courses as the new studios phased in, replacing the second semester of Freshman English with a sophomore-level studio. This experience, and the stories and reflections surrounding it, constantly problematized the nature of a studio course, the differences and progressions between successive studios, and the nature and sources of change in students from studio to studio, year to year.

In deciding content for a writing course independent of a writing curriculum, or without conscious reference to its cognitive and affective matrix in a broader academic life, teachers can make unconstrained assumptions about the portability and lasting impact of learning. Without opportunities to follow students into other contexts or to watch what happens next year, teachers have no reality checks on their implicit theories and hopes for their students. Under these circumstances, there is little pressure to doubt or to seek support for the developmental (or antidevelopmental) assumptions of textbooks and tradition, or even to wonder what is really "basic" and what "skills" really are.

This situation changes strikingly, though, when teachers form an intellectual community whose members treat the whole writing and learning curriculum as an interactive system, take responsibility for its diachronic and synchronic interdependencies, and do so by talking and writing together about their teaching experiences in a program-wide, ongoing conversation. We call this communal process "reflective practice" (Schon). Program instructors observe, argue about, and deal directly with the continuities and developmental changes in students taking writing studios over time, informed by students' own narratives and reflections on studio experiences. Through these ongoing student contacts and through experiences as consultants working with colleagues and students in other units, teachers also learn about the complex and varied nature of the texts and tasks their students deal with as writers and readers at the university.

As noted, instructors in the Writing Program invent their own course plans from semester to semester, relying on an extensive orientation and mentoring system when they are new teachers. The program-wide information exchange in talk and writing, especially in co-teaching arrangements and weekly meetings of small teacher groups, further guides concrete, day-to-day decision making about studio content. Within that stream of ideas, attention in the community ebbs and flows, concentrating inquiry and teacher talk around questions and topics that teachers describe as "hot points": the most intellectually exciting, intense, difficult, and vividly experienced problems of practice. Over a semester or yearly span, these questions set what we call "intellectual tasks" on a written program-wide agenda for curriculum development, teachers' professional development, and program research.

Here is just a sample of specific questions raised by the practical experience of teachers trying to implement a developmental, context-sensitive curriculum. What are, or should be, the continuing features of studios over the college years? How should these features change at different levels? What theories and evidence should guide these decisions? Where in studios may we look for developmental leaps to occur, and what would they be? Assuming the course content is designed to count on these leaps at certain points, what about developmental lags? How do we deal with the range of developmental variation in skills within each studio, and with the unevenness of development within any individual? When and in what areas of instruction do we need to spiral back to earlier goals and activities? How should we anticipate, or pre-teach, for later learning? What do students resist in each studio, and what do they like, want, or need? How much should their responses determine our own purposes and tactics? What writing tasks challenge students in different colleges and departments? At what point do students in different curricula become familiar enough with their own discipline's discourse to contrast its rhetoric to others? How can we activate the potential to transfer studio skills to new writing contexts, and what educational practices at the university encourage, motivate, or hinder this process?

To answer many of these questions, and especially to frame them in practical terms, I find the terms "basic" and "skilled" apt and suggestive, given their root meanings, common usage, and application in other fields. What we teach is both basic—being fundamental to intellectual work— and skillful—involving smoothly integrated, purposeful actions. As I will try to show, a redefinition of "basic skills" for composition teaching can work simultaneously on a theoretical level, where it represents a concept of writing as a symbolic tool, and on a curricular level, where it translates into a set of intellectual processes and activities, supported by writing, that students develop and practice differently over the course of their education.

There are strategic as well as intellectual and pedagogical arguments for rehabilitating rather than contesting the notion of basic skills on our own campus. At Syracuse, we face the need to rewrite legislation in a Liberal Arts Core that justifies writing requirements now fulfilled by writing studios. This statement, first approved in 1977, supports instruction and continuing practice in "basic skills of expository writing," which were defined then by the College of Arts and Sciences as clear communication of ideas based on organization, adherence to accepted norms of language, and control of writing conventions.

The Gates Committee, which reviewed writing instruction at Syracuse in 1983-85 and recommended creation of the new Writing Program, criticized this idea of basic skills as reflecting an impoverished notion of writing: "This definition is based on the familiar and misleading conduit metaphor of language, in which a person when writing is assumed to already have 'ideas' which he or she must then learn to 'communicate clearly,' such communication being further defined in terms of organization, accepted norms of usage, and problems of grammar" (Gates 8). The practices of the new studios have already changed this understanding of writing operationally, within the Writing Program courses and beyond; now we must do so explicitly by formulating and winning approval from other faculty for a new policy statement. Attacking this traditional conception of basic skills—and thus implicitly devaluing the legitimate concerns of its proponents—is bad rhetoric; I would rather try to persuade my colleagues to enlarge and enrich their interpretation to emphasize the intellectual skills basic to literacy and learning at the university.

Rethinking the Concept

In this essay I offer an operational definition of basic skills as a set of intellectual processes translated into socially situated practices that teachers ask students to engage in and to study. This definition makes concrete and teachable a theoretically grounded conception of writing as a symbolic tool—one of several perspectives on written language that have shaped curricular choices for the Syracuse Writing Program. We have found this notion of skills useful especially in introducing new teachers quickly to a complex practice of "teaching studios." Ultimately, however, "skills" (however defined) provide an incomplete notion of "what is basic" even at the concretely heuristic level, as I will discuss.

As I have noted, when the studio curriculum compelled us to take our own teaching seriously—to believe it makes a difference to what students do or learn in later studios and in concurrent writing contexts—we faced, with a much more vivid sense of consequence, the problem of what is basic: literally, what comes first. (And then, what continues, what changes, what is added at different points, and so on.) It is astonishingly different to design not a freshman English course but an introduction to a program of literacy education; one must have the whole sequence in mind as well as the broader context of the student's academic and professional experience, now and to come. This point—the need for a concretely informed developmental perspective in both directions—became clearly visible when we struggled to deal in the same Studio 2 classes with a mix of students coming from Studio 1 and from the previous freshman English program; and when teachers trying to reinvent the two upper division courses (populated still by students from the old program) ended up teaching versions of Studios 1 and 2. Clearly we had already succeeded in defining and teaching something basic that was missing in the repertoire of most students lacking the early studio experience: what was it?

In thinking through this question, I first asked myself what criteria one might apply to judge something basic in any college curriculum. For convenience, let me refer to course content, meaning the experiences, activities, information, and ideas that a teacher offers as a basis for student learning in a given course (I prefer to speak this way because the term "goals" implies some predictable end point of learning, either in cognition or in written products). Here are two criteria, either of which is sufficient to call (studio) course content "basic": first, it is significantly prerequisite or instrumental to further learning (over some nonspecialized range); second, it addresses a broad, fundamentally important intellectual structure or activity capable of continuing development and growth.

By examining the experiences and reflections of our teachers during the first year of teaching Studios 1 and 2, including a program-wide project in which teachers examined their own practices to characterize evolving generic features of studio teaching (Howell), I concluded that a central dimension of the studios qualifying as basic is the mediation of intellectual work through writing. Writing studios, particularly Studios 1 and 2, introduce and identify key intellectual processes and strategies that students continue to use and develop throughout their education. These literate habits are skills in the sense that they are ways of doing writing or ways of using writing to do things, as distinct from conceptual knowledge *about* something. Such skills are at once cognitive potentials (perhaps structures or schemas for activity) and practices that one can plan for students to engage in—partly observable, nameable processes and actions involving literate language as a tool.

Composing as a process of textualizing meanings or working spontaneous, partly nonlinear thought into particular discursive forms is a good candidate for a basic, general skill of literacy—the one usually meant by teachers who say they teach process. However, by "composing text," I do not mean here just any writing experience, for example keeping a journal, taking notes in class, or even the inquiry writing (like field notes) that may eventually become a paper. I mean more narrowly the process of deliberately shaping ideas and prior writing toward and into publicly accessible text forms. Studios initiate students into composing as a self-reflective, deliberate, self-managed process distinct from spontaneous, unplanned writing. While students may have engaged in this process before with more or less sophistication, studios ask them to practice it reflectively and to take it as an object of inquiry. In this respect studios follow the mainstream in contemporary writing instruction; the difference is that we regard composing text as only one basic skill—and we *call* it a "basic skill." Other "basic skills," like certain forms of focused talk, may have their own ends independent of text production.

What makes composing text and other activities listed here *skills* is that they have the structure of tools, what Michael Polanyi calls the "from-to" structure through which a tool becomes the instrument for attending to or accomplishing something else (*Tacit Dimension* 16). One composes text in order to accomplish other purposes—epistemological, psychological, esthetic, social, political. Acquiring a skill is a matter of learning to in-dwell such an instrument until it becomes fluently available for smoothly integrated skillful activity in the future. In this sense, basic skills in writing are internalized forms and practices of language as a cultural tool.

One can break down an integrated activity such as composing text into any number of skill levels, involving both physical and intellectual technologies. I chose this level of description, rather than a more fine-grained one, because teachers and students need to work with wholes, with activities and processes that constitute naturally salient categories of experience (Lakoff 31-57). The skills to be listed here were chosen because teachers and students in our developing studios experienced them as phenomenologically distinct events that could be named, attended to, and worked at in classroom settings. Psychologically, skills are cognitive products of instruction, practice, and learning, representing an individual's ability or potential for integrated behavior (Bruner 246-54).

Teachers work, however, with the objective correlates of these cognitive formations—the contextualized, observable practices and activities in which they engage students through their plans and daily improvisations. These correlates are what I am calling here basic skills as studio content: the fundamental stuff of course designs and daily plans.

Defining skills in terms of their translations into concrete, socially situated activities leads to a much more practical understanding of how they can become "basic" to the curriculum than when we understand them as individual performances and textual outcomes. In the first place, one can define some achievable goals in terms of studio practices: for example, in lower division studios, to give students sufficient experience in practicing and attending to intellectual strategies that they will be able to engage in them with familiarity and fluency in later classes (thereby possibly changing, over the long run, teachers' expectations for their work in other disciplines). Notice that from a curricular goal-setting perspective it is not necessary that every student complete each studio with a particular competence or level of achievement. What is important is that literacy skills are communally represented to some critical level within any student cohort, so that in subsequent classes teachers can count on students to practice them as forms of intellectual work. For example, a teacher should reasonably be able to expect studio-prepared sophomores to be able to participate in peer workshops on drafts, to annotate and reread texts, and to identify and list concepts in oral or written material.

If studios merely practiced strategies of this sort, though, they would not be studios as we define them. Studios are distinguished by reflexivity and by communicating to students the understanding that specific tactics like outlining or using invention heuristics fit into the broader integrations I have called here "intellectual skills." An explicit theoretical assumption of studios is that writing is like other symbolic systems in being a cultural tool that serves to extend and amplify human capacities like vision, reach, and grasp. Jerome S. Bruner describes intellectual skills as the internal counterpart to cultural inventions, including both abstract technologies like mathematics or writing systems and physical implements like pens or computers (327, 438-440, 470-477). The capacity for linking ourselves to these "alloplastic devices" is realized individually through the development of "personal skills" (Polanyi, *Personal Knowledge*), which have a genetic basis in, for example, opposable thumbs, binocular vision, and linguistic intelligence. I am in turn suggesting that we make these internal tools visible and facilitate their learning by enacting them in the classroom as distinct events and experiences concretely accessible for examination and description. Writing plays a special integrative role in this effort because it is simultaneously practice, reflective object, and means of reflection.

The New Basic Skills of the Writing Studios

On the basis of teachers' reports and reflections on their practice in the first year of the Writing Program, I proposed a scheme for thinking about ten basic skills that had emerged as studio-specific, well-defined classroom practices: five general modes whereby literate behavior mediates intellection and five related special skills (social, technical, and metacognitive). There is nothing sacred about these categories: there are many other ways to divide up and name such teaching practices. On the other hand, the categories are not arbitrary; they are chosen to reflect the ways our teachers talk and think about studio concepts, goals, and experiences.

This scheme presumes that each intellectual strategy has the potential for development toward more skillful use (increased fluency, accessibility, control, integration, flexibility, technical expertise, effectiveness, and so on). Its initial, important heuristic use has been to help characterize, generate, and evaluate generic studio practices, especially at the point of entry for new teachers (and their freshmen students). But this sense of "genre" forms the ground for pursuing the developmental and contextual questions asked earlier. For example, in articulating transitions between Studios 1 and 2, or between Studio 2 and upper division studios, teachers have studied students' retrospective perceptions of studio content as ideology and practice. The teachers then constructed transitions at beginnings and ends of studios to help students express and analyze the continuities and discontinuities in their experiences of the writing curriculum and its relations to other aspects of their education. They are tracing these mediating skills in the intellectual tasks students encounter in various disciplines and professions, as perceived by both students and faculty: for example, in a joint project on undergraduate research between the Writing Program, the Honors Program, and the School of Management. Specific skills in this scheme are elaborated in diverse contexts: for example, assessing and self-assessing development of teachers through their own portfolios; linking writing with technology through a Hypercard project on punctuation as design; examining in a graduate seminar or teaching group the portability of skills as a fundamental question about epistemology, to be raised explicitly in the redesigned upper division studios;

engaging in particular forms of structured talk as a practice for reading student writing or theory texts. The skills named in this scheme are, in other words, diffusely represented in the ongoing conversations and work of the Writing Program.

BASIC SKILLS AS GENERIC PROCESSES TAUGHT IN STUDIOS

GENERAL SKILLS	SPECIAL SKILLS
composing text	working collaboratively
learning from others through writing	editing documents for publication
making inquiries through writing	assessing the work and writing development of others
making writing-reading connections	linking writing with technologies and other symbol systems
engaging in focused forms of conversation	making skills and knowledge deliberately portable

GENERAL BASIC SKILLS

1. *Composing text*: Turning ideas and prior writing into public text and using this process heuristically to discover or connect ideas; managing one's own thinking and writing processes to deliberately compose meanings into discursive structures and genres to make them public for particular audiences, purposes, and situations. Encompasses strategies of process pedagogy including invention heuristics, planning, drafting, mapping one's own ideas or text, audience analysis, and so on.
2. *Learning from others through writing*: Using informal, semiprivate modes of writing actively to comprehend, remember, record, transform, reflect on, and evaluate the organized knowledge made systematically available by texts and others (e.g., in textbooks, readings, lectures, workshops). Concrete activities include keeping double-entry journals, annotating text, taking class notes; paraphrasing, glossing or listing concepts, digging out underlying assumptions, questioning.
3. *Making inquiries through writing*: Using informal modes of writing to aid in pursuing inquiries firsthand to discover, invent, or organize knowledge using methods like search, observation, experimentation,

interviewing; making connections among ideas by means of intellectual processes like patterning, hypothesizing, categorizing, comparison, metaphoric transformation, reasoning from evidence. Writing modes include field notes, lab observations, interview notes, observational narratives, speculative journals, clustering and mapping.

4. *Making writing-reading connections*: Connecting writing to reading in various relations of ends and means, especially the following:

   a. *Writing to read (better)*: With comprehension, with appreciation; to remember reading content, to organize or reorganize information and ideas, to contrast and combine, to challenge. Includes such practices as prereading and rereading; listing, mapping, glossing, paraphrasing, summarizing, questioning; reading for concepts, gist, issues and arguments, values, rhetorical tone, etc.

   b. *Reading like a writer*: To learn, or to imitate, writing techniques, strategies, and possibilities from models; to analyze and evaluate textual performances as skillful and effective. Imitative writing.

   c. *Reading to write*: Using conceptually difficult texts as starting point (stimulus, source, or object of inquiry): to respond to, interpret, or critique a text; to be stimulated to write; to derive information and ideas from multiple sources so as to construct an original argument or interpretation. Reading logs; high and low-tech strategies for manipulating information and glossing, synthesizing ideas from multiple sources. Note: Readings include a broad range of texts and genres including some imaginative and literary writing, with emphasis on those presenting intellectual challenges and requiring sophisticated reading strategies.

5. *Engaging in focused forms of conversation*: Practicing special forms of literate talk including argument, debate, role-playing, "crits" or "deep talk," a structured practice for collectively describing student texts as cultural works (Himley).

SPECIAL BASIC SKILLS

1. *Working collaboratively*: Participating with awareness of group dynamics in workshops and projects where ideas and writing are shared, criticized, sometimes jointly authored; using structured forms of talk and task-sharing.

2. *Editing for publication*: Modeling the handling of grammar and style issues after the copy-editing processes used in professional publication; stylistic editing based on the psychology and rhetoric of reading

along with document preparation techniques like formatting and document design. Class magazines are an illustrative activity.

3. *Assessing the work and ultimately the writing and intellectual development of others and oneself:* Providing feedback and critical judgments to others as reader and coauthor; playing this role for oneself in processes of revision; tracking, evaluating, and thus planning and managing one's own development as a writer, reader, and thinker. Organized around portfolios maintained by students throughout the college years.

4. *Linking writing with technologies and other symbolic systems:* Not merely using word processors but practicing, creating, and studying new links between writers or thinkers and technologies like computers and video—tools that challenge and revise the notion of text and make texts intertextual and multi-modal (Smith and Smith). Also connecting and comparing writing with other symbolic modes like speech, pictures, animation, or computer programming.

5. *Making skills and knowledge deliberately portable:* Actively researching and contrastively describing new discourse tasks, their contexts, their specific demands and expectations; using systematic questioning, observation, peer feedback, consultation of authorities and models, analysis, imitation, and other means to describe for oneself and begin practicing new discourse tasks and genres; adapting basic or portable skills to different needs and contexts with the aim of becoming independent of formal instruction for further growth in writing and thinking skills.

The Dangers of Teaching Basic Skills

Setting aside the historical connotations of basic skills for composition, let me anticipate some substantive grounds for objecting to the approach I have described here: grounds that hold equally for any program based on teaching intellectual or literate processes. Indeed, this objection applies comprehensively to the very idea of teaching composition and to rhetoric in general. It is simply this: to teach any generic skill—any symbolic tool—is either impossible or unethical or both since, by definition as an instrument rather than an end, it is divorced from both content and values. I will speak to several closely related forms of this critique, first focusing on the relationship between form and content and second on the relationships among skills, content, and values. My cases will be fictitious though I will refer to a few well-known advocates of the different views.

The first challenger says that we should not teach basic skills because it cannot be done; skills do not exist apart from content. At one level this is simply the observation that people do not learn such processes (of language or creative activity) deductively, through abstract description or prescription, but only through activity. But the critical point is that learning something by doing it does not create any general, transferrable skill or autonomous cognitive structure immediately available for a different task. Students have simply learned context-dependent skills (for example, how to read a particular engineering text) that are closely tied to local knowledge and do not tell them how to read a literary text or an anthropology text. This question is thoroughly reviewed by D. N. Perkins with respect to the value of heuristics in creative thought, leading him to mixed conclusions supporting some useful role for general heuristic principles in creative thinking.

Recent research in many disciplines tends to support the idea that intellectual and symbolic processes are far less general than had been thought. Problem-solving, invention, literacy, and similar activities are highly dependent on expert local knowledge of specific content and context. Skills in writing and thinking are not monolithic cognitive structures available *in toto* for new tasks; even if there are such structures at some level (e.g., a cognitive structure for a story schema), they do not automatically transfer to new tasks. On a practical level, teaching writing across the curriculum has sensitized writing teachers to the remarkable variety of discourse contexts and the formidable difficulties of integrating and transporting skills from one writing/learning situation to the next. All these findings raise doubts about the possibility of teaching writing so as to facilitate development of general skills.

E. D. Hirsch provides a strong example of this first critique when he attacks the idea he calls "educational formalism," defined as

> the theory that the aim of education in the schools, and particularly in English classes, is to develop large generalized skills. The aim of "English," according to this view, is to teach students *how* to read (including how-to-read literature) and how to write, and these are not primarily for the particular substance of the texts read, for these can be any appropriate texts, but rather for the sake of learning general skills for later use outside the school." ("Formalism" 372; see also "Cultural Literacy")

Hirsch criticizes this view severely as it applies to both literature and composition; in the case of composition he makes the traditional assumption described earlier, that the skills taught are purely technical and linguistic, not intellectual. (But I believe he would argue even more strenuously against the idea that writing courses should or can teach intellectual skills.) He concludes (based on scientific studies of reading) that "educational formalism is inadequate even on its own technical ground, since concrete, shared information is essential both to reading skill and writing skill. The purely abstract elements of those skills are slender indeed. (One thinks of Strunk's eleven short maxims of composition.) Literacy is not an empty form or skill. It is content and [cultural] knowledge" (375). Hirsch therefore condemns the teaching of "formal" knowledge (by which he paradoxically means processes and practices) in favor of the informational content he has come to call "cultural literacy."

This is not the place to undertake a scholarly analysis of this fascinating, difficult issue in the study of human cognition and the philosophy of knowledge. The curriculum designer, informed by a range of theoretical reading, has to make practical assumptions. My assumptions are as follows:

- There *are* generic principles relevant to thinking, learning, writing, reading, rhetoric (the opposite position reduces to the absurd proposition that there are no consciously accessible general schemas for activity).
- These principles do not represent unified cognitive structures and are not automatically available in one context simply because they have been learned or practiced in another. The notion of a skill is functional and abstract, summarizing potentials for future action.
- Skills are learned initially only in context, where they are tightly bound to expert knowledge of topic, discipline, rhetorical occasion, etc. Skills (procedural knowledge) and content (propositional knowledge) are interdependent; one must have skills to learn content and know something to exercise a skill.
- It is natural for human beings to abstract schemas from events and adapt them for new purposes, but one cannot count on this happening in given instances.
- It is reasonable to hypothesize that we can assist such abstractive processes and students' efforts to derive and consciously apply principles by providing opportunities for focused practice and reflection as well as by explicitly stating principles at appropriate teaching moments.
- The need for the student to learn new expertise (in the topic, dis-

cipline, situation, etc.) limits the portability of principles without support from experts in that topic, field, and discourse.

A strong argument for my account of basic skills in the face of the first objection is that writing instructors need not teach them out of context or divorced from meaning-content. The core of a studio class (as the analogy with art studios suggests) is learning by doing. Studios are deliberately context-sensitive, bringing into the classroom work from other content courses taken simultaneously (especially in Studio 2, which introduces contrastive rhetoric by examining differences among academic discourse communities) and engaging increasingly in upper division studios the problem of how to relate generic skills to cultural and disciplinary knowledge. In collaborative projects on writing in the disciplines, our Writing Resource consultants address these questions directly with the teachers and students in classes or projects requiring expert knowledge of topics from the perspective of a discipline or profession. Students, who are (in Catherine Smith's phrase) "walking studios," use skills actively to learn, integrate, and critically examine subject matter.

Part of the objection to skills is that they are defined as cognitive processes detached from experience. However, I have not defined skills at the level of cognitive process but rather phenomenologically, in terms of experienced events and practices treated as concrete equivalents to the intellectual processes being learned. These lived events of writing, reading, and thinking engage students in the same sense that a game involves its players and thus provides the opportunity for them to learn, say, the rules and principles of bridge. In addition to engagement, studios provide opportunities for reflection, as players might discuss a bridge hand to identify techniques and strategies for effective play. In such discussions, the bridge player or the studio player becomes self-aware that she is practicing intellectual strategies that may be usable or adaptable in other situations; then, as the games go on, the players discuss how the previously recognized principles apply to new situations and abstract new ones. At times, players of bridge—or of studios—may consult books and experts making more abstract statements of strategies, tactics, goal-setting, and so on.

Let me turn now to the second challenger. This one invokes Plato's critique of rhetoric as an instrument or means to an end that, being detachable from an ethical context, can be abused by those who wish to put it to bad purposes. The sophists were held culpable for teaching such a technology without caring about how it might be applied. Similarly, instructors teaching intellectual principles and processes may be seen as modern-day sophists, since they teach methods independent of any context of values, or transportable into any value framework. One of our studio teachers questioned whether it was right to put such powerful weapons into students' hands, after one of his engineering students used the rhetorical principles learned in a studio to successfully argue a position (on nuclear plants) which the teacher thought morally reprehensible—and, I believe, in a context where the argument could make a material difference in what happened.

In this instance, the objection is that writing teachers are dangerously amoral because they do not explicitly inculcate a set of values to guide applications of conceptual and communicative skills. But the obverse perspective on values and skills comes to a similar impasse. Ideology critique, which denies the very possibility of teaching that does not "favor one version of economic, social, and political arrangements over other versions" (Berlin 479), cannot sanction any notion of teaching "basic skills" (even in a greatly enriched version, as here) because its theorists see such a project as serving conservative ideological interests. By teaching students to participate in their culture skillfully, they argue, writing classes reproduce the social status quo which they wish to teach students to question and oppose. Thus this challenge holds that in teaching skills we are guilty, first, of blindness to our own ideological embeddedness and, second, of divorcing processes from their historical, political, and cultural contexts.

I shall reply again on a practical level. One must acknowledge the intrinsic problems that seem logically inescapable in teaching any form of activity. Any effort to abstract and articulate general principles from the matrix of practice activates these problems and provokes critique. Abstraction is by definition an act of decontextualization. In the case of activities, one abstracts strategies from the contexts of purpose and meaning and thereby treats acts as instruments to ends rather than ends in themselves. It takes another step to reinsert them into contexts of judgment, where one decides how they fit into structures of goals and commitment.

In that sense, there is no answer to these critiques, just a constant effort to work and rework the questions as tensions within practice. With respect to values, studios do not teach skills innocently and uncritically. But neither do they make ideology critique a central practice primarily because ideology critique, when turned against writing as a practice, tends inexorably to replace it as the central activity of the classroom. In James Berlin's revealing words, "Ideology is here foregrounded and problematized in a way that situates rhetoric within ideology, rather than ideology within rhetoric" (479). One can translate this statement as "The practice of political critique [especially, the critique of writing] displaces and subsumes the practice of writing." In so doing it defeats its own purpose by making it impossible for students to think and write critically about the dogma of critique (Knoblauch).

The Writing Program, aware that studios practice a particular rhetoric, regards any rhetoric as value-laden. We attempt as a community of teachers to articulate the values that animate the Writing Program as a project, to describe them as a rhetoric, and to subject them to critical examination and constant evaluation in the ways they shape decisions about the curriculum, administration, and research. In my own view, studio teachers have two direct responsibilities to students concerning values. First, they should recognize that as persons they cannot help but enact personal values, which have many sources and are culturally situated. Teachers must decide freely for themselves when to make such beliefs and commitments explicit for students, how to render them self-critical, and how to express the relationship between personal values and those of the program or university culture. But they should be held responsible to refrain from teaching their beliefs as dogmatic truths and especially to avoid making students' purposes as writers, readers, and thinkers instrumental to their own political or ethical goals, for this would amount to treating students as tools rather than as persons (see Johnstone on the ethics of rhetoric). Instead, teachers' decisions should be guided by their best judgments about students' educational needs, constantly informed by students' own perceptions of those needs and critically examined through exchanges with their peers.

The teachers' other responsibility to students is more fundamental: that is, to draw attention to the relationship between skills and values as one that calls for students to make informed, self-critical choices. Earlier I pointed out that the idea of basic skills is incomplete even as a simple heuristic without certain complements. I would like to end by showing how we situate a notion of basic skills in relation to a broader framework of "basics" (which in turn fits into the complex, dynamic system of ideas, values, practices, and patterns of activity we call a writing program).

Basic skills are one leg in a triad of "basic" elements that organize studio content. The triad is described thus in an internal program document written for new teachers:

> Writing Studios assume that students must acquire basic intellectual *skills* and develop conceptual *knowledge* about language in order to master writing as a multi-purpose tool. Skills represent "know-how": ways of *doing* things with discipline, purpose, inventiveness, and flexibility. Students learn skills by participating in inquiry and communication, which become the central focus of studios. Through study and reflective thinking, students also form concepts and test theories *about* writing and its relationships to cognition, historical and cultural contexts, and technologies. The third element in the triad is *judgment*, the ability to relate skills (ways of acting) to cultural or disciplinary knowledge (content) and to apply them wisely in view of the writer's values and experience.

The document goes on to say:

> The principle of teaching the "new basics" is that each basic element has equivalents in concrete classroom activities, experiences, and events. It is these equivalents in their detail, rather than a verbal definition of the basic element, that specify the meaning of each basic element and guide the teacher in planning studios.

Here is a summary of these equivalents:

BASIC ELEMENT	TRANSLATION IN THE CLASSROOM
intellectual and symbolic skills	activities and processes of writing, reading, talk
conceptual knowledge	the terms or "keywords" used to discuss writing and thinking
judgment	the process of applying skills and knowledge across contexts in light of one's commitments and purposes; an effort to articulate the strategic and ethical bases for choices

The concept of keywords is developed further in another Writing Program document by James Zebroski, which discusses the emergence of a language within the community of the Writing Program that (like all languages) is a cultural repository for conceptual knowledge, in this case about the domain of writing and rhetoric ("Eleven Keywords"; see also "Keywords of Composition") and about the processes of learning and teaching language skills (cf. Williams: keywords are "significant, binding words in certain activities and their interpretation; they are significant, indicative words in certain forms of thought" [15]). Just as classroom activities are the embodied expression of skills, the keywords of the studios become teachable representations of the program's shared or contested conceptual knowledge. Judgment is, on the one hand, a dimension of the activities involved in using skills. But also, concretely, it is a type of reflective conversation or second-order talk layered into the studios, with students moving up what Donald A. Schon calls the "ladder of reflection" (114-17) from reflection-in-action to examining, with more critical distance and perspective, the studio activities themselves. Teachers refer to this kind of reflection as occurring in "teachable moments," when one "freezes the frame" to recognize the ways that values enter into decisions about writing or reading, and shape the discourse of teaching and learning.

Ultimately, one cannot judge a proposal to reclaim basic skills except in relation to the goals it serves. Those goals may be different from one program or educational environment to another. In the writing studios at Syracuse, a new concept of basic skills fits into a transformed curriculum in which it helps to specify for teachers and students a much richer, more generous conception of writing and of students' intellectual potential. The array of skills I have defined reflects important values of American culture and American universities, among them cultivating an educated mind to reason critically and make value judgments (Schrag). In teaching literacy the Syracuse writing studios help students prepare to participate constructively as members and makers of their culture. At the same time, as both critical and self-critical instruments, basic skills (as defined here) open not only that culture but also the very concept and function of these skills to dialogue and question within a community of thinkers. In our attempt to practice this concept as reflective teachers, we court, paradoxically, both dangers inherent in teaching socially effective instrumentalities: that they do reflect cultural norms and values and that they make it possible to question them. Thus the practice advocated here for reclaiming basic skills walks the edge between critics on the left and right, mindful of the dangers on both sides. ❧

ACKNOWLEDGMENTS

I wish to thank my colleagues for the dialogues through which they helped me construct this essay, oftentimes by offering vigorous challenges to its ideas. The concept of studio here is deeply indebted to contributions and insights from Margaret Himley. She, along with other members of the 1987 Summer Team led by Faith Plvan, helped to reshape my discussion of basic skills in the direction of accounting for their relationship to values. James Zebroski helped me to articulate a concept of key words and a program language as the concrete equivalent of propositional knowledge. Finally, the teachers of the Writing Program, through their practice and reflections, especially in the Genre Project of 1986-87, made it possible to think these thoughts at all.

WORKS CITED

Berlin, James. "Rhetoric and Ideology in the Writing Class." *College English* 50 (1988): 479-94.

Briggs, Lynn, and Rob Faivre, eds. *Sourcebook: A Guide to the Writing Program at Syracuse.* Syracuse, NY: The Writing Program, Syracuse U, 1989.

Bruner, Jerome S. *Beyond the Information Given: Studies in the Psychology of Knowing.* Ed. Jeremy M. Anglin. New York: Norton, 1983.

Emig, Janet. "Hand, Eye, Brain: Some 'Basics' in the Writing Process." *The Web of Meaning: Essays on Writing, Teaching, Learning and Thinking.* Eds. Dixie Goswami and Maureen Butler. Upper Montclair: Boynton/Cook, 1983.

Gates, Robert, et al. "Final Report of the Ad Hoc Committee To Review Writing Instruction." Syracuse U, 1985.

Himley, Margaret. "'Deep Talk' as Knowing." *Shared Territory: Understanding Children's Writing as "Works."* Oxford U P, forthcoming.

Hirsch, E. D., Jr. "Cultural Literacy." *American Scholar* 52 (1983): 159-69.

——. "'English' and the Perils of Formalism." *American Scholar* 53 (1984): 369-79.

Howell, Charles, ed. *The Genre Project: A Survey of Studio Teaching Methods. Reflections in Writing* 7 (Dec. 1988).

Johnstone, Henry W., Jr. *Validity and Rhetoric in Philosophical Argument: An Outlook in Transition.* University Park PA: Dialogue P of Man & World, 1978.

Knoblauch, C. H. "Rhetorical Constructions: Dialogue and Commitment." *College English* 50 (1988): 125-40.

Lakoff, George. *Women, Fire, and Dangerous Things: What Categories Reveal about the Mind.* Chicago: U Chicago P, 1987.

Langer, Susanne. *Philosophical Sketches.* Baltimore: Johns Hopkins P, 1964.

Lawton, David L. "Composition Courses for College Freshmen Are Ineffective; They Should Be Abolished." *Chronicle of Higher Education,* 21 Sept. 1988: B1-2.

Perkins, D. N. *The Mind's Best Work.* Cambridge: Harvard U P, 1981.

Phelps, Louise Wetherbee. *Composition as a Human Science.* New York: Oxford U P, 1988.

——. "Developmental Challenges, Developmental Tensions: A Heuristic for Curricular Thinking." *Developing Reading and Writing During Adolescence and Adulthood.* Eds. Richard Beach and Susan Hynds. Norwood, NJ: Ablex, forthcoming.

——. "Practical Wisdom and the Geography of Knowledge in Composition." *Ms.,* 1989.

——. "The Spiral Curriculum." Writing Program Document. Syracuse U, 1987. Rpt. in *Sourcebook.* 35-40.

Plato. *Phaedrus and the Seventh and Eighth Letters.* Tr. Walter Hamilton. Middlesex, Eng.: Penguin, 1973.

Polanyi, Michael. *Personal Knowledge: Towards a Post-Critical Philosophy.* Chicago: U Chicago P, 1962.

——. *The Tacit Dimension.* 1966. Garden City: Doubleday, 1967.

Schon, Donald A. *Educating the Reflective Practitioner: Toward a New Design for Teaching and Learning in the Professions.* San Francisco: Jossey-Bass, 1987.

Schrag, Calvin O. "Liberal Learning in the Postmodern World." *Key Reporter* 54 (1988): 1-4.

Smith, John B., and Catherine Smith. "Writing, Thinking, Computing." *Ms.*, 1988.

Williams, Raymond. *Keywords: A Vocabulary of Culture and Society.* Rev. ed. New York: Oxford U P, 1983.

Zebroski, James. "Eleven Keywords of the Writing Program." Writing Program Document. Syracuse U, 1987. Rpt. in *Sourcebook.* 46-56.

—. "Keywords of Composition: A Discipline's Search for Self." Penn State Conference on Rhetoric and Composition. University Park PA, 9 July 1988.

🐦 7

Looking Under the Table: The Shapes of Writing in College

Carmen B. Schmersahl
Byron L. Stay

Imagine a group of artisans walking by a table laid for an elaborate seventeen-course feast. As they pass, they cannot help scrutinizing the handiwork. The silversmith, frowning, examines the cutlery. The weaver turns up a corner of the tablecloth. Finally, the carpenter stoops down, taps the underside of the table, and announces the whole structure unfit for use.

We wondered about the table of writing in the disciplines, especially at our own college. What are the dishes of the feast our students sample as they move through the core curriculum which constitutes half their academic work? And what about the major? What dishes and utensils do they need for their feast? What kind of writing course would provide the most adequate preparation for them? What kind of writing program would best support our table?

Similar questions have been raised nationally about the design of freshman writing courses and writing programs. Some of the impetus for questioning what is appropriate for freshman composition comes from the Writing Across the Curriculum movement and the increased contact with other disciplines that it has generated. That contact suggests expectations of other teachers often are markedly at odds with those of English teachers. Similarly, studies of writing in nonacademic settings (e.g., Odell and Goswami) have shown that the standards and practices of good writing for English classes are not universal. These two new ways of defining writing have suggested that writing courses which once claimed to give students skills transferable to any other setting may in fact have prepared them only to write in other English courses.

Although such trends and studies have made the status quo seem obsolete, finding a replacement for freshman composition has proved difficult, partly because of the growing influence of social construction and discourse community theory, which emphasize that what defines the discourse of a discipline is more than simply a set of easily teachable conventions. Instead, those conventions reflect different ways of seeing the world, defining and solving problems, and deciding what counts as knowledge (see Bruffee and McCarthy for useful bibliographies and summaries of these theories and their implications for rhetoric).

This problem may be subject to oversimplification by metaphors like Elaine Maimon's "student as tourist," which could be interpreted to imply a superficial approach to writing in the disciplines. The metaphor seems to suggest that writing for other disciplines is a fairly concrete and easily teachable skill. To travel through the curriculum students need learn only a few phrases like "Where's the bathroom?" "How much does it cost?" and "Thank you." But there may be more fundamental ways in which this metaphor disguises rather than clarifies the nature of disciplinary writing. Like discourse community theorists, the metaphor assumes that students will be asked to write papers modeled on scholarship in their fields. Further, it implies that those scholarly conventions are clear, concrete, and readily definable. In addition, as Joe Harris has recently argued, discourse communities may turn out to be cities instead of communities, places of "both consensus and conflict," that "hold room for ourselves, our disciplinary colleagues, our university coworkers, *and* our students."

We suspected that the nature of writing in the undergraduate disciplines, at least on our campus, is more complicated than some traditional WAC models would allow. In an effort to understand the nature of disciplinary writing at Mount St. Mary's College we have, over the past two years, been studying the ways professors use writing in their classrooms. Mount St. Mary's is a small liberal arts college in northern Maryland with fourteen hundred students and a little over 80 full–time faculty members. Like many similar small colleges, the major focus here has traditionally been on general undergraduate education, with faculty devoting most of their teaching time to core courses designed for nonmajors. Furthermore, faculty contact across departments is frequent, and professors, while often active as scholars, have less time and fewer facilities for research than they would at a university.

For each of the past two years we have conducted hour–long interviews with 22 full–time Mount professors, none of them writing teachers. These professors come from nine departments (art, English, history, philosophy, theology, sociology, education, business, and biology) and range in age and experience from a young assistant professor to a full professor with over 30 years at the Mount. They were selected because they include nearly all those who regularly assign writing in their classes. In these interviews we have explored how professors use writing in the classroom, in their departments, and in their disciplines. We discussed how they saw themselves as writers (including writers of dissertations) and how they use writing to meet the goals of the classes they teach.

What we found is that, at our small liberal arts college, writing is used in ways that are more imaginative and less discipline–defined than we expected. In fact, much of the writing assigned at our college serves general instructional purposes without conforming to the conventions and practices of specific disciplines.

Since our contacts with WAC programs and our reading of social construction had convinced us that academic writing is heavily discipline–specific, we were surprised to find only two departments where writing assignments consistently imitate professional genres: English and biology. Both departments use writing models and content primarily to enhance the students' understanding of texts and observations. These assignments are characterized, more than anything, by the requirement that students focus attention clearly within a disciplinary construct and use written formats native to scholarship in the field. In the English department, four out of five surveyed professors require student papers that are based on the analysis of literary texts and expect students to use the traditional format of literary criticism: introduction, argumentative thesis, and support based on quotation and explication. Even those who balk at typical literary critical style usually require students to mimic it. "In the sense that it's jargon," one professor said, "I don't want them to have anything to do with it.. . . . [But] any language that is the language of logical argumentation . . . [is] tainted with the jargonistic dimension."

The biology department is unique among the departments in the study in that the three professors we interviewed all explicitly connected their uses of writing and collaboration with the goal of preparing students to enter a profession. They require students to write up lab reports and do research projects using the traditional scholarly format (survey of literature, materials and methods, results, and discussion). In addition, in the upper–division courses, biology professors regularly collaborate with students on research and encourage students to participate in off-campus conferences. Biology is one of only a few departments at Mount St. Mary's that explicitly and consistently defines itself as pre–professional. Yet it is the only one to use writing consistently to train students in the habits of the field. (The other sciences—physics and chemistry—enroll so few students that generalizations about their teaching are not possible.)

In other departments discipline–based writing tends to be confined to specific courses or, rarely, professors. In most of those cases, professors understand that they are doing something unusual in assigning writing for discipline–based reasons. A theologian assigns a research paper in one course he teaches, for instance, because he thinks his students, as majors, should learn to do "research in the service of theology," and he knows that they will be asked to do that in no other course. A sociologist has his students do a formal research project and report only in his methods course, feeling students should know how sociologists work. But since he dislikes social science style (he "hated doing the technical writing" of his dissertation and found it "boring") and knows that hardly any of his students will practice sociology, he uses more non-discipline based assignments in his other courses.

Except among the English professors, we found a high degree of self–consciousness among faculty who ask students to imitate the models of their disciplines. They justify that practice, in the biology department, by saying "that's how biologists work," and the department sees itself as preparing future professionals. In other departments—history, theology, sociology, education—on the rare occasions when discipline–modeled writing is requested, its purpose is to give students an experience they would not have in most other courses in that department.

Our instructors seem to view writing more as a way to clarify content or engage students (and, rarely, to evaluate students) than as a way into a discipline. Most often, we found that instructors tend to draw on assignments that demand thinking about and manipulation of material: application, synthesis, and personal response. Instructors who use these assignments, whether in core or majors courses, often want to engage students personally in the material being studied. These assignments constitute new "student genres," tied at least as much to the types of thinking and learning that are valued as part of general education as to the habits and values of specific disciplines.

The most commonly used type of writing assignment, especially in lower division or core courses, can be described as application of theory. Sometimes such application is expected to be highly personal, with students drawing from their own experience. Members of the theology and philosophy departments, the most acutely conscious of having students connect classroom study to their personal lives and values, frequently require personal application. A philosophy professor treating Sartre's concept of "bad faith," for instance, has students write about bad faith in the dorms. At other times such application is less personal, as when a sociology professor requires students to trace theories of social change through Steinbeck's *Grapes of Wrath*. Assignments calling for the application of theory are also used in business, education, theology, and art history courses. Professors repeatedly indicated that these assignments, in addition to interesting both faculty and students, help students forge links between instruction and the culture around them.

Other widely used assignments require students to summarize primary or secondary source readings, often synthesizing or evaluating them. We expected these assignments to be generic research papers; they are instead highly individualized and clearly defined tactics for getting students to read and synthesize materials beyond the course texts.

What our professors have told us has raised doubts about whether undergraduate writing, at least at a liberal arts college, does or should imitate professional models. Our professors often do not follow what we or they think of as the normal disciplinary model, and they seem to have compelling reasons for what they do. Five explanations came up repeatedly. Two of these come from dissatisfaction with student abilities or performance: discouragement with student inability to handle discipline–specific tasks and frustration with plagiarism. Clearly, those are not particularly good reasons for calling for a reexamination of the nature of undergraduate writing in the disciplines.

Our instructors' other explanations for their assignments are well worth scrutiny, however. Two of them come as a way to reach instructional goals: the desire to have students connect course content meaningfully with their own lives or beliefs and the desire to find creative ways to spark student interest. The fifth reason that instructors avoid discipline–based assignments comes from a disenchantment with their discipline's discourse as it is normally defined in scholarly publications.

Some instructors use nondisciplinary writing assignments because such assignments interest students in a course's content and a discipline's truths. A professor of philosophy recognizes that students come to her classes with a strong prejudice against philosophy stemming from deep insecurities. "Philosophy makes them feel inferior," she says.

> They view it as something that scholars do, not [something] that they're equipped to do. So a lot of my writing [assignments require] placing philosophy on a level at which they can get engaged. . . . The writing assignments . . . are geared toward somehow convincing them [that] philosophy is not an abstract discipline.

Such assignments serve the dual purposes of generating interest and of helping students overcome feelings of inadequacy.

This kind of emphasis on instilling confidence and increasing commitment to the course explains why students are so frequently asked to apply course theory or insights to themselves. As one theology professor says, one of his main goals is to encourage students to explore "the connections between the course and their own lives." In order to accomplish that goal he realizes that he needs "to help teach them that they have something to say and to get them thinking on maybe a new level about things that have been part of them that they haven't thought about very much." Similarly, one English instructor wants to get his English majors

> to see the relationship between literary invention and invention in other parts of the culture, since most of our graduates are not going to be literary critics for a living. I'd like to make them conscious of the fact that the culture that they live in is something that they have to, at least in some degree, invent rather than just inherit or buy. And so I want to keep trying to make those bridges.

An education professor insists that students apply disciplinary theory to personal experience because otherwise "it's pre-occupational technique, and I think that's dumb. It just creates stupid people and stupid students."

Clearly, one of the motivations for our professors' assignments comes from their commitment to teaching undergraduates, most of whom will not become practitioners in their professors' fields. A second explanation comes from the sometimes problematic relationship the professors have with the discourse of their disciplines. Often, in fact, our professors dislike the scholarly conventions they must follow. Further, even the most active scholars do a high proportion of their writing for audiences outside their disciplines (other faculty, the college administration, parents, alumni, students, the general public). Again and again they spoke of that writing with more enthusiasm and energy than they felt for their scholarship. The professor who disliked the disciplinary conventions of sociology said, "What I like most doing is writing opinion pieces, like rhetoric, like arguments—polemical stuff." Several talked of valuing their research, but not the forms they must use for reporting it. A philosopher said she wishes she could "write on philosophy and yet not write for a philosophy journal" because she doesn't like the way philosophy is written: "It's a dry type of structure; . . . [they] pare things down just to argument."

These kinds of unease lead some professors to explicitly value writing that dares to subvert the commonplace and traditional. One theology professor, whose dissertation was criticized as reading like a novel, now wants almost more than anything for students to write in their own voice. The sociology professor who finds sociological writing "technical" and "boring" asks students to write very "free–form and subjective" think pieces.

So if our professors often do not get models for student writing from their scholarly communities, where do they get them? One of the most pervasive sources of our professors' models for undergraduate writing, whether shaped by their discipline or not, is the professors' own experiences as students at all levels from elementary school through the dissertation. Some professors who "loved to write" in high school and college value students' developing strong opinions and being creative in their writing. These are often the faculty who feel most constrained by the type of writing style they must use as scholars. Some professors use assignments that imitate those they themselves had as students or observed professors using. A philosophy professor who loves "creative" assignments connects them to a freshman-year experiment living in a communal academic environment. A theology professor has adapted both the highly personal theological approach and the teaching style of a mentor from graduate school. Both of these instructors publish regularly in their disciplines, but both have other writing interests as well.

Even more interesting to us were the professors who shape assignments in response to painful experiences they themselves have had as writers, especially as writers of dissertations. A history professor whose publisher called the dissertation unfocused and unclearly argued now most strongly emphasizes students' ability to shape and support an argument. Similarly, an English professor wants his students to be able to fashion a coherent argument because "that was the one thing I hadn't learned in college." This tendency of teachers to want to help students avoid their own weaknesses occurs even at the level of surface features; the business professor who complains vociferously about students' poor editing admits that he himself is an uncertain speller and an insecure writer.

We do not have the answers to our initial questions yet, but we have many more questions and some tentative insights. Our study has made us question our own assumptions about writing in the disciplines and about our work with faculty in other departments. We have learned that student writing at Mount Saint Mary's is assigned for a variety of purposes and in a variety of forms, only sometimes fitting into the kinds of disciplinary or preprofessional categories we had expected from reading about writing across the curriculum. We know that this is so at least partially because some professors' teaching goals are frequently articulated in terms of general or liberal education rather than in terms of their discipline, so that writing assignments are frequently designed for (often implicit) course goals that aim at making students' learning critical, reflective, and personal. We have learned that our faculty's feelings about their own writing have been shaped by a variety of experiences as both students and teachers. We have learned that C. P. Snow's well–known division of the scientist and the humanist does not describe much of the world our students move through in our curriculum, and that Maimon's metaphor of the tourist applies to only some of the courses our students take. Finally, we've learned that our faculty often have good reasons for what they do, and that their responses to the interaction among student, faculty, discipline, and subject are often highly imaginative and individual.

Our study has a number of theoretical and practical implications. It suggests that there may well be a general academic community of discourse as well as those defined in terms of the various academic disciplines: the "general educated audience" may really exist in the college classroom. It also suggests that we need to do more talking with faculty at our own institutions about their uses of writing before we can begin generalizing about writing in the disciplines: we need to be anthropologists of our own cultures. Such discussions can provide us an occasion to help faculty begin a discussion within and across departments so that the range of types of assignments and expectations can be explicitly defined. Rhetoricians stand in a useful position to help define and resolve some of the contradictions and inconsistencies within and across departments.

We do not yet know whether our findings are representative of what admissions folk call "peer schools" or are an idiosyncratic picture of one group of faculty at a particular moment in our school's history. At the very least, though, our interviews raise the possibility that when rhetoricians have gone into the kitchens of our institutions, we may find that there are really two (or more) tables, one for research–oriented universities and one for small colleges. Perhaps at research universities where professors identify almost entirely with their own departments and scholarship and spend most of their instructional time with majors and graduate students, student writing is more clearly domain–specific. Our interviews suggest, however, that writing and learning may be defined differently at small liberal arts colleges where the focus has traditionally been on general undergraduate education, where professors have time and facilities for much less research, where most of our students are enrolled in our core rather than majors courses, and where contact across departments is a way of life. Perhaps we in writing programs need to invite our colleagues in other departments to sit at our table—listening to what they say as well as looking at what they write—before we define what writing in the disciplines is or writing across the curriculum should be. ❦

WORKS CITED

Bruffee, Kenneth A. "Social Construction, Language, and the Authority of Knowledge: A Bibliographical Essay." *College English* 48 (1986): 773–90.

Harris, Joseph. "The Idea of Community in the Study of Writing." *College Composition and Communication* 40 (1989): 11–22.

Maimon, Elaine. "Maps and Genres: Exploring Connections in the Arts and Sciences." *Composition and Literature: Bridging the Gap.* Ed. Winifred Bryan Horner. Chicago: U Chicago P, 1983. 110–125.

McCarthy, Lucille Parkinson. "A Stranger in Strange Lands: A College Student Writing Across the Curriculum." *Research in the Teaching of English* 21 (1987): 233–65.

Odell, Lee, and Dixie Goswami, eds. *Writing in Nonacademic Settings.* New York: Guilford, 1985.

❦ 8

Technology as a Catalyst for Educational Reform in English Classes: Computer-Supported Writers' Conferences

Cynthia L. Selfe

Although computers are now a fact of life in many English departments, and few colleagues need be convinced any more that these machines have a place in the curriculum, we have not left the battles of the computer revolution behind us. In fact, English teachers have just begun to recognize some of the more sophisticated and critical decisions connected with our use of technology.

We have begun to realize, for instance, that what we do over the next few years, as technology continues to transform our society (Bravermann; Heim; Ohmann; Olson; Weizenbaum), will determine whether we use computers to support the current system of teaching literacy skills or whether we use the new technology to address some of the inequities that plague that system, especially as they are manifested in English composition classrooms (Selfe).

Without some creative thinking on our part, without some careful reconsideration of our goals as literacy educators, the introduction of

150

computer technology into our classrooms will not change a single thing. Students will learn to write with computers, just as they learned to write with pens. But unchanged, unaffected, as scholars like Richard Ohmann and Paul Olson point out, will be those social and political problems our profession has been struggling with over the last decade: among them, the marginalization of individuals because of race, age, gender, and handicap; the unintentional and the intentional silencing of certain segments of our population; the unequal distribution of power within economic and social groups represented in our classrooms. If we continue to integrate computers into our current system without considering these problems, our use of technology will only calcify existing social and political inequities.[1]

Thus, while critics agree that new technologies are potentially powerful catalysts for social and educational change (Bravermann; Lanham; Ohmann), the realization of that potential in English classes remains a responsibility of our profession. For teachers of English, then, the real value of computers during the next few years may lie as much in their power as catalysts for social and political reform as in their power as tools of communication.

But *calling* for action is never as difficult as *producing* action. How can teachers of English composition use computer technology to bring about positive changes in our educational system? On a large scale, given not only the inertia of our vast and complex educational system but also our relative inexperience with integrating computers into schools, the problem demands a long-term professional commitment, one that no one teacher can address or begin alone.

On a smaller and more specific scale, however, individual teachers can start immediately to develop computer strategies to move our classrooms in the right direction. Teachers can, for instance, begin to insist on computer networks and networking strategies—within and among schools—that will support collaboration rather than competition among groups of individual writers (Bernhardt and Appleby; Holsten; Holvig; Ludtke; Pfaffenberger; Spitzer "Writing Style"). Teachers can also work to develop computer-conferencing activities that will provide marginalized students in composition classrooms a new and powerful kind of forum for finding and using their voices as writers, one not bounded by the usual constraints of traditional classrooms (Selfe).

This essay focuses on one of these computer-based strategies—the use of electronic conferences as forums for on-line conversations among writers and readers—and speculates about how teachers can employ this technique as a catalyst for positive change within traditional writing courses. In subtle but important ways, computer conferences can complement discussion and intellectual exchange in traditional classrooms. Teachers can use conferences to increase dialectic and dialogic exchanges in a forum under students' own control, increase students' egalitarian participation in such intellectual exchanges, accommodate a multiplicity of interpretive perspectives, and encourage both collaborative and divergent involvement in discourse production.

Current Practices in Traditional Writing Classrooms

While many English composition teachers would subscribe generally to such goals, few are entirely satisfied with the progress they have made toward achieving them within traditional writing classrooms. Often the existing barriers between teachers and students make such frank and open exchanges difficult to set up. Although many writing instructors try to downplay their role as teachers, to support students' contributions, and to minimize the threat of grading, patterns of dialogue and exchange remain basically traditional in most composition classes. When teachers talk, students listen; an instructor's very presence is a constant visual reminder that he or she is different from students. As teachers, we are older than many of our students and we dress differently. Even when teachers and students sit in a circle to disguise the fact that they are different in status, a teacher's presence and contributions are privileged in such traditional settings.

These facts also make us react to our students in predictable ways during class discussions. Students who are verbally articulate about their knowledge of the readings are rewarded by the smiles and nods of other students and by the teacher's attention. Generally, those who are assertive about their views get rewards. While these reactions are not necessarily problematic, they do characterize a forum in which only certain kinds of students excel.

In such forums, whether teachers of English want it to happen or not, we must also recognize that other students are silenced and oppressed. Women, who traditionally speak less than men (Rich; Spender) and are interrupted more often (Zimmerman and West), are often at a disadvantage, as are students less articulate in oral than in written discourse. Students who want to take time to think about their response before they offer it or students who are merely polite may also be out of luck. The discussion in many traditional classroom sessions tends to proceed at a breakneck pace and, sometimes, in a competitive manner. Hence, older students who may be hesitant to add their views, students who speak English as a second or third language, or students with physical handicaps, who cannot verbalize, are also at a disadvantage in such a setting—especially when students' performance in class discussions are figured into teachers' grading systems or, even more common, when teachers unconsciously allow their overall evaluation of students to be diminished by a lack of participation in oral classroom discussions.

It is in these ways that traditional classroom environments, regardless of our intentions, mirror and sustain certain inequities in our society. In subtle and not so subtle ways, despite our best efforts as humanists, English composition classrooms generally favor students who are mainstream, verbally articulate, assertive, and confident. These students succeed within our classrooms as they do within our culture.[2]

However, if English composition teachers have made only moderate progress in addressing these issues in traditional learning environments, they have come to recognize that alternative learning environments—for instance, those that are computer-supported—may, if created and used carefully, provide new opportunities for success. Computer-based environments and electronic conferences, for example, can serve as forums that complement the learning that goes on in traditional writing classrooms. In these new forums, students can exchange ideas electronically rather than through face-to-face conversations. Generally speaking, because these environments are electronic, they are not bound by the same social and political conventions that inform our usual interpersonal exchanges (Hiltz; Kiesler, Siegel, McGuire; Pullinger). As a result, these conferences—if they are shaped by a critical analysis of educational goals and traditional pedagogy—can provide a mechanism for teachers and their students to alter some, although certainly not all, of the problematic social and political patterns inherent in traditional classrooms. At the same time, they may complement and augment those discursive exchanges our profession has always encouraged in writing courses.

The Characteristics of Computer-Based Conferences

Why does this particular computer-based strategy have such potential as a catalyst for change? And how is such change effected? To answer these questions we need to examine how computer-based conferences can function in the contexts of real writing classrooms.

For a specific case study we can focus on an early computer-based conference held at Michigan Technological University. This conversation was conducted within the context of a graduate-level course in professional grammar and editing that I taught in the spring of 1988. Although it was a graduate course, the general patterns of electronic conversation it produced—the involvement of students who did not speak frequently or openly in class, their frank engagement with course texts and concepts, their humor and intellectual divergence—have proven typical of similar on-line conversations in many other graduate and undergraduate courses I have since taught. The twelve students in this particular course, seven men and five women, were generally representative of the population in this mid-sized, midwestern university: all were white; none would be considered minorities. However, as in most classes, there were students who were silenced or marginalized by the traditional patterns of classroom interaction. Discussions, for instance, were dominated by a few verbally articulate students—mostly, but certainly not exclusively, the men. There were both men and women who seldom found or took advantage of opportunities to participate in such conversations: an older woman returning to the classroom after almost a decade of teaching, a man who was unusually reticent and shy in oral exchanges, a younger woman who was quiet and simply preferred not to speak up unless asked direct questions. These students were bright and capable learners, but not central contributors to the group's daily exploration of concepts and issues covered in class texts.

The students and I met in traditional classroom sessions twice a week. We also met twice a week in an electronic environment. Everyone in the class, including me, contributed to a computer-based conference, or conversation, in which we discussed our responses to the issues raised in traditional class sessions or by the assigned readings. Class members were allowed to contribute to the electronic conference at their convenience as long as they did so at least twice a week, and they were invited to use pseudonyms to identify their entries. At the end of the course, students wrote a final conference entry evaluating the on-line conversation and its place in the course. In postcourse interviews, students also told me which pseudonym(s) they had used and provided additional commentary about the conference forum.

The patterns of conversation and interpretation that existed in these two environments—that of the traditional classroom and that of the electronic forum—differed in critical ways. In part, this difference was visible on the surface level of the conversations. The following series of excerpted exchanges (ellipses my own), for example, suggests some of the stylistic features characteristic of the electronic conference. The original exchanges, which seldom went through systematic revisions in the way that formal papers do, are quite a bit longer and more rambling.

17 March
. . .When I think of grammar, I think first of my eighth-grade English teacher, the legendary Mrs. Turnquist. She force-fed us grammar until we all had appositives and prepositions coming out the ears. . . . . I can still hear her take on something of the aura of a Marine drill sergeant as she used to shout out her seven coordinating conjunctions ("And-but-or-nor-yet-for-&-so") or the principle parts of the verb "to be" ("Is-are-was-were-be-been-&-am"). . . . I still remember the day she told our class that one of her great ambitions was to have none of us spell the word "truly" wrong. . . .

Mark

21 March
Are we going to be ANY different from Mark's Ms. Turnquist when we finish this course? Can one teach grammar—give individuals the power of controlling standard usage—and yet help establish a culture where people aren't "lost" because they lack power in this area? . . .Will we learn grammar just to pass along the oppression or learn it to pass along the power? Or are the two inseparable?. . . .

Worried-but-ready

21 March
As a partial answer to "Worried," I think you have a good point about the power and the oppression being inseparable. . . . What I think I'm trying to say is, . . . [a knowledge of] grammar can liberate us by giving us more options for how to say what we're saying. But we can't forget that, before we can figure out how we're going to say it, we must have something to say in the first place. Looking back on most of the writing instruction I've gotten, I got lots of emphasis on grammar, little on how to develop ideas . . . . I try hard not to resent it, but it's difficult. . . .

My biggest concern now is that I don't want to help pass on the oppression. I definitely want to help pass on the power, though. . . .

Decided

2 April

Like Worried-but-ready, I am confused about the whole grammar issue. Not only am I confused, but I'm also feeling rather guilty. . . . [W]e have heard so much about these oppressed and silenced sections of society who do not have a handle on STANDARD ENGLISH. These people come from a variety of cultures. In many cases, not only do we ask them to use a different language than they're accustomed to, but we actually ask them to think differently. All of this effort for what?? To make them more like us—the mainstream, the allegedly enlightened. . . . I know I'm sounding grossly ideological, but we can't ignore these issues when we're taking a grammar class.

Susan 1234

5 April

Do you think that for most people in our society grammar is some nebulous, meaning-less activity associated with school?. . . . "Proper English" was mandated in my home as I grew up. . . . I was indoctrinated into standard English. I knew there was a connection between the English I spoke at home and the grammar I learned at school, but it was a long time before I learned the implications of the connection.

As I look back I realize that I never associated grammar with anything but restrictions. . . . Grammar became almost a moral issue always associated with right and wrong, correct and incorrect, success and failure—just as in our society. In retrospect, I realize that I never associated grammar with the beautiful language I read in books and enjoyed so much. I never associated it with the plays and book readings I heard. Grammar had nothing to do with creativity, beautiful language, or the wonderful picture images created inside my head by the words of others. It was never associated with the ideas I might want to express. . . . I didn't know language and grammar skills could empower me. In our society, even the "privileged" are not really empowered.

Pauline

In some fairly obvious ways, the entries in this conference look and sound much like traditional epistolary exchanges. Entries, for instance, were generally composed by individual students who wrote them in a public computing facility on our campus, although at least two entries composed for this class were collaborative efforts by two or more students. Each student writer also expected some reply to his or her entry from participants in the group conference. Unlike traditional letters, however, the on-line exchanges reveal discussions and responses that happened daily rather than occasionally. Also unlike letter exchanges, the entries are marked by their function as public discourse; individual participants wrote to all the conference members each time they added an entry rather than to a single correspondent. Hence at some points the entries manifest a more formal and distanced, less intimate tone than typical letters. Certainly, the electronic entries demonstrate an intellectual synergy that reflects collaborative group work. In conferences like this one, participants have a "dialogue" in writing; they respond directly to what others say, build on previous arguments, or disagree with particular interpretations within the conversation. In still other ways, the entries seem like journal material because they often contain expressive, informal language and show evidence of a frank engagement with the material frequently lacking in students' academic papers.

While these surface-level characteristics help us define the genre of conference conversations they cannot accurately convey the important potential of such conferences as catalysts for social and political change within composition classrooms. To understand this broader effect, the conference and the writing class must be considered in a contextual frame of political and social issues. Such a frame prompts the following questions, among others: Did the conference affect the control of power and its exercise within the classroom? If so, what effects did this shift in power have on students' intellectual activities and their risk-taking? How did students express divergence and dissent in the two environments? What does this behavior imply about the learning that went on in the two environments?

Power and Control

Our profession has known for some time that computer-based conferences in industrial settings eliminate some of the face-to-face cues that convey information about social status and power and, hence, that they encourage more equal participation among individuals engaged in problem-solving tasks (Kiesler, Siegel, McGuire). And while anecdotal reports of electronic conferences in academic settings have hinted at similar results (Spitzer "Computer Conferencing"; Selfe), few teachers who begin using on-line conferences to support writing-intensive classes fail to be surprised by the different kinds of power and control structures possible in electronic discussions. The teacher-centered structures that mark most traditional classrooms frequently contrast starkly with the student-centered exchanges that characterize on-line forums designed to encourage less directed, more freewheeling discourse. In part such efforts are possible because electronic forums are not rooted in traditional academic value systems and because change, exploration, and divergence exist already as central values associated with the medium (Fjermedal; Levy). If within traditional writing classrooms, as Robert Brooke points out, students commonly assert power and initiate their own brand of interaction through "underlife" exchanges, it is possible to make these activities sanctioned and central within learning forums represented by electronic conferences. For this course, my purpose in setting up the electronic conference was to create a student-centered learning "space" that would complement the more traditional forums of classroom discussions, lectures, and written assignments.

In the sample conference we are examining here, student-centered power structures that characterized the conference are evident in two areas. First, the students as a group control the subject matter being discussed, the direction of the discussion, and the etiquette of responses. For this conference, the only explicit directions I gave were to use the issues we discussed in the course as points of departure and to contribute regularly to the conversation in the conference.

This kind of open-ended invitation to take control of the class differed from traditional in-class sessions. In the regular classroom both the students and I were bound subtly and not so subtly by mutually accepted conventions. Habitually, as the teacher, I assumed most of the responsibility for controlling the issues we covered, the pace and the depth of our discussions, and much of the reading material introduced. Habitually, as students, they listened when I talked and initiated discussions at my invitation. And while this traditional mode of operation was useful in some respects, giving both my students and me a sense of comfort and continuity born of our collective educational histories, it limited the discussions and the learning that took place in the classroom in the ways outlined earlier.

The conference conversation, while also limited in its own way, provided an alternative forum for discussion. It took place outside the classroom, thus lending itself naturally to a new set of conventions determined by the students themselves. Reinforcing this situation was the fact that everyone who contributed to the conference, including the teacher, could use a pseudonym. Hence, there was no visible "teacher" in that electronic environment. In the absence of an instructor or central authority, the participants themselves collaboratively took control; they, as a group, negotiated the direction and focus of their discussion and decided whether to stay with a topic or abandon it.

The nature of control and power, however, cannot be represented simply as student-centered. Power also shifted away from those students privileged in the traditional classroom setting and toward those marginalized in that setting. Because the conference took place in an environment that was electronic and asynchronous, the conversation was more like a public letter exchange than a concurrent, real-time conversation. As a result, every member of the class had the opportunity to "speak," without interruption, for as long as he or she wished, and this characteristic of the conference became important. In such an electronic conversation, those quieter members of the class and those who wanted to mull over their responses before they contributed were no longer interrupted or silenced, consciously or unconsciously, by the constraints of face-to-face discourse and discussion. Hence, those individuals marginalized in the traditional classroom assumed a new kind of authority, power, and centrality within the conversational exchanges of the computer-based forum.

Similarly, by eliminating visual identification of contributors, the conference also removed some of the cues of status (gender, race, accent, clothing, paralinguistic cues) that contribute to the unequal distribution of power and control in the traditional classroom.

This particular characteristic of conferences seemed especially appealing to individuals who noted—both in their final evaluative conference entries and in postclass interviews—that every student did not receive equal amounts of "floor" time within a traditional class to explore topics in ways that satisfied them intellectually or creatively.

Reduced-Risk Environment

The shift of control to students as a group and as individuals, however, would still have been impossible had the conference not also represented a reduced-risk environment for dialogue, one in which individuals were not identified as they were in face-to-face conversations and discussions. What comes to count in such a setting, as Michael Spitzer has observed ("Computer Conferencing"), is the quality of an individual's thinking. What is said and how it is said becomes more important, at least for a moment, than who said it.

Associated with this anonymity was a change in perspective. Students who participated in the conference gained both a new intellectual distance from their ideas by "publishing" their work in a public forum and, at the same time, a new freedom to associate such ideas more closely and frankly with their own experiences. Discussions in the electronic forum, as a result, became more emotion-laden, more personal, and even more argumentative than face-to-face discussions in the classroom—a finding supported by researchers who have studied other types of on-line conversations (Kiesler, Siegel, McGuire; Spitzer "Writing Style"). The use of pseudonyms in the conference, for example, allowed participants to reveal personal anecdotes or emotional ties to issues without the embarrassment usually attached to such information and, thus, to make frankly personal connections with the subject matter of the course that were not necessarily supported within the traditional classroom.

Anonymity also made it easier for students with divergent or unpopular views to express those views or to try out opinions, ideas, and arguments in a public arena. One student remarked, "I think I was more willing to stick my neck out on the conference than in class—still in a wishy-washy, weenie sort of way, but that's my personality. . . . This was the first writing that I really felt was dangerous. . . . What we were writing was actually getting people mad! We were causing reactions; we were talking about the thing in the hallways. . . ."

And while the use of pseudonyms did not eliminate linguistic responsibility in the conference, it certainly changed its nature. Although participants did not have to identify who they were in a traditional sense, specific opinions and ideas became attached to individual pseudonymic personalities. Thus, participants in this conference could assume public responsibility for an idea without fear of being identified personally. They could argue for an unpopular opinion, put forth a dissenting interpretation, try on a perspective in an atmosphere of reduced personal risk.

This characteristic of conferences can be illustrated by example. The topic of the following discussion, while mentioned originally in the classroom, did not generate the frank discussion in that face-to-face environment that it did in the electronic environment, and the reason is evident:

25 March

This week, I had the opportunity to read an eleven-page curriculum insert . . . which has been sent to hundreds of schools throughout Ontario. . . . The document contains creative ways to introduce the topic of peace to students in grades 5-8, including a game for the children to play. When I examined the game, I was horrified at the manipulation of language the author uses to cast a positive light on socialist philosophy. At one point the author suggests that unemployed parents and state aid are something to be celebrated. . . . I deeply resent the world view that is being thrust upon these children through the manipulation of carefully chosen language. The political implications of this material are frightening to me.

Angry

25 March
ANGRY, I was wondering about some of the language you use in your entry. You state: "I deeply resent the world view that is being thrust on these children. . . ." Excuse me, but it seems to me that you, too, are being manipulative with language—we all are.

YOU USE WORDS AND PHRASES LIKE . . . "MANIPULATION," "THRUST," "FRIGHTENING," "HORRIFIED" IN CONNECTION WITH "SOCIALIST PHI-LOSOPHY," ALL OF WHICH ALSO REPRESENT A "WORLD VIEW" (LIKE YOU BELIEVE THE . . . GAME DOES). AND, PLEASE EXCUSE ME AGAIN, BUT THIS MIGHT BE TERMED "PROPAGANDA," TOO. ARE YOU TRYING TO GET US TO LOOK AT THE GAME OBJECTIVELY AND RATIONALLY, OR ARE YOU USING LANGUAGE THAT APPEALS . . . TO EMOTIONS AND INSTINCTS?

. . .I have trouble with your entry because when you accuse the authors of the game of using carefully chosen language to manipulate, I see you doing the same thing.

A mirror

26 March
They should be ashamed of themselves those socialists in Ontario. . . . Why can't they be like other people, people who don't play grammar games, people who never manipulate language to make things appear other than they really are, people who never use words like a magician uses smoke and mirrors, distracting and confusing the audience while the truth vanish-es, only to reappear as fiction.

The Masked Grammarian

"Angry," an older woman who did not often participate in oral class dis-cussions of controversial matters, chose the reduced-risk environment of the electronic conference to express a forceful opinion about a rather sen-sitive topic and to explore her feelings about it. The conference environment also allowed "Angry" to see and evaluate her peers' strong reactions to her opinion—without a face-to-face confrontation. The electronic discussion that "Angry" started continued over several days of the conference and included all twelve members of the class, with "Angry" as a frequent participant. In this and similar cases, the computer-based conference offered a "place" for a frank and meaningful discussion about important topics that might never have occurred in class or outside of class in face-to-face exchanges.

Divergence and Dissent

The reduced-risk environment represented by the conference also had a noticeable influence on the nature of divergence and dissent in the online class discussions. Afforded a new distance from and perspective on their intellectual exchanges, a new sense of authority, and the optional protection of anonymity, participants became at once more playful and creative in their writing and less overtly concerned about expressing dissenting ideas on various kinds of linguistic and political issues.

One of the primary ways in which students assumed control within the conference was by establishing the appropriateness of divergent language within the conversation, by ruling out a strict adherence to formal academic prose, and by rewarding informality, humor, parody, and creative exploration, as the following entries demonstrate.

25 March
. . .Why am I always passive in my dreams? Why can't I be a strong, active verb? A verb like "pounce," "supersaturate," "personify"? No, I dream I am "kept," "lost," or "froze." If I dreamt I were a noun, I probably would end up being . . . a nominalization. I have come to the realization that my life needs a transformation, but I hold little hope of potentialization of maximum character formation.

AYYYYY

7 April

ME:	What would you like to do this weekend?
SO:	It's up to you. I have a lot of reading to do.
ME:	Why don't we take a ride?
SO:	Sounds good, I could read in the car.
ME:	In the car! In the car! That's a prepositional phrase! Do you know you just said a prepositional phrase?

	This is really exciting! Let me explain to you how a preposition phrase functions! Let me explain to you how to recognize a prepositional phrase!
SO:	Cripes!
ME:	Cripes? The ways you said "Cripes"—I think that's an interjection! I never realized you knew so much about grammar

ME

15 April

Certain professors continue to demand that the Masked Grammarian . . . grapple with philosophical questions concerning grammar . . . take a stand on something. "Until you do so" they say, "we will continue to maintain residence atop your back."

To accommodate his back's growing population . . . the MG would have to build an infrastructure capable of sustaining a community of college professors. This would mean roads; sewer and water hook-ups; homes with lots of bookshelves. . .; movie theaters showing the latest . . . foreign films; and plenty of lounges in which to hold intellectual discussions

Needless to say, such a nightmarish situation is unacceptable . . . to have the MG abandon his visceral approach to writing and submit to the tyranny of professorial opinion, the oppressive chains of intellectual duty. . . .

Masked Grammarian

Central to the humor of these entries is their irreverence. In them, for example, the students have established a dissenting standard of linguistic appropriateness: ruling out a strict adherence to formal academic prose, rewarding humor, and poking fun at the gravity accorded the subject matter of "grammar" in the traditional classroom discussions. This humor provides evidence that the students in the class—midwestern, white, and mainstream—were beginning to cut across the grain of convention and rethink the course material for themselves in their own terms, questioning the relationships among formal and informal language learning, grammar instruction, and writing skill. These were activities they were invited to do, but seldom felt free enough to do, within the confines of the traditional classroom setting where discussions were typically more staid.

The extent to which students assumed control over the conference discussion became itself a means of dissent within the structure of the course and one which will prove interesting to study in future conferences. Once students became used to setting their own agenda for the conference, they resisted suggestions made in class designed to influence the nature of the on-line discussion. The students had assumed control of their alternate forum, and they did not welcome efforts to impose the structures of the traditional classroom on the electronic environment.

Given the opportunity to dissent in such a forum, students also became willing to question the opinions of authorities featured in the course and the opinions of individuals within the conference itself. Frequently, individuals used a quotation from a class reading or a reference to a previous entry to establish a point of contention or differing interpretations. I will venture to say here that the best part of the conference was, as one of the students pointed out, that it was always "full of people arguing." This particular aspect of conference discourse is very different from journal discourse, and I suspect this difference is due to the synergistic effect of conversation, dialectic, and exchange. In ways that are impossible within traditional classroom forums, given current constraints (Cooper), electronic conferences can encourage a healthy measure of considered dissent in writing courses, the chance for students to disagree with their classmates' and their teacher's vision of the world—to assert their own views in a logical sense as well as their own voice in a linguistic sense.

This new habit of divergence and dissent proved, in my opinion, to be the most profitable export from the electronic conference to the traditional classroom. Students, after exploring differing viewpoints in writing within the conference and gauging the effectiveness of their arguments against the benchmarks of their peers' responses, became more confident in disagreeing with each other, with me, and with the authors of their texts in classroom discussions. The frequency and the nature of these incidents, of course, differed as widely as the personalities of the students, but they seemed most valuable to me as a teacher when they involved students who were reticent to enter oral conversations within the traditional classroom. One such student, for instance, refused to participate in oral class discussions unless someone made a point of asking him a direct question. Within the electronic conference, however, he offered articulate responses to the group conversation, using his own name as a signature and often expressing opinions that diverged from those expressed within the more traditional forum. As the term progressed, other students would refer during class discussions to a point he had made cogently in the electronic conference and use the reference to back their own arguments or would ask him to elaborate on the opinion he had expressed in writing. Because the students wrote so frequently within the conference, these references and queries became increasingly noticeable and valued in the class. I suspect this situation would not have occurred in a traditional classroom—although my evidence for this claim is based simply on my experiences as a teacher. I do know that my past efforts to encourage reluctant class members to contribute to discussions have met with limited success and that no other group of students I have worked with would have made such a consistent effort to involve one quiet class member in group conversations—both written and oral.

Conclusion

This discussion of dissent brings us back to the challenge of using technology to make a difference in our classrooms. Teachers of English can sit back and let computers be introduced into our writing programs in quiet ways that will change little—our students will then use computers in isolated study carrels to do grammar drill-and-practice programs or labor alone with word-processing programs to complete their papers. But none of this work will change the essential hegemony in our classrooms or encourage students to engage in classroom discourse that runs counter to the dominant mind set or world vision. *Or* we can try to develop computer-based strategies that offer students the opportunity to effect change, to see things from different perspectives.

I am not suggesting that electronic conferences represent the only direction in which we can or should move with regard to our computer use in writing- or reading-intensive classes, but I do believe they represent healthy complements to the traditional composition classroom. Computer-based conferences have their own problems—they are expensive, difficult to manage, prone to abuse by eavesdroppers and teachers who value lockstep curricula. However, such environments, when they are shaped by reformist theoretical perspectives—such as Marxism and feminism, for instance—can be designed to value attempts to reconstruct and rethink existing social structures and visions. If we cannot eliminate oppression, bigotry, or racism from our traditional classes on a large scale because of social inertia, we may be able to set aside small electronic spaces in which traditional rules do not apply in quite the same ways. And in these reduced-risk spaces, students can discover or evolve different patterns of power and linguistic exchange, some of which will run directly counter to those that have become habitual in our traditional classrooms.[3]

Once students experience these new patterns, as I can attest, they bring them back into the traditional classroom and change that setting for the better, modifying the habitual balance of power between teachers and students and among various groups of students, inviting marginal participants into the center of discussions, and encouraging increased intellectual divergence and even dissent.

If computer networks encourage egalitarian dialogue in educational settings, they are indeed revolutionary tools, especially from a teacher's viewpoint. As Paulo Freire points out, change begins with honest, non-hierarchical exchanges that turn the existing hegemony into open dialogue,

> Through dialogue, the teacher-of-the-students and the students-of-the-teacher cease to exist and a new term emerges: teacher-student with students-teachers. . . . They become jointly responsible for a process in which all grow. In this process, arguments based on "authority" are no longer valid . . . . (67)

This active, frank dialogue, Freire continues, supports an increasingly "critical consciousness" (19) and the "practice of freedom" (15) through a "liberating education" (67). If we use computers to accomplish these ends, then we can inspire a computer "revolution" of the most meaningful kind—not one concerned with hardware and software but one concerned with people, education, and change. ❦

NOTES

[1]Here I am working from two related assumptions: first, that technologies such as the personal computer are artifacts of a particular culture; and second, that, as artifacts of a culture, technologies are naturally shaped by and imbued with particular cultural values. As a result, our uses of technology tend to support our cultural status quo. I am also working from a third important assumption: that this situation is neither inevitable nor desirable. We as teachers *can* and *should* think critically about our culture, about technologies and their uses. I am hopeful that by

doing so we can design technology applications that resist the status quo, that begin to address some of the cultural problems plaguing our education system. Although such optimism is not shared by many cultural critics (Bravermann; Marcuse), it forms the basic work that many computer and composition specialists do within our profession, and it is the experiences of these colleagues that encourages my own thinking. For further reading computers' potential for supporting and even exacerbating current inequities in our society and our educational system see Olson; Livingstone; Ohmann; Becker; Chen; and Gomez.

[2]For more thorough discussions of how we as writing teachers consciously and unconsciously silence and oppress students in composition classrooms, I suggest the essays in Caywood and Overing; or Cooper.

[3]Rich notes, for instance, that women (and, I can add, other oppressed minorities) will find their voices when "they begin to move out toward what the feminist philosopher Mary Daly terms a 'new space' on the boundaries of patriarchy" (49). Computer networks may provide such spaces, electronic and cultural "lacunae" (Wittig) in which we learn to listen to multiple voices and thus, in Gilligan's words, learn the importance of "different truths" (156). In these spaces, we may be able to recapture from women and other "silenced" (Olsen) minorities, perspectives that we have lost.

WORKS CITED

Becker, H. J. "Using Computers for Instruction." *BYTE* (February 1987): 149-162.

Bernhardt, S., and B. Appleby. "Collaboration in Professional Writing with the Computer." *Computers and Composition*, 3 (1985): 29-42.

Bravermann, H. *Labor and Monopoly Capital: The Degradation of Work in the Twentieth Century*. New York: Monthly Review Press, 1974.

Brooke, R. "Underlife and Writing Instruction." *College Composition and Communication*, 38 (1987): 141-153.

Caywood, C., and G. Overing. *Teaching Writing: Pedagogy, Gender, and Equity*, Albany: State U of New York P, 1987.

Chen, M. "Gender Differences in Computer Use and Attitudes." Paper given at the 35th Annual Conference of the International Communication Association, Honolulu, 1985.

Cooper, M. "Why are We Talking about Discourse Communities? Or Foundationalism Rears Its Ugly Head Once More." Paper presented at the Conference on College Composition and Communication, St. Louis, 1988.

Fjermedal, G. *The Tomorrow Makers: A Brave New World of Living Brain Machines.* New York: Macmillan, 1986.

Freire, P. *Pedagogy of the Oppressed.* Trans. M. B. Ramos. New York: Seabury, 1968.

Gilligan, C. *In a Different Voice: Psychological Theory and Women's Development.* Cambridge: Harvard UP, 1982.

Gomez, M. "Equity, English, and Computers." *Wisconsin English Journal,* 29 (1986): 18-22.

Heim, M. *Electric Language: a Philosophical Study of Word Processing.* New Haven: Yale UP, 1987.

Hiltz, S. "The 'Virtual Classroom': Using Computer-Mediated Communication for University Teaching." *Journal of Communication,* 36 (1986): 94-105.

Holsten, V. "What is Macy's Anyway? New York Comes to the Indian Reservation Via E-Mail." Paper given at the annual meeting of the National Council of Teachers of English, Los Angeles, 1986.

Holvig, K. "Voices Across the Wires through Breadnet and Clarknet." Paper given at the annual meeting of the National Council of Teachers of English, Los Angeles, 1987.

Kiesler, S., J. Siegel, and T. McGuire. "Social Psychological Aspects of Computer-Mediated Communication." *American Psychologist,* 39 (1984): 1123-1134.

Lanham, R. "Convergent Pressures: Social, Technological, Theoretical." A paper presented at the conference on "The Future of Doctoral Studies in English," Wayzata MN, 1987.

Levy, S. *Hackers: Heroes of the Computer Revolution.* New York: Dell, 1984.

Livingstone, D. ed. *Critical Pedagogy and Cultural Power.* South Hadley MA: Bergin, 1987.

Ludtke, M. "Great Human Power or Magic: An Innovative Program Sparks the Writing of America's Children." *Time* (14 Sept. 1987): 76.

Marcuse, H. *One Dimensional Man: Studies in the Ideology of Advanced Industrial Society.* Boston: Beacon, 1964.

Ohmann, R. "Literacy, Technology, and Monopoly Capitalism." *College English* 47 (1985): 675-689.

Olsen, T. *Silences.* New York: Dell, 1978.

Olson, P. "Who Computes?" *Critical Pedagogy and Cultural Power.* Ed. D. Livingstone. South Hadley MA: Bergin, 1987. 179-204.

Pfaffenberger, B. "Research Networks, Scientific Communication, and the Personal Computer." *IEEE Transaction on Professional Communication: Special Issue on Computer Conferencing.* Ed. V. Arms. *PC-29* (1986): 30-33.

Pullinger, D. J. "Chit-Chat to Electronic Journals: Computer Conferencing Supports Scientific Communication." *IEEE Transaction on Professional Communication: Special Issue on Computer Conferencing.* Ed. V. Arms. *PC-29* (1986): 23-29.

Rich, A. *On Lies, Secrets, and Silence: Selected Prose: 1966-78.* New York: Norton, 1979.

Selfe, C. "Computers Through the Lens of Feminist Theory." Paper presented at the Conference on College Composition and Communication, St. Louis, 1988.

Spender, D. *Man Made Language.* London: Routledge, 1980.

Spitzer, M. "Writing Style in Computer Conferences." *IEEE Transaction on Professional Communication: Special Issue on Computer Conferencing.* Ed. V. Arms. *PC-29* (1986): 19-22.

———. "Computer Conferencing: An Emerging Technology." Unpublished manuscript. New York: New York Institute of Technology, 1988.

Weizenbaum, J. "Not Without Us: A Challenge to Computer Professionals to Bring the Present Insanity to a Halt." *Fellowship* (1986): 8-10.

Wittig, M. *Les Guerilleres.* New York: Avon, 1969.

Zimmerman, D., and C. West. "Sex Roles, Interruptions and Silences in Conversation." *Language and Sex: Difference and Dominance*, Ed. B. Thorne and N. Henley. Rowley MA: Newberry, 1975. 105-129.

III

How Writers Develop

This section consists of two essays that raise questions about the nature of development in student writing. Evangeline Marlos Varonis challenges the prevalent assumption that errors or problems that crop up in a student's text at the end of a writing course signal that the writer has not learned the relevant writing skill or strategy—indeed, that the student's writing ability, rather than steadily rising as expected, has stalled or even degenerated. Drawing on psychological and linguistic research, she argues that apparent backsliding may actually represent a normal stage of skill development, which rather than following a steady upward course, often looks more like a U-shaped curve. In some cases, backsliding may be a consequence of sophisticated restructuring of writing strategies, similar to that typically experienced by second language learners. In other cases, students may backslide in previously mastered skills because they are concentrating their efforts on mastering a new writing skill. After analyzing three suggestive cases of apparent backsliding, Varonis concludes that students need continuing varied opportunities to practice their skills, as some institutions provide in writing-across-the-curriculum programs. She also suggests that writing assessment and placement procedures should take account of this irregular course of skill development by basing evaluation on portfolios rather than single samples of student writing.

Varonis's essay reminds us that the students in a writing class begin and end the semester at different points of development and that development may not be linear and straightforward. Like language acquisition, writing ability is a discrete skill that develops over time and incorporates many subskills, new dimensions, and applications that continually require more learning. Backsliding may occur within a semester or over longer periods of time, but these incidents of backsliding should resolve themselves with practice. One implication of this view is that teachers must be patient with students as they master new skills, and they must refrain from too quickly assuming that a deficient performance is due to ignorance, inattentiveness, or misinterpretation of the demands of the task. Backsliding also can occur at various points in the life of any writer—though perhaps not in relation to the same particular skill—as the writer takes on different and more complex tasks. Certainly, as teachers, we may experience our own variety of professional backsliding while developing effective classroom practices: for instance, when paying special attention to encouraging class participation, we may not allocate class time as well. While it is not radical to prescribe practice for overcoming skill deficiencies, Varonis's essay reminds us that, in the best of circumstances, learning to write takes a long time. All the *techne* in the world does not guarantee a perfect product every time a student writes.

Whereas Varonis considers development in terms of the rise and fall (and rise) of proficiency in particular writing subskills, Janice Hays and Kathleen Brandt focus on another aspect of development. They examine the development of rhetorical competence as a reflection of the socio-cognitive maturity of high school and college students. They report on a study of students who wrote two versions of an argumentative essay, one addressed to a friendly audience and the other to a hostile one. They looked for relationships among the students' socio-cognitive maturity (as measured by the Perry scheme), the quantity and quality of rhetorical moves toward audience in the papers, and the holistic scores the papers received. They found first that students made more audience accommodation moves when writing to hostile than to friendly readers. However, in general, students who scored lower on the Perry scale were less effective at accommodating their readers. When attempting to respond to hostile audiences, for example, they became hostile in return, making inaccurate, irrelevant, or pejorative comments. In contrast, students who scored higher on the Perry scale acknowledged the legitimacy of readers' objections and attempted to address them. One conclusion that emerges from this study is that rhetorical competence is strongly associated with socio-cognitive maturity. Thus, in order to improve at audience accommodation in their writing, students may need more experience at interacting with people of differing views in social and discipline-specific settings. To foster this development, students may need to practice adversarial role playing as well as developing potential objections to their own arguments. Development of rhetorical competence, then, is different from recovering from backsliding in writing skills. Rhetorical competence is unlikely to result simply from more practice at particular writing skills; it is the result of a broader kind of rhetorical education.

The development of rhetorical competence differs from skill development in another way. Backsliding occurs in any situation in which humans practice skills, but only certain kinds of educated readers consider the inability to accommodate to hostile audiences a deficiency. Taking rational account of opposing views is the rhetorical stance that our culture prefers. It represents an ideal goal of education in Western secular culture, one that reflects a particular, culturally influenced view of "enlightenment." The Perry scheme, then, does not represent an essential, universal progression of human cognitive development; it describes *socio*-cognitive development, where the social context is a norm reinforced by our system of higher education.

The Perry scheme grew out of a study of Harvard undergraduates and how their intellectual stances changed during college from unthinking acceptance of authority to a commitment to beliefs that emerge from careful evaluation of evidence and alternative perspectives. This change results from a combination of cognitive development and social, moral, and intellectual instruction at the university. Many freshmen come to college believing in authority and absolute right and wrong answers at least in part because that is what they have been trained to believe. In our culture, institutions of higher education often aspire to challenging these beliefs with the goal of creating graduates who are critically aware.

Because the Perry scheme is a product of cultural and social preferences, we must be careful not to apply it directly as a yardstick of intellectual maturity. If development along its progression were identical to maturation, we would not expect to find adult fundamentalists. But of course we do. Adults may even take different intellectual stances in response to different aspects of their lives: some may be committed relativists with respect to intellectual concerns but absolutists with respect to moral or religious principles. Once we acknowledge that development along the Perry scheme represents a social and cultural norm rather than some necessary byproduct of maturation, we can see the importance of rhetorical education for achieving the goal. In order for students to learn to accommodate arguments to audiences, they must first have reached an appropriate level of socio-cognitive maturity, but they also require instruction and corroborating experience within a community that prizes this ability.

The two essays in this section emphasize two different aspects of the development of writing ability. Learning to write well involves both cognitive and social development, but development does not follow a steady progression toward some fixed or inevitable goal. Individual writers at every stage may be confronted with new demands that call for reshaping their strategies and writing processes. In the course of this reshaping, well-learned practices may disintegrate while new ones develop. As writers develop within an intellectual community, they must learn how our culture prefers people to deal with opposition to their beliefs. A student's socio-cognitive maturity will affect his or her readiness to respond to appropriate instruction. Part of a rhetorical education should be the recognition that one never finishes learning to write.

❦ 9

U-Shaped Behavior in Basic Writing: The Case for Backsliding

Evangeline Marlos Varonis

Introduction

In recent years, writing theorists have shifted from regarding writing as a product to emphasizing the interactive writing process. They argue that the writing process is dynamic, that meaning may be created in the act of writing itself, and that writing should be seen not merely as an end but also as a means to that end. Writers write and rewrite, negotiating meaning with their audience in the process, just as interlocutors may negotiate meaning (Varonis and Gass) in face-to-face interaction. In this way, revision is viewed not as the tool of the inexperienced writer who couldn't get it right the first time but as an essential part of a creative act. Viewing writing as a problem-solving task, in the words of Linda Flower and John R. Hayes, "allows for the disorderly dynamics of serious thinking and encourages an analytical and experimental attitude in the writer" (461). Thus empowered, the writer may move beyond the demands of surface revision and participate in the creation and exploration of new ideas.

Often, however, it seems that practicing writers lose ground as they gain experience. A student who is focusing on one writing problem while revising an existing text or creating a new one may show less control than she previously demonstrated over a completely different aspect of her writing. This is the phenomenon that I refer to as "backsliding." I will argue that backsliding may not necessarily be the trademark of a lazy, unfocused, or incompetent writer but rather evidence of a practicing writer who is restructuring her composing strategy in response to the increased demands of the writing task. Such loss of skill may be apparent rather than real: when restructuring is complete, the writer may reassume her original competence as well as demonstrate a new one. Thus, backsliding in basic writing students may be seen as an intermediate stage in the restructuring process of practicing writers, a process that has been described in the literature of cognitive psychology as "U-shaped behavior" (Strauss and Stavey). The writer seems to move through three distinct phases with respect to a particular ability: 1) competence; 2) lack of competence; and 3) regained competence reflecting a reorganized system. I will argue that backsliding is merely the second stage of such U-shaped behavior.

In this paper I focus on backsliding in the writing of basic writers. In order to clarify the concept of backsliding I will first present an example of backsliding in one of Mina Shaughnessy's students, a revising basic writer who succeeds only in destroying the text that he is struggling to create. Second, in order to explore potential causes of backsliding, I will discuss backsliding in the context of such cognitive psychology concepts as learning shock, cognitive strain, and automaticity. Third, in order to show that backsliding is a general phenomenon outside of basic writing, I will discuss the notion of U-shaped behavior as it applies to first- and second-language acquisition, arguing that backsliding in basic writing is in fact one stage of such behavior. Fourth, I will return to the case of basic writing and present examples of backsliding in pairs of essays—assessment exams and subsequent unsuccessful post-tests—of students enrolled in introductory tutorial classes at the English Composition Board of the University of Michigan. I will apply the work of contemporary writing theorists to a discussion of these essays. Finally, I will suggest some strategies for dealing with this phenomenon in all basic writers and note the implications of backsliding for writing-across-the-curriculum programs.

Revision and the Basic Writer

Teachers of composition will agree that viewing writing as a process, and specifically emphasizing the value of revision, has had a positive impact on writing pedagogy. However, the act of revision itself is not problem-free. A number of recent reports suggest that many students do not revise

---

Figure 1. *Shaughnessy, 1977*

Start 1: Seeing and hearing is something beautiful and strange to infant.

Start 2: To a infant seeing and hearing is something beautiful and stronge to infl

Start 3: I agree that seeing and hearing is something beautiful and stronge to a
  infants. A infants heres a strange sound such as work mother, he than acc

Start 4: I agree that child is more sensitive to beauty, because its all so new to him
  and he apprec

Start 5: The main point is that a child is more sensitive to beauty than there parents, because its the child a inftant can only express it feeling with reactions.

Start 6: I agree a child is more senstive to seeing and hearing than his parent,
  because its also new to him and more appreciate. His

Start 7: I agree that seeing and hearing have a different quality for infants than
  grownup, because when infants comes aware of a sound and can associate it with the object, he is indefeying and the parents acknowledge to to
  this

Start 8: I agree and disagree that seeing and hearing have a different quality for
  infants than for grownups, because to see and hear for infants its all so
  new and mor appreciate, but I also feel that a child parent appreciate the
  sharing

Start 9: I disagree I feel that it has the same quality to

Start 10: I disagree I fell that seeig and hearing has the same quality to both
  infants and parents. Hearing and seeing is such a great quality to infants
  and parents, and they both appreciate, just because there aren't that
  many panters or musicians around dosen't mean that infants are more
  sensitive to beautiful that there parents.

---

or do not significantly improve their texts when they do (Sommers,
Zamel). Stephen Witte has shown that many who do revise may focus
solely on surface-level considerations, with no attention to content. Even
more discouraging, both Shaughnessy and Sondra Perl have shown that
many revisers succeed only in making their texts worse. As an example,
consider the text from Shaughnessy (7-8) in Figure 1. For an initial class
essay, the writer, enrolled in the City University of New York, is attempt-

ing to contrast the ways infants and adults see the world. As the writer composes and rejects one beginning after another, the syntax becomes more twisted, the discourse more tortured, the point more obscure. From the relatively forceful statement of the first attempt: "Seeing and hearing is something beautiful and strange to infant," the writer seems to back away from an assertive voice. Start 3 begins "I agree," as if the writer is trying to avoid conflict with an audience that has already made up its mind about the matter. Worse yet, Start 8 begins "I agree and disagree," as if the writer is trying to avoid conflict by invoking the voice of Pollyanna. Note also that as the writer struggles to find a stance that will offend no one, the syntax of the passage falls apart. As one example, contrast the language in Start 4: "its *all so* new to him" with the language in Start 6: "its *also* new to him" (emphasis mine). In this case, an increasing inattention to the forms of words results in writing one homophone for another, producing not a grammatical mistake but a meaning different from what was intended. Shaughnessy calls this phenomenon "disintegration." As she says, "so absolute is the importance of error in the minds of many writers that 'good writing' to them means 'correct writing,' nothing more" (8). Such students let their obsession with surface errors interfere with the expression of meaning. Thus, those students whose writing is in greatest need of revision may find themselves least able to integrate developing skills as they approach subsequent writing tasks. As a result, in the process of developing as writers, they may find themselves "backsliding," losing control over previously mastered aspects of writing as they sacrifice one type of writing concern for another.

Research in Cognitive Psychology: Learning Shock, Cognitive Strain, and Automaticity

In the previous section I suggested that, for basic writers, obsession with error may interfere with other aspects of the writing process. Such a hypothesis presupposes a model of human information processing that involves a number of cognitive subprocesses governed by a central processing unit—the monitor (Hayes and Flower) or executive system (Bereiter and Scardamalia). Basic writers may not have developed composing strategies that allow them to run the numerous subprocesses of the writing task simultaneously; as a result, one processing demand may be "swapped out" as another is "swapped in." Such a model of the writing process is based on notions most strongly developed in the field of cognitive psychology.

Much psychological research has been devoted to the study of memory and forgetting. Early studies in interference, for example, document the effect of retroactive inhibition on previous learning. Retroactive inhibition is the process by which learning new associations causes one to forget old ones; in other words, old and new responses compete, resulting in forgetting (DeCecco). While these early studies focused on mechanical tasks such as learning word lists, the results may be extended to more comprehensive types of thinking. Thus, David P. Ausubel and Floyd G. Robinson describe "learning shock" as "a postulated type of resistance and general cognitive confusion which occurs when unfamiliar ideas are introduced into cognitive structure" (111). They add that learning shock is gradually dissipated as new ideas become more familiar and less threatening. When the learning shock is in effect, however, it elevates what they term the "threshold of availability"; in other words, it impairs a person's ability to *apply* an idea even though that person may be able to *recognize* the idea if applied elsewhere.

In a similar vein, Peter Lindsay and Donald A. Norman describe the phenomenon they term "cognitive strain." While the early interference theories and the theory of Ausubel and Robinson address learning, Lindsay and Norman are concerned with decision making. There is an obvious parallel here with current views of the nature of writing as a problem-solving process. Lindsay and Norman argue that "a major factor in a person's ability to make a decision or do any mental task, such as that of problem solving, learning, or thinking, is the amount of strain that these operations place on his cognitive capacities" (533). Limitations in short-term memory will affect the way a decision maker approaches most tasks. "Although he might understand the sensible rules that ought to be followed in reaching a decision," they argue, "the load they impose upon his memory capacity makes it quite likely that he will simplify them enormously when actually faced with a real situation" (534).

If we cast the writer in the role of Ausubel and Robinson's learner or Lindsay and Norman's decision maker, it is easy to see how the load the "sensible rules" place on the writer's memory capacity could result in learning shock or cognitive overload. While focusing on learning one new technique of the writing process, the basic writer avoids making other decisions about the apparent blooming, buzzing confusion by simply disregarding it because it has not reached the threshold of availability. Since the basic writer may not have adequately internalized many of the so-called rules of writing, she suffers the consequences of overanalysis and copes only by focusing on a limited number of concerns at a time. The particular concerns being focused upon are not necessarily the same for every writing effort; thus, the writer appears to backslide.

A key issue here is the *capacity* of the writer's central processing unit, monitor, executive system, brain. Is it limited or limitless? Cognitive psychologist John R. Anderson cites a linguistic study of child speech (Levin, Silverman, and Ford) in support of his hypothesis that it is *limited*. Children asked to describe an event exhibited fewer grammatical errors than children asked to explain it. Since explanations are more demanding cognitively, Anderson argues, "such research implies that processing capacity is limited and must be divided between construction and trans-formation. When the demands for construction (planning) increase, the quality of linguistic transformation suffers" (*Implications* 388). Ann Brown and her collaborators also address this controversy, distinguishing four uses of capacity: mental space, basic processing operations, knowledge base, and strategies (100-102). They argue that total processing capacity (mental space) changes little after four years of age, but that capacity can be functionally increased by "the structure of the knowledge base, the use of strategies, and the efficiency of basic processes" (102). The issue then becomes how to make the existing capacity more efficient.

One way of making capacity more efficient is offered by W. Schneider and R. M. Shiffrin, who distinguish between automatic and controlled processing. Automatic processing occurs when a person, through practice, develops control over a complex task. It is "a fast parallel process that is not limited by short-term memory, that requires little subject effort, and that demands little direct subject control," in contrast to "controlled pro-cessing," which is "a comparatively slow, serial process that is limited by short-term memory constraints, that requires subject effort, and that pro-vides a large degree of subject control" (Brown et al. 111). In automatic processing all items in short-term memory may be processed at once without taking capacity away from other ongoing processing, while in controlled processing all items in short-term memory are examined indi-vidually, consuming more capacity.

I would like to argue that the complexities of the writing task make the basic writer, at least initially, a controlled or serial processor, capable of focusing on one or only a few items at a time. Carl Bereiter and Mar-lene Scardamalia point out that such factors as spelling, punctuation, word choice, purpose, organization, and reader characteristics are among those the writer must consider *simultaneously* (133). Only when basic writers automatize the skills required by the writing task can they process all of them together. And how does this come about? "Only with a great deal of practice . . . can controlled information processing become automatic," says Anderson (*Architecture* 127).

Bereiter and Scardamalia argue that one way novice writers cope with the many demands of the writing process is by engaging in "knowledge telling" (5), which allows them to rely wholly upon their natural language skills and basic social experiences. Though it may be an effective style for such discourse schemata as narratives of personal experience, knowledge telling is limited in that it does not allow the writer to *re-process* knowledge—this ability is the privilege of the knowledge-transforming model (6) and the more expert writer. Knowledge telling normally involves a *metamemorial* search, "a diffuse, topic-related search of memory" (65), while knowledge transforming typically requires a *goal-directed* search, "a top-down search, directed toward some goal such as proving a point, amusing the reader, or preparing an introductory lecture" (65). The authors cite a series of studies on school-age children to show that the movement between knowledge telling and knowledge transforming is developmental: "It appears that outgrowing knowledge-telling may depend on developing memory search strategies that are so effective that they give the knowledge-telling process more material than it can handle" (69). In other words, the knowledge-telling capacity cannot be "overloaded"; when it reaches its limits, some other strategy must be found. Bereiter and Scardamalia note that mastering the knowledge-transforming model depends upon the writer's developing "executive control" of the writing process and reorganizing her own knowledge along the way.

U-Shaped Behavior in First- and Second-Language Acquisition

The notion of reorganization of knowledge also appears in the literature relating to U-shaped behavior, specifically with respect to first- and second-language acquisition. Susan Ervin describes how children pass from the stage of correctly producing irregular past tense forms—e.g., *came, went, broke*—through the stage of producing these forms with regular past-tense morphology—*comed, goed, breaked*—and finally to the stage of again producing the forms correctly. She suggests that the first stage is the result of imitation, the second stage the result of oversimplified analysis, and the third stage the result of reanalysis. Only after sufficient practice is the child able to distinguish irregular forms from the rule-governed regular forms. Such behavior may be termed U-shaped, as the speaker passes from a stage of correct performance to a stage of deviant performance and then back to a stage of correct performance. Similar results have been recorded by Melissa Bowerman with causative and reversative verbs and by A. Karmiloff-Smith with the differentiation of meaning between synonyms. S. Strauss and D. Stein argue that such results should not be seen as attrition in linguistic competence but rather as a "cognitive advance" compatible with the notion that the learner has gone "beyond success" by reanalyzing her own system.

Several studies in the second-language acquisition literature corroborate the idea of U-shaped learning. The work of Eric Kellerman, for example, on Dutch learners of French and German, describes three different grammatical phenomena that may be explained as U-shaped behavior. Kellerman ("If at First You Do Succeed. . .") explains that in Stage 1 the learner's output is successful from both a linguistic and situational point of view. In Stage 2, however, "the learner now sets about to reorganize his or her mental representations of these structures into a system within the relevant linguistic subdomain" (352), resulting in utterances which become deviant during the process of reorganization. In other words, the learner backslides.

The learner, then, moves from analysis to reanalysis, from a narrow consideration of the problem-solving task to a deeper one. How does this occur? As Brown et al. note, "Progress comes only when the inadequate partial theory is well established and the learner is free to attempt to extend the theory to other phenomena" (120). And how does this inadequate partial theory become well established? Through practice. Through practice it becomes automatized and thus capable of further testing by the learner. This further testing may then lead to a restructuring of the system that allows the learner to consider more variables—simultaneously—than before.

Backsliding in Basic Writing

I now extend the notion of backsliding and U-shaped behavior to written composition by analyzing three sets of essays written by students enrolled in tutorial classes at the University of Michigan.

All entering freshmen and transfer students at the University of Michigan are required to take a 50-minute placement exam that assesses their writing proficiency. Based on a holistic evaluation of their writing, students are then exempted from freshman composition, with or without an accompanying writing workshop for individualized instruction; placed into freshman composition, again with or without a writing workshop; or placed into a tutorial class offered by the English Composition Board. The tutorial is an intensive seven-week class, with four hours of class time and one-half hour of individualized instruction with the course instructor every week. At the end of the tutorial class, students are given a post-test identical in form to the placement exam. Like the placement exam, the post-test is read by at least two English Composition Board instructors, with the stipulation that instructors do not evaluate their own students' writing. Possible placements resulting from the post-test are identical to those resulting from the assessment.

The three sets of essays I analyze here had identical outcomes: the students were placed into the tutorial as a result of the assessment exam and then placed back into the tutorial as a result of the post-test. It would seem, then, that these writers showed no growth as a result of their intensive tutorial class. I argue instead that these writers *were* learning but that their concentration on one aspect of writing in post-test essays caused them to backslide with respect to another. The post-test caught them in the act of restructuring their writing processes; although the students clearly needed more practice in the specially designed tutorial classes, their post-test placement should not be regarded as a total lack of growth.

Consider first Essay 1 in Figure 2, which represents the response of Wei-Nee, a native speaker of Cantonese, to an assessment exam stimulus about sexual experimentation. For this stimulus, as with every other assessment stimulus, the first sentence is given to the writer as well as a choice of three second sentences. Thus, Wei-Nee's own writing begins with the third sentence of the essay, on Line 6.

The essay suffers from a weak, one-paragraph argument: Wei-Nee spends more time discussing the causes of sexual experimentation than she does the problems of sexuality, as set forth in the chosen second sentence. Although she does return to the problems of sexuality in Line 18, the treatment is perfunctory. The essay seems to consist more of assertions than support. In addition, there are numerous surface errors that, although not interfering with meaning, certainly disrupt the flow of the argument.

In contrast, consider Wei-Nee's Essay 2 (Figure 3), a post-test written seven weeks later. In this essay, she narrows her thesis by adding a more specific sentence to the first paragraph and sticks closely to her thesis in developing a three-paragraph argument with points neatly marked by

---

Figure 2. *Non-native Speaker Essay 1: Wei-Nee*

Sexual experimentation is widespread among high school students, yet most states have laws that prevent minors from obtaining contraceptives or treatment for veneral disease without their parents being notified. While these laws do intrude to some extent into their private lives, young people are often unable to deal with problems of sexuality and need the help their parents can provide.

First of all, let us discuss about what sexual experimentation is so widespread among high school student. Nowadays, ~~many parents~~ it is very common ~~tat~~ that both parents are ~~wer~~ working. Even though the mothers ~~is not work~~ are not coming out to working, they usual join ~~certainly~~ kind of clubs ~~and~~ or hold important positions in some organization. (I know a couple that their family get to ~~gat~~ gather for dinner only once every week.). Since the parents do not have much time gather with their children, gaps generate. ~~And when there s is something happened, the children will not find their parents are trustful people to turn to. These children, when they find that they are neglect by their parents~~ While, these children, when they find that sweet home is no longer a sweet home, they will find somewhere to go to. They may gather ~~o~~ in bars, cinemas or find something wonderful to do such as sexuality. Besides, during their high school year, they ~~did~~ do not get a significant education in sexuality. Therefore these student are incapable of handling things like veneral disease, abrotion. Furthermore, the problem is not as simple as ~~getting~~ getting treatment, ~~we we~~ they must get help in order to stop the same thing to happen again. If they are able to handle, these problem ~~wou~~ will not exist.

If we want to stop social problems like this, the best thing is to improve the parent-children relationship, so the youngsters always ~~have~~ have somebody to turn to.

---

transitional phrases. Each paragraph is unified around a topic sentence, with other sentences clearly supporting the main idea. In addition, Wei-Nee spends some time revising, as evidenced by text (here separated by carets) that was written above the original. Despite the obvious improvement in organization and content with the second essay, both essays received the same scores and the same placement, namely tutorial. Upset with the results, Wei-Nee wrote her instructor a note:

> Last night I was thinking about the two exams. I thought that even though my first composition exam was real lusy, the grammetical mistakes that I made ~~is~~ ^was^ not as bad as this time. ~~I th~~ Do you know the reason why? It is because when I was doing the first exam, I didn't have to worry

Figure 3. *Non-native Speaker Essay 2: Wei-Nee*

A recent study of the effects of television violence on children in grade six through eight found that aggressive behavior increase when television viewing is frequent. From their experience of television, many young viewers learn that aggressive behavior is expected and accepted by society. Thus, this leads to an increase in children's violence behavior, and also an increase in children's crime rate, and rape rate.

The increase in children's violence behavior is reflected by school records. In the Michigan grade school, there is an increasing in ^the cases^ of the students fightings. Two years ago, the cases of fightings among ^grade six to grade eight^ students was twenty. With compare to the new record, which is eighty-three this year, we can see a great increase of the aggressive behavior of students of grade six to eight.

On the other hand, the children's crime rate ^for chidren between twelve and fifteen^ also raise tremendously within this two years time. The Michigan court reported that, there is an increase in the rate of children penalties. Two years ago the rate is 0.23%. However after the amount of violence shows has increased, the rate of children penalties also climb to 1.05% From the above statistic, we shall believe that the violence in television has an effection on children.

Finally, the children's aggressive behavior can also be reflected by the increasing rape rate within the last two years. The rape rate for children in grade six through eight is increase by almost 13%. From the Michigan Daily yesterday, a grade eight girl in Detroit high school was raped by one of her classmates. However, this same thing was very rarely happened two years ago. Thus, this is another example of the effect of the violence in ^the^ television programs.

In conclusion, the children's aggressive behavior such as fightening, commiting crime, raping has increased in the last two years after the amount of violence in network programs has increased. This is especially true for children in grades six through eight.

Note: Carets indicate text written above the original.

things like structure, organization, gave support etc., so I wrote freely—that is whatever I could ~~thing~~ ^think^ of at that moment. Besides, I was not under pressure, because I almost sured I would not make the exam. ~~at that time~~. However, the exam last week would ~~decide~~ either make me back into tutorial class or to freshmen ~~comp~~. comp. Therefore I was very tense, even though the sturture, organization etc ~~is~~ was alright, but the grammer ~~is~~ was lusy.

This was a provocative idea. Was Wei-Nee right? I analyzed the grammatical errors in each of the two essays in order to find out. Essay 1 contained a total of 208 words, not including words crossed out as the result of editing. I calculated errors on both the constituent level (e.g., topic-comment constructions, incorrect complements, fragments, missing or incorrect conjunctions, and missing direct objects) and the word level (e.g., nouns, including lack of a plural /s/ morpheme or other mistakes in form; verbs, including incorrect infinitive form, missing second person singular /s/ morpheme, or other mistakes in form; and incorrect or missing prepositions, functors, adverbs, relative pronouns, and articles). There were 21 errors in Essay 1, for an error-to-word ratio of 21 to 208, or approximately 10 percent. In contrast, errors in essay 2 totalled 23 out of 292 words, for an error-to-word ratio of 8 percent. At first glance Wei-Nee's hypothesis that she made more errors in Essay 2 is not borne out. However, closer examination of the data yields an interesting phenomenon: in Essay 1, only 10 of 21 errors involve a noun or verb, while in Essay 2, a full 20 of 23 errors involve one of those parts of speech. In fact, Wei-Nee committed two mistakes with nouns and verbs in the simple rewriting of the first sentence of the stimulus, a fact that did not enter into my analysis. Since nouns and verbs are the most salient parts of a sentence, Wei-Nee appears to be right: Essay 2 marks a significant decline in her grammatical proficiency with these forms ($\Xi^2 = 7.83$, $p < .05$). Such a finding is consistent with that of Suzanne Jacobs in her work with premedical students, who committed more grammatical errors when the writing task required complex, relational sentences in order to maintain coherence. Anderson (*Implications* 388) notes that "speakers usually plan their meanings as they generate their sentences. Many of the awkward or grammatically deviant sentences that occur in discourse reflect the conflicting demands of these two ongoing processes of construction and transformation." Thus, attention to one aspect of the discourse process results in difficulty with another.

Contrast Wei-Nee's performance on Essay 2 with that on Essay 3 (Figure 4), a post-test written seven weeks later after a second tutorial class. Like Essay 2, the third essay shows a narrowed thesis and well-developed argument. There are only nine errors in this essay of 385 words, for an error-to-word ratio of just over 2 percent. Six of these errors involve nouns or verbs. I argue that Essay 2 caught Wei-Nee in the act of backsliding with respect to grammar; given the opportunity with additional practice to reorganize and establish automaticity, she managed to pull

Figure 4. *Non-native Speaker Essay 3: Wei-Nee*

The 1977 Clean Air Act responded to public demands for environmental protection by forcing car manufacturers to reduce engine emissions. But the control of emissions stands is a partial solution; Congress must examine other alternatives such as development of mass public transportation. Being a foreigner, I know how important it is to develop a good syustem of mass public transportation. Let us take a look at the transportation system in Hong Kong, where I am from, and how it does to help the pollution problem.

The public transportion can be divided mainly into two parts, on land and in sea. Let us look first at the transportation system on land. The means of transportation on land are buses, trains, and mass transit railway. Of course, the mass transit railway is the fastest of all because it is built underground, therefore, even though there is a traffic congestion above the ground, the mass transit railway will not be affected. The other two means of transportation, buses and trains may have some troubles when there is a traffic jam. However, the buses and trains are running so frequently and the charges are so low that they become popular tools of commuting. The average time for waiting a bus or a train is five to ten minutes and the average cost is U.S. $.15.

With such a good transportation system, a lot of people there really consider taking the public mass transportation instead stead of keeping cars. Since both the trains and the mass transit railway use electricity as fuels instead of gasoline, the problem of air pollution by engine emissions is almost not existed there.

Another major mass public transportation is the boats since Hong Kong actually consists of a group of small islands. It is not uncommon for people there to commute by boats instead of cars. Besides, the mass transit railway connects the two main islands, Hong Kong side and Kowloon side by a under sea tunnel, therefore a large part of daily transportation is taken cared. The boats, too, are running very frequently and the charge is very cheap. It will never take you more than fifteen minutes for waiting and the charge is less than U.S. $.20. Once again, with such a transportation system, it is not worthwhile for people to keep their own cars, therefore, air pollution is always not very serious problem there.

In my conclusion, in addition to force the car manufacturers to reduce engine emissions, congress may consider to develope a good mass public transportation system like the one in Hong Kong.

together the many demands of the writing situation on her subsequent attempt in Essay 3.

Two essays of second dialect speaker James provide very different support for the notion of backsliding in basic writing. Consider first James's Essay 1 in Figure 5. One immediately obvious problem is James's unfamiliarity with the conventions of paragraphing. Note that he forms a second complete paragraph from the given second sentence option; the remaining three paragraphs are not unified; and although there is a one-line conclusion on lines 36-37, it is not explicitly marked. Rick Eden and Ruth Mitchell note that "this is a common problem of the average college freshman, who knows that prose should be indented at regular intervals but may not understand that the reader infers substantive unity from visual" (425).

In addition to showing a lack of overt structure and paragraph unity, this piece of writing is an example of what Judy Kirscht and Emily Golson term the "chaotic essay." James's first main paragraph deals with the importance of drugs to students, presumably the focus of the essay. The final paragraph, however, deviates from the theme: consider the shift in direction in lines 18-20, the philosophizing in lines 25-30, the attempt to return to the thesis in lines 30-32, and the extension of drug use to legislators in lines 34-36. My former colleague at the English Composition Board, Cheryl Johnson, has described this essay as jazz-like—variations around a theme (personal communication). And, like a jazz musician, James seems to be having a great deal of fun improvising. The language is colloquial and effective, the images vivid, the voice strong. As Peter Elbow might put it, this essay has "'juice'—a combination of magic potion, mother's milk, and electricity" (*Power* 286).

Contrast this essay with James's Essay 2 in Figure 6, written less than seven weeks later. Here he demonstrates more of the structural conventions of essay writing. He narrows his thesis by adding an extra sentence in line 5: "Children believe everything they see on television." He controls his paragraphing better, although as evidenced in the first three body paragraphs, lines 6-15, he may be hypercorrecting in the sense William Labov describes, as he separates material that could in fact be profitably combined. However, his next paragraph, devoted to parents, is neatly marked in lines 16-20. Then James returns to the idea of the Action for Children's Television (ACT) interest group that began the essay, building an argument for more ACT control of program content. Finally, his conclusion is clearly marked in lines 34-35.

Figure 5. *Second Dialect Speaker Essay 1: James*

Recently the Michigan Daily reported that campus use of marijuana and alcohol is as prevalent now as it was a decade ago.

This report is probably accurate because drugs are a significant part of contemporary life.

Today college community has a lot of free spirited young men and women. With todays economical and social problems young people are going to a way of relief. Somewhat of an escape out of the world or reality and in to the world of just (cool). Life in the contemporary college community is more outgoing then in the past. Like in the past marijuana and alcohol was just for parties and to get a little loose. Now students use it all the time not just at parties or just too get loose. We use it as a uper for a busy class day or just to get up and motivated. Some students find alcohol more enjoyable then marijuana and they also sometimes over indulge in it. Both of these drugs are easy to get by college students and they sometimes abuse thier privilige to purchase these drugs and it gets them in troble.

College students are more into the party side of things than in to the just siting around type high. College campuses are reporting more drinking and smoking then they ever seen.

Even with all the drugs poping up on campus thier still not a great decline in college students. This is good because it showe the students are handling thier drug all right. I should say some of the students, there are some that can not handle it and hurt themself very bad. Drugs has become apart of life and a way of life. People make livings off the drugs and people can not live without the drugs. Marijuana is so easy to get till the police sometimes does nothing if they find it on you. You must have a great deal of it on you or you might be driving car or some other way that you might hurt someone other than your self. Drugs Sex and Rock-n-Roll seems to be the cliche of the time in this contemporary life. Everything is starting to be a (controversy) wheather it is right or wrong. There is no more private joys everything is Rock-n-roll. At the rate the eighties are going we are heading for more then a contemporary life style we are going to the age of do what you want, and do it when you want too. Drugs will be a big part of it though, it will be refined and more stronger then before. People will go to drug for a escape road out of the real worlk and in to the world of (cool). Some of our top government officials might just have a little sniff session with a few cabinet members just to say up and witty. A significant part of the working class, college class and high school student are acustom to the drug scene and it might not get better in a way of stopping, but, in a way of handling the drugs. Drugs will always stay a significant part of life, why people enjoy it too much to let it go.

Figure 6. *Second Dialect Speaker Essay 2: James*

Action for children's televion (a.c.T) has 11,000 volunteer members who lobby for more control of program content during family viewing time.

Act should increase its efforts because children are unable to project themselves against questionable content or the influence of commercial advertisement. Children believe everything they see on television.

If you take the adverage child and set him in front of a television set he will pay attention to that. He will understand somethings that ~~are~~ going on and something he will not. is

For a child to watch a program made for his age group is good as long as the content is not to strong. Like watching electric company, and they are counting to 10 and all of a sudden they jump to 50 without first slowly moving toward it.

The content of a children's program is very important to the child. Children believe more on television then anything else. If the content is to weak or strong the program is useless.

During that time of family ~~hour~~ hour parents are watching and rating the program also. They are evaluating the program on purpose and content. They do not want their child to watch a program that will not make them a little bit curious about learning. Nor ~~t~~ do they want a program that is to dramtic in their teaching manner.

The A.C.T. should have a good commercial break. After they have tried to teach the child how to count or say different words. They should not have commericals that are none relavent to what they have just taught. This is a very important part for the ~~child~~ Program to have a commerical that will also be some help to the watcher. To have a commicial about Calvin Klien jeans is very distracting to the watcher.

Commercial ~~should be~~ are some what of a break so the ~~eh~~ watcher can think about what they have just ~~read~~ saw. That is ~~of~~ why they should ~~be~~ be relavent to the program.

I think that the (A.C.T) should have more power over the content and commercial. So that they can be more helpful to the child. The parent of America should write and speak on this after all it is their child.

Parent do care about what their child is ~~writting~~ watching on television. ~~S~~

So give the control over to the A.C.T. so they can help prepare the children for a brighter future and a better day. A mind is a terrible thing to waste.

But something is missing here. Gone is the jazz musician jamming at 3 a.m. in a smoky bistro. Instead, we find what I have previously termed a faceless writer ("Expert") with a voiceless voice: he is not willing to take risks, not willing to reveal himself. Kenneth Boulding has noted that in public expressions and especially in scientific writing, "high value is placed on dullness, obscurity, and lack of wit" (136); James seems to have internalized this notion.

Strong argues that developing writers "internalize images of those who will read their prose" (23), creating schemata for the *reader-at-work* who has outer-directed or social motives and using these schemata as they plan and revise their texts. However, Strong argues, there is a second kind of reader: "This is the reader of our childhood—a curious, irreverent self who is not afraid to ask 'what next?" or 'so what?' This is the *reader-at-play*" (24). Strong's reader-at-play is linked to Elbow's notion of "best self," the reader who "thrives on new connections and untrammeled language" (Strong 24). In Essay 1, James writes for his reader-at-play, oblivious to conventions, reveling in language; he is what I may term a writer-at-play. In Essay 2, James writes for his reader-at-work, intent on communicating, striving to be "recognized or approved" (24); he is a writer-at-work. He has improved in overall argumentation and at least acknowledges some of the conventions of formal writing, but such improvement has not come without cost: his voice has backslid into oblivion.

It might be argued that James could have "jazzed" here but chose not to, perhaps because of the subject matter of his second essay. But of greater concern is what eventually became of James: he dropped out of the university shortly after his tutorial class was completed and thus never took the opportunity to try again.

My final example of backsliding appears in the essays of Barbara, a native speaker of English. Her first essay, in Figure 7, is poorly argued and supported. Her support consists of only one weak body paragraph. Her conclusion simply picks up the idea offered by an alternative second-sentence option—one she did not choose—concerning the rights of the unborn child. Her final sentence is almost a direct repetition of her thesis. (I should point out that in this assessment stimulus, unlike any other, two sentences are given and the third sentence represents a choice among three alternatives, so Line 4 that begins her body paragraphs and ends her essay was actually not written by Barbara herself). While this essay is weak, it exhibits a certain awkward competence at the sentence level:

Figure 7. *Native Speaker Essay 1: Barbara*

According to <u>Newsweek</u>, "All across America abortion is under greater attack than at any time since the Supreme Court legalized it in 1973." Congress has extended the attack by eliminating ~~the~~ Federal Medicaid funds for abortion.

I think that abortion should be a private matter between a woman and her physican. The ~~Ac~~ American Democracy has always been acclaimed for freedom of choice; to deny a ~~ti~~ woman the choice of having an abortion would, according to some people, be a ~~inf violation~~ infringement of her free will. ~~Because abortion is a such a contriversal issue many~~ In the last 20 years, the subject of abortion has received much attention. In order for a women to decide ~~on wetth~~ wether or not she should have an abortion, she must ~~w~~ consider both the positive and negative aspects of its outcome, (~~result~~) In a private meeting between a woman and her physician, areas ~~such~~ ^such^ as her martial status, financial income and emotional stability are explored. ~~These~~ This information allows one to know if the woman is, in fact, capable of accepting the responsibilities she will be forced to encounter as a mother.

Because Congress has extended the attack for abortion by eliminating ~~f~~ Federal Medicaid funds, many women which desire abortions can not afford them, whereby bringing unwanted children into the world and further increasing the population. This however is only one side of the story~~,;~~ ~~other thin people think by eliminating Federal Medicaid funds for abortion s~~Some ~~people~~ ^think that abortion^ advocates ~~that abortion~~ want to deny the human rights of the unborn child. Although the debate over this contre^ve^rsal issue continues, I feel abortion should be a private matter between a woman and her physican.

Note: Carets indicate text written above the original.

---

there is some editing and false starting, but not much.

Contrast Essay 1 to Essay 2 in Figure 8, Barbara's post-test essay. Her argument in Essay 2 is much more sophisticated, incorporating cause and effect while considering alternatives to the chosen (third sentence) option. Notice, however, her battle with syntax: she crosses out a good deal of prose but inserts much more; these inserts appear as underlined text between carets. While such editing is frequently the mark of a problem-solving, process-oriented writer, in Barbara's case the revising does not seem to improve the text but instead reveals a counterproductive overconcern with form. As a result, her fluency suffers. Barbara was placed back into tutorial after her post-test. Seven weeks later, she had

Figure 8. *Native Speaker Essay 2: Barbara*

Experts believe that graduating college seniors will be unable to compete for many entry-level job opportunities because of improper education or training. Although these experts are probably right, fear of future unemployment should not unduly influence what a student takes in college; college should be preparation for a full life as well as preparation for a career.

The problem of unemployment has been ^largely^ prevalent in the last 10 years; ^it will not ^ however ^~~dissipate paper~~ disappear due to the courses a student takes.^ Often times the degree in which students ~~graduate~~ receive~~s~~ upon graduating from a college or university has no influence on the jobs they eventually obtain; therefore ~~to pick courses~~ in choosing one's curriculum, a students should take those courses he/she finds stimulating. ^In addition, this stimulation usually increases students performance.^

Many students feel bound and trapped because they are ~~placed~~ "caughtup" in 6 year medical and other type programs. ~~Because~~ These students are cramming ~~2~~   8 years of ^college and^ medical shool into their ^6 year^ ~~undergraduate~~ program. ~~Many~~ ^They must take classes set within the rigid boundaries of their programs^ and ^most^ are often unable to pick up a new language or additional English course that he/she desires.

~~Some~~ ^~~Many~~^ ^Some^ alternatives ^do^ exists for "learning" outside of the classroom ^for those students ~~free to try new and different courses~~ not locked into a fixed curriculum.^ Such programs as "Project Outreach" and "Project Community", allow students to reach out and help those around them ^thru volunteer work.^ This type of education is very useful in finding jobs in the future ^because it allows people to come in contact ~~with others~~ and learn about other kinds of people.^ When looking for a job, the employer is usually more concerned with the types of experiences ~~you have~~ ^the candidate has^ had in dealing with others, ~~rather~~ then ~~your~~ in ones final grade point average.

For students who have taken a variety of courses, many additional ~~opt~~ job opportunities exists. A student interested in hotel administration ~~and~~ or food management may work in the ^dorm^ cafeteria; a student who has found a particular course exciting can have an intership with that professor or do research for him.

~~As society~~ is continually advancing, new and different job opportunities arise. For example, a psyc ^If however a student does choose a narrow course of study, he may be able to broaden^

(continued)

(Figure 8 continued)

If however a student does c^h^oose a narrow ~~course~~ path of study, he/she may be able to broaden ~~their~~ his/her opportunities when looking for a job ^after college years.^ Society is continuously changing ^and^ new options are being presented. With a p^s^yschology major, for example, a person can teach, have a private practice, do research, work in a clinic or myraids of other alternatives.

Although one can always broaden their interests "later" in life, many students have rightly choosen to begin during their college years. The open-minded student will emerge better off and ^their ~~wi~~ broader and more varied experiences will be^ ~~be~~ ranked higher ~~when finding a job, to the narrow-minded ones.~~ then those of the narrow minded student when finding a job.

Note: Carets indicate text written above the original.

---

completed a second tutorial class and, based on the post-test, was successfully placed into freshman composition. (This latter post-test was not available for analysis.)

Wei-Nee, James, and Barbara thus demonstrate the phenomenon of backsliding in three very different ways: Wei-Nee loses her grammatical competence, James loses his voice, and Barbara loses her fluency. Obviously, backsliding is not a monolithic phenomenon; it must be approached qualitatively rather than quantitatively because it is manifested in different ways by different writers.

Conclusion

I have drawn upon the fields of learning theory, cognitive psychology, first- and second-language acquisition, and writing theory to document the phenomenon of backsliding and have shown how backsliding may be realized in different ways in the writing of basic writers.

A popular notion offered by researchers of second-language acquisition is that as learners move between their native language and the target language, they construct interim systems known as interlanguages that tend to approximate the target language more and more as the learner progresses. I believe that basic writers pass through similar developmental stages, constructing and deconstructing writing interlanguages that move closer to the desired norms of academic writing. Similar to sociolinguistic change, variation in the occurrence of the accepted or "prestige" writing norm is natural and indicative of change in progress. Although sampling these writers at an intermediate stage may reveal regression, I argue that this regression may be more apparent than real.

Given the existence of backsliding, how can writing instructors deal with it? First, instructors should view backsliding not as a random problem but as an artifact of a developmental stage, the midpoint of U-shaped behavior. Backsliding is a natural if not inevitable phenomenon, indicative of a stage in which the writer cannot respond to all the cognitive demands placed upon her by the complex writing task while she practices a new skill. At its worst, such cognitive strain results in an unsuccessful writing project and a frustrated writer. At best, the writer responds to the increasingly complex task by increasing "capacity."

Developmental psychologist Jeff Shrager (personal communication) notes at least five different hypotheses about ways in which capacity can be increased: by moving procedural subunits from controlled to automatic processing (Schneider and Shiffrin); by substituting remembered results for procedural subunits (Newell and Rosenbloom); by strengthening and associated speed-up or collapse of procedural subunits (Anderson *Architecture*); by restructuring or reprogramming procedures (Cheng); or by lifting some of the burden of skill acquisition off the learner through an external mediator. An example of the latter in composition might be a software program to guide the writer through some of the decision-making steps in writing. Presumably, any of these procedures could result in an increase in the capacity of the writer, at least until she faces another new challenge. Obviously a fruitful area for further research would be to move beyond behavioral observation to an examination of just how college writers move from failure to success.

An important corollary of this discussion is to suggest that a post-test may not be the only or even the best method of evaluating student progress in a basic writing class. Elbow and Belanoff point out two problems with a typical proficiency examination: it involves "having a serious topic sprung at you" (336) with no chance to read, reflect, or discuss, and it allows only one draft with no opportunity for "sharing or feedback or revising" (336). I offer a third: the examination may catch the student in the act of backsliding, thus masking any real progress that the student has made. Elbow and Belanoff argue that a writing portfolio offers a more sensible solution to the problem of how to evaluate writing competency and recommend that such a portfolio be evaluated not only by the student's own teacher but also by at least one other teacher who does not know the writer. Since the time that I began this research at the University

of Michigan, the English Composition Board has begun considering portfolios in making the decision to pass students along.

The implications of backsliding go far beyond the issue of evaluation. What can instructors do on Monday morning? For one thing, we can
encourage the practicing writer to achieve greater capacity by teaching
specific writing skills and providing ample opportunity for guided revision, fresh assignments, as well as unstructured writing. Only frequent
and sustained practice, including multiple drafts of the same paper, will
enable writers to internalize the rules of the many complex subsets of the
writing task and to use developing writing competencies simultaneously
rather than sequentially. Furthermore, such practice should expose students to "a variety of composing styles and actions, a variety of possibilities for planning, inventing, arranging, and revising" (Selzer 282) in order
to help them adjust their writing strategies to the peculiar circumstances
of the writing task.

The existence of backsliding provides an indirect argument for the
use of a journal or diary in writing classes. Students who pay too much
attention to the conventions of academic writing may forget that writers
write because they have something to say. One basic writing student
expressed shock when I complimented her on the organization of her
essay but noted that she really did not say anything. "You mean it's not
just the form, it's the content that counts?" she asked in amazement.
Elbow ("Teaching") has noted that "when we pay attention to our writing,
it is as though we are looking out the window but focusing our gaze on
the pane of glass. Imagine the relief that comes from letting our focus
pass *through* the pane to the green scene outside—the relief that comes
from doing lots of writing in a course but not thinking about it as writing"
(234). Allowing students the opportunity for expressive as well as transac-
tional (Britton), writer-based as well as reader-based (Flower), knowledge-telling as well as knowledge-transforming (Bereiter and Scardamalia)
writing may provide them with the nonthreatening environment they
need to look through the pane and pull together their developing skills as
writers.

Another nonthreatening environment is one that allows students to
serve as each other's critics, small group work in which students read and
respond to first drafts before they submit final drafts for instructor feedback and a grade. As Bereiter and Scardamalia point out, one problem
with the move from conversation to increasingly more academic forms of
writing is the loss of an immediate audience and the corresponding loss

of feedback. Encouraging students to respond to the writing of their peers thus serves two purposes: reading and responding to the work of class-mates helps students become part of the community of writers to which we all belong and helps "socialize" them to norms of appropriateness; and receiving feedback (akin to Bereiter and Scardamalia's "production signals") on their own writing gives students some helpful external cues for reconstructing both the particular text they are working on and their writing strategies in general.

A final implication: backsliding occurs not just within an individual course but also throughout a person's development as a writer. With a task as complex as writing, the U-shaped curve has the potential of recur-ring as often as the writer confronts a new writing challenge. This chal-lenge could be linked to an increase in world knowledge or to the writ-er's growing intellectual abilities that enable him to see many sides of an issue instead of just one. For example, during a discussion at a session on longitudinal studies of undergraduate writers at the 1987 Conference on College Composition and Communication, Janice Hays noted that "growth in the intellectual processes results in the falling-off of the writing compo-nent." In addition, as upperclassmen, many students face the challenge of writing within a specific discipline. The practice of writing, then, must continue beyond freshman composition, and backsliding is likely to occur again. With a task as complex and limitless as writing, perhaps the sine-curve—suggesting an initial gradual approach to early competence and repeated restructuring—is a more appropriate symbol than the U-shaped curve. Jeff Shrager (personal communication) points out that the damped sine curve may be more appropriate yet: the successively flatter troughs or minima suggest that as the learner acquires skills the bottom is just not as deep as it used to be.

A second argument for continued writing practice is simply that stu-dents' skills may erode if they do not practice. As far back as 1963, Albert Kitzhaber noted that Dartmouth students wrote worse in their senior year than in their sophomore year as a result of decreased writing practice throughout their undergraduate careers. More recently, Francelia Clark, Frances Zorn, and Eleanor McKenna have shown that University of Michi-gan writers do not improve on the assessment examination described here over three or four years, although they argue that holistic reading measures are not sensitive enough to measure growth at a level beyond that of freshman composition.

Clearly, then, an argument for the existence of backsliding in writing is also an argument for writing across the curriculum. Developing writers need as much opportunity as possible to practice and restructure their writing skills, especially in contexts in which it is not the writing itself but rather the content area of the class that is at issue. With sufficient opportunity to practice their developing skills, writers learn to internalize and make connections between their various subskills, thus moving closer to the desired norms of academic prose and achieving—and reachieving—the upswing in the U-shaped curve. ❧

ACKNOWLEDGMENTS

Many thanks to Josh Ard, Francelia Clark, Sue Gass, Liz Hamp-Lyons, Cheryl Johnson, Barbara Nodine, John Reiff, and Jeff Shrager for discussing with me various issues presented here and especially to Ted Sheckels for invaluable criticism of earlier drafts of this paper. I am indebted to my anonymous reviewer, whose comments guided me from a knowledge-telling revision to a knowledge-transforming one. Finally, thanks to Orestes Varonis for his enthusiastic support throughout and, of course, to Wei-Nee, James, and Barbara.

WORKS CITED

Anderson, John R. *The Architecture of Cognition.* Cambridge: Harvard UP, 1983.

——. *Cognitive Psychology and Its Implications.* New York: Freeman.

Ausubel, David P., and Floyd G. Robinson. *School Learning: An Introduction to Educational Psychology.* New York: Rinehart, 1969.

Bereiter, Carl, and Marlene Scardamalia. *The Psychology of Written Composition.* Hillsdale: Erlbaum, 1987.

Boulding, Kenneth. *The Image.* Ann Arbor: Ann Arbor Paperbacks, 1971.

Bowerman, Melissa. "Starting to Talk Worse: Clues to Language Acquisition from Children's Late Speech Errors." *U-Shaped Behavioral Growth.* Ed. S. Strauss. New York: Academic, 1982.

Britton, James. *Language and Learning.* Middlesex: Penguin, 1980.

Brown, Ann, et al. "Learning, Remembering, and Understanding." *Handbook of Child Psychology.* Ed. Paul Mussen. 3 (1983): 77-166.

Cheng, P. W. "Restructuring vs. Automatizing: An Alternative Account of Skill Acquisition. *Psychology Review* 92: 414-423.

Clark, Francelia, Frances Zorn, and Eleanor McKenna. "Studying the Longitudinal Study." Paper presented at the Conference on College Composition and Communication, Atlanta, 1987.

DeCecco, John P. *The Psychology of Learning and Instruction: Educational Psychology.* Englewood Cliffs: Prentice, 1968.

Eden, Rick, and Ruth Mitchell. "Paragraphing for the Reader." *College Composition and Communication* 37 (1986): 416-430.

Elbow, Peter. "Teaching Writing by Not Paying Attention to Writing." *Forum: Essays on Theory and Practice in the Teaching of Writing.* Ed. P. Stock. Upper Montclair: Boynton, 1983. 234-240.

——. *Writing with Power: Techniques for Mastering the Writing Process.* New York: Oxford UP, 1981.

——, and Pat Belanoff. "Portfolios as a Substitute for Proficiency Examinations." *College Composition and Communication* 37 (1986): 336-339.

Ervin, Susan. "Imitation and Structural Change in Children's Language." *New Directions in the Study of Language.* Ed. E. Lenneberg. Cambridge: MIT, 1964.

Flower, Linda. "Writer-based Prose: A Cognitive Basis for Problems in Writing." *College English* 41 (1979): 19-37.

——, and John R. Hayes. "Problem-Solving Strategies and The Writing Process." *College English* 39 (1977): 449-461.

Hayes, John R., and Linda Flower. "Identifying the Organization of Writing Processes." *Cognitive Processes in Writing.* Ed. L. W. Gregg and E. R. Steinberg. Hillsdale, N.J.: Erlbaum, 1980.

Hays, Janice. "Problems and Opportunities in Writing and Intellectual Development Research." Discussion at Conference on College Composition and Communication, Atlanta, 1987.

Jacobs, Suzanne. "Composing and Coherence: The Writing of Eleven Pre-Medical Students." *Papers in Applied Linguistics: Linguistics and Literacy Series 3.* Ed. Roger W. Shuy. Washington: Center for Applied Linguistics, 1982.

Karmiloff-Smith, A. "Children's Problem Solving." *Advances in Developmental Psychology 3*. Ed. M. Lamb, A. Brown, and B. Rogoff. Hillsdale: Erlbaum, 1984.

Kellerman, Eric. "If at First You Do Succeed..." *Input in Second Language Acquisition*. Ed. S. Gass and C. Madden. Rowley: Newbury, 1985. 345-353.

Kirscht, Judy, and Emily Golson. "Essay Thinking: Empty and Chaotic." *Journal of Advanced Composition* 4 (1983): 13-23.

Kitzhaber, Albert. *Themes, Theories, and Therapy: The Teaching of Writing in College*. Report of the Dartmouth Study of Writing. New York: McGraw, 1963.

Labov, William. *The Social Stratification of English in New York City*. Washington: Center for Applied Linguistics, 1966.

Levin, H., I. Silverman, and B. Ford. "Hesitations in Children's Speech during Explanations and Description. *Journal of Verbal Learning and Verbal Behavior* 6 (1967): 560-564.

Lindsay, Peter, and Donald A. Norman. *Human Information Processing: An Introduction to Psychology*. New York: Academic, 1972.

Newell, A., and Rosenbloom, P. "Mechanisms of Skill Acquisition and the Law of Practice." *Cognitive Skills and their Acquisition*. Ed. J. R. Anderson. Hillsdale: Erlbaum, 1981.

Perl, Sondra. "The Composing Processes of Unskilled College Writers." *Research in the Teaching of English* 13 (1979): 317-336.

Schneider, W., and R. M. Shiffren. "Controlled and Automatic Human Information Processing. I. Detection, Search, and Attention." *Psychological Review* 84 (1977): 1-66.

Selzer, Jack. "Exploring Options in Composing." *College Composition and Communication* 35 (1984): 276-284.

Shaughnessy, Mina. *Errors and Expectations: A Guide for the Teacher of Basic Writing*. New York: Oxford UP, 1977.

Sommers, Nancy. "Revision Strategies of Student Writers and Experienced Adult Writers." *College Composition and Communication* 31 (1980): 378-388.

Strauss, S., and Stavey, R. "U-shaped Behavioral Growth: Implications for Theories of Development." *Review of Child Development Research*. Ed. W. W. Hartup. Chicago: U Chicago P, 1982.

Strauss, S., and D. Stein. "U-shaped Curves in Language Acquisition and the Learning of Physical Concepts." *Die Neueren Sprachen* 3 (1978): 326-340.

Varonis, Evangeline M. "The Writer as Expert." Paper presented at National Endowment for the Humanities Conference on Writing in the Humanities, Philadelphia, June 1983.

——, and Susan M. Gass. "Non-native/non-native Conversations: A Model for the Negotiation of Meaning." *Applied Linguistics* 6 (1985): 71-90.

Witte, Stephen. "Topical Structure and Revision: An Exploratory Study." *College Composition and Communication* 34 (1983): 313-341.

Zamel, Vivian. "The Composing Processes of Advanced ESL Students: Six Case Studies." *TESOL Quarterly* 17 (1983): 165-187.

❦ 10

Socio-Cognitive Development and Students' Performance on Audience-Centered Argumentative Writing

Janice N. Hays
Kathleen S. Brandt

Much student academic writing is argumentative: it puts forth propositions, buttresses them with warrants, and supports them with data and evidence. Although such writing does not usually seek to move an audience to a particular action, it does hope to persuade the reader—often, the writer's instructor—to at least consider the writer's point of view. The skills involved in this argumentative process are also central to the social, professional, and political discourse that students will have to produce, evaluate, and act on after college. Thus their argumentative writing in college is doubly important—first as a means of understanding and communicating about complex subject matter and second as training in the critical-thinking processes upon which responsible citizenship depends.

Yet although argumentative writing is a common genre of academic discourse, for students it is difficult. An important study directed by Charles Cooper suggests that, as freshmen, students are not adept at argumentation. Cooper and his colleagues analyzed the persuasive writing performance of an entering class at SUNY-Buffalo on a topic of general social concern: affirmative action practices in a business context. This writing task was not narrowly academic; thus it did not require students to work within the conventions of particular disciplines. Nevertheless, the broad skills it elicited were generically similar to those required for general academic discourse. In connection with the study, Cooper observes:

> More than perhaps any other type of writing, the persuasive mode should invite a consideration of opposing points of view and involve a concern for the audience. Alternative views need to be examined, if only with the intent of disproving them and thus strengthening one's own position. What we observed instead was a consistent failure to do so: only 16 percent [of students in the study] addressed the opposing point of view. . . . The uniformity and naivete of [the] essays persuaded us that these students had been *actively* taught [by parents, teachers, and television] to fear and shun complexity, and especially to deny moral and legal ambiguity. (Cooper, Cherry, Copley, Fleischer, Pollard and Sartisky 40, 44)

As Cooper suggests, and as Marie Secor has emphasized, argumentation presupposes an audience. Thus it is preeminently a social activity, contingent not only upon interaction with a conceptualized reader but also upon the context in which it takes place. It requires writers to move dialectically between their own and a reader's inferred knowledge and perspectives, negotiating between them while referring to a context common in some way to both writer and reader. In addition, argumentation is a cognitive process. Conceptualization of an audience requires epistemic reasoning and perspective-taking ability (more broadly, empathy). A considerable body of research has established that both these abilities are aspects of socio-cognitive functioning and development (e.g., Benack; Clark and Delia; Flavell, Botkin, Fry, Wright, and Jarvis; Kitchener; Perry; Rubin). The socio-cognitive structures that enable both epistemic reasoning and mature empathic functioning grow out of complex interactions between individuals' internal cognitive processes and the demands and responses of the context in which those individuals function. Empathy and epistemic reasoning appear to be parallel: as the former increases, the latter becomes more complex, and vice versa (Benack 350-56). The capacity for "post formal-operational" dialectical thinking also parallels the emergence of higher-level epistemic reasoning (Benack and Basseches). In the American academic setting, complex functioning in these areas— epistemic reasoning, empathic responses to others, and dialectical thinking—becomes possible during the college years (Basseches; Kitchener and King; Kohlberg; Perry).

Developmental psychologists have conducted extensive research on the general subject of socio-cognitive "evolution" during the young adult and adult years. Less is known, however, about relationships between socio-cognitive development and college-level writing. In composition, the two most influential current paradigms—the individual-cognitive and the social-contextual—tend to ignore the impact of socio-cognitive development upon college writers' performance. For example, there may be some truth to Cooper's claim that much in the American scene promotes conformity and simplistic thinking. Yet he does not consider the possibility that poor student performance in the Buffalo study may also have reflected immature social cognition that made it difficult for writers to respond to the writing task, a richly social one, in fully mature ways. To assert the possibility of a developmental dimension to students' writing performance does not exclude the impact of either teaching or socialization on that performance; the domains are not mutually exclusive.

Much research on socio-cognitive development and writing has focused on writers' adaptations to their readers, generally finding that such adaptations are related both to social cognition and to argumentative writing performance. In this study, we posited a strong connection between writers' adaptations to their readers, their socio-cognitive development, and their overall argumentative writing performance, focusing upon their audience-centered activity as they wrote to two different readerships. In an initial phase of this project, we examined the performance of an entire group of high school and college students along these lines and found that our expectations were correct: there were, indeed, strong predictive relationships between socio-cognitive development and writing performance (Hays, Brandt, and Chantry). However, that study looked at the response of the group as a whole. Now we want to examine audience-centered activity within the three socio-cognitive subgroups identified in this study in order to look for systematic differences in the nature of their arguments to different audiences. If there are distinctive differences in writing performance between students at different levels of socio-cognitive development, these differences clearly have profound implications for teaching.

Overview of Study

Subjects. The study involved 52 high school and college students: 24

freshmen and sophomores (46 percent), 16 juniors and seniors (31 percent), and 12 high school seniors (23 percent); 29 participants majoring in liberal arts (56 percent), 12 in business (23 percent), and 11 in engineering (21 percent). The high school students, who were selected from a group of college-bound seniors, were assigned to these major areas on the basis of their reported probable major in college. The participants' median age was 20, with most ranging from 16 to 36 years; a few participants were over 36. Approximately half of the participants were female.

Writing Task. The subjects were asked to write two impromptu argumentative papers. To encourage revision, students were offered up to six hours to complete each assignment. While a few wrote for four or five hours, most finished in under three. In the first essay, students were directed to take a position on tougher drunk driving laws and to write to a friendly audience—that is, one that would generally agree with their position. In the second task, subjects were asked to write to an audience that would on the whole be hostile; several such readerships, all of them adults, were suggested (see Appendix A).

Normally, research methodology would have dictated our counter-balancing the order of these two topics—that is, assigning half of the students in each session to the friendly audience topic and half to the hostile. However, in designing the project, we were heavily influenced by D. G. Winter, David C. McClelland, and Abigail J. Stewart, who believe that the ability to think flexibly under pressure (for example, time pressure) indicates higher-order thinking: they tested for such flexibility by asking students to argue in favor of one side of a current social issue and then, with very little notice, to support the opposite side. Similarly, in our study we expected that the friendly audience/hostile audience paradigm would confront writers with almost opposite perspectives on the drunk-driving issue and so demand cognitive flexibility of them. In order to prevent students from revealing the nature of the second topic, we had to give all students the same topic at each session.

Holistic Scoring. After identifying information was removed from the papers, three raters evaluated the essays using a criterion-referenced scale. The rating scale included four categories: quantity and quality of the paper's ideas and development, including depth of development and elaboration of ideas; clarity and logic of structure, organization, and focus both in the essay as a whole and within sections; clarity and appropriateness of the paper's arguments for its intended readers; and correctness and felicity of syntax and usage. Each category was rated from 1 to 4, and individual ratings were summed to achieve a total paper score; these ranged from 13 to 44, with higher scores indicating better performance.

Perry Scheme Rating. In order to ascertain subjects' levels of socio-cognitive development, we submitted their papers to the Syracuse Rating Group, a research team that uses an instrument based upon Perry Scheme criteria to assess subjects' levels of intellectual and ethical maturity. The Perry Scheme is a structural model that describes the development of epistemic reasoning during the college years (see Appendix B) as first observed by William Perry at Harvard University. The Perry Scheme traces students' movement from an initially "dualistic" view of reality, in which situations and people are perceived as good or bad, right or wrong, true or false. This dualism gradually gives way to "multiplistic" thinking, in which students recognize that many perspectives exist, but because they are unable to evaluate them, they adopt the attitude that "everyone has a right to her own opinion." Finally, students move to "committed relativistic" thinking, in which they realize that some viewpoints are more tenable than others and are able to evaluate and choose among competing ideas. Although the Perry Scheme includes nine positions, in practice most college students place in positions two through five (Moore 2). After a preliminary reading, the Syracuse Rating Group decided that it was unnecessary to rate both sets of papers. They elected to evaluate the hostile audience papers, which they felt provided an especially rich source of Perry Scheme data. When the Syracuse ratings were returned, we used them to identify clusters of students who were placed at three Perry Scheme positions: position two, multiplicity pre-legitimate (n = 12; mean age = 18.6; mean grade level = 12.5); position three, multiplicity subordinate (n = 24; mean age = 24; mean grade level = 13.8); and position four and beyond, multiplicity legitimate and relativism (n = 16; mean age = 25.9; mean grade level = 14.5).[1]

Audience Coding. Our research team independently analyzed the papers to determine the amount and kind of audience activity that students engaged in. The coding scheme grew out of recent theory and research (e.g., Berkenkotter; and Flavell et al.). It also reflected textual cues to audience adaptation that we saw consistently recurring in this sample. The coding scheme had five major categories: Naming, Context, Strategy, Response, and Inappropriate (see Appendix C). For the analysis, the essays were divided into T-units (see O'Hare), and each audience-centered characteristic or "move" was labeled as it appeared. Therefore, one T-unit might have two, three, or even four different codes, others none at all. To tabulate a writer's audience activity scores, we counted the number of times each coding appeared and divided by the number of T-units in the paper. For the group of writers as a whole, the total number of audience moves per T-unit nearly doubled from the friendly to the hostile paper. That is, students engaged in more audience-related activity when writing for an adversative reader than they did for a friendly one. Our prior statistical analyses established that the Strategy activity on both papers and the Response activity on the hostile paper were the strongest predictors for overall paper performance (Hays et al., "Friendly and Hostile"). In all these areas, we found significant differences in performance according to Perry Scheme position (Hays, Durham, Brandt, and Raitz, "Argumentative Writing"). However, in order to deal with these categories in sufficient detail, we will focus here on Response and Inappropriate activities, using primarily descriptive statistics. We have discussed Strategy moves elsewhere (Hays, Durham, Brandt, and Raitz, "A Sense of Audience") and will address overall writing performance in yet another paper.

Results: Response Moves—Windows on Writers' Dialectical Activity

Performance in the Response category reflected the degree to which writers acknowledged and responded to a point of view different from their own, the kind of activity that Cooper suggests should be at the heart of argumentative writing. Response moves consisted of three categories: Stating Concerns, Reasons for Concerns, and Rebuttal. Stating Concerns refers to the writer's explicit statement of the reader's concerns about the topic; Reasons for Concerns refers to the writer's speculations about the reader's reasons. Mean scores show that for all students, Response moves accounted for only 10 percent of total audience activity on the friendly-audience paper, increasing to 23 percent on the hostile-audience essay (see Table 1).

For both papers, the number of Response moves increases across the three Perry Scheme positions (Table 2). However, on the friendly paper, the increase is slight between positions two and three, but marked in position four, and is linked to the increased Perry Scheme score in that range. Prior statistical analyses have established strong relationships between dialectical activity (Response) and Perry Scheme score on both papers (while characteristics such as age, grade level, and area of academic concentration were not significantly linked to Response). For the hostile audience paper, the number of Response moves was the strongest

Table 1. *Audience Moves in Argumentative Writing, Entire Cobort*

Audience Moves[a]	Friendly Paper		Hostile Paper	
	Mn	% Total Moves[b]	Mn	% Total Moves[b]
N Naming	.08 (.11)[c]	14.0	.35 (.32)	31.0
S Strategy	.26 (.27)	45.0	.30 (.27)	26.0
C Context	.13 (.10)	23.0	.11 (.10)	10.0
R Response	.06 (.13)	10.0	.26 (.26)	23.0
I Inappropriate Appeals	.05 (.15)	8.0	.12 (.19)	10.5
Total Audience Moves	.58 (.28)	100.0	1.14 (.39)	100.0
Total T-Units	33.23 (11.04)		33.37 (11.17)	

[a]Audience activity is tabulated in number of codings per T-unit.
[b]Numbers have been rounded and so may not add up to exactly 100%.
[c]Numbers in parentheses indicate standard deviations.

predictor of holistic paper score (Hays et al., "Friendly and Hostile"). While position two writers engaged in little Response activity, those in position four devoted 40 percent of their audience moves to Response.

Response Activity—Friendly Paper. For the friendly paper, Response moves would not seem especially important, since presumably writers and their audiences held similar positions on the drunk-driving issue. Yet the increased Response-friendly activity in position four, together with the pattern of that activity, suggests some significant differences in the approach to readers between position four writers and those in positions two and three. Some position two writers ignored the audience on both papers and simply articulated their own ideas; most of them, however, acknowledged their readers. Even these apparently saw little reason, in

Table 2. *Audience Strategies by Perry Scheme Position*

Variables	Position Two n=12		Position Three n=24		Position Four ± n=16	
	Friendly Aud. Mean	Hostile Aud. Mean	Friendly Aud. Mean	Hostile Aud. Mean	Friendly Aud. Mean	Hostile Aud. Mean
Paper Score:	19.75	18.58	26.83	24.79	31.63	31.87
T-Units	29.92	32.58	33.08	31.67	35.94	36.50
Pos Moves/TU	0.31	0.60	0.56	1.02	0.66	1.32
Naming/TU	0.05	0.21	0.08	0.41	0.10	0.35
Context/TU	0.17	0.12	0.13	0.09	0.11	0.14
Strategy/TU	0.07	0.16	0.31	0.31	0.33	0.39
Response/TU	0.03	0.10	0.04	0.22	0.12	0.44
Negative/TU	0.15	0.30	0.00	0.08	0.04	0.04
Total Aud Moves/TU	0.46	0.90	0.56	1.09	0.70	1.36

the friendly paper, to suppose that these readers might differ on some points from the writer. In short, writers in positions two and three seemed to assume almost complete identification between themselves and their readers. Consequently, they made few Response moves. The larger percentages of friendly Response activity in position four probably reflected these writers' increasing abilities to differentiate between themselves and others who were like them in some ways but not in others. For instance, in position four especially, some writers recognized that readers who supported the proposed laws might still worry that their enforcement could add to citizens' tax burdens. Specifically, in position four, the bulk of Response activity is devoted to Rebuttal, and this increase suggests that position four writers more clearly understood that even friendly readers may have doubts and questions that must be addressed.

Response Activity—Hostile Paper. In the whole group, the percentage of Response activity more than doubled from the friendly to the hostile paper (see Table 1). With the exception of position one, in which the difference in Response moves between friendly and hostile papers was slight (see Table 2), Response moves increased dramatically with the hostile audience. Clearly, except in position one, the adversarial audience made students aware that whether or not they questioned their own positions, others might.

The pattern of types of Response moves in the hostile papers reflects both the effect of audience and socio-cognitive development (Table 3). In positions three and four, Rebuttal exceeded the Stating Concerns activity (a change in the pattern of Response moves from the friendly paper). There were also more Reasons for Concerns in the hostile papers, again suggesting the impact that the hostile audience had in making writers more fully consider points of view other than their own and readers' possible reasons for holding those views. However, in many of the position two and three papers, readers' objections to the law (Stating Readers' Concerns) were articulated mostly as straw men to be handily toppled—that is, writers rushed from what was often a token statement of those objections to much fuller rebuttals of them. Often the rebuttals had either an imperious or a facile quality, suggesting that the writer had not fully considered the reader's point of view but was, rather, going through the motions of doing so.

Such reasoning falls short of being fully dialectical, and in fact resembles that stage in Perry Scheme development when students have become aware that there are many different ideas on important issues but

Table 3. *Response and Inappropriate Moves by Perry Scheme Position*

Variable	Entire Cohort N=52		Perry Position Two n=12		Perry Position Three n=24		Perry Position Four ± n=16	
	Friendly Paper Mean	Hostile Paper Mean	Friendly Mean	Hostile Mean	Friendly Mean	Hostile Mean	Friendly Mean	Hostile Mean
Response/TU	.06	.26	.03	.10	.04	.22	.12	.45
R1 Concerns	.03	.06	.03	.03	.02	.06	.05	.09
R2 Reasons	.00*	.03	.00	.02	.00	.03	.01	.05
R3 Rebuttal	.03	.17	.01	.05	.10	.14	.06	.31
Inappropriate./TU	.05	.12	.15	.30	.00	.08	.04	.04
I1 Pejorative	.00*	.02	.00	.03	.00	.02	.00	.02
I2 Ineffective	.04	.08	.14	.23	.00	.05	.03	.01

* Less than .01

do not concede genuine validity to those views. Thus, students still adhere without question to their own view, finding it difficult to imagine how those who differ have reached their conclusions. Even at the next level, students have trouble truly weighing and evaluating multiple viewpoints. Either they do not commit themselves to any position, or they do so arbitrarily and often illogically. The preponderance of Stating Concerns over Reasons for Concerns in position three and even four implies difficulties with fully grasping opposing viewpoints. Writers understood what readers on the other side of the issue thought but not *why* they thought it; hence the rush to rebuttal.

This pattern suggests some of the same kind of "one side only" reasoning about issues that Cooper found in the Buffalo study, and we believe that this characteristic was related to students' levels of socio-cognitive development. That is, these writers' rebuttals consisted of denials that the problem was genuine—often on the basis of the writer's handy and not-too-closely questioned solution. Such sequences ran something like this: "You [tavern owners] may think that the new laws will cut down on your profits, but they won't because you can do x, y, or z"—for example, call taxis for drunk patrons or install breathalyzers in bars so that drinkers can monitor their blood alcohol levels. Essentially these are closed-system views, implicitly predicated upon assumptions (probably largely unexamined) that there *are* simple solutions or Right Answers to the problem. Yet the cursory quality of these dialectical sequences is not surprising; Suzanne Benack and Michael Basseches have established that genuine dialectical thinking does not emerge until a point that corresponds with position five on the Perry Scheme. We also note that this focus on pragmatics, on the "practical, active nature of knowledge" (Basseches 94-97)—as distinct from the reifications of knowledge found in most position two writers—parallels some of Basseches' early dialectical schema.

Only in position four do we find some writers genuinely exploring views opposing their own—and the number who did so was small. In those papers, dialectical responses to readers differed in ways that do not show up in simple frequency counts of Response moves. One large difference was that these writers, the most socio-cognitively advanced in the study, genuinely credited the validity or partial validity of readers' concerns instead of dismissing them with quick, easy ploys. In short, they conceded that the new laws would, for example, adversely affect tavern owners' profits—or, on the other side, that in the short term the legislation might reduce the number of drunk driving accidents. Their phrasing of the adversarial reader's position suggested that they better understood its basis than did most writers in the study.

The way in which they conceded or rebutted those objections also differed from the approach of writers in lower Perry Scheme groups. Socio-cognitively advanced writers admitted that the laws would change the context in which, for example, members of the beverage industry conducted business and that these changes would not all be positive. However, they often went on to suggest that short-term losses would be outweighed by long-term gains—that, for example, losses in revenues would be balanced by gains in public relations for the alcohol industry and that such gains, in turn, might well forestall harsher governmental controls.

Basseches argues that a major characteristic of dialectical thinking is a conception of reality not in terms of unitary, static, and inexorable laws and structures but in terms of dynamic change in systems (98). In other words, the assumption of change itself becomes the constant in one's thinking about reality, which now recognizes that reality is contingent upon the system in which it is embedded. Such understanding was a marked characteristic of the few students in this study whose audience responses approached genuine dialectical thinking. Students who had not yet achieved this level seemed more intent upon denying the reality of change: "Profits will stay the same in spite of the new laws," or "The new laws won't make any difference anyway because they won't be enforced." However, even though the dialectics of less mature writers have a ritualistic quality, they are still important both to argumentative-writing performance and to socio-cognitive development. Both Perry and Norma Haan suggest that by grappling with opposing points of view, students eventually build more complex socio-cognitive structures. Even if that struggle is not fully successful in the early stages, it is part of a process that will ultimately lead to success. The threefold whole-group increase in Reasons for Concerns between friendly and hostile papers suggests the degree to which writers thoughtfully considered opposing views on the hostile paper, even though their responses to those views were frequently glib and superficial.

Inappropriate Moves—Windows on Writers' Empathic Functioning

Inappropriate activity also increased in the hostile papers relative to the friendly ones. These moves increased from 8 percent of all audience activity on the friendly paper to 10.5 percent on the hostile one (Table 1), and this increase was statistically significant (see Hays et al., "Argumentative Writing"). The pattern of inappropriate moves in the three socio-cognitive groups was almost opposite to that governing Response moves. That is, for the friendly paper, there was a linear decrease in the Inappropriate category from position two to position four. For the hostile paper, this pattern is even more pronounced. These figures suggest that if the hostile audience elicited increased audience adaptations in general and dialectical activity in particular, it also stimulated some Inappropriate responses to readers, especially from less socio-cognitively developed writers.

The increase in Inappropriate activity suggests writers' limitations in perspective-taking or empathy, which are both facets of socio-cognitive development. In her Perry Scheme-related work on relationships between epistemic reasoning and empathy, Benack contends that empathy involves "two complementary functions": first, letting go of one's own perspective in order to "imaginatively take the role of the other" and, second, distinguishing between one's own "imaginative experience and [the] other's actual experience of the situation" (343-344). In short, we must imagine ourselves having someone else's thoughts and experiences but must also realize that our imaginary construct will not be identical to the other person's actual experience. If we cannot make that distinction, we mentally distort the other person's experience through overidentification—that is, we assume that the other person's experience is exactly the same as ours.

The Inappropriate category included Ineffective Argument for the specified reader and Pejorative, or insulting, references to the reader. Inappropriate moves revealed some telling differences between position two students and their position three and four counterparts, and these differences shed light on limitations in the formers' empathic behavior.

Ineffective Argument—Friendly Paper. In the friendly paper, position two writers engaged in substantial amounts of Ineffective Argument. Some papers in this group consisted of what Linda Flower calls "file dumps": in effect, the writer says, "Here's everything I know on this subject. *You* [the reader] sort it out." We coded such material Ineffective Argument only when it was clearly irrelevant to the specified reader. For example, some high-school writers devoted much of their friendly papers to discussing the general effects of alcohol on teenagers, sometimes without even linking this material to the driving issue. While such information might be of general interest to those specified readers who were parents—members of Mothers Against Drunk Driving, for example—these writers typically failed to make causal connections between teens' drinking habits and drunk-driving accidents involving teenagers. In the case of writers who adopted such strategies while writing to the Colorado Highway Patrol, the relevance of material unrelated to driving was even more questionable, and we coded some of it as Ineffective Argument. In many such instances, writers appeared to be writing to themselves or perhaps to fellow students rather than to the community audience specified on the assignment sheet (see Appendix A).

Ineffective Argument—Hostile Paper. In their hostile papers, position two writers tended to drift away from the specified readership. Clearly, dualistic thinkers had some difficulty identifying with their hostile readers. We interviewed about half our writers after they had completed the second writing session. A number of the dualistic position two writers—not all young high school students—told us that they had had no idea what their hostile readers would think, so they had decided simply to state their own ideas. Perhaps they assumed that those ideas would automatically interest a reader. Or perhaps, finding the task of addressing the hostile audience cognitively difficult, they simply avoided it. Other dualistic writers claimed in the interviews to have been aware of their readers' perspectives, and yet their papers too showed considerable Ineffective Argument. These results suggest that some high school and college students may indeed have had difficulty viewing reality from a perspective other than their own—at least in a situation in which they had limited time to attend to both the topic and the reader—and so misconceptualized their readers' probable responses in ways that adversely affected their writing performance.

Perhaps such writers conceptualized and addressed their readers inappropriately (from the standpoint of what the assignment asked) in part because they had had little experience with discourse situations and readerships like those asked for by the research task. However, many of these writers had been in college for one or two years, and so presumably they were familiar with some forms of argumentative writing. We believe that, in part, less developed socio-cognitive structures also limited their resources for apprehending and responding to the essay task. Further, Benack links empathic understanding to level of epistemic development: the dualistic thinker (Perry positions one and two) believes that external reality is absolute and fixed; therefore, dualists believe that all people perceive it alike—or that if they do not, they are "wrong" or in some way deviant. However, the dialectical thinker (Perry positions five and beyond) recognizes that the nature of experience is contextual, that "reality" depends upon the vantage point from which it is seen, and that there are "multiple subjective perspectives on common situations," some of which overlap and some of which do not (Benack 345). Thus a dialectical conception of reality involves responsible mental negotiation among those perspectives. Benack contends that relativistic epistemology enhances the ability to understand another's experience, citing a cross-domain study in which relativistic thinkers performed more empathetically than dualistic ones—that is, were both more willing and more able to assume another's perspective.

We also suspect that in the single writing session with its time constraints, simple cognitive overload was probably considerable for all except the most socio-cognitively advanced writers. Some recent work on audience indicates that writers may find it more useful to attend to the audience at later stages of the composing process, focusing upon content during earlier ones (Elbow; Roen and Willey; Rafoth). In a study of persuasive writing that manipulated structural versus content constraints, Shawn M. Glynn, Bruce K. Britton, Denise Muth, and Nukhet Dogan found that in students of average verbal ability, relaxing structural constraints facilitated idea production during early drafts of a persuasive argument perhaps because of decreased cognitive demands. However, students with low verbal ability produced fewer arguments in either situation. This finding suggests that the low verbal-ability writers had a narrow fund of ideas to draw upon; therefore, freeing up metacognitive "space" by relaxing structural constraints did little to augment this limited repertoire of ideas. Recent work by Dawn E. Schrader suggests that in young adults and adults, metacognition itself is developmental—that is, it emerges in a predictable sequence that culminates at the post-formal operational level. Thus less socio-cognitively mature students may not yet have fully developed the metacognitive ability to take advantage of increased space for metacognitive activity. In any event, in our study, less proficient writers experienced the greatest difficulty with the hostile audience, as evidenced in their Inappropriate activity.[2]

Pejorative Activity—Hostile Paper. In their hostile papers, position two writers also made Pejorative references to the audience. According to Benack, dualists believe that "only one interpretation of events is correct," and so they experience "moral opposition to adopting 'false' beliefs or 'wrong' feelings as though they were 'true/right'" (348)—even when temporarily adopting them for the sake of trying to understand them. Position two writers' pejorative moves suggest such moralistic approaches to the hostile reader.

We coded as Pejorative those remarks that obviously would insult or alienate the audience—statements that, for example, said to members of the beverage industry, "You don't care how many people get killed; you just want to make money" or to bartenders and tavern owners, "It's your fault that people are being killed on the highways." Whether or not these allegations are true, such statements would be more likely to antagonize readers than to enlist their support for the proposed laws. While members of the beverage industry obviously want to make money, one could also argue, as some of our high-scoring writers did, that on this issue they might profit by aligning themselves with the good guys. Further, those making money from alcohol also have concerns as parents and citizens, a fact that many writers in positions three and four perceived and tried to use as a basis for argument.

Writers in position two did not make even these distinctions about their hostile readers, treating them pretty much as agents of the devil. We suspect that these students found it too threatening to consider that the hostile audience might have had some legitimate reasons for opposing the laws—such as wanting to make a profit by catering to a strong, legal consumer market for alcoholic beverages. Even when these writers were not actively insulting their readers, their papers had an absolutist and moralistic tone offensive to their audience—for instance, unqualified and unargued claims that "drunk driving is a sin," and so on. This kind of moral absolutism, very different from reasoned moral conviction, is typical of Perry positions two and even three; according to Benack, it implies a genuine resistance to considering other perspectives, especially on issues about which people may have intense moral beliefs.

We suspect that absolutism took the form it did in our study because Colorado Springs is strong in religious fundamentalism, and fundamentalists often view alcohol in morally pejorative ways. In parts of the country where such views are less prevalent, we would expect students to mount different kinds of arguments on this issue. However, we also believe that moral absolutism would show up in any dualistic thinker's papers; it would simply take a different form. Ten years ago, one of us conducted research at a private liberal arts college in upstate New York, one that attracts children of the affluent. Although politically conservative, these students had more liberal attitudes about personal behavior than do many in Colorado Springs. They wrote for a general community audience (not a hostile one) on the topics of abortion and marijuana. Most student writers were pro-choice and favored legalization of marijuana. Yet the lower scoring papers in that study manifested the same kinds of absolutism, often with a moral flavor, that we found in the Colorado project. What differed was the content: the New York writers made discrete, unargued claims such as, "Nobody has a right to tell a woman what she can do with her body," or "Smoking dope is the individual's decision. The government has no right to interfere," and so on. In short, the differing socio-economic and cultural context produced different forms of absolutism and moralism, but the general structure of such thinking appeared similar in the Andirondacks and the Rockies—and such forms of reasoning evidently make it difficult for student writers to assume the perspectives of readers who differ from them.

Teaching Implications

Response. The marked increase in Response moves between the friendly and hostile papers suggests that the adversarial audience stimulates increased dialectical activity. However, in position two, that increased dialectical activity was offset by "interference" that evidently contributed to the counterproductive Inappropriate moves. We suspect that for writers in this position, the hostile audience specified by the study's writing task was too intimidating. That is, these writers had to write to adult businesspeople whom dualistic perceivers would tend to regard as Authorities. Yet in the eyes of dualists, these readers' positions on the topic would also automatically make them Bad Authorities. Thus dualists' tendencies to regard authorities as unquestioned sources of "Truth" would conflict with their propensity to reject "Wrong Ideas" as beyond the moral pale. Reconciling this conflict imposes a heavy cognitive load for dualists. Although the act of writing to an adversarial reader stimulated these students to increase their dialectical activity, the status differences between writers and their adult readers evidently made it extremely difficult for them to identify with their hostile audience long enough to consider their perspective.

Research in developmental psychology strongly suggests that the clash of moral and social ideas among peers stimulates socio-cognitive development (e.g., Berkowitz). A key phrase here seems to be "among peers," although our research also indicates that students nearing position four in the Perry Scheme coped effectively with the non-peer adversaries. Position three writers found it more difficult to empathize with an adversarial adult audience but also were also challenged to think creatively about ways to dodge the issue's implications. A productive teaching strategy for position three writers might be to analyze the validity of such "problem-solving" suggestions. For position two learners, however, an audience of peers (rather than adults) who held opposing views might well stimulate dialectical activity and at the same time be more manageable than the readership specified by the research topic. In-class small-group activities in which students on opposing sides of issues thrash out their ideas should help prepare writers for such assignments.

In addition, our research suggests that students in all three Perry Scheme positions would benefit from activities requiring them to pay more attention to "opponents'" reasons for their perspectives. Listing a hostile reader's probable objections to the writer's position and spelling out the reasons for those objections—perhaps to the satisfaction of a peer who supported the opposite side of the issue—might stimulate more mature dialectical behavior than that observed in this study. Simulations in which students assumed the role of those with whom they disagreed should also be helpful. Developmental research and our own teaching experience suggest, however, that progress would be slow and that such exercises would need to be repeated. Yet given present concerns about American students' limitations in critical thinking—concerns evident in the remarks of Cooper cited earlier—we think that such activities merit the highest priority, not only in the composition classroom but in many discipline-specific classes as well.

Inappropriate. We suspect that teaching and time for revision lessen students' tendencies to respond inappropriately to their readers. To the extent that Inappropriate behavior resulted from cognitive overload because of time constraints and the general difficulty of thinking about both topic and readers at the same time, we would expect a two-phase composing process to decrease Inappropriate activity. In particular, writers should initially concentrate on the topic and later on shaping their messages for their readers. To the extent that Inappropriate moves were linked to lack of academic or other experience, we would expect students to improve their performance as a result of classroom activities directed to broadening that experience. But to the extent that Inappropriate moves reflect more fundamental socio-cognitive structures, we would expect improvement to show a short-term ceiling effect and to be differential. We also suggest that a developmental approach to teaching might yield better results than a more global pedagogy—especially if the developmental approach not only made conscious use of what we know about both the general characteristics and writing behavior of students' performance at differing socio-cognitive levels, but also utilized some of the "challenge and support" principles of developmental/constructionist pedagogy (Sanford). 🐦

NOTES

[1] For further information on the Perry Scheme criteria and methods used in this study, see Hays and Hays, Brandt, and Chantry.

[2] Of course, even proficient writers often misinterpret a rhetorical context (see, for example, Kirsch); however, misalignments between writer and reader appear to be more extreme at lower socio-cognitive levels.

WORKS CITED

Basseches, Michael. *Dialectical Thinking and Adult Development.* Norwood, NJ: Ablex, 1984.

Benack, Suzanne. "Postformal Epistemologies and the Growth of Empathy." *Beyond Formal Operations: Late Adolescent and Adult Cognitive Development.* Ed. Michael L. Commons, Francis A. Richards, and Cheryl Armon. New York: Praeger, 1984. 340-356.

Benack, Suzanne, and Michael Basseches. *Dialectical Thinking and Relativistic Epistemology: Their Relation in Adult Development.* St. Paul: Perry Network Copy Service Document BENASB87A0292, 1987.

Berkenkotter, Carol. "Understanding a Writer's Awareness of Audience." *College Composition and Communication* 32 (1981): 388-389.

Berkowitz, Marvin W., ed. *Peer Conflict and Psychological Growth.* New

Directions for Child Development, No. 29. San Francisco: Jossey-Bass, 1985.

Clark, Ruth Anne, and Jesse G. Delia. "The Development of Functional Persuasive Skills in Childhood and Early Adolescence." *Child Development* (1976): 1008-1014.

Commons, Michael L., Francis A. Richards, and Cheryl Armon, eds. *Beyond Formal Operations: Late Adolescent and Adult Cognitive Development.* New York: Praeger, 1984.

Cooper, Charles, Roger Cherry, Barbara Copley, Stefan Fleischer, Rita Pollard, and Michael Sartisky. "Studying the Writing Abilities of a University Freshman Class: Strategies from a Case Study." *New Directions in Composition Research.* Eds. Richard Beach and Lillian Bridwell. New York: Guilford, 1984.

Elbow, Peter. "Closing My Eyes as I Speak: An Argument for Ignoring Audience." *College English* 49 (1987): 50-69.

Flavell, John. H., Patricia T. Botkin, Charles L. Fry Jr., John W. Wright, and Paul E. Jarvis. *The Development of Role-taking and Communication Skills in Children.* New York: Wiley, 1968.

Glynn, Shawn M., Bruce K. Britton, Denise Muth, and Nukhet Dogan. "Writing and Revising Persuasive Documents: Cognitive Demands." *Journal of Educational Psychology* 74.4 (1982): 557-67.

Haan, Norma. "Hypothetical and Actual Moral Reasoning in a Situation of Civil Disobedience." *Journal of Personality and Social Psychology* 32 (1975): 255-270.

Hannum, Bunny, Nan Jensen, Marty Nicholas, and Lois J. Zachary. *Working Cue Sheets for the Syracuse Rating Group.* Fayetteville, NY: Syracuse Rating Group, 1982.

Hays, Janice N. "Socio-cognitive Development and Argumentative Writing: Issues and Implications from One Research Project." *Journal of Basic Writing* 7.2 (1988): 42-67.

——, Kathleen S. Brandt, and Kathryn H. Chantry. "The Impact of Friendly and Hostile Audiences on the Argumentative Writing of High School and College Students." *Research in the Teaching of English* 22.4 (1988): 391-416.

——, Robert L. Durham, Kathleen S. Brandt, and Alan E. Raitz. "The Argumentative Writing of Students at Three Levels of Adult Socio-Cognitive Development." Unpublished manuscript, University of Colorado at Colorado Springs, 1989.

——, Robert L. Durham, Kathleen S. Brandt, and Alan E. Raitz. "A Sense of Audience in the Argumentative Writing of Students at Three Levels of Adult Socio-Cognitive Development." To appear in *A Sense of Audience in Written Communication*. Eds. Duane H. Roen and Gesa Kirsch. Sage, in press.

Kirsch, Gesa. "Experienced Writers' Representations of Audiences: The Cases of Three Writers." To appear in *A Sense of Audience in Written Communication*. Eds. Duane H. Roen and Gesa Kirsch. Sage, in press.

Kitchener, Karen S. "Cognition, Metacognition, and Epistemic Cognition: A Three Level Model of Cognitive Processing." *Human Development* 4 (1983): 222-232.

Kitchener, Karen S., and Patricia M. King. "The Reflective Judgment Model: Ten Years of Research." Symposium on Beyond Formal Operations 2. Harvard University, 22 June 1985.

Kohlberg, Lawrence. "Stage and Sequence: The Cognitive Developmental Approach to Socialization." *Handbook of Socialization Theory and Research*. Ed. D. Goslin. Chicago: U Chicago P, 1969.

Moore, William, J. "The Measure of Intellectual Development." Unpublished manuscript, Center for the Application of Developmental Instruction, Farmville VA, 1982.

Perry, William G. *Forms of Intellectual and Ethical Development in the College Years: A Scheme*. New York: Holt, 1970.

Rafoth, Benjamin A. "Audience Awareness among Good and Below Average Writers: First to Final Draft." Unpublished manuscript, Indiana U of Pennsylvania, 1988.

Roen, Duane N., and R. J. Willey. "The Effects of Audience Awareness on Drafting and Revising." *Research in the Teaching of English* 22.1 (1988): 75-88.

Rubin, Donald L. "Social Cognition and Written Communication." *Written Communication* 1 (1984): 211-245.

Sanford, Nevitt. *Self and Society: Social Change and Individual Development*. Chicago: Aldine, 1966.

Schrader, Dawn E. "Case Analyses of Differences in Moral Metacognition in Adolescence and Adulthood." Cornell University. Paper presented at the Fourth Annual Adult Development Symposium, Society for Research in Adult Development, Cambridge MA, 29 July 1989.

Secor, Marie. "Modes of Thinking, Modes of Argument." *The Writer's Mind: Writing as a Mode of Thinking.* Ed. Janice N. Hays, Phyllis A. Roth, Jon R. Ramsey, and Robert D. Foulke. Urbana: NCTE, 1983. 67-72.

Winter, D. G., David C. McClelland, and Abigail J. Stewart. *A New Case for the Liberal Arts.* San Francisco: Jossey, 1981.

APPENDIX A*
Topic B
Writing About Tougher Drunk Driving Laws for a Hostile Audience

Background
Last session, you wrote an essay in which you took a position on the issue of tough drunk driving laws. In that essay, you wrote to an audience that pretty much agreed with your point of view on the subject.

For this assignment, you are to write on the same topic, but this time for an audience that will <u>disagree</u> with your point of view and will probably feel some hostility towards it. Your job as writer is to persuade these unsympathetic readers to at least consider your point of view and maybe, even, change some of their own thinking on the issue of drunk driving laws.

If <u>on the whole you favor tougher drunk driving laws</u>, write your essay for the newsletter or magazine of one of the following groups; these groups will probably be opposed to tougher drunk driving laws:

Colorado Beverage Industry
Colorado Brewers Association
Colorado Springs Bar and Tavern Owners Association
Colorado Teamsters Union
Members of Playboy Clubs, Western Area

If <u>on the whole you are opposed to tougher drunk driving laws</u>, write your essay for the newsletter or magazine of one of the following groups; these groups will probably be in favor of tougher drunk driving laws:

Alcoholics Anonymous
Colorado Highway Patrol
Colorado Springs Council of Churches
Mothers Against Drunk Drivers

Underline the readers that you will write your essay for, and write the name of your readers here:

_____

Write your own name here: _____

Hand this sheet in with your essay.

Essay Assignment

Write a well-organized essay of around 1000 words in which you present your position on tough drunk driving laws to readers who will disagree with you. Be sure to support your position with examples and illustrations. Note: the 1000 word length is a suggestion only; if you can make an effective argument in a shorter paper, that's fine, or if you need more than 1000 words to construct your argument, that's fine too. Use your common sense about length.

Reminder

The proposed new drunk driving law would include a mandatory jail sentence of 24 hours for anyone found guilty on a first offense of driving under the influence of alcohol together with a stiff fine and suspension of the person's driving license for 30 days; second-time offenders would be sentenced to 30 days in jail, pay an even stiffer fine, and lose their driver's licenses for six months. They would also have to attend an alcohol education program for one year. Any person driving while under the influence of alcohol and involved in an accident resulting in a fatality would automatically be charged with manslaughter.

*An identical task was given for first paper except that the audiences were reversed.

APPENDIX B*
THE PERRY SCHEME
POSITIONS TWO THROUGH FIVE

STAGE TWO, MULTIPLICITY PRELEGITIMATE

In this position, individuals perceive alternative points of view. However, legitimate multiplicity is often rejected in favor of discrete units of knowledge. Authorities are the source of knowledge, but because individuals perceive alternative points of view, they are forced to separate authorities into Good Authority, which is truthful, and Bad Authority, which may be ignorant, wrong or misinformed. The individual is a passive knower who knows reality through Authority. Peers, like Authority, are bifurcated into those who support the reality of Good Authority and those who are bad, ignorant or wrong. In reasoning about reality, the individual is forced to confront the diversity perceived. Position Two subjects will rely on simple, often non-rational, solutions to the contradictions of reality in an attempt to maintain the Good.

STAGE THREE, MULTIPLICITY SUBORDINATE

In position three, individuals acknowledge the existence of different views and, further, acknowledge that the differences are legitimate. However, they perceive the legitimacy of diversity as temporary and hold out for the possibility of discovering the absolute nature of knowledge through Good Authority's hard work. As emulators of particular authorities, individuals view their own hard work as essential in knowing. Learners have become active. As active learners of the quantity of knowledge, they will embrace certain authorities for their personal characteristics—i.e., friendliness, clarity of thought, wisdom, good looks, dress, etc. Peers' views are recognized, but have little impact on knowing since learners view them from a reasoning stance incapable of distinguishing between bias and inference. As a result, experiences of diversity are expressed or reported as lists of unconnected events or opinions without logic or modifiers.

STAGE FOUR, MULTIPLICITY LEGITIMATE

Position four individuals recognize that in many areas they will never achieve certainty, but fail to generalize this insight to an integrative theory or view of knowledge. The realization that they may never banish uncertainty can on the one hand result in a cynicism towards authority—a sense of being let down, or failed, in their search for the truth. On the other hand, it can lead to a deeper embracing of authorities, particularly those who recognize the individual's particular genius. In either case, it is the individual who will generate her truth. For one, it is a lonely oppositional process; for the other, it is a partnership with an idolized authority. Peers are important to position four individuals. They are respected because they, too, have been left to generate their own truth. For this reason, one belief is as good as another. Individuals are able to see that evidence leads to hypothesis and conjecture rather than to absolute answers. But they are unable to endorse a conclusion unless it coincides with their own view. The truth which they establish for themselves becomes the absolute through which all judgments are made. The individual has created her own absolute world.

STAGE FIVE, RELATIVISM

With position five, a qualitative change has occurred in the individual's view of the structure of knowledge. It is as if the long personal history of accumulated quantities of data, experiences, and the like has resulted in a qualitative shift in the perception of reality. For the first time, the individual sees that the "big picture" depends upon understanding the frame of reference from which it is developed. Authorities are seen as experts who interpret reality and who have preferences and biases. For these reasons, it is possible for the individual to evaluate authorities qualitatively, distinguishing between authorities who have carefully weighed the evidence at hand and thus arrived at a considered judgment or point of view and those who have failed to approach with logic and passion the search for knowledge. Since all knowledge is viewed as relative, the self emerges as a consciously active partner along with experts in the process of exploring reality. In the educational context, the self emerges as the agent of its own learning. Because knowledge is viewed through the experiences of the self and because the individual understands the importance of exploring the context of experience, the individual realizes the legitimacy of others' considered judgments and thus may attempt to view knowledge and understand problems through the experience and perspective of others. This empathic ability brings about a recognition of the social/communal nature of knowledge. To this active, self-generated role in knowing, the individual brings a reasoning style characterized by logical inquiry and use of evidence to support her point of view. Unlike the position four learner, the individual in five can distinguish subtle differences in the evidence. Right/wrong, either/or thinking is no longer sufficient to the task of knowing.

* Based upon descriptions of stage positions in Hannum, B., Jensen, N., Nicholas, M., and Zachary, L.J. (1982), Working Cue Sheets for the Syracuse Rating Group. Fayetteville, N.Y.: Syracuse Rating Group.

APPENDIX C
AUDIENCE CODING RUBRIC
DEFINITIONS AND EXAMPLES

N – NAMING: recognizes that an audience exists by direct and indirect reference.
N1 – Direct reference "you"—speaks or writes directly to the audience.
    —"You would not want the drunk driver in your bar."
N2 – Indirect reference "They, their."
N3 – Names audience—appears in text when writer names the group to whom
    the paper is written.—MADD, Bar and Tavern Owner Association, etc.

S – STRATEGY: implements a strategy or tactic for reader.

S1 – Appeals to self interest vis-a-vis laws—how laws will help reader; how reader might benefit financially, socially; how business will benefit, reputation improve.
—"These laws will make your job easier."
—"ou will not have to put up with drunks in your bar."
—"Drunk drivers are not good for your business."

S2 – States readers' responsibility, obligation; what readers ought to do. Key words: "ought," "should," "your duty," "your responsibility."
—"Bar and tavern owners ought to be sensitive to these problems."
—"You should be a responsible citizen."

S3 – States readers' circumstances, beliefs, experiences, characteristics—their state of being. Key phrases: "you have seen...," "you might think. . .," "you put your family first. . .," "you are. . . ."
—"As bartenders, you see drunks all the time. . . ."
—"You come in contact with this. . . ."
—"Parents care about the well-being of their children. . . ."

S4 – Direct emotional appeal
—"What if you lost a child, spouse, or friend because of drunk driving?"
—"This tragic incident may occur to your child."
—"You might be affected personally."

S5 – Tells readers they have choices.
—"You have a choice. . . ."
—"These issues present us with choices. . . ."

S6 – Praises, supports, shows appreciation, flatters—calls readers "responsible people."
—"[Yours is] a prominent association. . . ."
—"We as upright citizens. . . ."

S7 – Use of shared features, aligns with audience—"we."
—"Just recently in our city. . . ."
—"We all want a better place to live. . . ."

S8 – Asks reader to take some kind of action or to support laws or to take action to solve the problem.
—"I urge you to support these laws. . . ."
—"You can ask your customers to drink less. . . ."
—"You can write your congressman. . . ."

C – CONTEXT: establishes context and gives background information for the reader.

C1 – Simply states own position but not as a summarizing statement or repetition of an earlier statement. This is the initial statement of the position—limited to first part of paper.
—"I'm here to argue against the proposed changes in these laws."
—"The state should pass and enforce tougher drunk driving laws."

C2 – Introduces self, establishes persona.
  —"I'm speaking to you as a concerned citizen."
  —"I know how law enforcement officers feel because my father was a policeman."
C3 – Gives reasons for own position (not general reasons; some variety of "I" statement).
  —"I feel very strongly about drunk driving because my best friend was killed by a drunk driver."
  —"One of my best friends was permanently disabled in an accident involving a drunk driver."
C4 – States issue or problem—what it is, why it's a problem; comes in the opening section only.
  —"The number of accidents caused by drunk drivers has risen sharply."
  —"The provisions of the present law are not enforced. Drunk drivers are let off with a slap on the wrist."
C5 — Gives specific information or clearly explains the proposed laws (does not give an opinion but clarifies what the terms of the laws are).
  —"Under the proposed law, anyone found guilty of drunk driving must enroll in an alcohol education program."
  —"One such bill provides for a mandatory twenty-four hour jail sentence, license suspension for thirty days, and a stiff fine."

R – RESPONSE; responds, accommodates to reader's concerns, values, beliefs.
R1 – Articulates readers' possible worries or fears or possible objections—that laws might affect business or financial position, that reader might see laws as extreme or unfair.
  —"Bar owners may feel that the laws will hurt business."
  —"You will probably believe that these laws are too costly."
R2 – Gives reasons for these fears, worries, etc.—often signalled by "because" clause.
  —"Some [tavern owners] fear these laws because they are afraid they will hurt business."
  —"Many [drivers] object to the new laws because they are afraid they will be caught driving drunk."
R3 – Answers objections, fears; rebuttal. Explains why the reader need not be concerned.
  —"The laws won't keep anyone from drinking but only from driving drunk."

I – INAPPROPRIATE APPEALS
I1 – Pejorative or negative references to readers. The writer blames the readers or attempts to make them feel guilty; negative representations of readers.
  —"You [bartenders] don't care what happens to people—you just want to make money."

—"Maybe you just don't care about how you drive. . . ."

I2 – Ineffective argument for audience. The argument would be ineffective with the specified audience.

   —"Alcohol is a depressant. It does not give <u>you</u> your judgement." [to Council of Churches]

   —"Those laws are a step in the same direction parents have tried to go all along where raising their kids is concerned." [to Bar and Tavern Owners Association]

   —"Drinking is popular among teenagers." [to Playboy Club]

I3 – Private or code references

I4 – Vague pronouns

I5 – All-purpose words

IV

How Writers Respond
to the Needs of Readers

The previous section considered the development of writing ability from social and cognitive perspectives. This section continues the focus on the skills necessary for effective writing, looking not at the development of writing skill in individual writers but at the ways in which writers must accurately anticipate the moment-by-moment comprehension process of readers. Of the three essays, the purpose of Jeanne Fahnestock's is most general: her study investigates the linguistic resources available for guiding readers' integration of each sentence of the text into a coherent structure. Fahnestock demonstrates that, even in the absence of explicit linguistic cues, readers have extraordinary powers to create coherence by reading backwards. In spite of their general ability to create coherence, the amount of effort readers are willing to expend to understand any specific text depends on its genre and their background knowledge. By describing the conditions that foster the reader's apprehension of coherence, Fahnestock's analysis helps writers anticipate the situations in which they need to supply readers with more or less explicit guidance. Her analysis has implications both for those writing to inexperienced or novice readers and for those addressing mature audiences. First, she poses a serious challenge to those who apply readability formulas to texts (e.g., school books), simplifying them by shortening sentences and in the process eliminating important discourse cues. Paradoxically, while the goal of readability formulas is to make texts easier to read, they can actually make the reader's job harder by suppressing cues to the relations between sentences. Second, her analysis suggests how writers—by playing with and against mature readers' expectations of cues—can transform coherence devices into generative tactics within a stylistic repertoire.

Whereas Fahnestock deals with the linguistic competence of mature readers and writers, Barbara Sitko's focus is more directly pedagogical. She develops and tests an exercise that enhances both the reading and writing skills of her students. In their role as writers, Sitko's students are given the opportunity to revise their texts in response to other students' reactions during reading. The exercise draws on readers' capacity to anticipate future developments even in unfamiliar and unpolished texts— the very capacity explored in the previous chapter by Fahnestock. To participate in this exercise, Sitko's students learn to become active readers—to pause at various places in the text, to summarize the preceding point, and then to predict what will come next. She then supplies her student writers with transcripts of these responses and observes how they use them to revise their texts. She finds that this exercise helps student writers make appropriate substantive changes that clarify their own intentions as well as make the texts easier for their classmates to read.

Clearly the research methods adopted by Fahnestock and Sitko are quite different. In the first place, they focus on writers and texts at different stages of development. Fahnestock looks for the most part at published professional text and the means by which a mature reader like herself makes sense of it. Sitko examines first drafts of students' texts, and her readers are peer reviewers, well aware of the unfinished status of the drafts. Therefore, they do not assume that their own unfulfilled expectations result from the writers' superior artistic intention and control. If, as readers, we assume that the text is polished and controlled by artistic intention then we are willing to labor to supply the implicatures or inferences necessary for coherence. In some cases, we are even willing to consider that effort part of the pleasure of reading, as in reading literature or in exploring some new subject matter.

Several factors, including genre and background knowledge, influence the reader's willingness and/or need to expend interpretive energy to create coherence. Readers of traditional literary genres, for example, are willing to work harder at building coherence than readers of technical writing, who place a heavier burden on the writer to show how each element relates to the purpose of the text. In fact, technical writers cannot often indulge in certain kinds of tropes, such as irony or periphrasis, which in other genres contribute to the pleasure of the text. To comprehend irony the reader must already be quite familiar with what the writer is likely to mean; to interpret periphrasis, the reader must work to recognize a reference to the same subject.

This is not to say that writers can or should make all coherence connections explicit. Much depends on the readers' background knowledge, as Fahnestock points out. Readers who have extensive background knowledge will automatically draw on what they know and fill in the necessary inferences, without even being aware of how much they are bringing to the text. Even disciplinary experts, however, do not always understand everything they read immediately. Just like novices, they will make frequent use of the technique of reading backwards. But for novices, this technique is a primary way to build up the necessary disciplinary knowledge that they lack. Most readers, neither experts nor novices, tend to read published discourse in areas that they already know something (but not everything) about. So they assume that the writers are practiced and that their own background knowledge will be sufficient to make the necessary inferences. Readers notice when these expectations are violated, and if the genre is one from which they expect immediate coherence (such as instructions), they get frustrated.

Melissa Holland asks the same question that Fahnestock does: is it possible to devise a formula that calculates the minimum amount of background information required to read a text? Holland, however, takes the perspective of the writer of instructions who must calculate what the reader knows and how much explanatory information to include. In her search for a generative model of readers' needs, she starts by reviewing current models of the writing process—primarily those of Flower and Hayes and McCutchen—to show that they do not go far enough. She then explores the potential contribution of intelligent tutoring systems and artificial intelligence which require explicit representations of readers' knowledge.

Holland's goal is to help writers of technical instructions select appropriate kinds and amounts of information to supplement possible gaps in their readers' background knowledge. The problems that these writers face are particularly interesting because readers of instructions are likely to be quite diverse: some will be anxious technophobes, others will be confident do-it-yourselfers. The instruction writer must aim at the least competent reader, whereas writers of other technical genres such as research articles often can assume a higher degree of competence and leave the less informed reader to struggle.

This section demonstrates the value of bringing diverse research methodologies and theories to bear on problems in composition. Fahnestock and Sitko both enhance our understanding of coherence, but their studies would rarely be juxtaposed because one is doing discourse analysis and the other experimental process research. Similarly, Holland's foray into computer science is one that few composition researchers could make, but she has brought back useful insights on assessing readers' needs that composition scholars can benefit from.

❧ 11

Connection and Understanding

Jeanne Fahnestock

The challenge to students of text structure was succinctly stated by Benoit Mandelbrot almost twenty years ago when he wrote that "human discourse is both something highly structured and something highly unpredictable" (550). Surely that is a paradox which experience supports. When I talk with a colleague or family member, or read an article in *College English* or *Sports Illustrated*, I cannot say beforehand precisely what the outcome or content will be. Even when I know something about a topic, I can rarely predict in any specific way what I am going to read. If I could, why would I read? And yet if I find a text coherent, I am in some way not surprised by it. If I am surprised to the point of being disconcerted or confused, I often turn that impression into a property of the text, calling it incoherent. But most often, what I read gives me new insight, information, or conviction. How is it possible not to be able to predict what a written text will be about and yet to be competent to read it?

The answer that many text grammarians have invoked here is world knowledge brought to bear on the text (van Dijk 37-38). World knowledge includes very local knowledge of the subject matter at hand, as well as very general knowledge of what it means to be human in our world. It is this kind of knowledge, for example, that enables a reader to perceive two sentences like "I finished my meal. The waiter brought me the check," as a coherent sequence because they describe two actions that normally follow one another in a restaurant, part of the world most twentieth-century Westerners are familiar with.[1] Without such "extra-textual," outside knowledge, this series would be as incomprehensible as the pair, "I finished my meal. With *Ac* in the genome, on the other hand, the mutation reverted in some cells." (To create this example I simply kept the first sentence and added a second lifted at random from a *Scientific American* article.)

But what kind of extra-textual knowledge and how much of it is necessary to make a particular text readable? Could we ever come up with a formula which calculated the minimum amount of background information required to read a text? And even if we could calculate the amount expected, would it matter? After all, readers rarely confine their reading to subjects they are familiar with. If they did, the consequences for learning would be disastrous. We all occasionally read a piece in an unfamiliar genre on a topic beyond our ken—the medical article, the engineering report, the poststructuralist interpretation—and yet the result is not total incomprehension. We do not find these texts incoherent even when we cannot bring to them the background knowledge the authors assumed their readers would have. We can often, by dint of re-reading and consulting a glossary perhaps, make significant headway at understanding a piece for which we are far from the ideal reader. What kind of knowledge enables us to do that?

If it is possible to read discourse without the background knowledge the author counted on, then surely we are dealing with some feature of the process of comprehension that sits above the actual content on the page and that is also distinct from the reader's world knowledge. In other words, there must be some kind of general mechanism, some kind of linguistic or discourse knowledge, that comes to the aid of readers, helping them in addition to their background knowledge.[2] Thus two individuals could conceivably have the same knowledge of things in the world, but the one without this linguistic knowledge would not understand connected discourse, even on a thoroughly known subject, while the other with this linguistic knowledge could. There are then at least two kinds of competence-enabling comprehension, linguistic knowledge and general knowledge. This paper will discuss one potential aspect of linguistic knowledge, describe the process of "reading backwards" that best demonstrates it, and, finally, point out some of its analytical benefits.

One part of this linguistic knowledge, this competence to create coherence, is the expectation that readers have about the kinds of inferences or connections they can make between pairs of clauses or sentences.[3] Readers are able to see what we might also call the functions of clauses in sequence, how the next in line works as an example or as support, etc., for the one just read. These functions or connections have been studied by linguists, rhetoricians, and investigators in artificial intelligence. We identify them with M. A. K. Halliday and R. Hasan's set of conjunctive relations, their sorting bins for transition words (242-243), and with Ross Winterowd's "grammar of coherence" (828-835) to mention just two of the most familiar of many discussions of these relations. However, although the reader's ability to make connections or inferences is related to transition words, inferring connections does not depend on their explicit presence. We can of course have a pair like the following:[4]

> A sudden change in the environment may eliminate a well adapted population or even a whole species. For example, several kinds of previously very successful Hawaiian birds were wiped out by diseases carried to the islands by introduced bird species. (Patent 18)

Here the relation is marked by an explicit transition, "for example." But we can also have a similar pair without any transition word.

> The third point to keep in mind is that chance is a large element in evolution. A seed which could develop into a particularly robust, healthy plant may well be eaten before it has an opportunity to grow. (Patent 19)

Even without the explicit transition word, the reader has no trouble understanding that the healthy seed devoured is an example of chance intervening in evolution. Since in real written discourse so many of the relations are not marked by transition words, readers must have a set of expectations about how sentences can be related. And they wait for these expectations to be fulfilled. This is part of the linguistic knowledge that makes comprehension possible.

Two related questions come to mind immediately: is the set of these possible semantic relations finite, and if so, how is that set organized (Dillon 76)? How the first question is answered depends a great deal on the level of abstraction we will accept in the answer. At one level, we can easily say that some clauses are entailed or predicted by the clause that precedes them and some are not. There we have created two exhaustive categories of possible relations between adjacent clauses.

At the opposite extreme, we could say that each pair of connected clauses represents a unique, unclassifiable relationship, a special conjunction of meanings exactly responsive to a particular context and to the precise wording and syntax, so that to change even one word or to rearrange words slightly would be to change the meaning relationship between the pair of clauses. Probably every writing teacher who takes pains to teach students sensitivity to precise wording and phrasing would agree to some extent with this view.

Is there any happy medium between these two ways: between two vague, all-encompassing categories—related or not related—and the acknowledgement that every pair of sentences is uniquely tied? A traditional approach to these connections has been through transition words. We can take transition words and phrases (sometimes even whole sentences function as transitions) as representing the potential connections or semantic relations that can hold between clauses or sentences. In other words, we can once again use the clues provided by the language itself. If we want to generalize, though still at a meaningful level, the best way is to use the explicit markers of relations that already exist, such as "therefore," "however," "because," etc. Furthermore (to use one of these natural connectors), we quickly discover that some of the transition words are interchangeable. "For instance," "for example," or a phrase like "to give an example"—and so on—are surely synonymous in most contexts. It is therefore possible to group the vast variety of natural transitions into fewer categories, each representing a semantic relation, as many have done, including Halliday and Hasan (242-243), Winterowd (828-835), Robert E. Longacre (chap. 3), Joseph E. Grimes (chap. 14), Jerry R. Hobbs (16-26), and even Fred N. Scott and Joseph V. Denney (24-33) and Alexander Bain (94-100) one hundred years ago.

But even within this reduced set of categorized relations based on the natural transition words, a pattern of symmetry or pairing is apparent. There seem to be sets of, in a sense, opposite relations, one member in each set being less predictable than the other and therefore more likely to be explicitly indicated by a transition word as an aid to the reader. Take a pair like "premise and concession."[5] A premise is generally a supporting statement; it can be a cause, a condition, or simply some enabling claim. Readers can infer the premise relation even when it is unmarked, as in the following example: "Therapy does him [Jennings in LeFanu's ghost story "Green Tea"] no good: he is victimized by something finally independent of his psyche" (Sullivan 21). This pair could obviously have an explicit transition word: "Therapy does him no good because he is victimized by something finally independent of his psyche." But suppose that instead of giving a supporting statement we weakened the initial claim by conceding that therapy does good to many. Now to get these two to follow one another we must use a transition word: "Therapy does him no good *although* therapy does good to many." When we follow with a less expected relation like "concession," the transition word seems necessary to prevent a flat contradiction (Fahnestock 406). Tones of voice could perhaps make the second sentence sound like a concession without the "although," but such "tones" are difficult to convey in written discourse. Of course certain rhetorical effects may be achieved by doing away with the "necessary" transition word. In general, however, writing lacks the intonational resources of speech, so writers must fall back on such cues as transition words.

A strong disclaimer is in order here about the kind of "coherence" produced by the connections between sequences of sentences. Like a physical chain that has connection but no necessary shape, a set of sentences all linked to one another may meander aimlessly, even in contradictory directions. Thus a text of related sentences does not necessarily constitute a coherent discourse overall. In reader's terms, the perception of connections between individual clauses does not guarantee the perception of overall coherence. This point has been made many times, but it is worth repeating to avoid any misunderstanding about what I am claiming about intersentence connections. According to Tanya Reinhart, in order for a text to achieve overall coherence, it must fulfill three conditions: connectedness, consistency, and relevance (164). Connectedness, in Reinhart's scheme, is only one of three elements and is divided into co-reference and linkage by the "semantic sentence connectors" that are the subject of this paper (168). To ease the terminological muddle caused by acknowledging levels of coherence, we can follow the standard practice of distinguishing local, linear, or sentence-to-sentence coherence from overall or global coherence.

An uncertainty remains about the various sets of intersentential relations that have been proposed by various scholars of text structure. If, as I claim, these relations do not depend on explicit transition words, does it follow that a relation can be identified between every pair of clauses? In other words, must such a relation be present for sentence-to-sentence coherence? Investigations by Gary Sloan and others suggest that there are certainly pairs of clauses in sequence that cannot be inferentially connected (453); if we try to link them with a transition word, the test for the presence of a semantic relation, no choice will satisfy.

When sentences are not inferentially connected, we may invoke two other sources of sentence-to-sentence or linear coherence that may still be present in inferentially connected sentences but that may sometimes have to carry readers from clause to clause without other aid. The first is the powerful topic/comment organization of many English sentences, the well-known tendency for speakers and writers to put known, topical, or thematic information at the beginning of a sentence, and so-called newer information toward the end; what is "new" in one sentence may then become "old" in the next, creating a chain of overlapping reference from clause to clause. The other possible source of linking are those surface features of textual cohesion, catalogued initially by Halliday and Hasan and recently refined by Sandra Stotsky (433-440). Readers may perceive a connection between sentences when they see the same words in both, or synonyms, superordinate terms, pronouns of clear anaphoric reference and so on, though it has been amply demonstrated that these surface features of cohesion are by no means a sufficient explanation of sentence-to-sentence coherence and can in fact be present in gibberish.

Another uncertainty about unmarked semantic relations is the degree of fixity or invariance with which they can be identified between a given pair of clauses. When we are dealing with humans, variance is a given. When readers are asked to parse a text according to possible relations, some will name a relation one thing, others will give it another name, though both identifications will come from the set of relations defined by transition words. An example will illustrate this point.

> She [the nineteenth-century French novelist George Sand] was not however short of "systemes" to expound in the next decade, up to the 1848 revolution. This was the period in her life when she was most deeply involved in politics, both theoretically and practically. (Thomson 4)

One reader will interpret the second sentence in this pair as essentially a restatement of the first: George Sand was not short of systems; in other words, she was deeply involved in politics. "Systemes" and "politics" are seen as roughly synonymous, so here are two ways of saying the same thing, one more general. Another reader may understand the second sentence as a premise in its relation to the first: George Sand was not without "systemes" *because* she was deeply involved in politics. Thus this pair of sentences could make sense to readers in slightly different ways as they build different models of this passage.

Furthermore, the ability to discover the appropriate connection between a pair of sentences depends very much on the context in which those sentences are found. The term "context" has several applications which should be sorted out, beginning with context in the sense of co-text, the other sentences around the two whose relation is examined. We can illustrate the influence of co-text by borrowing an example from Herbert H. Clark and Susan E. Haviland's essay, "Comprehension and the Given-New Contract." They make the point that when the given/new contract is violated, when an element in one sentence does not have an antecedent in a preceding sentence, readers are invited to make what they call an "implicature" between sentences. (These "implicatures" are not to be confused with Grimes's; Clark and Haviland have inferences in mind). The readers' ability to draw implicatures enables them to read a sequence of sentences like the following as coherent, even though the "Maxim of Antecedence," as they call it, has been violated: "Oscar had lipstick on his cheek. It was Olivia who kissed him" (Clark and Haviland 18). Clark and Haviland speak only of general implicatures, but we could say that the second sentence in this example was related to the first as a premise: "Oscar had lipstick on his cheek *because* Olivia kissed him."

Clark and Haviland warn, however, that the "holes" between sentences can be too large, "violating the computability requirement": "It is difficult, for example, to imagine how the ordinary listener would build a bridge between the two sentences 'George Washington was the father of our country. It was Olivia who kissed Oscar'" (19). Clark and Haviland argue that this sequence is unacceptable because it is impossible to find an implicature (i.e. semantic relation) that would connect the second sentence to the first. But it is possible to invent a co-text enabling readers to form an implicature linking these sentences. It might go as follows:

> Bernice claimed that George Washington is the Father of Our Country. Her friend Olivia denied it, nominating Thomas Jefferson instead and betting that whoever was wrong would have to kiss her pet frog Oscar. They looked in a history book. *George Washington is the father of our country. It was Olivia who kissed Oscar.*

This process of contextualizing a meaningless pair into meaningfulness has been demonstrated many times to prove beyond a doubt that the reader's ability to build a bridge between any two sentences can depend on what we may call their semantic environment (Edmondson 12-14). In this example, we expect a conclusion to this little story once a certain condition has been fulfilled, once the right answer has been found to

"Who is the father of our country?" Context in the sense of co-text creates expectations in this way and thus governs our ability to infer semantic relations between sentences, especially sentences without lexical cohesion or topic/comment relations between them. Theoretically, there is no gap between clauses that could not be bridged in a suitable context. (One wonders then why some made-up pairs seem comprehensible immediately, like the first example cited from Clark and Haviland, and others do not. The answer may be that some minimal sets of two sentences immediately invoke some familiar setting or frame and so in fact create contexts for themselves without the need for more co-text.)

The reader's perceptions are not, however, conditioned only by the semantic environment of the two clauses being linked. They are also determined by context in another sense, by the kinds of background knowledge the reader brings to the text. For many texts, the reader's ability to see the appropriate semantic links depends, in a sense, on a co-text larger than what is on the page; it depends on the reader and writer sharing background knowledge—more likely in the form of shared reading than shared experience. It also follows that the reader can make inferences the writer never intended or may fail to make those the writer counted on.

We can all demonstrate to ourselves this process of relying on background knowledge by picking up something we do not usually read and trying it out:

> A goal of current studies on the ribosome is to understand the relationships of its structural complexity to the parallel complexity of the process of protein synthesis. None of the approximately 55 macromolecular components of the ribosome alone has the ability to catalyze the formation of peptide bonds, even though the peptidyl transferase catalytic center is located on the large ribosomal subunit.

These are the very first two sentences of an article in *The Journal of Biological Chemistry* (Auron et al. 6893). In order to understand these sentences fully, the reader should know beforehand that the ribosome is the organelle in every living cell which makes proteins. More specifically, to understand that the second sentence in the passage essentially restates the first, the reader must know beforehand that "the formation of peptide bonds" is the key process in protein synthesis. With that knowledge, the reader immediately perceives the synonymy between "structural complexity" in the first sentence and "approximately 55 macromolecular components of the ribosome" in the second, and between "the process of protein synthesis" in the first and the "formation of peptide bonds" in the second. The synonymy between the first two clauses leads the reader to interpret the second as essentially a restatement of the first. Similarly, even though the subordinate clause in the second sentence is marked by an explicit transition word, the reader should already know that "peptidyl transferase" is the enzyme which catalyzes the formation of peptide bonds in order to understand what this clause concedes. All this background knowledge is necessary for full and immediate comprehension of the semantic relationships among the first three clauses in an article obviously speaking to specialists.

Reading Backwards

The explication of this passage from a scientific article demonstrates how the extralinguistic knowledge a reader brings to a text constrains the identification of semantic relations between clauses (though readers uninformed about the subject of the passage probably began to attack it anyway through using the parallelism that reinforces the synonymy in the first two clauses). But the experience of finding comprehension impeded by lack of background knowledge actually leads once again to an awareness of the role that linguistic knowledge plays. As an illustration of the role of linguistic as opposed to background knowledge, take these first two sentences from an article called "Basic Assembler" in the magazine *Nibble: The Reference for Apple Computing*:

> Shortly after purchasing my Apple II Plus, I realized that many applications that I wished to develop would need the speed and efficiency of machine code programming. I was disappointed when I found that the Apple II Plus did not contain the mini-assembler that the Apple II did. (Whitney 17)

Obviously, for ease of comprehension, for seeing that the second sentence could be linked to the first with a "so" or a "therefore," the reader should know beforehand that "machine code programming" depends on a "mini-assembler" so that without it there is disappointment (a fact unknown to this reader before reading these two sentences).

However, ignorance did not prevent me from comprehending these two sentences. I simply read them backwards. Instead of using prior knowledge to identify the semantic relations, I used the semantic relations to establish the knowledge. Unlike the isolated George Washington/Oscar sentences, these *Nibble* sentences have clues to their meaning relationship in the phrases "I wished" and "I was disappointed when." These phrases frame the content of a wish and the resultant cause of disappointment, a very predictable pair, part of our general world knowledge. For this example, we can also add the general knowledge that doing something with a computer requires some special program or piece of equipment. If the author who wants to do machine code programming is disappointed because he does not have a mini-assembler, then a mini-assembler is necessary for machine code programming. Following clues like these, readers can work on material initially unfamiliar and reason back to the special knowledge enabling inferential links, knowledge that the author probably counted on in the first place. Thus it is possible to learn from texts that do not deliberately state information for us as "unknowing" readers.

For another example of the power of the reader's expectations about connection, we can return to that incomprehensible sequence of sentences used in the very beginning of this piece: "I finished my meal. With *Ac* in the genome, on the other hand, the mutation reverted in some cells." Perhaps some readers of that pair immediately began to follow something of the process of "reading backwards" from linguistic knowledge. One of the basic expectations we can have about a pair of clauses is that they represent a sequence in time, the first clause naming an event or condition that comes before the second. That expectation would enable us to interpret a sequence like "I put on my hat. I put on my coat," as representing two time-ordered actions. We might almost call this relation of sequence the "default expectation"; it is the least we can suppose. Or we might prefer to call it a genre expectation, postulating that the piece we are reading is a narrative.

Suppose now that, reading backwards, I try to make this incomprehensible pair of clauses conform to my expectation of sequence. The only way I can do that is to imagine that the two sentences represent narrated acts, one physical and the other mental. Someone is telling what she or he has done: "I did this, and then I thought that." Now many different kinds of world knowledge build on that connection hypothesized on the basis of linguistic knowledge and help me to construct a scenario in which these two sentences could be related to one another in a plausible sequence. The "I" of this story is relating how some ideas, perhaps an insight, occurred during a meal, both levels of activity going on simultaneously perhaps, but ordered in the telling:

When the waiter brought the soup, it occurred to me that when Ac was absent, the mutations were stable. I finished my meal. With Ac in the genome, on the other hand, the mutation reverted in some cells.

Some familiarity with scientific biographies and accounts of insight enabled the construction of this sequence in what could become the latest TV game show craze: "Contextualize that Passage." What I have done here exactly parallels what I did with the Clark and Haviland example. But what enabled me to invoke the appropriate world knowledge in the first place? What was the seed of my contextualizing? It was specifically my expectation of what *could* be a possible connection between any two clauses, not just these two clauses. In effect, I said to myself, "I think I will relate these as though they represented acts in sequence, because that is a very plausible relation." Then and only then was I able to construct a plausible scenario. It was also another semantic clue, the presence of the "on the other hand" in the sentence lifted from the *Scientific American*, that enabled me to create the sentence representing the prior thought; then I applied semantic knowledge to help me construct a sentence that looked like a reversal. I could actually have picked any relation and tried to work backwards from it, attempting to make that second sentence into an example or consequence or premise or even a contrast to the first by taking that transition phrase, "on the other hand," to be an immediate connector. But the general knowledge available to me made those hypothetical connections dead ends; instead, I took the easiest path and invented a context that made an incomprehensible pair of sentences into elements in a narration. I read backwards (Warren et al. 24, 48).

This ability to read or reason backwards is a process that we should actually be quite familiar with from our reading of fiction and "artful" prose. Take these opening sentences from a chapter of William Warner's *Beautiful Swimmers*: "It can come anytime from the last week in October to the first in December. There will be a fickle day, unseasonably warm, during which two or three minor rain squalls blow across the Bay. . . [more weather description]. Then it comes" (33). That opening "it" once again violates Clark and Haviland's maxim of antecedence, the pronoun's need for a referent. One possible antecedent is the title of the chapter, "Winter," but by the time we get to the second "it" we realize that a more plausible reference is a yet-to-be-mentioned storm. Or "it" could mean both. At any rate, readers are patient with this kind of little reference mystery in artful prose, and they postulate and correct possibilities as they read along, much as they reciprocally use their background and linguistic knowledge to comprehend nonliterary texts. I would argue that what we do for fiction and poetry—setting up mental representations for pronouns temporarily without reference or immediately creating an entity when the determiner "the" is used instead of "a"—is a special case of what we do when we comprehend anything, reciprocally reading backwards and forwards.

The process of "reading backwards" also suggests that understanding a text may involve two stages. First, the reader recognizes the new knowledge acquired by "reading backwards," and then the reader integrates that knowledge with a storehouse of already accepted learning. In other words, readers may occasionally create something like a "buffer" or holding bin for the new knowledge they gain from reading backwards in order to comprehend a text. As in the example from *Nibble*, the new fact that machine code programming depends on an assembler may wait in a kind of limbo until it can be confirmed, either because it is consistent with what comes later in the same text or because other reading or experience reinforces it.

Perhaps we can see the need for this "temporary buffer" more readily if we consider what happens when an argument is read. In the process of expanding the enthymemes of an argument, readers must often temporarily postulate values and beliefs they do not hold. Thus they can understand an argument perfectly yet not be convinced by it because its assumptions contradict what they firmly believe. In much the same way, the knowledge postulated from reading backwards may undergo a probation before it is finally rejected or accepted. And just how tentative this new, indirectly acquired knowledge is obviously depends in part on how authoritative the source seems to the reader. Young readers are likely to sponge up uncritically the knowledge acquired both directly and indirectly through reading, while old and wary readers may make subtle distinctions according to the credibility of the sources of their information.

Connection and Rhetorical Analysis

If a reader's expectations about the kinds of connections that can link sentences are a firm part of the linguistic knowledge that enables comprehension, we can use these expectations to facilitate other kinds of textual analysis. In particular, we can see how the relations can operate between units larger than the sentence or clause, how certain rhetorical effects are achieved, and how the paragraph break is used. Finally, an awareness of the function of relations and the process of reading backwards has implications for the quality of reading material our elementary and high school students receive.

In particular, can the sentence-to-sentence relations help us describe how a text may be organized as it is read? Here we can try to see the relations operating on different levels in the way that Grimes, Christensen, and many others have. Can readers create groups of clauses and see these as related to other groups of clauses or single clauses using the same repertoire of connections that tie individual clauses?

To go back to a point made earlier, some relations can be described as more disruptive or "surprising" while other connections are more predictable and therefore usually more readily comprehended (Fahnestock 405). A restatement, for example, another version of a statement reinforcing by near repetition the point made in a previous clause, will be readily assimilable and not surprising. Thus a statement and its restatement can be taken as a unit. We can say the same about a statement-premise or statement-conclusion pair; their residual effect is that of a single reinforced statement. The same may be true of comparisons or additions in a predicted series. We can see how clauses tied by these relations can become units of meaning, ready in turn to be related to other units, perhaps more distinctly marked by the author. But the relations described as negatives do not invite the combination of sentences into a single meaning unit. Instead, they emphasize the break between sentences and draw the reader's attention to a discontinuity, a turn, and perhaps the formation of a new unit. We can see how this combination of units takes place by looking at a short paragraph.

> (1) When the complementary chromosomes of the mother and father line up in the sex cells of their offspring, they routinely recombine. (2) Groups of genes from the mother's chromosome will exchange places with similar groups of genes from the father's chromosome. (3) Sometimes, however, errors are made. (4) Pieces of DNA may be lost or duplicated or uselessly scrambled. (Chedd 55)

This sequence of four sentences simply says two things and says each twice. The first two sentences can be described as a statement followed by a restatement: genes recombine; in other words, they exchange places. The reader registers this process and the implication (perhaps created by the restatement) that that is the way things normally proceed. But now the writer wants to deny the implication that things always proceed normally, and to do so the author must use a transition word: *but* sometimes errors occur; (followed by another clarifying restatement) *in other words,* pieces of the gene, DNA, may be lost. This sequence of four sentences, then, breaks into two units around the transition word "but." A model of paired semantic relations helps us detect this scheme of arrangement. And this process of organizing units of meaning by using the same relations over and over can continue at the paragraph level, at the level of major divisions in the text, and even on up to where the reader schematizes the overall form of the piece from the relationships among its largest units.

An analysis of text structure based on using the same relations at different levels seems to violate the distinction made earlier between linear and global coherence (and the related distinction between top-down and bottom-up processing) by suggesting that the overall meaning of a text can be built up from connections between individual sentences. No such suggestion is intended. Instead, what I am focusing on here is simply the use of the same kinds of relations between larger blocks of text. The reader's perception of these connections or relations or functions between larger units is not necessarily constrained by the relations between small units down to immediately adjacent clauses. Indeed, how the local organization of a text influences the overall structure is, as Longacre recently observed, "one of the relatively unexplored areas of discourse structure" (xviii). When it is explored, I would only suggest that provision be made for the fact that readers can comprehend a piece without being familiar with the genre it belongs to (and hence the scheme of arrangement it follows), just as they can comprehend a text without a full complement of the background knowledge an author may have counted on.

With a model of the paired semantic relations in place, we can also make an attempt to describe the range of effects actually achieved by writers when they manipulate connections between sentences. Suppose we postulate first, for the sake of the model, that in their "natural" condition semantically linked sentences will use an explicit transition word. That will give us a text with transition words between every pair of independent or subordinate clauses. (There are real texts that come close to this model.) Such an overdetermination of meaning would reflect the writer's concern for the reader's ability to follow and may also be a subtle aid to reading backwards.

In the next phase, we can easily imagine a writer leaving out all the transition words that mark the more or less predictable semantic relations, relations which the writer assumes a competent reader can infer from context, be it co-text or background knowledge. Now we have a text that signals only the less predictable turns of thought with transition words like "but," "however," "although," "nevertheless," etc.

In the third phase, we can imagine that rhetorical effects come into play, and the writer may begin to put back those transition words which, so far as comprehension is concerned, could have been left out. They are put back for the sake of emphasis so that the writer can begin to achieve intonational effects. Now we have a text with the "negative" transition words in place and a few positives added for the sake of emphasis. The precise placement of any transition word is another "intonational" device left to the writer, as is the choice of which among several synonymous transition words and phrases to use. (Thus an initial "however" may achieve effects an initial "but" would not.)

In the fourth phase the author may also leave off certain "mandatory" transition words that normally flag for the reader the unexpected turns of thought. This is possible because other factors, including co-text, precise wording, punctuation, and even clause length help to produce the intonational pattern that puts emphasis where the usually necessary transition word would be. In order to see this effect working, we have to look at a slightly longer passage, in this case a paragraph taken from "The Validation of Continental Drift" by Stephen Jay Gould.

> (1) We now have a new, mobilist orthodoxy [plate tectonics], as definite and uncompromising as the staticism it replaced. (2) In its light the classical data for drift have been exhumed and proclaimed as proof positive. (3) Yet these data played no role in validating the notion of wandering continents; (4) drift triumphed only when it became the necessary consequence of a new theory. (166)

The second sentence follows the first here as a result follows its cause. In the logic of discovery that Gould has been at pains to establish, the data for continental drift are now proclaimed as proof *because* of a new theory and not vice versa. Next in sequence comes the unexpected reversal marked by "yet"; normally we expect that data or evidence precede theory, yet these data did not, a surprising reversal that is marked. The next and very last clause can be seen (in the particular scheme I advocate) as a "replacement," a proposition which substitutes for a preceding proposition. This relation is in a sense "negative," the opposite of a restatement, and normally it would be signaled by "instead": "Yet these data played no role in validating the notion of wandering continents; *instead* drift triumphed only when it became the necessary consequence of a new theory." It is highly unlikely that any reader misunderstands the relation between these clauses when the "instead" is removed because the sentence patterning produces, in effect, an intonation that supplies the correct implication. The semicolon suggests a close tie of some kind. In fact, semicolons are often used between clauses related as statement-restatement or statement-replacement, and elsewhere in this particular article, Gould uses the same device—a semicolon followed by an unmarked replacement—twice. The sentence patterning as well—the immediate, unmodified subject-verb combination coming just after the semicolon— helps produce the emphasis that "marks" this relation intonationally. The reader is also likely to understand this relation without the transition word because, although it is a replacement for the immediately preceding clause, it simply restates the point of the opening two sentences, which in turn restate the point of Gould's whole article: data are inert without theory. Thus the paragraph closes by reiterating its own opening point, a not uncommon circularity in paragraphs.

A model of paired semantic relations also gives us a new way to look at paragraphing. Basically, the confusing accounts of paragraphing can be grouped into two camps: those who look for features of paragraphs and those who look for principles of paragraphing. Admittedly, these two approaches are not mutually exclusive, but those who look at features tend to think of paragraphs as isolated units with their own laws of development, while those who look at paragraphing start conceptually with a continuous stream of text and then ask why it is broken at certain points by paragraph indentations. Both approaches have their validity, but it is the latter question that I am asking here. In terms of the semantic relations, we can say that texts are frequently broken where no inferential connection is possible between immediately adjacent sentences—as in the following example:

> The need for scribes to learn Sumerian led to the preservation of much Sumerian literature by the schools; it also meant that an enormous number of lexical lists (word lists in the two languages) were compiled.
>
> Many cuneiform texts are very long, and it seems impossible to understand how so much could be accommodated on small lumps of clay. (Clapham 37)

We are used to calling such a break between paragraphs a change of topic, despite the inadequacy of definitions of "topic" to cover such subtle text divisions. It is easier instead to describe a paragraph break like the one above as the point where no inferential link between immediately adjacent sentences is to be made. The two sentences on both sides of the paragraph division in our example are tied by lexical collocation, nothing more. Here then we have a norm for purposes of a model: ideally paragraph divisions are placed wherever inferential links between immediately adjacent sentences are impossible. An inferential link may be made between the beginning of the new paragraph and a sentence earlier than the immediately preceding one. At any rate, a break between unconnected sentences leaves us in our model with paragraphs as units of text internally made of semantically linked sentences.

It is easy, however, to find texts where a semantic relation crosses the paragraph boundary. I cannot pretend to a statistical analysis of representative texts, but paragraph breaks at the point of the "negative" or discontinuous relations seem to be preferred. My evidence is the preference given to these points when students and fellow teachers paragraph what is presented to them as continuous text. Since the paragraph break is a tool for emphasis, creating stress on both the last sentence of the preceding paragraph and the first sentence of the next, a tendency to throw emphasis on the reversals represented by "but," "yet," etc. should come as no surprise. The paragraph can also be used to mark any of the relations, particularly if the newly emphasized first sentence of the second paragraph initiates its own chain of semantically linked sentences. When the paragraph break does come between semantically linked sentences, however, it is more likely that a transition word will mark the relation, whether positive or negative.

The importance of the semantic relations and reading backwards cannot be too heavily stressed when we consider "text" in its common signification as the book that students read in a class. The poverty of our elementary and high school texts has become a scandal of national proportions; students now read science or social studies texts that have been simplified into virtual gibberish in the name of formulaic readability. Authors are forced to shorten sentences and simplify vocabulary, and the result can be a series of cryptic predictions whose connections with one another are unclear. According to one school official, "'Because of the way readability formulas operate, you won't find the word 'because' in a standard K to 8 textbook series'" (Fiske).

If we realize that the process of learning from texts includes reading backwards from the clues deposited in part in the transition words, we can see that the danger from absurdly simplified textbooks is more than the danger of boring students with "lowest common denominator" content. Their very ability to learn the art of reading, forwards or backwards, is jeopardized in two ways. First, in order to learn the expected semantic relations in the first place, children have to read texts that mark the relations so they become familiar with them. Texts that leave out all the "becauses" are not going to teach connection. Although students may read more narratives in "unengineered" texts, an exclusive diet of narrative will probably not provide enough instances of relations like "premise," "exception," or "conclusion." Second, once students eventually pick up a working knowledge of the inferential relations possible between sentences, they should begin to practice reading backwards in more challenging texts that require them to puzzle out connections. In this way they will come to "revelations" while reading: "Oh, if the book says x then y must be true." Or, as they become more sophisticated, "Then y may possibly or probably be true."

Most discussions of cohesion, coherence, and planning seem to emphasize how much readers must already know before a text can be comprehended. They must know the particular subject matter, its general frame of reference in the world, and the specific genre of the piece being read. Of course no one can deny the substantial correctness of this position. But the characterization of the reader's work has gone so far that the text seems an inert substance in many accounts, almost an inconvenience in the reader's creation of meaning. Surely what we want to describe instead is the interaction of the two, how reading experiences condition the reader's mind so that in each fresh encounter with yet another text something of that previous experience informs the new experience, while at the same time the text cues the reader to what new knowledge to invoke. But descriptions of the art of reading sometimes go so far the other way that they can reach a position like that espoused by E. D. Hirsch. Frustrated by his inability to guarantee readability by the manipulation of text alone, he has turned to arguing that what we must do is improve our minds rather than our texts (165-169). Following the logic of Hirsch's position, the entire revision industry, based on the premise that texts can be made more comprehensible as well as readers more comprehending, can go out of business.

Ultimately the separation between mind and text seems to be based on a very limited notion of the relation between knowledge and language. Part of the knowledge a reader brings to a text may be physical knowledge—a memory of what it feels like to catch an invisible cobweb on a bare arm—but much of it is specifically linguistic knowledge, like learning to expect certain interclausal connections or accept the cueing of transition words when provided. Or it is knowledge that exists as the memory of other semantic webs. Language is knowledge, and the two cannot be so easily separated that knowledge—out there—is somehow brought to bear in the act of reading language—down here—on the page. Obviously what we want to understand is the interanimation, backwards and forwards, of the two. 🍎

NOTES

1 I am of course invoking the familiar notion of a cognitive "script" for frequently repeated actions (Schank and Abelson 40, 41, 67).

2 Both Joseph E. Grimes (272) and Robert E. Longacre (xvi) postulate an independent element in a speaker's language capacity for comprehending what they call respectively "cohesion markers" and "prediction combiners."

3 The unit of analysis in the identification of semantic relations or connections here is not the T-unit. Instead, independent and subordinate clauses are considered for connection but relative clauses are ignored. In a sense, I am interested only in what advances a passage "adverbially"; anything that can be embedded as the modifier of a noun is bypassed. Whole sentences can be embedded in preceding sentences, and these drop out of consideration when a chain of semantically linked sentences is constructed to represent a passage. I should also note that I am not concerned with inferential connections between sentences *per se* but rather with connections between the knowledge structures represented by the sentences.

4 As a rhetorician, my methodological preference is to find illustrations in real texts and not to work from artificially constructed examples.

5 By premise I mean what would be *either* data or warrant in the Toulmin model. In other words, the premise is the supporting half of an enthymeme.

6 An ingenious system for schematizing the relations between all

sentences in sequence, whether they are adverbially or adjectivally related to a preceding one has been put forward by Jerry R. Hobbs in "Why is Discourse Coherent?" and in "On the Coherence and Structure of Discourse." I wish to thank Professor Hobbs for allowing me to see copies of his papers.

7 See Willis Edmondson (12-13) for similar contextualizations of supposedly "ungrammatical" pairs of sentences. Edmondson makes the point that what is at issue is not "distinguishing 'text' from a 'non-text,' but distinguishing between coherent and non-coherent suprasentential stretches of language, and further that the critical issue is *interpretability as discourse*" (14).

WORKS CITED

Auron, Philip E., Kathryn J. Erdelsky, and Stephen R. Fahnestock. "Chemical Modification Studies of a Protein at the Peptidyltransferase Site of the *Bacillus stearothermophilus* Ribosome." *Journal of Biological Chemistry* 253 (1978): 689-693.

Bain, Alexander. *English Composition and Rhetoric. Part First: The Intellectual Elements of Style.* London: Longman, 1901.

Chedd, Graham. "Genetic Gibberish in the Code of Life." *Science 81* 2 (Nov. 1981): 54-59.

Clapham, Frances M., ed. *Ancient Civilizations.* New York: Warwick, 1978.

Clark, Herbert H., and Susan E. Haviland. "Comprehension and the Given-New Contract." *Discourse Production and Comprehension.* Ed. Roy O. Freedle. Norwood NJ: Ablex, 1977.

Dillon, George. *Constructing Texts: Elements of a Theory of Composition and Style.* Bloomington: Indiana UP, 1981.

Edmondson, Willis. *Spoken Discourse: A Model for Analysis.* London: Longman, 1981.

Fahnestock, Jeanne. "Semantic and Lexical Coherence." *College Composition and Communication* 34 (1983): 400-416.

Fiske, Edward B. "Quality of Textbooks is the Focus of Debate." *New York Times* 29 July 1984: 1.

Gould, Stephen Jay. *Ever Since Darwin.* New York: Norton, 1977.

Grimes, Joseph E. *The Thread of Discourse.* The Hague: Mouton, 1975.

Halliday, M. A. K., and R. Hasan. *Cohesion in English.* London: Longman, 1976.

Hirsch, E. D., Jr. "Cultural Literacy," *The American Scholar* XX (1984): 165-169.

Hobbs, Jerry R. "Why is Discourse Coherent?" *Technical Note 176, Stanford Research Institute.* Menlo Park: Stanford U, 1978.

——. "On the Coherence and Structure of Discourse." *The Structure of Discourse.* Ed. Livia Polanyi. Norwood NJ: Ablex, 1985.

Longacre, Robert E. *The Grammar of Discourse.* New York: Plenum, 1983.

Mandelbrot, Benoit. "Information Theory and Psycholinguistics." *Scientific Psychology: Principles and Approaches.* Eds. Benjamin Wolman and Ernest Nagel. New York: Basic, 1965.

Patent, Dorothy Hinshaw. *Evolution Goes on Every Day.* New York: Holiday, 1977.

Reinhart, Tanya. "Conditions for Text Coherence." *Poetics Today* 1 (1980): 163-172.

Schank, Roger C., and Robert P. Abelson. *Scripts, Plans, Goals and Understanding: An Inquiry into Human Knowledge Structures.* Hillsdale NJ: Erlbaum, 1977.

Scott, Fred N., and Joseph V. Denney. *Paragraph-Writing.* Boston: Allyn, 1895.

Sloan, Gary. "Transitions: Relationships Among T-Units." *College Composition and Communication* 34 (1983): 447-453.

Stotsky, Sandra. "Types of Lexical Cohesion in Expository Writing: Implications for Developing the Vocabulary of Academic Discourse." *College Composition and Communication* 34 (1983): 430-446.

Sullivan, Jack. *Elegant Nightmares: The English Ghost Story from LeFanu to Blackwood.* Athens: Ohio UP, 1978.

Thomson, Patricia. *George Sand and the Victorians.* New York: Columbia UP, 1977.

van Dijk, Teun. *Macrostructures: An Interdisciplinary Study of Global Structures in Discourse, Interaction, and Cognition.* Hillsdale, NJ: Erlbaum, 1980.

Warner, William. *Beautiful Swimmers.* New York: Penguin, 1983.

Warren, William H., David W. Nicholas, and Tom Trabasso. "Event Chains and Inferences in Understanding Narratives." *New Directions in Discourse Processing.* Ed. Roy O. Freedle. Norwood, NJ: Ablex, 1979.

Whitney, John. "Basic Assembler." *Nibble: The Reference for Apple Computing* 5 (1984): 17-20.

Winterowd, W. Ross. "The Grammar of Coherence." *College English* 31 (1970): 828-835.

❦ 12

Toward Improving Models of Writers: Searching for Models of Audience

V. Melissa Holland

Technical documents that communicate effectively are notoriously hard to create (Duffy; GAO; Lewis and Mack). Traditional solutions to this problem treat only the product. Text design guidelines usually address sentence structure, paragraph organization, graphical format, and other formal features of text (Felker et al.; Hartley; Kieras *Computerized Readability*). Although these guidelines are empirically derived from studies of how text features affect readers' memory and performance, it is unclear how well they work when writers attempt to apply them.

We can look at the adequacy of text design guidelines from two angles: First, how effective is naturally produced text that follows these guidelines? Second, what are the consequences of violating these guidelines?

We can answer the first question by examining a type of text whose effectiveness is relatively easy to measure—that is, a text that gives instructions for carrying out procedural tasks, such as operating a computer or assembling an object from parts. Tests of instructions produced by professional writers, even writers knowledgeable about design guidelines, reveal surprising flaws (Holland, Rose, Dean, and Dory; Kieras "Reading"; Lewis and Mack). Users of the instructions make many errors and may not even complete the procedure. However, when these instructions are examined as text, they not only appear factually accurate (they do not present wrong information about the task), but they also conform to empirically derived guidelines (with short sentences, informative headings, goal statements, and other prescribed features). Their deficiency appears to lie in a more elusive aspect: they fail to present all the information that users need.

Two examples of instructional texts will illustrate. One involves a set of sign-on instructions for new users of a computer, described by C. Lewis and R. Mack. The instructions said to type an assigned password and then to press the RETURN key, but they did not specify where the RETURN key was. A typical user inferred that she should type out the word "return," a response that prevented her from signing on. A second example involves assembly instructions for a model car, described by V. M. Holland et al. One set of instructions began, "Form the chassis by selecting the large flat piece with notches on either side." This description happened to fit two different pieces, one square and one oblong. About half the users chose the wrong piece, building a misshapen frame and nonfunctional car.

In both examples, the writers of the instructions knew the procedure and wrote skillfully in terms of document design criteria, but they produced ineffective instructions by inadvertently omitting information needed by the reader. Thus, in the first example, inserting information about the RETURN key (e.g., it is on the right of the keyboard and is labeled with a bent arrow) might have resolved the ambiguity. In the second example, elaborating the description with a phrase like "the piece that is longer than it is wide" might have clarified the reference. In fact, when that specification was added to the instructions, readers consistently chose the right piece.

The same phenomenon was demonstrated by K. A. Schriver for articles in *Scientific American*. The kinds of flaws that most hindered readers in her study, but were least visible to writers, were information gaps: missing examples, ambiguous titles, undefined terms ("laser-illuminated"), and cryptic analogies ("holography is like photography"). As Schriver noted, writers revising such texts dealt better with "what was on the page . . . [than with] what was not on the page."

In addition to **insufficient information,**[1] other informational flaws can also create difficulty. Procedural instructions sometimes contain **too much information**, and the depth of detail confuses readers (Holland et al.). Procedural instructions sometimes even have the **wrong kind of information**. L. M. Reder, D. H. Charney, and K. I. Morgan as well as M. Nystrand found that the effectiveness of different kinds of elaboration varied not only with the task but with the reader's expertise.

Informational variables of the sort described above are not addressed by guidelines for text design, which are inherently limited to issues of form. Content, however, is situation-specific and eludes capture by general rules (Lyons; Nystrand).

Thus, missing or inappropriate information might be considered theoretically trivial by producers of guidelines because there are no ready theories of context to motivate guidelines. A content guideline might be, "Describe each piece in an assembly task so that it cannot be confused with other pieces," as implementable through the more specific rule, "For pieces to be selected from an assortment of abstract-shaped, three-dimensional objects, describe the desired piece on all three dimensions." But we don't see many writing rules of this sort because content can vary infinitely in texts.

Rather than in content, document design is grounded in form-based theories of syntax and text structure—features common across a range of text content. And it draws on psychological theories of reading, which address letter recognition, lexical access, and construction of semantic representations. Neither set of theories considers how readers relate representations to a referential domain in order to comprehend it or to act on its objects. Although some psychological research is exploring readers' representations of content in terms of memory structures like schemas and scripts, it usually explores the structures of canonical events—social exchanges, such as what to do in a restaurant—rather than the physical configurations readers encounter in carrying out procedural instructions. Again, the difficulty lies in the huge number of world and text variables that have to be manipulated to gather relevant observations. To be useful, such theories would have to explore how informational arrays in text influence readers' perceptions, interpretations, and actions. Thus, neither text-design guidelines nor the theories underlying them address the content issues needed to explain or help with readers' informational difficulties. Simply requiring instructions to conform to these guidelines does not guarantee success.

A second perspective on the adequacy of design guidelines concerns the practical consequences of text that violates them. The formal features targeted by guidelines, such as sentence structure and line length, have the expected effects on reading speed and memory when tested experimentally. But when analyzed across studies, these effects account only slightly for the observed variance in reading performance, a phenomenon attesting to the "robustness of the reading process" in the face of text-feature manipulations (Kieras, "Reading in Order"). In authentic instructions, moreover, the adequacy of the content consistently swamps the effect of such stylistic variations on measures like accuracy and completeness of task performance (Foley). It appears that adult readers can negotiate cluttered layout, awkward syntax, and inefficient sequence to extract core content with only small losses in reading time.

In summary, violations of traditional design guidelines, derived from data on how readers deal with form, appear to account for few of the significant problems in naturally occurring technical text. Design guidelines ignore the pervasive problem of what kind and how much information to specify. Clearly, writers have difficulty solving this problem, and the consequences for readers are crippling.

An alternative approach is to consider the problem from the perspective of the writing process. We look at the writer, rather than at the text or the reader, because writing processes are potentially general and generative. That is, a small set of maladaptive processes might underlie a host of specific informational deficiencies.

What aspects of the writing process are implicated? Intuitively, it is easy to understand why writers leave information gaps. A writer who already knows the material does not think of everything a reader might not know. How the writer considers the reader is clearly key. Manuals for functional writing give voice to this intuition when they advise writers to "start by analyzing the audience," "avoid ambiguity," and "provide readers with information that meets their needs." However, this advice is too vague to tell writers what kind of information or how much of it to include. If writers draw on a deficient model of audience as they write, practical guidebooks say little about what should go into such a model.

Theories of writing are potentially more specific. Cognitive theories provide research-based models of the mental processes involved in writing, and much of the research emphasizes how the writer thinks about the reader. For example, expert writers tend to refer to audience more often than novice writers do when composing (Berkenkotter; Flower). Outside of writing, theories of talking and tutoring may also be relevant. They treat selection of information as a general problem of communication—a problem of creating and refining the content of a discourse or lesson. Cognitive science shapes these theories into explicit models of natural language generation and of intelligent tutoring.

These three fields may shed light on how technical writers use considerations of audience to select information: first, cognitive models of writing; second, models of natural language generation; and third, systems for intelligent tutoring. This paper will probe that potential. How do theories in these three fields explain competence in communicating information? What does each reveal about the nature and use of knowledge about audience in this communication? How do these accounts complement each other? What can they contribute to helping writers of instructions better accommodate readers? The obvious place to seek an account of how writers select information is in cognitive models of writing. Two sets of models are representative: the Hayes and Flower model and the McCutchen model.

The Hayes and Flower Process Models

J. R. Hayes and L. S. Flower ("Identifying"; Hayes, Flower, Schriver, Stratman, and Carey) have identified basic mental processes in composing and revising and have developed descriptive models of how these processes are organized. One model breaks the overall process into the following components: planning (setting goals and generating ideas), translating (producing text), and reviewing (rereading and editing). Based on evidence from think-aloud protocols, the model depicts these processes as goal-driven and recursive, controlled by a higher-level monitor. Thus, one process may interrupt another as cycles of planning and translating may occur within reviewing, or reviewing may be embedded in planning.

This framework is useful for capturing differences in how expert and novice writers order the processes of composing. For example, experts engage in more extensive monitoring, ordering their processes hierarchically. They plan more and revise continually and cyclically. They may postpone consideration of some types of goals, such as grammatical refinement, for later cycles of review. Novices are less systematic, planning less and revising less. They appear to lack strategies for setting goals and allocating attention over the course of composing. Thus, their processes are more linear, more subject to external control by text or topic. Similar kinds of differences are illustrated in a model of revising. Hayes et al. find that experts make global plans, surveying and subdividing the revising task and working on subtasks separately. Novices display less flexibility and control over planning, editing at superficial text levels and considering faults in the order they appear in the text.

Thus, process models reflect the global structure of composing and revising and the strategies for planning and managing those processes. But they do not address questions of information selection: how writers invent content in composing and how they diagnose faults in revising.

In focusing on internal control mechanisms and strategic organization, the Hayes and Flower models isolate process from text and reader and thus cannot handle content problems. This focus is deliberate. Flower and Hayes adopt what they call a "rhetorical perspective" as opposed to a "linguistic perspective" (e.g., Matsuhashi), that would yoke process to text. Although Hayes and Flower's rhetorical perspective references rhetorical goals and audience needs, it tends to treat writing as an abstract mental process parallel to problem-solving in formal domains. In addition, this perspective tends to overlook local choice points in a text where information selection often occurs. As noted in one study (Holland et al.), strategic differences in planning and managing writing may be irrelevant to writers' effectiveness in determining readers' needs for information at particular locations in the text. In that study, writers who plunged into instruction writing with little or no planning were as effective as those who planned extensively. Viewing writing as a flow of problem-solving processes may contribute little to understanding the question of concern here, which is writers' difficulty with selecting information in technical text.

McCutchen's Dual Component Model

The linguistic perspective rejected by Flower and Hayes can be found in a cognitive model of writing developed by D. McCutchen, who embeds Hayes and Flower's composing processes in a description of the writer's knowledge, as schematized in Figure 1.

This knowledge consists of a high-level **planning component**, following Hayes and Flower, which monitors strategy, coordinates processes, and chooses discourse schemas. Subordinate to this component is a **discourse component**, with linguistic knowledge in the form of sentence generation procedures and discourse schemas. Parallel to this component is a **content component**, with domain knowledge in the form of networks of concepts with labeled links that match those in the discourse schemas.

Figure 1. *A Model of the Writer: Integration of Hayes and Flower's Planning Component with McCutchen's Knowledge Components*

PLANNING COMPONENT

DISCOURSE COMPONENT ⟶ CONTENT COMPONENT

In McCutchen's scheme, a writer's goal (e.g., to write an essay) stimulates the planning component to select a relevant schema from the discourse component. The discourse component then activates content knowledge relevant to the writing topic (e.g., an essay on baseball). Content knowledge is then retrieved and restructured by insertion into the pre-existing discourse schema. McCutchen offers developmental evidence that the content and discourse components develop independently and contribute separately to the quality of writing. For example, the content component is largely responsible for the writer's ability to elaborate a topic, the discourse component for maintaining coherence between elaborations.

Still, McCutchen's account of how writers select information remains incomplete. Two texts can fill a given discourse schema equally well but vary widely in informational adequacy. Thus, a schema for instructions would include slots for steps linked in correct sequence. The writer could fill the slots with procedural knowledge, creating a correct and coherent text that is still unfinished, because the discourse schema does not specify the categories of information or the level of detail for each step. These specifications must grow out of the communicative context, including the reader's goals, situational constraints, and likely misunderstandings. McCutchen's model lacks a notion of how developing writers' growing awareness of audience helps to structure information.

The elaboration and coherence measures that McCutchen takes from essays are relatively autonomous aspects of text that an external judge can assess. Information, however, can be assessed only by reference to the reader's task. Like the Hayes and Flower model, the McCutchen model treats text more as an output of abstract problem-solving processes than as an ongoing transaction with readers. Thus, neither model raises the issue of information selection. While both models posit "knowledge of audience" as a major contribution to writing, neither model says what that knowledge consists of or how it comes into play in writing. This view of writing as cognitive process can be complemented by the view of writing as discourse implicit in some models of natural language generation.

Models of Natural Language Generation

Research on natural language generation applies methods of artificial intelligence to build computational models of the rules governing sentence and discourse production—rules assumed to describe the competence of language users. If fully captured, these rules could automatically generate coherent and sensible text. Because these rules are stated explicitly, they can be inspected, compared, and tested on a computer. This approach complements cognitive models, much as models of competence complement models of performance. An example of this approach, K. R. McKeown's model of connected discourse, explains textual form partly in terms of the interactive principles that link reader and writer as participants in a discourse.

McKeown's model of text generation seeks not only to derive the lexico-syntactic form of sentences but also to explain how content is selected and ordered in paragraphs. This model is broadly consistent with that of McCutchen: both models assume that content and discourse knowledge contribute independently to the form of the text produced, that content knowledge consists of concept nodes with labeled links like cause-effect, and that content knowledge is selected to fit a discourse frame. But McKeown's knowledge representations go beyond the cognitive model and describe precisely the structure and function of the discourse component. Her description can be integrated into our evolving model of the writer as shown in Figure 2.

In McKeown's account, discourse knowledge consists of strategy and tactics. The strategic component contains discourse schemas and focus rules. Discourse schemas are standard patterns of propositional relationships, typically realized in paragraph form, used to achieve particular discourse goals, like defining something or comparing one thing with another.

Analyzing naturally occurring paragraphs, McKeown formally describes schemas for several discourse goals. Labeled slots in the schemas represent relationships between propositions such as attribution, analogy, and contrast. Thus, instead of a global essay schema, McKeown's

Figure 2. *A Model of the Writer: Integration of McKeown's Discourse Rules*

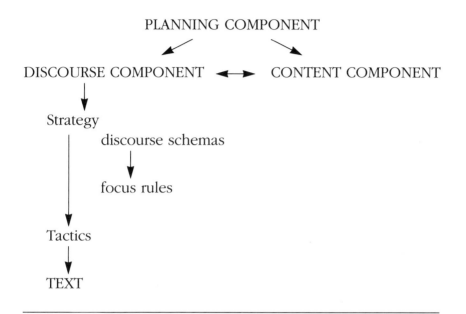

account proposes a specific essay strategy such as definition or compare-and-contrast. While discourse schemas determine what to say, focus rules determine when to say it. Focus rules constrain topical shifts between sentences or propositions and prevent a text from jumping sporadically between topics. Together, schemas and focus rules provide a kind of grammar of the prototypical paragraph—the constraints on selecting and ordering propositional relationships and rendering the text cohesive. Operating on this grammar, the tactics component contains syntactic and lexical rules that determine how propositions are to be phrased.

The components of the text-generation model interrelate as follows. The writer starts with a rhetorical goal, such as answering a question: "What is a frigate?" or "What is the difference between a frigate and a steamer?" Stimulated by the rhetorical goal, the content component activates propositions in the knowledge base relevant to the question topic ("frigate" and "steamer"). The discourse component then activates a schema appropriate to the goal: "What is a frigate?" → definitional schema; "What is the difference between a frigate and a steamer?" →

Figure 3. *A Model of the Writer: Integration of a Model of the Reader*

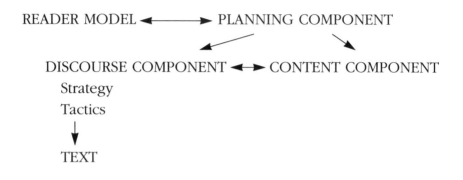

READER MODEL ◄───────► PLANNING COMPONENT

DISCOURSE COMPONENT ◄──► CONTENT COMPONENT
Strategy
Tactics
↓
TEXT

compare-and-contrast schema. To answer the second question, a compare-and-contrast schema would pull from content knowledge just those features about frigates that contrast with steamers. The output of the model at this point consists of an abstract text base—that is, a series of connected propositions. After focus rules are applied, the tactics component converts propositions and focus markers into words.

McKeown has tested this model by running it on a computer. The ultimate test is whether it yields discourse. While it can produce garden-variety paragraphs, McKeown acknowledges that the model fails the test. At issue are, first, the final selection of propositional relationships (what to do when the schema offers a choice) and, second, the depth of propositional recursion (when recursion is necessary). This second issue concerns the appropriate level of detail, for example, the problem of how many attributes are required to identify a concept unambiguously. The missing ingredient—the "test for recursion"—is, according to McKeown, "an assessment of the user's knowledge." In other words, how much the writer says is determined by what he or she thinks the reader already knows. Echoing our conclusions about the cognitive models, McKeown notes that "in order to develop a comprehensive theory [of text generation] . . . a full-scale user model must be developed" (39).

A model of the user or reader such as that sought by McKeown might fit into our evolving model of the writer as shown in Figure 3. McKeown leaves the development of such a model to future research in natural language generation. However, another field of artificial intelligence is already engaged in developing models of audience: research on intelligent tutoring systems.

Systems for Intelligent Tutoring

A natural place to seek audience models is in accounts of the knowledge involved in teaching. Detailed representations of this knowledge can be found in work on intelligent tutoring systems (ITS) (e.g., Clancey; Psotka, Massey, and Mutter; Sleeman and Brown; White and Frederiksen).

These systems stand as alternatives to simple computer-based training, which presents instructional frames and test questions, records the learner's response, and delivers immediate feedback. This feedback may branch the learner to a remedial frame triggered by an errant response. But frame-based programs present canned segments of instruction and use only a few predefined answer choices to categorize learners' responses. They also tie remediation to single questions rather than drawing inferences about learners' misconceptions based on patterns of response.

Tutoring that is coherent and individually tailored requires more sophisticated representations of the learner and of the knowledge to be taught, as attempted in the design of tutoring systems through artificial intelligence methods. What is the relevance of these systems to the concerns of instruction writers? Can the insights and issues coming out of ITS help in understanding the writer's problem of selecting information?

Relevance of ITS to writing. As a process of selecting and sequencing content in the service of clear description and explanation, teaching is fundamentally like writing. Indeed, there are striking parallels between the architecture of ITS and the requirements of a writer model as outlined above. In particular, ITS rely on explicit models of the audience or student, and student modeling is a central issue in developing these systems.

The following components are common to ITS: first, a higher level monitor to plan and control processes; second, an expert system, which encodes content knowledge for the domain to be taught; third, pedagogical knowledge, including strategies for how to organize teaching topics and tactics for how to illustrate points, when to interrupt, what feedback to give; fourth, a student model, which covers the student's knowledge and reasoning process. The correspondence between these components and those of the writer model are shown in Table 1.

Thus, pedagogical strategies parallel rhetorical strategies—both deal

Table 1. *Structural Correspondence between Intelligent Tutoring System and Model of Instruction Writer*

Intelligent Tutoring System	Instruction Writer Model
Planning Component	Planning Component
Content Knowledge	Content Knowledge
Pedagogical Knowledge	Rhetorical/Discourse Knowledge
Student Model	Reader/User Model
(knowledge, process)	(knowledge, process)

with what to say, when, and how. Similarly, the tutor's model of the student parallels the writer's model of the reader—both are aimed at anticipating audience response.

Structure of ITS. The components of ITS are formally defined and computationally represented. Their design can be run on a computer, producing inspectable teaching protocols and outcomes. Content knowledge may be formally represented as a system of if-then or condition-action rules defined in terms of when they apply and what they do (Anderson). This kind of representation is common for domains of procedural skill such as arithmetic. For factual or declarative domains, like medical diagnosis or meteorology, expert knowledge can be a network of concepts or propositions connected by cause-effect and other relations, as in McCutcheon's and McKeown's frameworks. In ITS, this network may be more or less "articulated" in terms of first principles—beliefs about laws of logic and physical phenomena that warrant facts and give rise to connections (Wenger). For example, knowledge can be articulated by encoding causal or teleological justifications for domain events.

Knowledge in the student model is often represented as a subset or overlay of the expert's content knowledge, using the same formalisms. The student model also represents procedures for operating on knowledge—rules for reasoning, making inferences, solving problems, drawing conclusions. These rules are usually domain-independent and designed to capture reasoning processes revealed in studies of learners. The formal description of the student's knowledge must also include general psychological principles for interpreting and integrating new information, such as forming analogies. Finally, the model ideally incorporates perceptual and memory constraints for the effective presentation of material, like the number of distinctions a learner is assumed to be able to assimilate at once. The representation of basic cognitive principles and constraints constitutes a kind of tutor's theory of learning.

These structural components support critical ITS functions. Representing content knowledge as a system of rules or linked concepts allows knowledge to be decomposed into primitive skill or conceptual units. This decomposition permits knowledge to be reorganized into learnable form for a novice. Indeed, a contemporary issue in ITS development concerns characteristics of knowledge that make it communicable, for example, the requirement for articulation imposed by the need to explain (Wenger).

In the same way, the structure of the student model supports adaptation of pedagogical action to the learner's changing cognitive needs. To grasp the complexity of this enterprise, consider systems with rudimentary audience models, such as the typical intelligent help system designed to answer computer users' requests for guidance or clarification.

The help system employs templates to profile stereotypical computer users, such as stock market executives or beginning statisticians. The templates are completed with empirically derived lists of features relevant to choices like vocabulary and presentational mode. For example, a user template might include a word list with each word tagged with an estimate of the probability that it will be familiar to the user. Also listed might be the user's preferred styles of presentation—visual or auditory, graph or pie chart. But the established preferences and lexical probabilities are inflexibly linked to a limited set of design choices. There are no explanatory principles, no anticipation of the user's needs, no generalization beyond the fixed triggering of a given design feature by a given template feature.

For ITS, the situation is more complex. To select and adapt instruction, the tutor must anticipate what the student is likely to understand and misunderstand. This anticipation, in turn, requires forming and testing hypotheses about the knowledge base the student is constructing. It is helpful to characterize this knowledge base as a subset of expert knowledge in order to highlight where to concentrate instruction, that is, on elements of knowledge outside the overlay. But tailoring effective instruction requires structuring the knowledge to be taught as a genetic graph, depicting a kind of natural hierarchy of learning. While this hierarchy could be built into ITS by a human designer, some designers attempt to encode the principles for deriving hierarchies (Wenger). A system that encodes such principles has a resident epistemology that can forecast the states of knowledge learners pass through, and on that basis, it can organize knowledge for teaching.

Moreover, intelligent presentations do not rely on canned chunks of instruction; rather, they adjust instruction moment by moment to the student's errors and misconceptions. To enable diagnosis and anticipation of errors and misconceptions, the system traces the student's evolving knowledge by applying a representation of reasoning and learning rules to a description of the student's current knowledge, then calculating the changes in knowledge that the new information is expected to produce. The system can verify a hypothesized knowledge state by calculating the responses, errors, and questions predicted to result from it and comparing these predictions with observations.

To help with error diagnosis and to focus remediation at the right level, some ITS have *a priori* accounts of errors—how they manifest themselves and where they originate, such as deviant rules or "bugs," broad misconceptions, or faulty planning (Brown and Burton). For example, systems may be equipped with a catalog of bugs compiled from studies of real students. These systems usually fall short because they cannot predict or account for new bugs. Moreover, referring a user's errors to a list does not rationally explain their cause or tell how to correct them. While a detected bug may set off prestored remedial actions, those actions are not necessarily linked to the level at which they are needed. As an alternative to bug catalogs, some systems employ a generative theory that explains how bugs arise from underlying misconceptions or from combinations of primitive units of action or from incomplete plans. Remediation is then aimed at the diagnosed source. Instead of merely correcting an error, the tutor may need to address the underlying goals in the student's plan for problem solving.

In summary, intelligent tutoring systems diagnose interactively, tracing observed student errors back to hypothesized sources and predicting further errors and responses based on these hypotheses. Unlike intelligent tutoring systems—and unlike real tutors—writers lack direct access to readers' ongoing responses, so they cannot empirically match observed with hypothesized problems. In fact, the writing process reverses the diagnostic process. Writers must predict misinterpretations and errors from what they already know of the audience, and they revise text based solely on these predictions. Still, both reader models and student models are detailed enough to allow anticipation of responses, errors, and questions, so we can expect instructive parallels between them.

Contributions of the Tutoring Analogy to a Model of the Instruction Writer

What do the aspects of tutoring revealed in these formal models contribute to understanding instruction writing—in particular, to understanding writers' skill in selecting information? Arguably, a writer has a theory of reading and understanding, just as a tutor has a theory of learning and knowing. By this assumption, a writer's model of the reader would represent the reader's relevant knowledge as well as processes for operating on text to derive semantic interpretations. These processes would include procedures for parsing text, extracting propositions, drawing inferences from prior knowledge, constructing a connected text base, and isolating referents—basic components of reading identified in cognitive studies (Kintsch and van Dijk). Moreover, a writer's theory of reading would include general cognitive and memory principles that constrain processes. In addition, the writer's model of the reader would also include rules for forming a plan of action from the semantically interpreted text and for executing the plan. Thus, both writers and tutors can be assumed to model the rules by which the reader/student uses prior knowledge to operate on text/instruction in acquiring and acting on information.

Thus, just as the tutor tracks the student's knowledge and goals, so the writer can be seen as continually monitoring the imagined reader's construction of the emerging text. The writer does this by applying rules to text in order to calculate the reader's interpretations, just as the tutor applies rules to instructional sequences to calculate changes in student knowledge. It is precisely in this way, the model suggests, that writers assess informational sufficiency while developing a draft. For example, having composed or planned a segment of procedural text, the writer projects possible responses based on assumptions about how instruction users interpret text. The projected responses—understanding, confusion, error—are used to select or shape the presentation. The writer who anticipates confusion may add, delete, or change information, using tactics drawn from discourse knowledge to repair ambiguities..

The picture that comes into focus shows a writer engaged in active, minute manipulation of information, simulating a reader's manipulation; it shows a writer who constructs solutions instead of using canned solutions to informational problems encountered during composing. This ongoing modeling of a reader steps beyond the global audience analysis taught in technical writing manuals. Audience analyses list global characteristics like reading level, age, interests, vocation, role in the organization—dimensions likely to be rhetorically relevant but not sufficiently operationalized to participate in local text decisions. What evidence is there that writers do the dynamic simulation and on-the-spot adjustment suggested by the tutoring analogy?

Think-aloud protocols from a study of instruction writing (Holland et. al.) suggest that effective writers often assess local choices of content by anticipating the user. In the following excerpt, a writer of assembly instructions is developing a description of two pieces to serve as wheels:

> So I've said "pick out the two small, round pieces with a hole in the middle that resemble buttons." But now that I'm looking at this, somebody could think those pieces for the axle look like buttons. I don't know. Plus if they pick out those axle pieces, they'd find that they fit, so they'd think they made the right guess. So I better go back and say "the pieces that resemble buttons or a pillbox hat, with a steep rim."

This writer, who produced successful instructions, appears to be engaged in a kind of internalized testing of the text by reference to the predicted responses of a reader. As with tutoring, these predictions form a continuing basis for selection of content and level of detail. This internalized reader testing is to be distinguished from blind role-play of the reader, which as Flower and Hayes have noted is not evidenced in mature writers' verbalizations. Rather, reader testing is a selective simulation that appears to be deliberately deployed to assess informational adequacy at critical choice points in the developing draft.

This excerpt also supports the hypothesized components of a reader model. The writer can be seen first presupposing the reader's text base (the reader is assumed to have encoded the description of "small round pieces"); second, constructing the action plan (the reader is seen as surveying task objects and finding extraneous pieces that match the description); and third, simulating the execution of the plan (the reader is seen as trying these pieces and finding that they fit). Moreover, the writer uses explicit representations of the reader's relevant knowledge (the reader knows nothing about this task but knows what buttons look like—an import from another domain) and of the reader's processes (the reader maps piece descriptors to the entire array of task objects).

Evidence of internalized reader testing appears in the text of procedural instructions as well. For example, the writer who inserts a "be sure not to. . ." warning has anticipated a specific action by the reader. Thus, the data suggest that the writer generates informational arrays, tests them against the reader's imagined response, and uses the results locally to select or refine information.

To support internalized reader testing, the reader model must be detailed, dynamic, and flexible enough to enable prediction of reader reaction to ever-changing presentations. Data from the assembly study indicate that the reader model and the constructions it supports can reflect enormous cognitive detail. Instruction writers in that study could anticipate readers' alternative sentence parses and propositionally based misinterpretations. However, this capability does not mean that reader modeling is coldly algorithmic, exhaustively generating the reader's derivations of each text proposition. Instead, the writer can be seen as following the ITS precedent, adopting heuristics to identify and focus on uncertain or task-critical chunks of information. Also likely to enter the reader model are general cognitive constraints like memory capacity as well as the meta-rules by which readers construct communicative frames: the reader's understanding of text conventions (the reader takes numbered steps to mean a sequence of actions), reading strategies (the reader will reread if a first reading is unclear), and contractual assumptions (the reader expects to see relevant information). Data from the assembly study further indicate that the procedural instruction writer represents the reader's processes for relating semantic interpretations to a physical task domain in order to perform actions. The reader model would thus include constraints on perception and action that allow the writer to estimate the reader's visual perspective and to block the prediction of implausible performance errors.

Like ITS, the writer's model of the reader could also include an account of reading "bugs"—typical misinterpretations readers make. We can reasonably hypothesize that this account is both generative, predicting bugs from a theory of how misreadings arise, and enumerative, cataloging bugs the writer has noticed and remembered or has pulled from guidelines.

Given these insights into how effective writers select information, what other benefits might come from the tutoring analogy and from attempts to articulate in detail the audience models writers are assumed to posit? One benefit would be to illuminate differences between effective and ineffective writers. In addition to the differences in rhetorical planning, problem definition, and monitoring strategies found by Hayes et al., writers may vary in the precision and elaboration of the audience model or in techniques for manipulating the model. For example, writers who cannot recognize ambiguity in their drafts may be anticipating audience at the wrong level. They may employ too gross a "grain size" in representing and decomposing knowledge, an error that is a demonstrated cause of failure in intelligent tutoring systems. Defining a structural root of writers' ineffectiveness could motivate testable solutions. It might also help explain the effectiveness of certain kinds of elaborations, based on the kinds of articulated knowledge discussed in ITS (Wenger). For example, the elaborated versions of Reder, Charney, and Morgan's computer operating instructions call on teleological justification to define procedural applications and on fine-grained decomposition to illustrate procedures. E. E. Smith and L. Goodman's effective instructions for electronic troubleshooting draw on causal justifications. Successful writers in the Holland et al. study describe assembly pieces with structural similes, evidence of articulation by integration.

A second benefit of explicit models of audience would be to characterize what writers learn from audience sensitization procedures. Studies by Schriver and Holland et al. demonstrate that technical writers can improve their texts when shown written protocols or videotapes of a reader who is voicing difficulties. Schriver's writers not only learned to write better but transferred their learning to new text genres. What these writers learned may be best describable in terms of structural features of a model of audience.

Summary

The three theoretical frameworks reviewed here—cognitive models of the composing process, artificial intelligence models of natural language generation, and intelligent tutoring systems—illuminate complementary aspects of technical writing competence. While the first two fields make many contributions, they say little about information selection because they say little about knowledge of audience. The fullest account of how knowledge might be organized and how the audience can be modeled to guide choices of content comes from intelligent tutoring systems. Advances in these systems suggest that information selection goes beyond the slot and filler models of McCutchen and McKeown to involve deep reorganization of domain knowledge and ongoing simulation of the processes by which readers or students operate on text or instructions. These suggestions draw support from studies of writers thinking aloud, and they stimulate hypotheses for further study. They can also motivate programs to assist instruction writers beyond the standard document-design guidelines.

By drawing explicit models of the reader analogous to the student models developed for tutoring systems, we may get a better grip on what is meant by "audience awareness" and "anticipating the reader." Explicit models may also reveal differences between more and less effective instruction writers. They may help define what writers learn when they learn to write better. We need precise, articulated models of audience in order to explain why readers' misunderstandings are understandable. ❦

NOTES

[1]The difficulties resulting from insufficient information have also been demonstrated with instructions produced in the lab, where categories of information are deliberately deleted (Bieger and Glock).

WORKS CITED

Anderson, J. R. *The Architecture of Cognition.* Cambridge: Harvard UP, 1983.

Berkenkotter, C. "Understanding a Writer's Awareness of Audience." *College Composition and Communication,* 4 (1981): 388-399.

Bieger, G. R., and M. D. Glock. *The Information Content of Picture-text Assembly Instructions.* (Technical Report No. 5). Ithaca: Cornell U Dept. of Education, 1981.

Brown, John Seely, and R. R. Burton. "Diagnostic models for procedural bugs in basic mathematical skills." *Cognitive Science 2* (1978): 155-191.

Clancey, W. J. *Knowledge-based Tutoring: The GUIDON Program.* Cambridge: MIT P, 1987.

Duffy, T. M. "Preparing Technical Manuals: Specifications and Guidelines." *The Technology of Text*. Ed. D. Jonassen. Vol. 2. Englewood Cliffs NJ: Educational Technology Publications, 1985.

Felker, D. B., F. Pickering, V. Charrow, V. M. Holland, and G. Redish. *Guidelines for Document Designers*. Washington: American Institutes for Research, 1981.

Flower, L. S. "Writer-based Prose: A Cognitive Basis for Problems in Writing." *College Composition and Communication* 41 (1981): 19-37.

Flower, L. S., and J. R. Hayes. "The Pregnant Pause: An Inquiry into the Nature of Planning. *Research in the Teaching of English* 15 (1981): 229-243.

Foley, J. P. *Description and Results of the Air Force Research and Development Program for the Improvement of Maintenance Efficiency*. (Report No. AFHRL-Tr-72-72). Brooks Air Force Base, TX: Air Force Human Resources Laboratory, 1973.

GAO. *Improved Management of Maintenance Manual Needed in Department of Defense*. (Report No. LCD-79-105). Washington: General Accounting Office, 1979.

Hartley, J. *Designing Instructional Text*. New York: Nichols, 1985.

Hayes, J. R., and L. S. Flower. "Identifying the Organization of Writing Processes." *Cognitive Processes in Writing*. Eds. L. W. Gregg and E. R. Steinberg. New York: Academic, 1980.

Hayes, J. R., L. S. Flower, K. Schriver, J. Stratman, and L. Carey. *Cognitive Processes in Revision*. (Technical Report No. 12). Pittsburgh: Carnegie-Mellon U Communications Design Center, 1985.

Holland, V. M., A. M. Rose, R. Dean, and S. Dory. *Processes Involved in Writing Procedural Instructions*. (ONR Final Report). Washington: American Institutes for Research, 1985.

Kieras, D. E. "Reading in Order to Operate Equipment." Paper presented at the 1984 meeting of the American Educational Research Association, New Orleans, LA.

———. *An Advanced Computerized Readability Editing System: Final Report*. (Report No. 22). Ann Arbor: U Michigan College of Engineering, 1985.

Kintsch, W., and T. A. van Dijk. "Toward a Model of Text Comprehension and Production." *Psychological Review* 85 (1978): 363-394.

Lewis, C., and R. Mack. *The Role of Abduction in Learning To Use a Computer System*. (Report No. 44388). Jackson Heights NY: IBM Watson Research Center, Computer Science Department, 1982.

Lyons, J. *Semantics One*. Cambridge: Cambridge UP, 1977.

Matsuhashi, A. "Explorations of the Real Time Production of Written Discourse." *What Writers Know: The Language, Process, and Structure of Written Discourse*. Ed. M. Nystrand. New York: Academic, 1982.

McCutchen, D. "Domain Knowledge and Linguistic Knowledge in the Development of Writing Ability." *Journal of Memory and Language* 25 (1986): 431-444.

McKeown, K. R. "Discourse Strategies for Generating Natural Language Text." *Artificial Intelligence* 27 (1985): 1-41.

Nystrand, M. *The Structure of Written Communication: Studies in Reciprocity between Writers and Readers*. New York: Academic, 1986.

Psotka, J., L. D. Massey, and S. A. Mutter. *Intelligent Tutoring Systems: Lessons Learned*. Hillsdale NJ: Erlbaum, 1988.

Reder, L. M., D. H. Charney, and K. I. Morgan. "The Role of Elaborations in Learning a Skill from an Instructional Text." *Memory and Cognition* 14 (1986): 64-78.

Schriver, K. A. "Teaching Writers To Predict Readers' Comprehension Problems with Text." Paper presented at the 1986 meeting of the American Educational Research Association, San Francisco CA.

Sleeman, D., and Brown, J. S., eds. *Intelligent tutoring systems*. New York: Academic Press, 1982.

Smith, E. E., and L. Goodman. "Understanding Written Instructions: The Role of an Explanatory Schema." *Cognition and Instruction* 1 (1984): 359-396.

Tannen, D. "What's in a Frame? Surface Evidence for Underlying Expectations." *New Directions in Discourse Processing*. Vol. 1. Ed. R. O. Freedle. Norwood NJ: Ablex, 1979.

Wenger, E. *Artificial Intelligence and Tutoring Systems: Computational and Cognitive Approaches to the Communication of Knowledge*. Los Altos CA: Morgan Kaufman, 1987.

White, B. Y., and J. R. Frederiksen. *Progressions of Qualitative Models as a Foundation for Intelligent Learning Environments*. (Technical Report No. 6277). Cambridge: Bolt, 1986.

❦ 13

Writers Meet Their Readers in the Classroom: Revising After Feedback

Barbara M. Sitko

The technique helped because I went back and listened to the comments on tape. I'd have two comments on the same paper, and I'd listen to them to see where I needed to make changes. When I used to talk to you and you told me something about a paper wasn't clear, I'd go back, and look at it. I thought I understood but when I looked at it, I didn't revise. It made sense to me. It sounded clear to me, I guess, because I wrote it. And I'd forget why it didn't sound clear to you. But when I had Darryl read it, I wanted him to read aloud because then I could tell if he didn't understand it. Like in one place he stumbled, and I thought, "you don't understand that paragraph; you don't understand that sentence." So I made changes at that point.

As Tanya, a freshman writer, talks with her teacher, we hear her describe a method of getting feedback that will be specified in this essay. Tanya's words raise important issues about revising after feedback. One important issue is the difficulty writers have detecting problems in their own texts. Tanya reports that she remembers from a teacher conference that there are unclear places in her text and that she knows where those places are. But later, when she attempts to revise, she finds that the text "sounds clear" and "makes sense" to her. At the point where she must make a decision about changing her text, she has only her own interpretation to guide that decision. Because at that point she sees no problem and remembers no specific difficulty, she takes no action. A second important issue raised by Tanya's words is the control she demonstrates over her method of seeking relevant information from a reader. As a writer, she has composed words that, so far as she can tell, meet her intention. But she needs to know whether that intention is met when someone else reads her words. So Tanya follows a method, asking her partner to read the text aloud so that she can observe clues to misunderstanding, such as stumbling or rereading. Given this information, she knows at what point to make changes.

Writers revise when they detect something "wrong" with their text (Flower, Hayes, Carey, Schriver, and Stratman). The detection may come from two sources. Writers might themselves notice problems such as errors or mismatches between their written texts and their intended versions. This kind of detection often occurs during a composing session while a writer is rereading text in progress (Flower and Hayes). Alternatively, writers may use the feedback of other readers to detect problems.

Feedback is useful, as Tanya suggests, because it helps writers to detect where other readers do not comprehend a text. Reading on their own, writers perceive the text as a series of clues to their intended meaning. Real text and intended text interact to form meaning for writers (Bartlett). Feedback, however, provides new information about a text and brings writers to a decision point. If feedback is functioning as intended, it should help writers improve their texts by alerting them to their readers' needs. Feedback should thus function to help writers develop the alternative perspective typical of another reader. It is this perspective that students often lack and that experienced writers demonstrate (Sommers).

Unfortunately, both instructional experience and research indicate that using feedback to help writers improve their texts is fraught with difficulty. Research with student writers indicates that they typically need more explicit information than feedback sometimes provides (Ziv). Students struggle to match comments to text (Hayes and Daiker), have difficulty maintaining authority in the face of suggested alternatives (Berkenkotter), and must decide among conflicting responses that arise from different types of readers (Newkirk). When interpreting the feedback becomes the problem to be solved, student writers' attention is diverted from the more important problem of revising the text.

When feedback is viewed in this way, a major educational task becomes how to devise a method by which students can get *useful* commentary that provides them with needed information without unduly diverting their attention. One possibility is to embed feedback firmly in instruction, providing a consistent focus (Hillocks). Another possibility is to provide commentary so explicit that writers are spared potential misinterpretation (Ziv). A third possibility is to educate the "reader" within the student writer (Murray). A fourth possibility is to arrive at a group consensus so that teacher and peer feedback are congruent (Freedman). This essay adds another method to this repertoire, one based on natural reading processes, that has the added advantage of being simple and accessible to student writers.

The method is grounded in theories that describe reading as a process of constructing meaning (Spivey). Readers do not passively receive information but rather fashion from the printed text a mental version into which they further incorporate ideas. The act of reading is thus dynamic and interactive. Reading comprehension is obviously influenced by the organization of the printed text, which functions to guide readers in this constructive process (Meyer). Comprehension depends, however, on the knowledge and expectations that readers bring to the text. It is obviously important for writers to understand how their words influence the varied interpretations of readers. But student writers normally have no experience in observing these processes. I hypothesized that given an opportunity to observe the processes of readers actively making meaning from their texts, students would use this information to revise.

In this essay I will describe two studies. The first, a protocol study, explores how more experienced and less experienced writers worked with ongoing reader feedback, what they paid attention to, whether they made changes based on the feedback, and what types of changes they made. The second study describes how the findings might be applied in a classroom. In both studies, the broad research question addresses how students revise their texts after observing readers' reactions.

Study One: How Writers Use Feedback

This study was designed to explore the activity of writers as they revise their own texts following feedback from members of their intended audience. The focus was not so much on visible changes made to texts as it was on the thinking and decision-making processes that writers engage in when confronted with readers' comments.

Thirteen participants—six experienced instructors of writing or professional writers and seven college freshmen enrolled in introductory composition—wrote a piece of advice to a twelfth-grade student having difficulty composing a college entrance essay. In the paper, they were asked to identify one problem that such a student might have and to suggest several strategies the student might use to solve the problem. Writers were given one hour to write their essays.

One week later the writers received a copy of their original essay to revise. The revision session consisted of three parts: writers made any initial changes they wished, then they read transcripts of readers' feedback, and finally they made additional changes. The initial revision was included for two reasons. First, pilot studies had indicated that writers wanted to read through their own texts before looking at the feedback and that during the course of this reading they spontaneously made changes to the draft. Second, because the purpose of the research was to link writers' revisions to feedback, I wanted to eliminate insofar as possible revisions in response to problems that writers detected on their own.

Following this initial revision, writers received the feedback of two twelfth-grade readers. The students had audiotaped their readings, which consisted of periodically summarizing the main point of the text and predicting what was likely to follow. This reading method was based on research (Olson, Duffy, and Mack; Stauffer; Vipond and Hunt) suggesting that good readers engage in these specific activities as they move through a text. Stauffer's Directed Reading and Thinking Activity, for example, is designed to engage students in interactive reading with the text. Of particular interest to this study was the "thinking" step in which students predict future text based on their ongoing interpretation.

In the transcripts, the readers' feedback was inserted into the writer's text in a smaller contrasting typeface at the locations where the readers had produced it. Thus the writers had specific information about their readers' constructive processes while they were reading. They saw an ongoing record of their readers' attempts to orient themselves within the text by making sense of the developing point and speculating about future development.

The following is an excerpt of the feedback transcript one writer received. The writer's text is printed in italics; the feedback is in boldface. In this example the reader is attempting to identify the main point of the paper.

> *A problem a student in 12th grade may have in writing an essay about a book that has influenced him is that the student may not see any connection or similarities between the topic of the book and himself.* **Which is a real problem. It must be the problem the writer will talk about. It probably goes on to say what to do in this case.** *A student may choose to react to the influence of an autobiography by Julius Irving, Dr. J. of the Philadelphia Seventy-Sixers.* **Which is not right because it went on to say that the student may react to the influence of an autobiography by Julius Irving? And I would not—I would never have guessed that to come next. The point of this then is probably going to be focussed around Julius Irving.**

After seeing the feedback of two readers, the writers revised their texts, recording think-aloud protocols (Ericsson and Simon). Writers were given approximately one hour to revise.

Analysis and Results

This study addressed how writers used feedback to revise. Writers chose whether to revise; and if they revised, they chose whether to refer to the feedback. Three writers, one experienced and two inexperienced, made no changes. The other ten writers made changes ranging from one word to several paragraphs. These writers tended to select one comment or cluster of comments referring to the same idea and to use it as the basis for revision. Not surprisingly, this "focal" comment often appeared at the end of the first paragraph, as the reader was summarizing the writer's main point and predicting the shape of the paper to come. Protocols provided evidence of what the writers were thinking about as they processed their readers' feedback and made a decision to revise. These ten episodes, one per writer, formed the data for the analysis.

An example of a revision episode from a protocol follows. Ellipses indicate elapsed time rather than elision. Normal typeface indicates the writer's oral response to the feedback; underlined italic indicates the writer's addition to the original text. No words were omitted.

> **Writer:** (reading feedback) **And I would not—I would never have guessed that to come next.** What was the matter with that? (rereading text) *A problem a student in 12th grade may have in writing an essay about a book that has influenced him is that the student may not see any connection or similarities between the topic of the book and himself. A student may choose to react to the influence of an autobiography by*—OK—to clarify this, we could throw in something about . . . like basketball, if the student was a

basketball player, OK. (adding new text) *If the student . . . was a basketball player . . . he may choose* . . . OK That will take case of that. Should be all set.

Results delineating specific revision processes are reported in detail elsewhere (Sitko). However, three general conclusions can be drawn from these results: writers detected where readers were experiencing difficulty in understanding the text as intended; writers made specific changes in their text to remedy reader confusion; and the changes were substantive rather than surface modifications. Observing readers' processes appeared to be beneficial to writers. It remained to be seen whether students in a normal classroom could make effective use of this kind of feedback. The second study explored that possibility.

Study Two: Instructional Application of the Reader Feedback Method

The instruction in revising after feedback followed the method of the first study and used the same materials. I worked with freshmen in an introductory writing class, meeting with them for two regular class periods. During the first session, they learned the method for reading the papers, examined protocols of writers working with feedback, and discussed the cognitive and decision-making processes involved in revision. During the second session they observed a partner using the reading method with their texts, audiotaping the session for reference. On their own, if they wished, they recorded a verbal protocol of their own revision session.

In the first part of the instruction, the students discussed illustrations of how other readers used the "point-predict" reading method described above. They examined examples of both a text and a transcription of readers' responses to the two questions: "What is the point of this section?" and "What do you predict might come next?" They observed how readers typically form an initial version of a text and then use it to incorporate further points from the printed text. The following excerpt illustrates materials discussed by the class. It shows how a reader summarizes a point and predicts expected text.

> **Text**: *One problem a 12th grade student might have in writing this essay is the problem of understanding what the essay assignment is asking the student to do. For example students might think that the assignment is asking them to describe in detail an entire book before they begin to write about its influence on them.*

Reader: (point) **The problem is obviously in the first sentence. The one problem is making sure you answer the question—well, really it's understanding what the question is.** (predict) **I'm assuming that what will come next is how to do this.**

Text: *So before students begin to think about what they might write, it would be good to help them break down the task for themselves.*

Reader: (point) **OK, my interpretation was right. The point of this section is to make sure that the student understands the question and to write an answer to the question, and not to go off on a tangent somewhere.** (predict) **I expect that an example will come next.**

From this and similar excerpts, students discussed the process by which the text cued the reader's ongoing interpretation. Students noted how the reader matched the actual text to her expectation. They could see that far from being a passive activity, reading is an active engagement with a text.

Readers may not grasp an author's point for several reasons. First, readers bring their own prior knowledge and experience (however limited) to the text, including, for example, knowledge of genre and of the specific topic. Second, they bring general expectations about how texts operate. The reader in the illustrative material expects an example to follow the author's statement of the problem. Readers' knowledge and expectations interact with the text as they continue to read, with the result that readers construct mental versions of the text into which they then integrate new information. Although they are guided by the words on the page, they are influenced by much more than those words.

After discussing their observations about the reading process, the students turned to revision, specifically the cognitive and decision-making processes involved. They examined an extended excerpt from a think-aloud revision protocol of a writer detecting a problem, considering alternatives, and making decisions. The class looked for specific examples of the ways in which this writer evaluated information from reader feedback, generated alternatives that fit his own goals, and made decisions about both the content and location of a change. An excerpt from the instructional materials follows. The writer reviews his text, reads the reader's comment, and then thinks aloud as he revises. The original text is italicized, changes are underlined and italicized, responses are printed in boldface, and the writer's thinking aloud is represented by plain text.

Text: *Writing a college essay requires several crucial methods. The most* *important part of writing a college application essay it to make it stand out to the reader. When an essay asks you to choose a book that has influenced you, the book you choose must be unique. Also important for writing the essay is that you use good grammar, clear and concise language, and a style that's fun to read.*

Reader (summarizing the point of the text as a whole): **I think the points that came up were too obvious. If you're writing an essay for college, some of this is just—you have to know anyway.**

Writer: Well, but everybody doesn't get in. Hm— let's see—maybe I should pull—maybe I'll pull the idea of "balancing" in first. OK; it comes into the third paragraph now. Let's see if we can pull it into the first. (rereads) *The most important part of writing a college application essay is to make it stand out to the reader*—OK, have to bring balance in early—make that the key point. OK. Back to the first paragraph—you must choose—no—(adds) *The book you choose must balance the rest of the application.* OK, *Also important for writing the essay is that*—OK, let's see—to quit boring this person we could drop the whole grammar and concise language paragraph, and really shorten this thing down—OK, (rereads) *The most important part in the essay*—Let's read it without those things in it. OK, (rereads) *Writing a college essay requires several crucial methods.* Which no longer would be my topic sentence. Well, OK, *Writing a college essay . . .* is like a balancing act. Good old analogy (adds) *is like a balancing act.*

In this illustration students could see the writer in the process of reconsidering a decision made very early during planning, namely, to order the suggested strategies from least important to most. Reading the feedback, the writer is presented with evidence of the reader's lack of interest in reviewing what the writer intends to be the least important material. Faced with this resistance, the writer elects to move what he considers his most important point from the third paragraph to the first. In so doing he reconstructs the major organization of his paper and creates a new thesis.

After examining these and other illustrations, the students worked with a partner, each reading aloud the other's text. These texts had been composed as a class assignment. The students were to describe how a familiar group could be considered a discourse community. In reading their partner's texts, students followed the method they had observed in the first part of the instruction. Readers paused periodically to summarize the point as they understood it and to make a prediction about forthcoming text. Writers audiotaped these readings so that they would have access to them as they revised.

In the last part of the instruction, writers revised their texts in light of the feedback. To record their revision process, they talked aloud as they revised. Some chose to make concurrent verbal protocols, turning on their tape recorders as soon as they had reviewed the tape of their partner's in-class reading. Others chose to revise their texts with tape recorders off and then tape their commentary about the changes, taking a kind of retrospective self-interview. As part of their participation in the research, students permitted me to make copies of their tapes, including the readings and revision sessions.

Analysis

This study addressed the connection between observing reading processes and revising texts. To establish the connection between reading feedback and revision, I needed to see whether writers had revised their texts at the places where readers had shown difficulty. To answer this question, I compared those places at which the reader provided feedback with the places at which the writers revised. Data for analysis consisted of the original and revised drafts as well as the readers' tapes. Complete data was available for five students. Working with the original drafts, I first marked the places where readers had stopped to summarize the point or to make a prediction; next I next marked the places where the writers had subsequently made changes. Places at which a reader commented and a writer revised were designated "revision points." An example follows:

> **Original:** *The basis for the designs of these books can be seen in various factors of writing such as content, style, structure, and layout.*
>
> **Reader**: (point) **And then she identifies factors in the way that these books want to say, and** (predict) **she's probably going to end up comparing the differences in these four ways as they relate to the discourse communities.**
>
> **Revised text:** *The basis for the designs of these books can be seen in various factors of writing such as content, style,* (strikes out "structure") *and layout.*

By deleting "structure" from her list, the writer indicates her response to the reader's expectation that these four words were functioning to forecast the text. The reader's inaccurate prediction apparently influences the writer to inspect the paper and see that the text develops only three of the four original points. Such text changes appear to be fairly straightforward reactions to reader comments. However, I could not infer from this data alone whether writers were taking the feedback into account as they revised. It is possible that the writer in the example may have detected the mismatch independently of her reader. To address the question of whether writers were responding to the observed needs of their readers, I examined the protocols for converging evidence.

The revision protocols required a different type of and thus a different unit of analysis. The think-aloud protocols typically included three kinds of activity: reading the text, summarizing the reader's feedback, and revising. As in the more controlled study, revising included several subprocesses, beginning with detection of a problem and ending with a decision to change the text. Revision episodes could thus be defined as clusters of related activities beginning with feedback and ending with text change. A new episode began when a writer moved to a new place in the text. As an example, the following revision episode matches the revision point indicated above.

> **Writer:** Now later on I didn't use any sort of example for "structure," so I'm going to eliminate "structure" as one of my factors.

Here the writer clearly indicates that her revision is intended to respond to her reader's misreading.

Results

The five texts yielded a total of seventeen "revision points," or changes between first and second drafts at places where readers had paused to comment. Protocols provided converging evidence for sixteen of the seventeen changes. In the seventeenth case, the writer changed the text without reference to the reader's comment.

Of the sixteen changes, fourteen can be linked directly to feedback, and two changes were made after the writer apparently detected a problem during the course of independently rereading the text. Of the fourteen changes that could be linked directly to feedback, thirteen were traceable to the feedback of the readers using the point-predict reading method, and one referred to a comment by the instructor. Clearly, the converging evidence of the protocols indicates that almost all of these changes were influenced by reader feedback. An example follows:

> **Text**: *There are some distinguishable items on the Macintosh which cannot*

> *be found on many—on most other personal computers. These items, since they are known to many people in the Macintosh user's community, are referred to in an informal manner.*
>
> **Reader**: Now what are these items?
>
> **Text**: *It is the uncanny reference which makes the user community a distinguishable discourse community.*
>
> **Reader**: Now, he starts talking about these items, but we don't know what these items are. Now, if he could state what these items are, maybe it'll be a little easier, because he refers to them. Like maybe windows, or icons.
>
> **Text**: *If you had never used a Macintosh before, would you be able to decipher these terms:*
>
> **Reader**: Oh, so now in the next paragraph he goes on to the terms. I don't know. He starts talking about it in the last paragraph, and then like cuts it off, and starts into the next. I don't know.

Arriving at the same point in his text during revision, the writer refers to the feedback and makes an adjustment in response:

> **Writer**: What I think I might have to do is move this fourth paragraph up, and I'm just going to read through it, and I'm going to kind of go over why I should do that. (rereads text) I'm thinking about a way I can somehow put these items from the fourth paragraph into the third paragraph, because I brought the idea in the third paragraph, and it might be a good idea if I elaborated on it there. (rereads text) Maybe what I should do is before the last sentence, I could insert the fourth paragraph. Yeah. That would work really good. Let me read that to see how it would sound.

To address the question of whether the changes writers made were substantive, a follow-up analysis classified the kinds of changes made by the writers during the thirteen revisions in response to feedback. These episodes indicated that the majority of changes were revisions of meaning. Writers made global as well as sentence-level and editing changes.

As indicated by Figure 1, the thirteen revisions can be categorized as structural, sentence-level, and surface changes. Of the four structural modifications, one formed a new global plan including a new thesis and topic sentences. Three writers matched their purpose or plan statements to their texts or vice versa. Sentence-level changes accounted for eight cases. In six of these, the writers added new information by elaborating

---

Figure 1. *Categories of Text Changes*

Structural Changes
1 New purpose statement, topic sentences
1 Match purpose statement to text
2 Match text to purpose statement

Sentence-level Changes
6 Explain/elaborate key words, claims
1 Correct inaccurate statement
1 Delete misleading text

Surface Changes
1 Edit

13 total changes

---

key words or key ideas. One change involved correcting an inaccurate statement and another the deletion of misleading text.

The following example illustrates how one writer made major structural changes based on his reader's feedback. The feedback episode begins with the partner reading the writer's first sentence following an introductory quotation defining discourse community. We hear the reader ask the first of the questions: "Is this the point of the essay?"

FEEDBACK EPISODE

> **Text**: *Like any other interest group, the sport of crew has its own discourse community. Crew, usually identified as rowing, is the action of moving a vessel through the water by using bladed sticks called oars.*

> **Reader**: **Do I think this is the point? No, not really. I think he is defining what crew is as a sport.**

> **Text**: *Crew is a sport that is catching on, but is still not practiced by all colleges and high schools. Being lucky to attend an institution that promoted crew as a means for physical exercise, I got an early start in the sport.*

> **Reader**: **I think here he has still not brought his point out clearly, but**

> **he's getting locked up in what crew is, and his experience in crew—and not so much the language used in crew.**
>
> **Text**: *Most rowers are usually tall and have somewhat short hair.*
>
> **Reader**: **Um, I think this sentence has nothing to do with the language at all.**
>
> **Text**: *During racing season most of them either get flat-top haircuts or very short army style crops.*
>
> **Reader**: **Um, I don't think this has anything to do with it either. I think he's—he's going off on all these tangents all of a sudden.**

The reader reasonably looks for the main point, which according to the assignment is to be a description of how a particular group familiar to the author forms a kind of discourse community. She finds instead a "tangent," a series of descriptive statements about the group's physical characteristics, but nothing about language. The writer's response follows. The original draft is italicized, new text is printed in underlined italics, and the writer's words are represented in plain typeface.

REVISING EPISODE

> **Text**: *Like any other interest group, the sport of crew has its own discourse community.*
>
> **Writer**: OK, I'm beginning to talk about crew after I define discourse community. (adds new sentence) *In crew rowers not only communicate orally, but they also communicate physically.* That I think is my thesis statement right there.

Continuing to revise, the writer creates a new topic sentence for the second paragraph. His protocol records the extent to which his decisions are influenced by his reader's feedback.

> **Writer**: (adds new sentence) *The rowing community speaks in technical terms during a practice session.* I'm relating back to my thesis. *The first common word one should familiarize themselves with when speaking of crew is "shell," which describes the boats used in rowing.* That's good because I'm introducing "shell," which is a word I'm going to be using throughout the rest of my paper, and by defining it right at the beginning I can already clear that—you know—the people that will be reading my paper will already know, so my audience will already be set with the word "shell," so I don't have to define it throughout the rest of the paper.

By adding a new thesis, the writer integrates the point of the assignment with the point he wants to make. Knowing the assignment, the reader expects to hear an account of how verbal communication marks group membership. The writer, however, wishes to establish that nonverbal communication also characterizes the group. He elects to specify the verbal communication first, in a series of definitions of technical terms. His new topic sentence envelops this first part of the text.

A second illustration shows how another writer responds to her reader's need. Her text discusses similar chapters in two physics textbooks. Text A is used by students of humanities and social sciences. Text B is used by students concurrently enrolled in calculus. The writer discusses how different treatments of the topic of velocity provide evidence that the texts are intended for different discourse communities.

FEEDBACK EPISODE

> **Text**: *This can be seen in the differences in content. The chapter on motion in Text A defines distance and displacement and shows how speed and velocity are derived from it. Text B assumes the reader can understand the concept of velocity equalling displacement over time directly and skips over a discussion of earlier topics.*
>
> **Reader**: **Now this sounds a little bit confusing, sort of. Let me think. Now I know that—I think what Text B actually does—it understands that you can understand the concept of velocity in a more complex manner and also the initial idea of velocity quicker.**

REVISING EPISODE

> **Writer**: She said that this needs to be clarified more, that the reader can't understand what I'm saying directly from this, and they have to think a little. So I guess what I'll say is—(adds new sentence) *The writer of Text A has predicted that the student needs to understand single dimensions before learning about vectors.*

The added sentence directly compares Text A with Text B, repeating the main point that we can deduce an author's intended audience through an examination of text.

Changes in successive drafts provide one measure of revision. Protocols provide converging evidence that writers changed their texts in response to reader feedback rather than solely by their own detection.

The high proportion of structural and sentence-level changes indicates that the writers were making new meaning as they responded to their readers' attempts to construct the sense of the text.

Discussion

Observing their readers' processes appeared to help the five writers who completed this study. Because I was not their teacher, I cannot comment on long-term effects. However, the changes that students made in their second drafts were, as the examples illustrate, appropriate. Without a control group I can only speculate about whether, on their own, the student writers might have detected the same problems and made similar changes. However, the research cited earlier, as well as teaching experience, suggests that because they read what they intend to see in their own texts, students have difficulty detecting these kinds of problems.

Several pedagogical implications can be drawn from this study. The first is that it is possible for students to elicit useful information about a text by listening to how readers attempt to make sense of it. The examples illustrate how students are stimulated to examine the structure of their essays, to add information at points where readers need it, and to delete text that is interesting (to them) but misleading (to the reader). All of these changes mark potential improvement. The second implication is that, given assistance in detecting problems, students are helped to access a repertoire of problem-solving strategies. Rather than representing the problem vaguely as "something wrong," they can see precisely how and where readers have difficulty. Readers' confusion thus influences writers' text representation. Just like the writers in the initial study, the students set new goals and used alternative strategies when confronted with reader misunderstanding, using problem-solving strategies. A third implication is that long-term benefits may result from this kind of direct experience. Provided with enough observations, students might come to represent their readers more accurately, understand how texts guide readers, and see how prior knowledge and expectations influence a variety of interpretations. Students might thus gradually approximate the behavior of more experienced writers.

This research suggests that simply by listening to readers' constructive processes, writers can get information that helps them to identify text problems and to take action at the structural level of their text. Further research is needed not only to identify more precisely what kinds of information are most useful to writers but also to determine the ways in which writers process this information. Such research could help the design of instructional methods to assist students in generating helpful feedback about their own texts. Over the long term students might develop a more elaborated representation of audience than classrooms conventionally provide. 🍂

WORKS CITED

Bartlett, E. J. "Learning To Revise: Some Component Processes." *What Writers Know: The Language, Process, and Structure of Written Discourse.* Ed. M. Nystrand. New York: Academic Press, 1982. 345-363.

Berkenkotter, C. "Student Writers and Their Sense of Authority over Texts." *College Composition and Communication* 35 (1984): 312-319.

Ericsson, K., and H. Simon. *Protocol Analysis: Verbal Reports as Data.* Cambridge: MIT P, 1984.

Flower, L., and J. R. Hayes. "A Cognitive Process Theory of Writing." *College Composition and Communication* 32 (1981): 365-387.

Flower, L., J. R. Hayes, L. Carey, K. A. Schriver, and J. Stratman. "Detection, Diagnosis and the Strategies of Revision." *College Composition and Communication* 37 (1986): 16-55.

Freedman, S. W. *Response to Student Writing.* Urbana: NCTE, 1987.

Hayes, M., and D. Daiker. "Using Protocol Analysis in Evaluating Responses to Student Writing." *Freshman English News* 13 (1984): 1-5.

Hillocks, G. "The Interaction of Instruction, Teacher Comment, and Revision in Teaching the Composing Process." *Research in the Teaching of English* 16 (1982): 261-78.

Meyer, B. "Reading Research and the Composition Teacher: The Importance of Plans." *College Composition and Communication* 33 (1982): 37-49.

Murray, D. M. "Teaching the Other Self: The Writer's First Reader." *College Composition and Communication* 33 (1982): 140-147.

Newkirk, T. "Direction and Misdirection in Peer Response." *College Composition and Communication* 35 (1978): 301-311.

Olson, G. M., S. A. Duffy, and R. L. Mack. "Thinking-out-loud as a Method for Studying Real-time Comprehension Processes." *New methods in reading comprehension research*. Eds. D. Kieras and M. Just. Hillsdale NJ: Lawrence Erlbaum Associates, 1984.

Sitko, B. "Writers' Cognitive and Decision Processes: Revising after Feedback." Diss. Carnegie Mellon U, 1989.

Sommers, N. "Revision Strategies of Student Writers and Experienced Writers." *College Composition and Communication* 31 (1980): 378-387.

Spivey, N. "Construing Constructivism: Reading Research in the United States." *Poetics* 16 (1987): 169-192.

Stauffer, R. *Teaching Reading as a Thinking Process*. New York: Harper, 1969.

Vipond, D., and R. Hunt. "Point-driven Understanding: Pragmatic and Cognitive Dimensions of Literary Reading." *Poetics* 13 (1984): 261-277.

Ziv, N. "The Effect of Teacher Comments on the Writing of Four College Freshmen." *New Directions in Composition Research*. Eds. R. Beach and L. Bridwell. Urbana: NCTE, 1984. 362-380.

V

How Discourse Communities Construct Readers and Writers

The previous sections dealt with the pedagogy of writing within different school environments, the development of the abilities of individual writers, and the ways in which texts construct or respond to the needs of readers. The next two sections adopt a slightly different focus; they examine the texts and processes of functioning adults for whom writing is a means of accomplishing their work and of defining themselves as professionals within discourse communities. Thus, the three essays in this section examine writing representative of discourse communities defined at various levels of generality: the writing of engineers designing refrigerator parts at a manufacturing plant (Mary Rosner); the citation and documentation practices of scientists, social scientists, and humanists functioning as members of larger academic communities (Diane Dowdey); and the self-presentation in annual reports of corporations operating as distinctive entities within American capitalist culture (Elizabeth McCord). Although addressing different aspects of professional discourse, these essays together demonstrate that a full understanding of the social forces that shape professional discourse requires analysis at various "grain sizes." That is, because any writer belongs to several concentric, overlapping, and even mutually exclusive discourse communities, an analysis that focuses on only one level can produce a misleading sense of unity or disunity. The essays in this section show how the choice of grain size affects the conclusions one can draw about the forces that shape writing in the work place.

The notion of discourse community is vexed and slippery. We all talk about discourse communities—and we all have a commonsense notion that they exist and can point to some—but no one has adequately described the necessary and sufficient conditions that determine what it takes to constitute a discourse community. Discussions of discourse communities that have not been based on substantive studies of particular groups are not ultimately very useful because they have tended to remain rather general and abstract. The real problem is that no one ever seems willing to say "This is *not* a discourse community," marking out some group that fails to meet the criteria. When the term "discourse community" is used so loosely, it becomes almost meaningless—lacking practical or theoretical teeth. Only if we can define discourse communities rigorously can we describe, predict, evaluate, and, ultimately, improve the writing practices of any group.

Because the term discourse community is so loose, it has been used to describe almost every kind of gathering. At one extreme, some have claimed that participants in a casual conversation or a collection of individuals at a conference panel are discourse communities. The logical extension of this view is that each writer is, potentially at least, an island, a discourse community unto herself (or himself). Although Mary Rosner focuses on the idiosyncratic writing processes of her two engineers, she skillfully avoids this trap. While the two engineers work in the same company, they respond differently to their institutional environment. But Rosner rightly avoids concluding that their discourse practices are so divergent that we cannot consider them members of both a larger engineering discourse community and a smaller community within their company. Certainly, any group or individual can develop distinctive discourse practices; few of us, however, would find it useful to define such small groupings as communities.

At the other logical extreme, one could say that groups consisting of all English speakers or all academics constitute discourse communities. In some sense this observation is true, but it is not very useful. Even if large scale comparisons could be drawn (say between academics and politicians in general), the generalizations would be so far removed from specific practices that any recommendations or conclusions would be useless. Although Diane Dowdey contrasts discourse practices at the level of large branches of academic inquiry—the sciences, the social sciences, and the humanities—she does not make the mistake of assuming that each branch speaks with one voice. Rather, she argues that each field takes a distinctive stance on numerous issues including the importance of verbal originality, the desirability of preserving the exact language of previous scholarship, the relative value of new and old contributions to the literature, and the appropriate strategies for adding to existing knowledge. These broad strokes paint a big picture of how families of disciplines conduct their discursive practices, but Dowdey also draws finer lines that distinguish among specific forums within each discipline. For example, she finds a surprising degree of stylistic variation among scientific journals, and even journals in the social sciences often deviate from the style guidelines laid down by the American Psychological Association (APA). Dowdey's study suggests that although broad generalizations about academic discourse communities are useful, more fine-grained analyses are also necessary if we wish to advise a chemistry student writing her first journal article.

In addition to the difficulty of defining discourse communities at the appropriate grain size, research on professional discourse also runs another risk. As participants standing within our own discourse community, we must be careful not to project its features onto the communities we study. Dowdey points out that the advice given in our writing textbooks exhibits this tendency. She shows that disciplines within the humanities usually abide by a single system of documentation and citation—that of the MLA. We therefore tend to assume that the sciences and social sciences will also conform to a single system. As Dowdey demonstrates, however, the APA is not the MLA—its style book is not nearly so widely used—and the sciences lack any institutional arbiter comparable to either. Reserving the right of poetic license to poets, our technical writing textbooks often discredit or ignore variations in science and social science writing that arise from non-artistic motives.

Despite the apparent unanimity of stance within the humanities, signalled by conformity to MLA's documentation and citation practices, we know that even within English studies there are discourse communities that seem to have little to say to each other. Elizabeth McCord's study builds a bridge between two such communities, new historicism and social constructionist rhetoric. She explores the strong philosophical commonalities shared by the recent scholarship on Renaissance literature and research on writing in non-academic settings. McCord shows that literary texts in the Renaissance and annual reports of today's corporations can be seen as both shaping and shaped by their cultures, as both supportive and subversive of their cultures' dominant ideologies. Obviously these approaches differ significantly in subject matter and methodology: social constructionists do not confine their attention to privileged literary texts, and new historicists must depend on surviving cultural artifacts—they cannot go out and interview the writers and readers of their texts. Nevertheless, McCord's analysis emphasizes the fact that every text has the potential to reflect and shape its political, social, and cultural context.

Studies of discourse communities have different implications for research and for teaching. As researchers, we may want to study discourse communities to test the adequacy of our rhetorical assumptions. Do classical constructs drawn from the rhetoric of public debate apply to the discourse practiced in specialized private institutions and academic disciplines? In answering such a question, we can take a wide or a narrow focus on any discourse community, but the value of our conclusions will depend on our ability to zoom in and out. If we examine individuals, we have to attempt to place them within a wider organizational perspective; if we examine institutions, we have to look at how broadly defined stances are played out in the writing practices of individuals or groups at lower levels.

In his *Rhetoric*, Aristotle advises us to seek in every subject the appropriate degree of precision. This is good pragmatic advice. It also applies to how we apply studies of discourse communities to the writing classroom. Students in advanced composition courses are poised to enter their academic and professional discourse communities. When, as teachers, we face a roomful of them, we must avoid both fragmenting and overgeneralizing. Our jobs would be impossible if we felt obliged to tailor rhetorical advice to each student's field. On the other hand, we would be irresponsible to unthinkingly impose on them the values and practices of one discourse community, even our own. Abstracting to the right level is a curricular challenge.

❦ 14

New Historicism and Social Rhetoric: From the Bard to the Boardroom— A Cultural Exchange

Elizabeth A. McCord

In recent years, theory in English studies has become interdisciplinary, to such an extent that both literary theory and rhetorical studies evidence a convergence of history, sociology, and psychology, as well as traditional disciplinary concerns in such areas as feminist criticism or poststructuralist linguistics. For some of us, the tie that often binds our otherwise diverse inquiries is a threshold unanimity: as interpreters of the human experience, we believe there is no such thing as an autonomous human nature independent of culture. The result of this commonality is that we approach our study of discourse, be it *As You Like It* or an annual report, from the premise that, as members of various cultures, writers participate in creating the interpretive constructs, the public significations, that inform their daily existence. Currently, this theoretical alignment is particularly apparent in the work of those literary critics most often called new historicists and those rhetoricians of nonacademic discourse who espouse a social perspective.

Unlikely though it may seem at first glance, the philosophical homes of these critics and rhetoricians (and thus their analytical perspectives) are remarkably similar, because, I believe, they share the sameness of their differences, to borrow from Levi-Strauss: they are complementary; their interlacing connections overpower their opposition. Thus it is illuminating for rhetoricians to review new historicism, particularly its methodology, with an eye to expanding our own discourse inquiry. What follows in this essay, then, is a look at new historicism as a culture-based critical method for studying texts. In order to do justice to the movement, I first provide some background on the theoretical context of new historicism and second consider its practical application. I also summarize contemporary social rhetorical inquiry for the purposes of comparing it to new historicism. In the process I hope to address the "So what?"—the "Why does this matter?" question, for both rhetorical theory building and research as well as for our pedagogy—because this persistent inquiry has informed my own exploration of this topic.

I have focused my comparison on new historicism as applied to Renaissance literature and social rhetoric as applied to contemporary nonacademic writing because I believe the participants in the twentieth-century marketplace, like the movers and shakers of the Renaissance, are extremely self-conscious about the "fashioning" of their identities, to borrow a new-historical term. I also believe our current marketplace structure provides a contemporary corollary for the Renaissance crown, for both were, and are, dominant forces of power dependent upon successful cultural representation for survival. Renaissance England and the post-World War II American marketplace were and are sites of tremendous expansion: geographic in the Renaissance; economic in this century; and scientific and ideological in both cultures. And in both societies, the shaping of mass culture has been facilitated by information explosions (in the Renaissance with the printing press, today through high-tech equipment). Because both societies were and have been full of unsettling, rapid-fire changes—and because discourse has played and plays an integral role in shaping the attitudes of large numbers of people from both cultures—the forces acting on contemporary nonacademic writers are in a large sense similar to those new historicists posit as influencing the belletristic writers of the Renaissance.

In 1980, Stephen Greenblatt published *Renaissance Self-Fashioning*, which set forth the foundations of new historicism. Starting from the premise that "[s]ocial actions are themselves always embedded in systems of public signification, always grasped, even by their makers, in acts of interpretation, while the words that constitute the works of literature . . .

are by their very nature the manifest assurance of a similar embedded-ness," Greenblatt goes on to assert that, in the sixteenth century, "there appears to be an increased self-consciousness about the fashioning of human identity as a manipulable, artful process" (5, 2). Appropriating the prevalent Renaissance definition of the term "fashion" as "the action or process of making, . . . a way of designating the forming of a self" (2), Greenblatt suggests that "fashioning" accurately describes the Renaissance concern with "representation of one's nature or intention in speech or actions" (3). He then proceeds to examine some of the leading "fash-ioners" of that period and the writing they produced. As he expressly states, he does not look solely at a given writer or product in a particular historical setting to see how writer or work were affected by the times; rather, he views the writer and his discourse as an implementing force, affected by and effecting his society. This dialectical expansion of the way literary critics look at the writer, particularly the emphasis on the writer as "affector," has become one of the significant characteristics of this mode of inquiry.

Since 1980, other literary critics have contributed to new historicism, a school of literary analysis which is greatly indebted (as Greenblatt acknowledges) to the work of Clifford Geertz and other cultural anthro-pologists. For Geertz, all humans are in and of themselves cultural arti-facts—products of particular cultures and affectors of culture who have a metaphoric grasp of reality (51), or as Geertz so poetically describes it: "man is an animal suspended in webs of significance he himself has spun . . . " (5). Thus our discourse, be it imaginative or not, is always culture-bound and embodies the predominant modes of conceiving and experi-encing, even if the writer is reacting to or challenging the status quo.

New historicists, then, approach their study of written discourse somewhat as social scientists, looking at writers and texts and their inter-action with members of particular cultures. Greenblatt, for instance, writes that literature functions within the cultural systems of contemporary meaning and is concerned with large "networks of meaning" in which both author and works participate (*Renaissance Self-Fashioning* 3-4). Another leading scholar, Jonathan Dollimore, argues that literature cannot be separated from other kinds of social practice (4); thus new historicists study the implication of literary texts in history as well as the effect the times had on the author. Louis A. Montrose perhaps best characterizes new historicist concerns when he notes that a work of literature assumes a dialectical function of cultural representation: those forces by which the work is shaped are also those to which the work gives shape ("*A Midsummer Night's Dream*" 69-70). However, despite my identifying new historicism as a "school" of literary analysis—a useful enough label for the purposes of this article—in fairness I should first place the movement in its broader context within literary studies and suggest ways that new historicists vary among themselves.

It is inaccurate to say *the* new historicism, because in fact several different critical practices fall under this rubric. Simply stated, new historicism is part of a larger critical movement to "rehistoricize" literary studies. There are differences and similarities among the growing field of scholars, and, arguably, there are at least two camps, reflecting the geopolitical roots of the early participants: the British, some of whom call their inquiry "cultural materialism" and who in general have forged a closer alliance with feminist and Marxist criticism; and the Americans, who have produced insignificant Marxist writing and whose works reflect more the thinking of Foucault and deconstructionist inquiry. Moreover, although the Renaissance has been, by far, the period most studied by the scholars engaged in new-historical methodologies, new-historical studies can be found on almost any period or genre, as well as many individual writers. Additionally, culture-based inquiry along the lines of new historicism has been extended to artifacts and experience beyond the literary text, as revealed by even a cursory look at any issue of the scholarly journal *Representations* (itself a new-historical journal co-edited by Greenblatt).

Undoubtedly, new historicism emerged as a reaction to the formalism that for so long informed most Renaissance scholarship; however, in pushing to reintegrate history with the text, the new historicists depart significantly from the "old" historicism, as epitomized by E. M. W. Tillyard and others who espoused an essentially positivist view of the past, with literature serving as a mimetic reflection of that objective world. By contrast, most new historicists assert they are not monological, focused on a single political vision (e.g., Greenblatt, "The Forms of Power" 5); rather, the new historicist premises any inquiry on the assumption that there are always competing centers of cultural power. In reconstructing Renaissance centers of power, new historicists may employ certain structuralist techniques in their close reading of texts and in their appropriation of the assertion that everything is a text. They draw on other theoretical modes as well.

The British, in particular, practice what one detractor has labeled "a kind of" Marxist criticism (Pechter 292) because of its focus on power, especially political power in its broadest sense. In fact, Dollimore, one of new historicism's leading voices, writes that cultural materialism (the British new historicism) is committed to changing an exploitative social order (*Political Shakespeare* viii). Dollimore further explicitly acknowledges the movement's debt to feminism as well as structuralist and post-structuralist theory, especially the work of Althusser, Macherey, Gramsci, and Foucault (*Political Shakespeare* 2-3). In addition to continental Marxist influences, however, new historicism has borrowed from Derrida, with his close attention to the text, his focus on linguistic deconstruction, and his blurring of the boundaries between literary and nonliterary, text and context; from Foucault, with his work on power and sexuality as well as his placing of the subject; and even from Bakhtin, who, arguably, was the first to explore the overlapping of literary history and popular culture.

But is new historicism in fact simply "a kind of" Marxism in disguise? In general I think not. While certainly new historicists are concerned with power and ideologies as well as with how writers of a particular period responded to power and in turn affected existing power structures—a dialectic recognized by both new historicists and Marxists—new historicists seem as a whole to recognize and allow for diverse ideologies, and, perhaps because of this, seek to *describe* the historical forces but not to explain them (through economic analysis or otherwise) or to privilege certain forces over others. To that extent, in my view, new historicists go beyond Marxism, at least in the normative sense, because they do not evaluate the "correctness" of a political stance, nor are they particularly concerned with economic or political cause and effect within a particular society.

However, as with any new movement once it has gained momentum, new historicism has now been critiqued and found lacking in certain respects. As I implied above, new historicists themselves occasionally begin to look like historical positivists because of their absorption with certain themes, which are inevitably based on our twentieth-century interpretation of certain images of the Renaissance world (e.g., colonialism, the power locus of the monarchy). In fact, the new historicists *are* looking back and deciding what the cultural forces were—and attributing evaluative labels to them (e.g., "dominant," "subversive"), which often they extrapolate from events or nonliterary texts without supplying additional evidence of the relative value of the identified power forces against society as a whole. This tendency is evident in Paul Brown's critique of *The Tempest*, which I discuss later in this essay. Brown premises his analysis of the play on an assumed connection among playwright, play, Renaissance audience, and certain cultural forces. He extrapolates these cultural dynamics from actual nonliterary texts and events of the period; however, he offers no evidence to show, for example, that Shakespeare was in fact aware of or influenced by these writings or events. Nevertheless, regardless of these and other problems with the inquiry, the new historicists' insistence that literature, no matter how "universal" or "enduring," cannot absolutely transcend its social order is, in my view, an important step toward creating a more encompassing (and thus more useful) methodology for literary studies. And the means these scholars have employed to explore texts in a social context—the methodology that is common to all new historicists—provide a useful comparison for social rhetorical study of nonacademic texts.

Social rhetoric—the positioning of any study of texts within the cultural framework of their production and use—is vital for the study of nonacademic (or marketplace) writing. Various scholars have articulated the assumptions and methodology of social rhetoricians, so it is useful here to examine how they frame their research. Beginning from the premise that writing is a social act, social rhetoricians (like new historicists) are concerned with the context in which writers create discourse—and the nature of those contexts. Thus the social rhetoricians who investigate nonacademic writing consider the large social contexts in which writing is produced in the marketplace. According to Lester Faigley, this social perspective examines how individual acts of communication define, organize, and maintain social groups and how the writer functions within those social relationships, which by definition contemplate more than the text as a physical object and the writer as an isolated strategist ("Nonacademic Writing" 35-36). Consequently, as Lee Odell urges, a rhetorician must consider the ways a discourse community influences writers' attempts to formulate and express ideas ("Beyond the Text" 249). Thus, nonacademic writing must be examined as a social act that changes as society changes, has consequences in the economic and political realms, and shapes the writer as much as the text is shaped by the writer (Faigley, "Nonacademic Writing" 236).

Clearly, the rhetorical methodology sounds remarkably similar to that employed by new historicists. Consequently, I offer the following extended syllogism, in which I deliberately fuse the descriptive scholarly language of new historicists and social rhetoricians:

- that writing, whether imaginative or not, is a social act;
- that writers are engaged in representing themselves and their world;
- that the enabling condition of representation is power—that is, writers seek to be "affective";
- that any study of writing and texts must seek to identify and understand the cultural signifiers through which discourse is empowered;
- that, by definition, then, writing is collaborative or collective because, at a minimum, writing involves a cultural exchange between the writer/text and the culture at large;
- that the act of writing and the text itself assume dialectical functions, since both participate in cultural representation and exchange;
- that, as a participant in a dialectical enterprise, the writer is constantly confronted with new cultural values, of both the dominant culture and subcultures;
- that, as a work is produced and given over to society, it in turn challenges, modifies, and even displaces some existing cultural forms, as well as supports and reinforces others;
- thus, a written text gives shape to its culture even as it is shaped by the culture.

And the rhetoricians would add:

- therefore, any study of texts must not only examine the individual writer but also follow the completed text, tracing its dissemination, its use, and its effects, both as to resulting actions and subsequent influence of the text.

For obvious reasons this last step is extremely problematic for a literary critic attempting to reconstruct the shaping events of the Renaissance; therefore, it is not usually attempted by these scholars—except inferentially.

How, then, do scholars apply this theory to writers and texts? As might be expected, new historicists (who do not have the option of conducting any ongoing study of text production) usually examine specific literary texts (although they can also focus on particular writers), juxtaposing a close intertextual analysis with a socio/historical context, which they often infer from contemporaneous nonliterary texts or historical anecdote. Thus the new historicists' analytical paradigm might be articulated as follows:

1. Identify and describe existing sources of cultural representation, including both written discourse and other artifacts;
2. Analyze these sources to determine the possible dominant and subcultural norms and their interplay;
3. Trace these cultural dynamics in a specific literary text to determine whether the text reinforces or subverts the prevailing cultural norms, or does both.

This is generally the approach used in Brown's analysis of *The Tempest*, entitled "'This Thing of Darkness I Acknowledge Mine': *The Tempest* and the Discourse of Colonialism." Because most new-historical studies depend on a tight interweaving of historical detail and intertextual analysis, most examinations defy succinct summary; thus the following examples of the application of new historicism are illustrative only.

After introducing his study with a detailed textual analysis of a letter from John Rolfe (of Jamestown fame), who is seeking royal approval of his marriage to Pocahontas, Brown uses this letter to posit what he sees as one cultural dynamic of the time: that the dominant posture toward colonialism hinged upon maintaining the tension between social order (i.e., England, the crown, civilized society) and the "other" (i.e., savagism, masterless society, antisocial behavior). Brown then reviews several additional nonliterary texts that perpetuated this cultural dynamic in the minds of the Renaissance populace (and, presumably, in Shakespeare's mind as well): descriptions of geographic areas of expansion (e.g., the New World), legal statutes aimed at reforming the British vagrant classes, and discourse advocating the virtues and vices of expanded British control into Ireland. He avers that these writings, which he labels "colonial discourse," demonstrate cultural tension between order and disorder, based on a shared perception of much of the unknown or different (e.g., unchartered geographical regions, godless Celts) as a disruptive "other," and that this "other" was essential for the continued justification of the colonial mentality. That is to say, the prevailing Renaissance culture of power could continue to claim superiority only if it could play off against a contrasting dynamic.

Brown then traces this complex relationship of colonialist discourse through *The Tempest* by looking at its narrative structure, its use of classical tropes, and its characterization. Through this analysis, Brown argues that, in fact, the play does not completely reinforce the dominant Renaissance concepts of power (which supported colonialist notions of, e.g., exploitation); rather the play shows considerable ambivalence on this issue and is thus no all-embracing triumph for the dominant cultural attitude toward colonialism. Implicit within Brown's analysis is the claim that the members of the Renaissance audience of *The Tempest* would have been required, at least temporarily (and perhaps subconsciously), to exchange their embedded notions of colonialism for those presented in the play, and, in fact, this exchange was possible only because the audience members were themselves familiar (at least tacitly) with the dominant cultural myths that legitimized Renaissance colonialist practices. Brown's analysis illustrates one rhetorical dynamic that new historicists explore: that of the writer as subverter of dominant cultural norms.

Montrose's essay on *A Midsummer Night's Dream* is perhaps a better known application of new historical criticism; however, it lends itself even less to summary. Nevertheless, it is representative of a new-historical analysis of a work which, Montrose argues, was not intended to subvert radically the prevailing culture (as was *The Tempest*) but rather to reinforce certain norms (in general, patriarchial supremacy) in the face of an aberrant but powerful cultural force to the contrary (a female queen). Montrose builds his analysis as follows. He first draws on collateral texts and identifies certain existing Elizabethan cultural forces that he asserts unequivocally shaped the play (e.g., the fascination with and fear of Amazonian societies). He then goes on to argue that in *A Midsummer Night's Dream* Shakespeare was not only influenced by these cultural forces, but also wrote to reinforce some of them (for example, Elizabethan private and public order) through an interweaving of private and public images of gender and power. Through close analysis of dialogue, imagery, characterization, and plot, Montrose then shows how contemporaneous Renaissance private values are reinforced (e.g., bonds of sisterhood are negated while bonds of brotherhood are strengthened), along with public ones (e.g., political stability is maintained through regulation of harmonious personal order).

Montrose therefore concludes that, even though *A Midsummer Night's Dream* does not attempt to subvert the general Elizabethan social order, nevertheless in this play too Shakespeare was required to craft the text subtly and deliberately to make his cultural statement because of the peculiar aspect of the prevailing Elizabethan culture, the gender-inverted body politic, which was diametrically opposed to traditional patriarchal order, both private and public. Montrose also draws on other Renaissance writers to support this point, writers who he says also participated in a dialectic on this unusual circumstance. He quotes extensively, for example, from *The Faerie Queene*, including this passage which, Montrose says, illustrates how Edmund Spenser carefully subverts the matriarchal social order in Book V of *The Faerie Queene* while simultaneously fashioning an "out" that allows for the possibility of a female queen in an otherwise patriarchal society:

> Such is the crueltie of womenkynd
> When they have shaken off the shamefast band,
> With which wise Nature did them strongly bynd,
> T'obay the heasts of mens well ruling hand,
> That then all rule and reason they withstand,
> To purchase a licentious libertie.
> *But vertuous women wisely understand,*
> *That they were borne to base humilitie,*
> *Unlesse the heavens them lift to lawful soveraintie.*
> (qtd. in "Shaping Fantasies" 47-48, emphasis added)

In essence Montrose says that the implication of these literary texts in history was to act as a preservative for a traditional patriarchal order that was, at least during Elizabeth's reign, somewhat threatened. Moreover, writers of this time were not anxious to disturb the relative political stability; therefore, private support for patriarchy could not be asserted at the expense of public order. Thus *A Midsummer Night's Dream* is more than a reflection of, for example, the Elizabethan court; this play, too, like other more "radical" work, contributes to an ongoing cultural dialectic which (albeit subtly) challenges some norms while supporting others.

These two illustrations of new-historicist approaches to literary discourse reflect what I would characterize as two stances a writer can take in any writing enterprise where the texts are intended for public dissemination, given the basic dialectical nature of any writing act: that of subverter or reinforcer of prevailing cultural norms. New historicists significantly depart from other sociological approaches to literary analysis, however, in their claim that writers are very aware of prevailing cultural norms affecting them and that their writings are intentional, knowing responses to these cultural influences. Specifically, new historicists explicitly factor in the concept of power and look for the role written discourse plays in maintaining or subverting various power structures. Thus Greenblatt's insistent appropriation of the term "fashioning" is well chosen for describing the Renaissance writer's conscious forming of a self, be it the public body politic or the private individual. I believe contemporary rhetoricians, particularly those of us who study nonacademic writing, have not yet grasped the full implications of writing as "fashioning," and I submit we can broaden both our research and our pedagogy by comparing the scope of our inquiry to that of new historicists.

Only recently have rhetoricians learned that today's marketplace writers are indeed aware of their immediate corporate cultures. Through the groundbreaking work conducted by Lee Odell and Dixie Goswami we have learned, for instance, that nonacademic writers make choices based on a fairly detailed understanding of their extended audiences and their needs (e.g., Odell et al., "Studying Writing"). We have looked at writers in particular discourse communities and learned, for example, that in some companies writers realize that it is acceptable, even important, to self-promote in written discourse (Paradis et al. 295-96). We now know that nonacademic writing is highly collaborative (Faigley and Miller). We also have common-sense understanding as to how, in corporate America, a writer may be required to perpetuate his or her corporate culture through discourse (e.g., from using letterhead stationery, which contains the company logo; to following structural constraints such as Procter & Gamble's "one-page memo" rule; to adopting certain stylistic conventions; to deliberately including preferred corporate metaphors and myths in the discourse). And, as the programs of any recent rhetoric conference will attest, we are constantly expanding our knowledge of marketplace writers and their cultures by studying diverse on-the-job writers as they write on the job (e.g., doctors, foreign business executives, dental hygienists, and CPAs). But we still have much to learn.

From new historicists we can see the importance of examining the much larger social nature of corporate discourse—its interplay within the marketplace as a whole. How, for example, are discourse and discourse production affected by the cultural dynamics of the larger communities of the American marketplace, as reflected both in discursive and nondiscursive influences (e.g., *The Wall Street Journal*, theories of management, political elections)? Can these sources of culture shaping be analyzed to determine dominant and subcultural influences and then applied to the writing of, say, a particular company or industry (both retroactively, at existing texts, and proactively, at text production)? Can we combine intertextual and social rhetorical analysis to see how particular marketplace writing reinforces or subverts broad cultural values? What, for example, are the dynamics that influence a particular company to create one self-image rather than another? What effect does Company A's choice have on the rest of the marketplace?

As rhetoricians we can begin our analysis by drawing on the comprehensive work of McKinsey and Co., a management consulting firm whose studies have shown that individual corporate cultures can be "diagnosed" by looking at intercompany manifestations of cultural values and codes (such written discourse as annual reports, quarterly statements, press releases; and other indices such as physical environment, interpersonal interactions, demographics of personnel) (Deal and Kennedy 129-39). For example, these consultants offer a sampling of corporate annual reports aimed at maintaining or promoting a certain image in the marketplace while subverting others. Consider these excerpts:

Delta Airlines: "There is a special relationship between Delta and its personnel that is rarely found in any firm, generating a team spirit that is evident in the individual's cooperative attitude toward others, cheerful outlook toward life, and pride in a job well done."

Dana: "The Dana style of management is getting everyone involved and working hard to keep things simple. There are no policy or procedure manuals, stacked up layers of management, piles of control reports, or computers that block information and communication paths. . . . The Dana style isn't complicated or fancy. It thrives on treating people with respect. It involves all Dana people in the life of the company. . . ."

Digital: "Digital believes that the highest degree of interaction in any of its activities needs to be in the area of customer service and support."

Johnson & Johnson: "Back in 1890, Johnson & Johnson put together the original first-aid kit in response to a plea from railroad workers who needed treatment on the scene as they toiled to lay tracks across America. Ninety years later the name Johnson & Johnson is still synonymous with home wound care" (Peters and Waterman 283).

Although these self-fashioned images are framed in general terms, each paints a picture that reflects certain deeply held values of its company, and each stresses a theme that complements the industry environment—the airline industry, for example—yet is distinct to the specific company—for example, Delta (Peters and Waterman 283). Moreover, the best and strongest companies consciously participate in this dynamic cultural exchange, for the benefit not only of the public but also of the company's employees (the better to engage them as participants in a strong, value-driven corporate culture), as the McKinsey experts have noted:

The rule seems to be: if you've got it, flaunt it. Companies with strong cultures recognize the importance of their values and their people and they continually report this to the world. When Wheelabrator-Frye goes to the trouble of producing a child's version of its annual report, people recognize that the company is a bastion of conservative free enterprise thought and has a culture that strongly reflects this religion. By contrast, companies with weak or fragmented cultures make much ado about the business and its performance—almost as though it operated without the help of human hands. What the company says about itself should be carefully checked for consistency. It is often possible to track company statements over time and watch how its culture evolves. . . . It can be done by simply tabulating the number of times a particular phrase or belief is articulated in the annual report. The surprise is that even such a simplistic analysis will show a clear trend in the evolution of a company's beliefs about itself. (Deal and Kennedy 131)

Others in management support the McKinsey analysis. In *Management and Statesmanship*, Richard Normann asserts that the most important process of any company is its continuing interpretation of historic events and concomitant redefining of its dominating business idea in light of ongoing cultural change (275). Implicit within Normann's analysis is the notion that each company's interpretation becomes a reinterpretation in the corporate community at large, thereby itself becoming an affective force.

In their chapter entitled "Reshaping Cultures," McKinsey's Terrence Deal and Allan Kennedy have identified five situations in which a company, because of changing circumstances, "should consider the reshaping of a culture as something close to its most important mission" (159): When the environment is undergoing fundamental change, and the company has always been highly value-driven; when the industry is highly competitive and the environment changes quickly; when the company is mediocre, or worse; when the company is truly at the threshold of becoming a large corporation—a Fortune 1000-scale corporate giant; and when the company is growing very rapidly. The recent television advertising of two companies who fall within the above categories reflects twentieth-century corporate self-fashioning in action.

AT&T, once the monopolistic giant of telecommunications, has experienced fundamental change since its antitrust break-up a few years ago. It is also, according to the McKinsey folk, highly value-driven (Deal and Kennedy 159). For years, Cliff Robertson was the spokesperson in AT&T ads. Within the past two years, however, AT&T has moved away from this type of self-promotion to ads that stress its difference from others in the field (a relatively new concern, since competition was previously nonexistent). At first its television advertising focused on the superiority of AT&T's products and service (e.g., a clumsy young suitor wreaks a path of destruction in his girlfriend's mother's house as he stumbles to use the telephone; "Don't worry," says the mother to her daughter, "it's an AT&T"). But competitors were doing the same (e.g., another company's ad features a telephone user speaking through a bull-horn into the phone, ostensibly because he is using an inferior system). These "We're better, you're inferior" ads were the logical first responses to the instant competition that followed the dissolution of the AT&T parent company, and the dialectical self-fashioning principle is clear. However, AT&T's most recent ads no longer focus on an overt "We're better" product approach; now, for example, ads profile employees who talk to an unseen interviewer about one of a myriad of services AT&T offers. The new image is clear: the old Ma Bell, oriented toward one product and individual consumers, is no longer; the new AT&T is concerned with providing a panoply of high-tech support services for the business community. No doubt AT&T's competitors will soon respond to this new image as well.

In an opposite market phenomenon, the computer industry has always had many players and no parent company at the forefront (IBM notwithstanding). This industry has always been highly competitive, characterized by quick and constant environmental changes. How each company fashioned itself was crucial to its success in gaining a hold on the market. For years Apple contented itself with being known as the "user-friendly, we're made for people" computer company. As a result, the business community considered Apple products to be consumers' toys. Recently setting out to refashion itself as a grown-up, capable of holding its own with the big guys, Apple has targeted its advertising toward gaining corporate respect. Thus a typical television spot shows shirt-sleeved, harried executives learning that their printer needs ten days to two weeks to put together an important report. A colleague pulls out an impressively bound document replete with slick color graphics. "Who did that?" someone asks. "We did," he replies. "How soon could we finish this report?" another asks. "This afternoon," he replies. The scene fades and the name "Macintosh" appears silently on the television screen.

These examples of corporate self-fashioning constitute the "macro" component we can appropriate from new historicism: the expansion of social rhetorical analysis to include a consideration of the dialectical nature of corporate discourse within the marketplace as a whole. Additionally, there is a "micro" component that complements the new historicist's concern with private self-fashioning against the sponsoring agent's public requirements.

New historicists have considered how belletristic writers responded to cultural constraints that may have run counter to their private beliefs. A new historicist would ask what happens when a writer is not in personal agreement with the public position he is required to take, because of, for example, his patronage obligations. Through such a query new historicists have considered whether (and, if so, how) individual writers have effected a compromise between private or personal self-fashioning that is in opposition to overt public statement. For example, Stanley Fish explores how Ben Jonson handled this dilemma. Fish argues that, although Jonson most often wrote in ostensible gratitude to his patrons, through conscious linguistic manipulation (e.g., syntactic juxtapositions, evocative "false starts") he created subtexts that had the ultimate effect of excluding his readers from full audience participation. Fish asserts that by exerting this type of textual control, Jonson was able to maintain some degree of independence from his world of patronage (261).

Curiously, Fish begins his article on Jonson with an observation relevant to my thesis. In writing about the Renaissance patronage system, he comments that "the two worlds of modern bureaucracy and ancient privilege are alike in at least one respect: they present their inhabitants with the problem of maintaining a sense of individual worth within the confines of a totalizing structure" (232). Contemporary social rhetoricians must consider what strategies are available to the individual writer who must communicate as a participant within (even a spokesperson for) his or her corporate world. Importing from new historicists, we can study whether there are any options available to a marketplace writer who wishes (for any of a number of reasons) to subvert the prevailing cultural values, or whether he or she is ever able to go against the demands of corporate authorial sponsorship and not get fired. We have begun to recognize that such a dilemma is an ethical one (Rentz and Debs); we must further study whether marketplace writers have devised strategies to effect a compromise (as the Renaissance writers did), or whether strategies are even available which provide legitimate ethical alternatives.

Even as we begin to explore these issues in our research, new historicism shows us further areas we need to address in our pedagogy, based on the premise that no writer is entirely autonomous. First, any student (whether a future marketplace writer or not) needs to be taught how to diagnose the particular culture in which he or she writes, be it a fresh-man composition classroom or a Big Eight accounting firm. As Patricia Bizzell has recognized, we teachers of writing therefore have a duty to introduce our students to a socio-anthropological awareness of the various communities of their worlds and to help them discover what they bring from their respective environments (237). We must also make explicit the tacit conventions that we impose on our students and their discourse. We further need to help them learn how to ferret out the different (and usually tacit) conventions that govern other cultures in which they will write (e.g., a philosophy class, the scientific research community). Once we have instilled in our students an awareness that they will always write as participants in a dialectical cultural exchange, then we need to help them develop strategies for producing discourse that can either reinforce or subvert given cultural requirements.

Such an expanded social approach to the teaching of writing will also affect the way we respond to our students' writing. Not only does a broad social perspective allow us to understand that each student brings to class a complex set of cultural influences (as, for example, Shirley Brice Heath has so aptly described), but it also forces us to reconsider how we respond to student writing: that is, what may first appear to be poor writing can in fact be a student's unconscious attempt at self-fashioning in a way he or she finds more comfortable than the picture we imposed. One example will illustrate this last point.

I often choose to have my first assignment in Writing for Business be one in which students must draw on autobiographical information. One writing situation I created recently asked each student to assume that he or she was applying for a scholarship, a university-wide grant given to "worthy students," those who demonstrated that they deserved this financial assistance. I explained in class that the criterion for obtaining a scholarship was not necessarily good grades; rather, "worthy students" could be variously defined (e.g., seriousness of intent), thus each should develop a persuasive personal statement which defined "worth" according to his or her particular strengths. Although I was well aware that writing about oneself is always difficult, even for expert writers, I was nevertheless surprised to find that one very capable student turned in a very poor statement. It was not until later in the quarter when we began to talk about writing and ethics, especially the concept that one must be able to "own" what one writes, and about the problems a marketplace writer faces when he or she is in conflict with the corporate values, that my student realized why she had been unable to write an effective personal statement. Because she was not financially self-supporting, because she felt she had no data which supported seriousness of intent, and because, having just begun her college career, she had amassed no significant accomplishments (by her standards), her self-image was at odds with my requirement that she argue in support of her worthiness for this scholarship; that is, she could not see to "fashion" herself in a manner that met the assignment. Moreover, since neither she nor I was aware of this cultural/ethical dilemma at the time, we were not able to consider whether there were strategies available to her for analyzing the cultural dynamics of the situation and completing the assignment in some other way that she could have ethically owned.

Increasingly I find I am most comfortable—as a writer, theorist and teacher—with a broad social approach to discourse which appropriates and fuses many of the tenets basic to new historicism and to social rhetoric. Such a theoretical home complements my basic existential view of the human condition, in that it is premised on viewing life itself as contextual yet defined by the exercise of affective, personal choice. And I support this convergence of analytical models within English studies, this continuation of the theoretical blurring of lines between poetics and rhetoric.

As I implied at the beginning of this article, my point is to show the links in theory and methodology in order to create a broad discourse dynamic, a dynamic that I believe will particularly highlight needed areas of rhetorical scholarship. In the process, I have come to believe that indeed rhetoricians and literary critics are moving away from traditional, mutually exclusive definitions of art and rhetoric, a view which, as Faigley has noted, especially limits literary theory to a study of the products of "solitary artistic genius rather than expressions of a culture" ("Nonacademic Writing" 236). Certainly new historicists adamantly assert that art is not simply mimetic or universal, and that in fact Renaissance literary art, as much as the written scientific treatises of the times, helped shape reality. Indeed it seems especially appropriate to recognize the rhetorical nature of the belletristic writers of the Renaissance, as it was their rhetorician contemporaries who reduced rhetorical study to a concern with form over substance. And as Robert Scholes has noted, the traditional "binary opposition" of rhetoric and poetics ignores the fact that no text is free of the reason/aesthetic, power/pleasure, information/expressive functions of discourse because every text is culture-bound.

At the very least, then, a comparison of new historicism and social rhetoric further illustrates the commonality between rhetoric and literary theory and tells us something about the nature of knowledge, what Carolyn Miller has called the "centrality of human interpretive activity to many fields" (32). In its broadest sense, I hope my discussion will also contribute to an ongoing dialogue among all of us engaged in culture-based inquiry, leading to what Bizzell has called "a new humanistic synthesis," which, she suggests, will rediscover rhetoric to be "the central discipline of human intellectual endeavor" (239). ❧

WORKS CITED

Bizzell, Patricia. "Cognition, Convention, and Certainty: What We Need to Know about Writing." *PRE/TEXT* 3 (1982): 213-43.

Brown, Paul. "'This Thing of Darkness I Acknowledge Mine': *The Tempest* and the Discourse of Colonialism." Dollimore, *Political Shakespeare*. 48-71.

Deal, Terrence E. and Allen A. Kennedy. *Corporate Cultures: The Rites and Rituals of Corporate Life*. Reading, MA: Addison-Wesley, 1982.

Dollimore, Jonathan, and Alan Sinfield, eds. *Political Shakespeare: New Essays in Cultural Materialism*. Ithaca: Cornell UP, 1985.

Faigley, Lester. "Nonacademic Writing: The Social Perspective." Odell, *Writing in Nonacademic Settings*. 231-48.

———, and Thomas Miller. "What We Learn from Writing On the Job." *College English* 44 (1982): 557-569.

Fish, Stanley. "Authors-Readers: Jonson's Community of the Same." Greenblatt, *Representing the English Renaissance* 231-263.

Geertz, Clifford. *The Interpretation of Cultures*. New York: Basic, 1973.

Greenblatt, Stephen. *Renaissance Self-Fashioning*. Chicago: U Chicago P, 1980

———, ed. *Representing the English Renaissance*. Berkeley: U California P, 1988.

———, ed. "The Forms of Power and the Power of Forms in the Renaissance." Special issue of *Genre* 15 (1982): 1-242. Norman: U Oklahoma P, 1982.

Heath, Shirley Brice. *Ways with Words: Language, Life, and Work in Communities and Classrooms.* Cambridge: Cambridge U P, 1983.

Miller, Carolyn R. "Public Knowledge in Science and Society." *PRE/TEXT* 3 (1982): 31-49.

Montrose, Louis A. "*A Midsummer Night's Dream* and the Shaping Fantasies of Elizabethan Culture: Gender, Power, Form." *Rewriting the Renaissance: The Discourses of Sexual Difference in Early Modern Europe.* Eds. Margaret W. Ferguson, Maureen Quilligan, and Nancy J. Vickers. Chicago: U Chicago P, 1986. 65-87.

———. "'Shaping Fantasies': Figurations of Gender and Power in Elizabethan Culture." Greenblatt, *Representing the English Renaissance.* 31-64.

Normann, Richard. *Management and Statesmanship.* Stockholm: Scandinavian Institutes for Administrative Research, 1976.

Odell, Lee. "Beyond the Text: Relations between Writing and Social Context." Odell, *Writing in Nonacademic Settings.* 249-80.

——— and Dixie Goswami, eds. *Writing in Nonacademic Settings.* New York: Guilford, 1985.

———, et al. "Studying Writing in Non-Academic Settings." *New Essays in Technical and Scientific Communication: Research, Theory, Practice.* Eds. Paul V. Anderson, R. John Brockmann, and Carolyn R. Miller. Farmingdale, NY: Baywood, 1983. 17-40.

Paradis, James, David Dobrin, and Richard Miller. "Writing at Exxon ITD: Notes on the Writing Environment of an R&D Organization." Odell, *Writing in Nonacademic Settings* 281-307.

Pechter, Edward. "The New Historicism and Its Discontents: Politicizing Renaissance Drama." *PMLA* 102.3 (1987): 292-303.

Peters, Thomas J. and Robert H. Waterman, Jr. *In Search of Excellence: Lessons from America's Best-Run Companies.* New York: Warner, 1982.

Rentz, Kathryn C. and Mary Beth Debs. "Language and Corporate Values: Teaching Ethics in Business Writing Courses." *The Journal of Business Communication* 24.3 (1987): 37-48.

Scholes, Robert. Keynote address. Penn State Conference on Rhetoric and Composition. State College PA, 6 July 1988.

❦ 15

Engineered Revisions in Industry

Mary Rosner

Several years ago, Lester Faigley identified three general lines of research in nonacademic writing: a textual perspective that analyzes the features of texts, an individual perspective that analyzes certain choices the writer made while composing, and a social perspective that analyzes how texts define and maintain organizations by their relationship to previous texts and to their present contexts (233-236). These perspectives help us see some of the complexity of "real-world writing"; and the more we see, the more likely we are to create complete and accurate pictures of the nonacademic writing and revising we teach.

We need these pictures. We all know, for instance, how *little* we know about how technical writers revise. This ignorance persists in spite of increased interest in technical writing and in spite of increased research in broad areas of composing that tells us again and again that writers revise on many occasions and in many ways. The generic revising strategies we now teach are certainly more sophisticated than the advice advocated in an old technical writing book directing the technical writer to synchronicity, to "the habit of regulating the speed of his [or her] writing so that it keeps step with the order of his [or her] thinking" (Rickard 166). Still, we need more than generic strategies. We need to acknowledge that specific writing communities may have *specific* revising strategies as well.

Thus, before we can teach revising to our technical writing students, we need to identify the kinds of revising technical writers do.

Unfortunately, we do not yet have enough research to generalize soundly; those very good studies we do have—because they are good and because they are few—give persuasive but distorted and contradictory views of what writers do when they revise—in part because their perspectives are limited. Paul Anderson has used survey research to argue that

> when writers on the job are preparing documents longer than ten pages, they spend substantially more time prewriting and revising than they do when composing shorter documents. Also, when preparing longer documents they are more likely to treat prewriting and revising separately from writing (rather than prewriting and revising simultaneously with their actual writing activities). (48)

Even with composing processes that are not necessarily recursive, Anderson's writers substantially revise their texts. The writers at Exxon ITD interviewed by James Paradis, David Dobrin, and Richard Miller similarly spent chunks of their writing-related job time, anywhere from 19 percent to 72 percent, in reviewing and editing (revising) completed drafts (285). But Jack Selzer's study of the texts produced and interviews given by one engineer indicates that he spent less than 5 percent of his time revising and that he defined the activity as little more than superficial editing occurring within the constraints of the organizational context and only after a draft had been typed. Moreover, his writing activities always fell "into mutually exclusive and consecutive stages" (185). As Selzer explained, "rarely does [his subject] begin to arrange or draft before his inventing or global planning are completed; rarely does he invent or revise while he writes his first draft; rarely does his revision include anything but final editing" (185). From Dorothy Winsor's broader research perspective, we find a possible explanation for the revising habits of Selzer's engineer: he may have needed to make few changes in his current document only because of the many changes he made in its earlier "lives": "Whether [this engineer] is seen as doing much revision depends upon what is taken to be his 'original' wording. On one hand, [he] made few changes once he had created his own draft, but, on the other hand, almost everything he did was revision of previously written documents" (277).

My study contributes to this picture of the revising process of technical writers with analyses of interviews, texts, and organizational context that reveal the revising practices of two engineers at a large manufacturing plant in the midwest: Joe Jones has worked for this organization for 16 years, Sam Smith for nine. (All names are pseudonymous.) Both have held their current positions for four years. Joe and Sam are Advanced Manufacturing Engineers responsible for—as Sam says—"automated equipment procurement with babysitting functions that go along with it. We identify projects, concept equipment, write specs, go out for vender quotes, build the machinery when it arrives, and debug it." In other words, both design new machines and hire people to build them; then they check out the machines and get them running efficiently at the plant. Sam is responsible for preparing product doors to receive insulation; Joe is responsible for assembling and insulating the doors. My research confirms that these two engineers are technical writers; and like professional writers in general, they seem to spend considerable time planning before they begin to write. But my results also suggest that because they see planning as part of composing—composing the concept rather than the text—they see revising as a large part of planning, not a separate activity. And for them, revising means not just editing but actually revisualizing and rethinking *during* prewriting as they are working with concepts and *during* writing as they are working with texts.

In collecting data for this study, a colleague and I conducted initial 40-minute interviews with 15 engineers within the manufacturing plant, asking them about the kinds and amount of writing they produced, their audiences, and their planning activities, as well as their criteria for the specific kinds of documents we had been hired to produce: equipment training manuals. I targeted Joe and Sam for follow-up interviews because of their interest in and ability to talk about writing. In preparation for the second interview, I asked them to collect copies of everything they wrote at work within a two-week period, including scribbles, notes, doodles, designs, outlines, rough plans, final drafts on paper or in the computer. I also asked them to collect the early notes, drafts, revisions, and final copy of any single document they had produced. Joe had copies of everything he drafted for every project he had worked on in well-organized files—sketches, drawings, form fill-ins, formal and informal proposals. After reviewing the material, I interviewed him about his revising procedures and followed with a third interview after I had analyzed the tape and transcription of the second. Sam had copies only of final drafts, so these were the subject of my second meeting with him. However, he also allowed me to observe him for more than an hour as he revised a final draft that he had created to document an earlier project so it would fit his current project; as he made these changes, I asked him questions that led him to articulate his rationales. The information presented in this paper comes from analyses of Joe's series of texts, Sam's original and revised final drafts, and my interviews with both of them as well as an analysis of an interview with the company's in-house text reviewer.

Conceptual revising

The company encourages engineers like Joe and Sam to see revising as part of planning. Following procedures at the plant, they participate in "Concept Reviews" early in their projects: in these formal meetings, engineers get feedback on their ideas from other members of the engineering team about what machines they need and what work they would perform. Eleven people with varied expertise and interests attended Joe's Concept Review for a typical project recently, and he received criticisms from most of them. Later, after revising his concept for a piece of machinery, he brought it to a local company and received further suggestions for revision, so that after five weeks and three or four different attempts, the company and Joe, working together, came up with a model that accurately fit his needs. The informal feedback that colleagues within the plant are likely to provide also leads to new and revised ideas. Because these engineers are housed in small open-door carrels on both sides of a single corridor, it is easy for them to exchange information, questions, criticisms, and drafts as they visit back and forth.

In addition to the advice that Joe and Sam happily invite from their colleagues as they are working out their ideas for machinery, they also use a strategy that previous studies do not mention: they draw. Like the scientist who noted that "the words of the language, as they are written or spoken, do not seem to play any role in [his] mechanism of thought" (Hadamard 142), these engineers acknowledge that visuals are more important than words as they work out their ideas. For them sketches and blueprints are tools for invention and revision, not simply a way of recording data. As Rudolf Arnheim has said, we need to "go beyond the traditional notion that pictures provide the mere raw material and that thinking begins only after the information has been received . . . *thinking is done by means of structural properties inherent in the image. . .*" (14, my emphasis). These visual images help engineers think, plan, and revise their plans. Joe explained to me that when he is working on a project, he visualizes procedures—first with doodles of parts, then of the whole. He said that he "likes to see what's going on . . . to massage it on paper" because that helps him think. Joe typically moves from a rough sketch, to a sketch identifying parts, to a detailed design; each of these stages may be refined repeatedly. On a recent project, for example, he revised his design 20 to 25 times *before* he started to draft his detailed description in prose.

This strategy clearly resembles Stephen Witte's "pre-text," defined as "a 'trial locution' that is produced in the mind, stored in the writer's memory, and sometimes manipulated mentally prior to being transcribed as written text" (397). Witte says that these "mental constructions" affect phrases, clauses, sentences, and sequences of sentences as the text is constructed. The engineers I interviewed treated *designs* as pre-text; they imaginatively juggled choices of materials, sizes, locations, complexity, and costs before transcribing their designs. And they continued to manipulate and revise their designs in the review and testing stages of their equipment as they moved from sketches to texts. Joe and Sam see these activities as occasions to modify and adapt—to revise.

Textual revising

The paperwork required to document each project as well as the length of time from project assignment to completion helps engineers like Sam and Joe to re-see and alter their plans when they finally get to the text stage. As the sign on one engineer's wall said, "Getting things done around here is like mating elephants: it's done at a high level; it's accomplished with a great deal of roaring and screaming; it takes two years to produce results." Two years is conservative. In February 1986 Joe was asked to design a simple machine that would automatically seat gaskets on product doors. After several false starts, Joe worked steadily on the project from March 1987 on. Here is a summary of Joe's designing and documenting activities as of April 1988:

3/8/87	Designs method to seat gaskets automatically.
	Writes invention disclosure.
6/1/87	Requests bids from a reliable company.
8/6/87	Changes Design after a concept review.
	Revises design.
	Writes a draft of Specifications.
8/11/87	Writes a Request for Material.

8/17/87	Writes to explain why competitive bids were not solicited.
8/20/87	Writes Purchase Order for Equipment Prototype.
8/27/87	Revises Specifications.
9/1/87	Writes a Request for Material.
	Writes an Acceptance Criteria Report, identifying what tests have to be run on the machines and with what results for the machines to be acceptable.
9/9/87	Writes a Purchase Order for two machines.
	Revises the Control Panel on the machines.
10/19/87	Completes an Internal Shop Order Form.
11/16/87	Changes design after a Design Review.
1/8/88	Writes a Request for Shipping.
1/26/88	Writes a Request for Bids to install the machines.
	Writes Specifications for installing the machines.
2/5/88	Writes a Request for Quotes to install the machines.
2/24/88	Writes a Request for Material to finance installation.
3/1/88	Writes a Request for Inspection of Machines.
3/15/88	Revises the design.
4/5/88	Discovers problems while operating machines and makes ongoing revisions in the design.

Over this 13-month period, Joe had six documented occasions to revise his design for the machine, the documentation describing the machine, and the machine itself. He expects to revise further.

Probably one of the most important texts that these engineers write at the plant are "specifications," which give detailed descriptions of equipment required for a project and identify precisely and thoroughly the standards that each new piece of equipment has to meet as it is built, installed, and operated in the plant. Creating wholly original sets of specifications requires the engineer to become part of a team, since he or she needs information from specialists in mechanics, quality control, safety, production, and so on in order to document each machine and its functions thoroughly. But just as the machines that the engineers build are often improvements on existing models, the texts that they write are often revisions of existing texts. I actually watched Sam spend over an hour "creating" specifications for a new conveyor system by—as he said—"cutting and pasting, rewording, adding, and doing whatever necessary" to the old spec so it accurately described his latest model. This process is typical of Sam's written revisions. He invariably starts a writing project by retrieving the specification of an earlier version of a machine from his file.

He uses a red pencil on an existing text to identify small changes he wants to make. For major revisions, he uses black pencil on lined paper, which he then cuts and pastes onto a copy of the old document. He revises each paragraph as he writes, and then the whole document; then he rereads and rethinks both the design and the text that his secretary has by then typed and checked for spelling, punctuation, and abbreviations. After the document receives a final internal review and a final revision, he destroys all earlier versions.

Because specifications become the basis for bids from vendors outside the organization, engineers know that they have to be accurate, complete, and clear. Sam is a careful reviser, interested in expressing his ideas accurately, in directing but not dictating to his audience, and in using the form prescribed within the organization. Sam's explanations of his revisions indicated that he was very conscious of both his professional image and his relationship to his audience, who are bidders for the job of creating and installing the equipment that would run his line:

4.2.1	He said he changed "move" to "relocate" because "relocate" sounds stronger, more serious.
4.2.1.1	He changed "required relocation" to "included is relocation" because he said that he did not want to require a vendor to follow a particular plan. Sam prefers broad specifications that allow him to get the benefit of the vendor's creative solution to a problem, rather than narrow specifications that restrict the vendor to carrying out Sam's solution.
4.2.1.2	He added information when he realized that he had to say something about using existing conveyors to fill the gaps in the new system so his instructions would be complete and his design would be economical. Sam explained that the first sentence he constructed in his head had "holes" filled with modifications. Before transcribing that sentence, he realized "you don't fill holes with modifications."
4.2.2	He realized that he needed to be more specific, so Sam added the qualifiers "Orange Belt Accumulating" to Zone.
4.2.3	To be more specific, Sam again added qualifiers: "Red Roller South." Then he looked at his drawing and realized that conveyors going in the direction he wanted could not be red, and so he revised for correctness to "Orange Belt Accumulating" Zone Conveyor South.

As this excerpt shows, while Sam was writing and revising this page, he first identified the general kind of information he needed, then refined that information with his specific context in mind. For instance, he knew he wanted Zone Conveyors in the production line because they are the standard for moving material at the plant—so he wrote down Zone Conveyors; but as he visualized the line and consulted his blueprints, he recognized that he needed to distinguish the kinds of conveyors he wanted at this specific location. This excerpt does not show how careful Sam was to be precise in his use of numbered subdivisions, always consciously reviewing the logical progression of numbers and information as he moved from step to step. He did far more than the "superficial editing" that Selzer reports his engineer practiced. Revising for Sam was hard work: it required rethinking throughout text production.

In spite of the hard work done by engineers like Sam who revised their specifications, they seem to feel little ownership of their products, perhaps because they have in a sense already coauthored both their designs and their texts as they responded to the advice received both formally and informally. As a result, some do not hesitate to scavenge from texts produced by other engineers, crossing out and adding where appropriate. For example, a third engineer, Scott, "wrote" his specification by revising an earlier one created by Joe. Scott relied so heavily on Joe's original text that the secretary, Bonnie, had to be reminded whose spec this was by a note on the bottom of the page: "Bonnie Pls Note Put in Scott's File."

In-house review

While these engineers say that they consider what they do *during planning* to be the most significant part of their revising, they also acknowledge that engineers new to the organization might spend as much time and energy revising completed drafts of documents, especially specifications, since the in-house review that a spec goes through can be intimidating. Ed Frame, the in-house text reviewer, is in effect a symbol of quality within the company because he is the man who created the four-inch-thick Blue Book—distributed to each engineer—that identifies the standards for all new machinery used in the plant. The Blue Book also identifies in detail the correct form and appropriate content for each specification. Ed's job is to make sure that all specifications for new machinery comply with the standards announced, that the specs are in the designated format, that they describe clearly what the machine should do, and that they are detailed enough to result in accurate vendor bids. To help the "strong-minded" engineers meet his expectations, he created a one-page checklist for generating and issuing specifications, keyed to the information in the Blue Book. The engineers I observed, however, referred to previously successful specs rather than to this checklist as they composed and revised.

Both Sam and Joe say that they have no trouble writing for this internal reviewer: they know what he is looking for because they have been under his review for four years. They also know that they can occasionally ignore his comments without penalty. But new engineers do not find this review so painless: they have no files of old specs that make writing easy, they are unfamiliar with the form used by the organization, and they lack the tacit knowledge that helps them distinguish between the significant and the insignificant. As Joe said, "[New guys] coming in [get] destroyed. . . . They don't know what [the reviewer] is looking for. They're writing down what they perceive to be the right things, but they are generally not. It's a matter of becoming familiar with the . . . guy upstairs." These new members of the organization have to learn their new culture—through the reviewer's criticisms, through models that circulate informally, and through any help they can get from the other engineers— so they can revise appropriately.

Implications

Studying engineers like these raises questions about the soundness of the general conclusions drawn from previous research. From the examples of Joe and Sam, we can see that studies of the composing processes of engineers need to take into account all the composing that goes on before engineers start to write, all the composing that is not verbal; the effects of the lengthy process of documenting their designs, which invites them to rethink and revise their previous design decisions and texts; and the important role that the organization plays in implicitly and explicitly training its workers to write. Studying engineers like these might suggest that we create a series of related assignments on a single project for our technical writing students so they can have the experience of rethinking and reevaluating that project as they write and rewrite it. It might suggest that our course be extended into a second semester, that we use visuals as a heuristic in our classrooms, that we encourage more sharing of documents and ideas. It might also suggest that we listen more to what professionals say about the writing they do—so that, for instance, we can determine whether engineers have definitions of "revision" that differ from our own. In other words, we have to analyze—and help our students analyze—the cultures they will enter, the special topics of their organizations.

As Carolyn Miller has explained, an organization can constrain what its members think and write about. The principles underlying Aristotle's special topics suggest that such topics have three sources: conventional expectation in rhetorical situations, knowledge and issues available in the institutions and organizations in which those situations occur, and concepts available in specific networks of knowledge (or disciplines). (67)

We too often restrict what we teach to the first source, the conventional wisdom. We need to help our students study the other two: the contexts of the organizations in which rhetorical situations occur and the key issues of those organizations. To do this, we need to recognize the limitations in our own field-dependent concepts. I have tried to do that in the study I describe here by replacing a common technical writing textbook definition of revising with the engineers' own definition. Revision for them is not just something that happens after a text is written, and it is not just something that concerns words on the page: a concept gets revised; so does a sketch.

We also need to beware of overgeneralizing the significance of the studies on which we base what we teach. After all, Joe and Ed are only *two* manufacturing engineers from one large organization; what I've learned about their revising procedures cannot be generalized to the revising of *all* engineers, since each organization has its own culture and constraints. We need broader studies that will give us reliable answers to questions like these:

- Do engineers typically have the long incubation stage exemplified by Joe as he revised his designs for seating the gasket?
- Do engineers in other fields use visual thinking for inventing and revising as these two men do?
- Do other organizations typically designate a reviewer to define its public face by suggesting revisions in important documents that go outside the organization? Are engineers able to reject the reviewer's suggestions?
- How do engineers learn to do the kind of writing expected from them as they move from organization to organization?
- How important are models? forms? checklists? existing texts?

Whatever answers we find to these questions, we need to go

beyond telling our students that technical writers revise for 5 percent, 10 percent, or 50 percent of their writing time; we need to help them understand how, when, and why writers do what they do. To accomplish this, we need to expand our research perspectives and our research base so that what we teach—about individual texts, writing choices, and the relationships between text and context—is supported by, and tested by, more studies. We need to analyze and help our students analyze the cultures they will enter, for, as Carolyn Miller says, those cultures can serve as "conceptual places that yield arguments possibly useful in a rhetorical situation related to the genre, institution, or discipline" (67), possibly useful to the revising they will do. And we need to embrace our responsibilities for helping our technical writing students revise conceptually as well as textually, even if this means we have to become educated in some basic heuristics of their fields. Too often—and too easily—we have followed Ramus in abandoning "responsibility for the materials and content of discourse that . . . fall within the province of the special sciences" (Kneupper and Anderson 318) and in limiting rhetoric to considerations of an already created text. As teachers and researchers, we need to revise what we do. 🐝

WORKS CITED

Anderson, Paul. "What Survey Research Tells Us about Writing at Work." *Writing in Nonacademic Settings*. Eds. Lee Odell and Dixie Goswami. New York: Guilford, 1985. 3-83.

Arnheim, Rudolf. "A Plea for Visual Thinking." *New Essays on the Psychology of Art*. Berkeley: U California P, 1986. 135-152.

Faigley, Lester. "Nonacademic Writing: The Social Perspective." *Writing in Nonacademic Settings*. Eds. Lee Odell and Dixie Goswami. New York: Guilford, 1985. 231-248.

Hadamard, Jacques. *The Psychology of Invention in the Mathematical Field*. Princeton: Princeton UP, 1945.

Kneupper, Charles W., and Floyd D. Anderson. "Uniting Wisdom and Eloquence: The Need for Rhetorical Invention." *Quarterly Journal of Speech* 66 (1980): 313-326.

Miller, Carolyn. "Aristotle's 'Special Topics' in Rhetorical Practice and Pedagogy." *Rhetoric Society Quarterly* 7 (Winter 1987): 61-70.

Paradis, James, David Dobrin, and Richard Miller. "Writing at Exxon ITD:

Notes on the Writing Environment of an R & D Organization." *Writing in Nonacademic Settings*. Eds. Lee Odell and Dixie Goswami. New York: Guilford, 1985. 281-307.

Rickard, T. A. *Technical Writing*. New York: Wiley, 1928.

Selzer, Jack. "The Composing Process of an Engineer." *College Composition and Communication* 34 (1983): 178-87.

Winsor, Dorothy. "An Engineer's Writing and the Corporate Construction of Knowledge." *Written Communication* 6 (1989): 270-85.

Witte, Stephen. "Pre-Text and Composing." *College Composition and Communication* 38 (1987): 397-425.

❧ 16

Citation and Documentation Across the Curriculum

Diane Dowdey

In the course of reading documented articles in many academic disciplines, I became aware that the traditions of research, citation, and documentation vary tremendously from one discipline to another; even within various disciplines there is more diversity than most of us trained in the traditional humanities are aware. As writing across the curriculum becomes more important, as English teachers work more with colleagues in other fields, as composition classes encourage students to do research in a variety of disciplines, it becomes imperative that we understand the traditions of research, citation, and documentation in other fields. We also need to understand that differences in documentation styles frequently reflect different ways of using citations and even the role of citation in the discourse of various disciplines.

Because the documentation style reveals the importance of citation within a discipline, it also reveals something about the method of research and the traditions of scholarship within the discipline. What counts as knowledge in a particular field is displayed by what is cited and how it is documented. James L. Kinneavy has called for a study of the rhetorical conventions of specialized academic discourse communities and "some general study of the methodologies, definitions, criteria of evidence, general axiomatic systems, and views of value systems" (19) within various disciplines. Obviously such a comprehensive study is beyond the scope of this essay, but by looking at a fairly narrow and straightforward aspect of a discipline we can address some of these issues.

Patricia Bizzell argues that "to help poor writers . . . we need to explain that their writing takes place within a community, and to explain what the community's conventions are" (230). To help students fulfill the expectations of their academic community we need to introduce them to the conventions of the various discourse communities within it. One of the most obvious conventions of a discourse community is its citation strategy and documentation style. Charles Bazerman shows that writers within an academic community know how to relate the text to "the object under study, the literature of the field, the anticipated audience" (362) through discipline–specific conventions governing vocabulary, implicit knowledge, and explicit citations. Erwin Steinberg cautions scholars of writing not to "think in terms of a single model [of the writing process], because if we do we'll find one and force everyone to use it" (163). This caution is also appropriate when teaching or discussing citation and documentation styles in disciplines. In fact, as a discussion of textbooks will demonstrate later, composition teachers in English departments do tend to impose a single model for citation and documentation.

Methodology of the study

In order to make some generalizations, I grouped various disciplines into the three major divisions of academic study: the humanities, the social sciences, and the sciences. However, conventions of documentation are usually discipline specific and not standardized throughout divisions, especially in the social sciences and the sciences.

In order to determine the standards for citation and documentation, I examined the policies of journals in various disciplines. According to a compilation of style sheets for theses and dissertations made by the Texas A&M library, most departments require students to use the style of various standard journals within the field, especially those published by their major scholarly association. To determine standardization within the academic divisions and within single disciplines, I conducted a random survey of every twentieth item in the *Directory of Publishing Opportunities*, 5th edition, 1981.

Citation and documentation in the humanities

What disciplinary expectations are revealed by the citation and documentation strategies used in literary and rhetorical criticism? These disciplines use the citation and documentation strategies of other humanities disciplines such as philosophy, fine arts criticism, and history. Citations in the humanities are frequently used as authoritative places to begin an argument. Articles often begin by naming an authority, and in the humanities we often give the person's credentials—academic affiliation, authorship, or in some cases the connection to someone else, such as identifying the cited person as the student of a recognized authority. Humanities scholars depend on shared background knowledge. For example, an article will begin with "James L. Kinneavy," and the author expects the audience to know who he is and why he is an appropriate authority to cite. Usually in humanities research, relevant passages are cited or the authority's position summarized.

For example, Daniel Hoffman, in *Form and Fable in American Fiction*, writes the following:

> Where some find the theme of [*Huckleberry Finn*] to be the search for freedom, another proposes the "theme of appearance versus reality." J. M. Cox suggests initiation and rebirth as its besetting theme, while Philip Young discovers that "an excessive exposure to violence and death" have produced the ideal symbol" for dying, namely, a "supremely effortless flight into a dark and silent unknown." Yet again "death and rebirth" and "Huck's journey in search of a father" are urged by K. S. Lynn as themes, while R. W. Frantz terms Huck a "creature of fear." As for motive, the ingenious Leslie Fiedler reads the book as a wish–fulfillment of homosexual miscegenation. On the other hand Mr. Trilling has made a definitive case for "Huck's intense and even complex moral quality." (319)

This kind of dense citation and quotation, usually early in the work, is characteristic of humanities citation patterns. Tying new interpretations into standard traditions is an explicit part of the citation process because the humanities tend to see knowledge as an accumulation of perspectives.

Humanities scholarship uses citations throughout the text both as authority and demonstration. It usually relies heavily on primary texts to provide demonstration and on authority to exemplify the approved assumptions in the community. For example, one article in *Philosophy Today* begins with a direct quote to substantiate the importance of the topic. Sixty–four percent of the author's citations are to direct quotations, many of them substantial in length (Dooley).

Privileging the text—accentuating the importance of exact words—is exemplified by both the citation conventions and the major documentation systems used in humanities research. I will focus here on the parenthetical style recommended by the *MLA Style Manual* of 1985 (see Figure 1). This documentation system makes it easy to refer to a specific passage by incorporating the page, scene, or line number into each instance of documentation. It encourages the use of notes that elaborate with additional material, caveats, or editorial commentary. For example, the previously cited article by Bizzell includes the following endnote:

> See Basil Bernstein, *Class, Codes and Control* (1971; rpt. New York: Schocken, 1975); and to correct the vulgar error that Bernstein is diagnosing a cognitive deficiency in working–class language, see "The Significance of Bernstein's Work for Sociolinguistic Theory" in Halliday, pp. 101–107. Many dangerous misinterpretations of Bernstein could perhaps have been avoided if he had not chosen to call working–class language–using habits a "restricted code" and middle–class (school–oriented) habits an "elaborated code." (242)

This note not only contains documentation but also tells the reader how to interpret Bernstein and even suggests what he should have done to prevent the error in the first place. That Bizzell, or her editors, clearly saw this information as secondary to the main point of the article is emphasized by its placement in a note. However, it is also clear that Bizzell thought it important to include this interpretation of Bernstein to remedy a misperception of his work.

What else does the MLA documentation style suggest? By using the complete name of the author, or the author's preferred form of address, the MLA style stresses the significance of the unique individual (see Figure 1). The title of an article is placed in quotation marks, recognizing that it is somebody's words, once again privileging the text. Journal titles are not abbreviated, suggesting that the audience is not likely to be familiar with all journals in the field. The place of publication tends to be just the city, assuming some audience familiarity, and only the first name of a publishing firm is given. This practice suggests that the audience knows the names of most publishers and will recognize "Holt" as an abbreviation for "Holt, Rinehart, and Winston." Publishing firms tend to be more substantial than journals, which perhaps accounts for the difference in treatment between journal names and publisher names. The date of the book

---

Figure 1. MLA Style Manual *guidelines for "Works Cited" lists*
Source: MLA Style Manual *103–104, 132–133.*

4.4 Citing Books: Information required

4.4.1. General Guidelines

An entry in a list of works cited characteristically has three main divisions—author, title, and publication information—each followed by a period and two spaces.

> Frye, Northrop. <u>Anatomy of Criticism: Four Essays</u>.
> Princeton: Princeton UP, 1957.

4.4.2. Author's name

Reverse the author's name for alphabetizing, adding a comma after the last name: Porter, Katherine Anne. Follow the name with a period and leave two spaces before beginning the next item.

Always give the author's name as it appears on the title page. Never abbreviate a name given in full. If, for example, the title page lists the author as "Carleton Brown" do not enter the book under "Brown, C." Conversely, if the title page shows an initial for a name (T. S. Eliot), do not spell out the name in full.

4.6. Citing articles in periodicals: Information required

4.6.3. Title of the article

Give the title of the article in full, enclosed in quotation marks (not underlined). Unless the title has its own concluding punctuation (e.g., a question mark), put a period before the closing quotation mark.

4.6.4. Name of the periodical

When citing a periodical, omit any introductory article but otherwise give the name, underlined, as it appears on the title page: <u>William and Mary Quarterly</u> (not The William and Mary Quarterly).

---

comes last, the place of least significance. The insignificance of the date is underscored by a study of citations in humanities journals showing that the vast majority of citations were to works published more than 10 years ago (Garfield 55). Although this study made no distinction between primary source material and criticism, examination of the October 1989 *PMLA* demonstrates that even with primary source material left out, most citations were to books and articles more than 10 years old. The range was from 78 percent older than 10 years (an article on James Joyce) to 39 percent older than 10 years (an article on dramatic and cinematic treatments of the Elephant Man story). The citation style demonstrates that recency is not a significant qualification.

There is a high degree of standardization in documentation styles in the humanities, which makes it different from the social sciences and the sciences. Most scholarly journals in the humanities, 74 percent in fact, referred contributors to a standard style sheet, such as those published by professional organizations like the Modern Language Association or the Linguistic Society of America, or the style manual published by the University of Chicago Press. Seldom does a humanities journal develop its own style sheet. However, a few journals acknowledge that these "standard" styles allow for some variation.[1] Although *The MLA Style Manual* recommends a parenthetical citation system, the book devotes 14 pages to the use of notes as an alternative system. *The Chicago Manual of Style* actually presents four systems:

> This chapter discusses and illustrates four methods used to document texts: (1) Author–date (name and year) references in the text with full citations in a reference list at the end of the book or article, a method long used by the biological and physical scientists and now rapidly gaining adherents in the social sciences and the humanities (15.4–35). (2) Endnotes (backnotes), like footnotes but placed all together at the end of the book or article (15.54–57). (3) Footnotes, still beloved by traditionalists, especially those in the humanities (15.58–64). (4) Unnumbered notes, and notes keyed to line or page numbers and placed either at the foot of the page or at the back of the book (15.70–73). (400)

The Chicago Manual of Style also demonstrates various bibliographic reference styles[2] (see Figure 2).

Apparently, all of the forms are equally "sanctioned," equally "correct," and all provide essentially the same information; the reason for the differences must be disciplinary style or rhetorical expectations. It is, however, worth noting that only the humanities disciplines seem to have some consensus on documentation style, as demonstrated by the general acceptance of standardized citation styles by most journals in a variety of different disciplines.

Figure 2. *Differences Between Chicago Style A and Chicago Style B Bibliography Formats*
Source: Carosso 252.

	Chicago Style A	Chicago Style B
names	Usually spells out the author's given name	Usually uses initials instead of the author's given name
date of publication	Places book date after publisher, journal date after volume number	Places date after author's name
capitalization	Capitalizes all key words in titles	Capitalizes only the first letter of titles and subtitles and any proper nouns
titles	Uses full titles	Often omits subtitles and sometimes omits article titles
quotation marks	Uses quotation marks around article titles	Does not use quotation marks around article titles
abbreviations	Usually uses full names of publishers and journal titles	Often abbreviates publishers and journal titles

Citation and documentation in the social sciences

Articles in the social sciences—business, economics, education, political science, psychology, and sociology—tend to cluster citations in the introduction and conclusion. Citations are used to appeal to authority, to serve as starting points for research, and to demonstrate accepted givens in the discipline. Of course, citing a reference can make it given. Direct quotation is not used as frequently as in the humanities. For example, an article on houses in Brazil in *American Anthropologist* has an introductory paragraph dense with citations but only paraphrasing the main ideas of the authors it is discussing.

Bourdieu's notion of *habitus* helps us clarify the complex relation of space and practice. Habitus is that array of commonsense, taken–for–granted social ways whose structuration of our practices often escapes us. Habitus simultaneously generates and is generated by social classifications reproduced in practice (Bordieu 1977:72; 1984:170). These structural properties of practices "are both the medium and the outcome of the practices they recursively organize" in the process of structuration (Giddens 1984:25). Structures and classifications are simultaneously produced and reproduced interiorized and exteriorized as the unintended consequences of both conscious and habitual pursuits (Certeau 1984:57; Giddens 1984:8–14, 1985:272–278; Sahlins 1985:ix; Touraine 1977:3–6). (Robben 570–571)

The point of such a paragraph is to demonstrate the commonality of the idea by scholars in the discipline, not to give their exact words. The author, Antonius Robben, assumes his audience is familiar with Bordieu, since no other information, even a first name, is provided. He also assumes that his audience will recognize the connection between Bordieu's work and that of Gidden, whom he briefly quotes. Like many social science articles, the two-page introduction of this piece contains 53 citations, while the rest of its 13 pages contain only 49 citations.

Similar use of citation without quotation to demonstrate accepted ideas within the discipline is found in an article by David R. James from *American Sociological Review:*

Class theories argue that local–state fragmentation serves the interests of dominant classes by protecting class privileges, and by managing social conflicts and demobilizing insurgences (e.g., Friedland, Piven, and Alford 1978; Cockburn 1977). Institutionalists argue that fragmentation hinders policy implementation and tends to make the metropolis ungovernable (e.g., Greer 1987; Yates 1977). Rational–choice or market models claim that local–state fragmentation serves democracy. If citizens are not satisfied with one local government, they may choose another in the metropolitan area that provides them with the public services they prefer (e.g., Peterson 1981; Ostrom, Tiebout, and Warren 1961). (963)

Neither of these examples shows the use of extensive quotation or even of brief quotations. It is not exact language that is privileged but ideas only. James also clusters citations in the introduction and in a section which begins "[n]umerous studies find that high black percentage is one of the most important causes for white exit from and nonentrance to desegregated public–school systems" (971). The entire article contains only one direct quotation.

Demonstration or proof tends to be provided not by citation of text but by quotations of surveys, statistical interpretation, or experimental data. For example, after quoting authorities to set up the context of the research, Robben provides census data about the number of inhabitants and how they earn a living. He also provides a description and diagram of these people's houses. The body of the article contains only two direct quotations, one of which claims that the plan of Brazilian houses has remained stable for several centuries. James's article also presents census information in tables and analyzes that data to prove his point.

Even in social science scholarship that surveys the literature, there is little direct quotation of studies or experiments. For example, in "The Powers of John Barleycorn: Beliefs About the Effects of Alcohol on Social Behavior," an article surveying and synthesizing previous studies rather than presenting new information, the use of direct quotations is minimal. Of the 185 citations in the article, only 33, or 18 percent, are to quotations. The majority of the 33 quotations establish historical belief or quote individuals' beliefs about how alcohol affects behavior (Leigh). Strategies of citation in the social sciences do not privilege text.

Although many English textbooks present the *American Psychological Association (APA) Publication Manual* system of documentation as standard in the social sciences, they are inaccurate. Only 32 percent of the journals surveyed in the *Directory of Publishing Opportunities* prescribe a standardized style sheet such as the APA style or *The Blue Book: A Uniform System of Citation* published by the Harvard Law Review Association. Most journals have an individualized style sheet that prospective authors can obtain by writing to the editor or can find published annually in the journal itself. In fact, according to the *Directory of Publishing Opportunities*, only six of the 54 journals listed under "Social Science—General" identified the *APA Publication Manual* as the style manual of choice. No journals listed under "Business and Economics" or "Political Science" specified the APA documentation style, and only one journal under "Sociology and Anthropology" did so. Obviously, the APA style is not widespread among the social sciences. Numerical systems of documentation are common. Even systems that use a parenthetical citation of author and date may have a bibliography style quite different from that of the *APA Publication Manual*, such as including the author's entire name, placing the title of the article in quotation marks, and placing the date last in the bibliographic entry.

The APA is, however, one of the few professional social science organizations to publish a complete style manual. Its documentation system reveals what it believes is important to document (see Figure 3). "APA journals use the author–date method of citation; that is, the surname of the author and the year of publication are inserted in the text at the appropriate point" (*APA Publication Manual* 107). The use of parenthetical documentation by author and date usually means that the entire text is being cited, rather than a specific passage. The prominence of the date establishes recency as an important criterion for citation. The social sciences as well as the sciences tend to view knowledge as progress, as a process of accretion, which explains the emphasis on recency (see Figure 3).[3] In the reference list, only initials of authors are given, a practice that decreases the sense of the individuality of the author. Article titles are not placed in quotation marks, a practice that de-emphasizes the source of the words. Capitalizing only the first word of a book title also decreases the emphasis on the language of the original author. Giving the entire journal title suggests that the audience may not be familiar with all pertinent journals in the field. This system does not recommend including supplementary material in notes, so authors are discouraged from including caveats or editorial commentary.

Bazerman, in "Codifying the Social Scientific Style: The APA *Publication Manual* as a Behavioristic Rhetoric," writes:

> The *Publication Manual* had adopted a reference style wherein the author and date of a cited work appear as facts or landmarks in the course of the article, visibly demonstrating the incrementalism of the literature. As anyone who has worked with this reference system can attest, it is very convenient for listing and summarizing a series of related findings, but it is awkward for extensive quotation or discussion of another text, and even more awkward for contrasting several texts in detail. The format is not designed for the close consideration of competing ideas and subtle formulations. (140)

As Bazerman suggests, the documentation strategies of the APA *Publication Manual* focus on the citation of ideas, on the major point of an article or book, not on its language. It demonstrates methodological association with the sciences by emphasizing recency of publication and de–emphasizing the unique contributions of the individual author. Text is not privileged in this system, nor is elaboration on tangential points encouraged. However, other documentation styles in the social sciences may more closely resemble humanities documentation styles.

Figure 3. APA Publication Manual*'s information on the reference list*
Source: APA Publication Manual *119–120, 123–124.*

Elements of a reference to a periodical
Spetch, M.L., & Wilkie, D. M. (1983). Subjective shortening: A model of pigeons' memory for event duration. Journal of Experimental Psychology: Animal Behavior Processes, 9, 14–30.

Article authors: Spetch, M. L., & Wilkie, D. M.
• Invert all authors' names; give surnames and initials for all authors, regardless of the number of authors. . . .
• Use comas to separate authors and to separate surnames and initials; with two or more authors, use an ampersand (&) before the last author. . . .

Date of publication: (1983)
• Give the year the work was copyrighted (for unpublished works, this is the year the work was produced). For magazines and newspapers, give the year followed by the month and day, if any.
• Enclose the date in parentheses. . . .

Article title: Subjective shortening: A model of pigeons' memory for event duration.
• Capitalize only the first word of the title and of the subtitle, if any, and any proper names; do not underline the title or place quotation marks around it. . . . .

Journal title and publication information: Journal of Experimental Psychology: Animal Behavior Processes, 9, 14–30.
• Give the journal title in full, in uppercase and lowercase letters; underline the title.
• Give the volume number and underline it. Do not use "Vol." before the number.
. . .
• Give inclusive page numbers. Use "pp." before the page numbers in references to newspapers and magazines, but not in references to journal articles. . . .

Elements of a reference to an entire book
Bernstein, T. M. (1965). The careful writer: A modern guide to English usage. New York: Atheneum.

(continued)

(Figure 3 continued)

Book title: <u>The careful writer: A modern guide to English usage</u>.
•Capitalize only the first word of the title and of the subtitle if any, and any proper names; underline the title. . . .

Publication information: New York: Atheneum.
•Give the city and, if the city is not well known for publishing or could be confused with another location, the state (or country) where the publisher is located.
. . .
•Give the name of the publisher in as brief a form as is intelligible. Spell out the names of associations and university presses, but omit superfluous terms such as Publishers, Co., or Inc. that are not required for easy identification of the publisher. . . .

Citation and documentation in the sciences

Disciplines in the sciences tend to cluster citations at the beginning of articles, in introductory sections, or in reviews of literature. Their practice is similar to that of the social sciences and quite different from that of the humanities, which use citations throughout articles. Each citation tends to list multiple references, blurring distinctions between texts. These citations are almost always to complete texts; they focus on ideas, not on specific language or passages.

For example, an article in the *Journal of the American Chemical Society* cites six numerically coded sources in a single sentence: "Ni(II) radicals and Ni(I) anions have been reported as reduction products[3–9]" (Renner 8618). An article in *Physical Review A*, a publication of the American Physical Society, contains the following sentence: "Much evidence[1,8,12,13,15] suggests that this may be done efficiently through the use of a few well–chosen Slater–type orbitals" (Beck 2887).[4]

Citations tend to be used to establish fact. Some known fact can also lead to the questioning of some other phenomenon as in the following article, where the citations establish the facts that nosocomial infections are transmitted by the hands of hospital personnel and that hand washing can alleviate the problem.

Organisms that cause nosocomial infections can be transmitted by the hands of physicians, nurses, technicians, and other hospital personnel.[1–4] Hand washing is considered the single most important procedure in preventing

> nosocomial infections, and it has been recommended after contact with every patient by both the Centers for Disease Control and the American Hospital Association.[5,6] The risk of acquiring organisms, transmitting them to others, or causing a nosocomial infection may vary with the susceptibility of the patient and the type of patient contact.[7] However, because patients in intensive–care units are highly susceptible to nosocomial infections,[7,8] it has been suggested that personnel working with these patients should wash their hands more frequently.[7] Compliance with these recommendations has not been evaluated. (Albert and Condie 1465)

Citations are rarely used to provide backing for assertions. On the rare occasions when a direct quotation is given, the number often appears before the quote. The idea demonstrated by the citation is more important than the words.

> According to testimony by General Ellis of the U.S. Strategic Air Command [135, p. 3834], "launch on warning is an option we have and must maintain. It remains a useful option because the enemy cannot be certain it will not be used. . . ." (Borning 118)

Except for this article, which surveys computer system reliability and the military's reliance on such systems to launch nuclear attacks, none of the science articles previously cited contain a single quotation. Relating the language of the original author is simply not important. Proof in science scholarship is almost always quantified data, not textual reference.

Documentation styles in the sciences tend to vary dramatically even within disciplines; the American Chemical Society *Handbook*, for example, gives three systems of documentation (see Figure 4). According to Robert Day, author of *How to Write and Publish a Scientific Paper*, a study of 52 scientific publications found 33 different methods of documenting sources (42). Even in disciplines with style manuals published by a professional organization (such as mathematics, biology, physics, or chemistry), these manuals are not recognized as standard by the majority of journals in the field. In my survey of 68 science journals, only nine referred to a standard style sheet, and the vast majority of these were journals published by a professional organization that had a style manual. For example, no physics journal that was not published by the American Institute of Physics referred to its style manual.

Many of the documentation systems use numbers that refer to a reference list. Each reference is cited and numbered only once, and each additional mention of the reference repeats that number. Notes are almost

---

Figure 4. *Citations in the text of the* ACS Style Guide
Source: The ACS Style Guide *106.*

Citing in Text

References may be cited in text in two ways: by number or by author name and date.

> Oscillation in the reaction of benzaldehyde with oxygen was reported previously.[3]

> Oscillation in the reaction of benzaldehyde with oxygen was reported previously (3).

> The primary structure of this enzyme has also been determined (Dardel et. al., 1984).

References are cited by superscript numbers without parentheses and without spaces in *Accounts of Chemical Research, Chemical Reviews.* . . .

References are cited by numbers on the line, underlined (for italic), in parentheses, and with spaces in ACS books, *Analytical Chemistry.* . . .

References are cited by author name in *Biochemistry, Industrial & Engineering Chemistry Fundamentals.* . . .

---

always strictly referential. There is no editorializing, and adding information is rare. Many documentation systems have cumbersome methods of citing exact text. For example, the American Medical Association *Manual,* which uses superscript numbers to refer to the citation, requires that page references to specific words be included in the superscript citation.

These documentation systems privilege only ideas. Even experimental methods tend to be mentioned but not documented. Readers unaware of the details of the method mentioned are usually offered no documentation to sources of further explanation. Offering only minimal information, these documentation systems imply an audience quite familiar with the materials and methods of the field and exclude the uninitiated (see Figure 5). The author's name is given in an abbreviated form, even omitting punctuation between initials. Using initials hides some personal characteristics of the author. This practice limits the usefulness of citation as an appeal to authority and reinforces the "impersonality" of the scientific method. If scientific information is truly obtainable by anyone, then it does not really matter who is responsible for a particular piece of infor-

---

Figure 5. JAMA *Reference Style*
Source: "Instructions for Authors." Journal of the American Medical Association *259 (1988) 2539.*

References: Number references in the order in which they are mentioned in the text; do not alphabetize. In text, tables, and legends, identify a reference with superscript Arabic numerals. In listing references follow the AMA style currently in use, abbreviating the names of journals in the form given in Index Medicus.

Examples:
1. Black DW: Laughter. JAMA 1984;252:2995–2998.
2. Weinstein L, Swartz MN: Pathogenic properties of invading microorganisms, in Sodeman WA Jr, Sodeman WA (eds): Pathologic Physiology: Mechanisms of Disease. Philadelphia, WB Saunders Co, 1974, pp 457–472.

---

mation. In the *Journal of Biological Chemistry* and some other science journals, the title of the article is not mentioned and journal titles are abbreviated (see Figure 6). Their style sheet also lists the publisher before the place of publication, thus de–emphasizing place as an identifier. The lack of specificity about author, title, and text in the majority of science documentation systems may make it more difficult to use the citation strategy as an appeal to authority.

Implications for the composition teacher

What does this diversity of citation and documentation strategies mean for writing teachers? One clear implication is that we need to be aware of the citation and documentation strategies of other disciplines. We need to make it clear to our students that there are several standards for the humanities, social sciences, and sciences. We also need to be aware that differences in documentation reflect differences in citation strategy and use. Differences in documentation styles reflect rhetorical strategies and reveal assumptions about the use of authority and testimony in the discipline. They also reveal what types of evidence or proof the discipline finds most convincing.

How aware are we as a profession of these implications? Not very, according to my own small survey of handbooks, research paper writing books, and technical writing books. The sample of my survey was one of convenience: I simply chose books to which I had access in my own or

Figure 6. Journal of Biological Chemistry *Reference Style*
Source: Journal of Biological Chemistry *255 (1980): 1–11.*

References may be cited in the text in either form recommended by the IUB Committee of Editors of Biochemical Journals. . . . For example: "The methods for the preparation were those previously described (1)." **or** "The methods for the preparation were those previously described (Smith and Jones, 1971)."

Regardless of choice of citation system in the text the recommended style for references to journals or books in the bibliography is given in the following examples:

Smith, A., and Jones, C. (1971) J. Biol. Chem. **246**, 127–131

Dixon, M., and Webb, E. C. (1964) Enzymes, 2nd Ed, pp. 565–567, Longman Green, London

Brachet, J. (1967) in Comprehensive Biochemistry (Florkin, M., and Stotz, E. M., eds) Vol. 28, pp. 23–54, Elsevier, Amsterdam

Abbreviate journal names according to Chemical Abstracts or Biological Abstracts List of Serials with (Biosis). Include first and last page numbers.

colleagues' offices, examining seven handbooks, seven research paper books, and seven technical writing books (see list Works Cited.)

Technical writing texts tend to acknowledge diversity among disciplines, often including lists of style manuals. However, these are not always an accepted standard in the field. It is simply incorrect to imply that all chemistry publications use the ACS style. Even these textbooks, then, tend to imply a standardization of style manuals that does not exist. Many technical writing texts also contain examples of parenthetical or numerical citation styles, and some refer to the American National Standard style published by the American National Standard Institute (ANSI). But again, these textbooks often send a contradictory message. On one page Kenneth Houp and Thomas Pearsall say, "There is a bewildering complexity of documenting systems from journal to journal, company to company" (232), and on another page, "as is typical of a scientific research article, this article is documented by parenthetical references" (447). In fact, diversity is typical.

When we look at handbooks and guides to writing research papers, we find even less acknowledgment of difference. Research paper guides, by and large, discuss both MLA and APA styles, suggesting that APA's position in the social sciences is equivalent to MLA's in the humanities. *The Holt Guide to Documentation and Writing in the Disciplines* states quite erroneously:

> Documentation format in the social sciences is more uniform than in the humanities or the sciences. The disciplines and journals in the social sciences almost uniformly use the documentation style of the American Psychological Association's *Publication Manual*. (Jussawalla 74)

Only three of these guides to writing research papers mention *The Chicago Manual of Style*. Some of the guides implicitly acknowledge that documentation style is related to content and citation strategies by having different sample papers to demonstrate the different styles. For example, *Writing the Research Paper* illustrates MLA style with a paper on "The Certainties of Hawthorne's Moral Ambiguity in *The Scarlet Letter*" and illustrates APA style with a paper on "More Funding for Autism." But sometimes, though they make distinctions, they are inaccurate. For example, *Research Writing* includes a paper on photovoltaic cells using APA style, which is not used in the sciences. One book presents an identical paper on the subject of hypnotism twice, once with MLA style and once with APA style. This book gives the paper two different titles so that it is not immediately obvious that the same paper is used twice. Such use refuses to acknowledge any difference in citation strategies or any reason for differences in documentation styles.

Handbooks, which are supposed to be reference tools, are even less precise about the diversity of citation styles. Several discuss only the MLA style, although some mention the APA style. Some of the sample research papers used MLA style with an appropriate topic, for example "Third Person Unbiased: The Generic Pronoun in English" in *The Confident Writer*. But most of the others used MLA style and the citation strategies of the humanities for papers on such scientific topics as "The Medical View of Cholera: 1832–1860" in the *Macmillan College Handbook,* "Disadvantages of Geothermal Energy" in *Handbook of Current English,* or social science topics such as "The Italian Family: 'Stronghold in a Hostile Land'" in *The Holt Handbook*. Encouraging students to believe that MLA style and citation conventions of the humanities are appropriate for all topics, whatever the discipline, is intellectually chauvinistic.

Obviously, as English teachers we cannot learn every documentation strategy for every discipline, let alone every journal. But we can acknowledge the diversity among styles and strategies. We can acknowledge that documentation styles reflect rhetorical practices within a field. We can acknowledge that our training encourages a false belief in standardization and ignorance of the diversity among and within other fields. If we want to help students join an academic discipline, if we want our suggestions about writing to be taken seriously by our colleagues in other disciplines, we must be willing to acknowledge that the conventions of citation and documentation in other fields differ from our own. ❦

NOTES

[1]One exception is the *Southern Speech Communication Journal* which says, "when the MLA style is used, authors must follow exactly the form for endnotes and footnotes prescribed on pp. 190–205 of *The MLA Style Manual.*"

[2]The *Chicago Manual of Style* explicitly mentions cost as a factor in determining which documentation style is preferable. "The system of documentation generally most economical in space, in time (for author, editor, and typesetter), and in cost (to publisher and public)—in short, the most practical—is the *author–date* system" (emphasis in the original, 400).

[3]There is a great deal of controversy among philosophers and sociologists of science about whether this is an accurate portrayal of science. However, it still has a tenacious hold on many practitioners. See I. Bernard Cohen, *Revolution in Science,* 369–404.

[4]I find the use of superscript numbers to refer to citations extremely cumbersome in the sciences, as many articles also contain equations with superscript numbers. As a novice reader of such articles, I find it difficult to tell whether a number is a reference number or something else. Thus, this use of documentation style may be a rhetorical strategy for excluding the uninitiated.

WORKS CITED

Albert, Richard K, and Frances Condie. "Hand-washing Patterns in Medical Intensive-Care Units." *The New England Journal of Medicine* 304 (1981): 1465-1466.

Bazerman, Charles. "What Written Knowledge Does: Three Examples of Academic Discourse." *Philosophy of the Social Sciences* 11 (1981): 361-387.

——. "Codifying the Social Scientific Style: The APA *Publication Manual* as Behaviorist Rhetoric." *The Rhetoric of the Human Sciences: Language and Argument in Scholarship in Public Affairs.* Eds. John S. Nelson, Allan Megill, and Donald N. McCloskey. Madison: U Wisconsin P, 1987. 125-144.

Beck, Donald R. "Wavelength, Oscillator Strength, and Fine Structure for the 4P 4S Transition of Mg-." *Physical Review A Third Series* 40 (1989): 2887-2893.

Bizzell, Patricia. "Cognition, Convention, and Certainty: What We Need to Know about Writing." *Pre/Text* 3 (1982): 213-243.

Borning, Alan. "Computer System Reliability and Nuclear War." *Communications of the ACM* 30 (February 1987): 112-131.

Cohen, I. Bernard. *Revolution in Science.* Cambridge: Harvard UP, 1985.

Day, Robert A. *How to Write and Publish a Scientific Paper.* 2nd ed. Philadelphia: ISI, 1983.

Garfield, Eugene. "Is Information Retrieval in the Arts and Humanities Inherently Different from that in Science? The Effect the ISI's Citation Index for the Arts and Humanities is Expected to Have on Future Scholarship." *Library Quarterly* 50 (1980): 40-57.

Hoffman, Daniel G. *Form and Fable in American Fiction.* Oxford: Oxford UP, 1961.

James, David R. "City Limits on Racial Equality: The Effects of City-Suburb Boundaries on Public-School Segregation, 1968-1976." *American Sociological Review* 54 (1989): 963-985.

Kinneavy, James L. "Writing Across the Curriculum." *Profession 83* (1983): 13-20.

Leigh, Barbara Critchlow. "The Powers of John Barleycorn," *American Psychologist* 41 (July 1986): 751-764.

Renner, M. W., et. al. "Electrochemical, Theoretical, and ESR Characterizations of Porphycenes. The [pi] Anion Radical of Nickel(II) Porphycene." *Journal of the American Chemical Society* 111 (1989): 8618-8621.

Robben, Antonius C. G. "Habits of the Home: Spatial Hegemony and the

Structuration of House and Society in Brazil." *American Anthropologist* 91 (1989): 570-588.

Steinberg, Erwin. "A Garden of Opportunities and a Thicket of Dangers." *Cognitive Processes in Writing.* Eds. Lee W. Gregg and Erwin Steinberg. Hillsdale NJ: Erlbaum, 1980. 163-165.

STYLE MANUALS CONSULTED

American Institute of Physics. Publications Board. *Style Manual for Guidance in the Preparation of Papers.* 3rd ed. New York: American Institute of Physics, 1978.

American National Standard for Bibliographic References, Z39.29-1977. New York: American National Standards Institute, 1977.

American Mathematical Society. *A Manual for Authors of Mathematical Papers.* 7th ed. Providence: American Mathematical Society, 1980.

American Psychological Association. *Publication Manual of the American Psychological Association.* 3rd ed. Washington: APA, 1983.

Barclay, William R., Therese Southgate, and Robert W. Mays, compilers. *Manual for Authors and Editors: Editorial Style and Manuscript Preparation Compiled for the American Medical Association.* Los Altos, CA: Lange Medical Publications, 1981.

Bishop, Elna E., et. al. *Suggestions to Authors of the Reports of the United States Geological Survey.* 6th ed. Washington: GPO, 1978.

Chicago Manual of Style. 13th ed. Chicago: U Chicago P, 1982.

Council of Biology Editors. Style Manual Committee. *CBE Style Manual: A Guide for Authors, Editors, and Publishers in the Biological Sciences.* 5th ed. Bethesda: Council of Biology Editors, 1983.

Dodd, Janet S., ed. *The ACS Style Guide: A Manual for Authors and Editors.* Washington: American Chemical Society, 1986.

MLA Style Manual. New York: Modern Language Association of America, 1985.

For other style manuals and authors' guides, see John Bruce Howell, *Style Manuals of the English-Speaking World*, Phoenix: Oryx, 1983.

TEXTBOOKS SURVEYED

Technical Writing Texts

Carosso, Rebecca Burnett. *Technical Communication.* Belmont: Wadsworth, 1986.

Houp, Kenneth W., and Thomas E. Pearsall. *Reporting Technical Information.* 6th ed. New York: Macmillan, 1988.

Kolin, Philip C., and Janeen L. Colin. *Models for Technical Writing.* New York: St. Martin's, 1985.

Olsen, Leslie A., and Thomas N. Huckin. *Principles of Communication for Science and Technology.* New York: McGraw–Hill, 1983.

Philbin, Alice I., and John W. Presley. *Technical Writing: Method, Application and Management.* Albany: Delmar, 1989.

Stuart, Ann. *The Technical Writer.* New York: Holt, 1988.

Zimmerman, Donald E., and David G. Clark. *The Random House Guide to Technical and Scientific Communication.* New York: Random House, 1987.

Guides to Research Papers

Farrelly, James P., and Lorraine M. Murphy. *A Practical Guide to Research Papers.* San Diego: Harcourt, 1988.

Jussawalla, Feroza. *The Holt Guide to Documentation and Writing in the Disciplines.* 2nd ed. Fort Worth: Holt, 1989.

Memering, Dean. *Research Writing: A Complete Guide to Research Papers.* Englewood Cliffs: Prentice, 1983.

Rivers, William L., and Susan L. Harrington. *Finding Facts: Research Writing Across the Curriculum.* 2nd ed. Englewood Cliffs: Prentice, 1988.

The Research Paper: A Common Sense Approach. New York: Harcourt, 1983.

Willis, Hulon. *Writing Term Papers: the Research Paper, the Critical Paper.* 2nd ed. Revised by Alan Heineman. New York: Harcourt, 1983.

Winkler, Anthony C., and Jo Ray McCuen. *Writing the Research Paper.* 2nd ed. San Diego: Harcourt, 1985.

Handbooks

Corder, Jim W., and John J. Ruszkiewicz. *Handbook of Current English.* 8th ed. Glenview: Scott, 1989.

Dornan, Edward C., and Charles W. Dawe. *The Brief English Handbook.* 2nd ed. Boston: Little, 1987.

Gefvert, Constance J. *The Confident Writer.* 2nd ed. New York: Norton, 1988.

Kirkland, James W., and Collett B. Dilworth, Jr. *Concise English Handbook.* Lexington: Heath, 1985.

Kirszner, Laurie G., and Stephen Mandell. *The Holt Handbook.* 2nd ed. Fort Worth: Holt, 1989.

Levine, Gerald. *The Macmillan College Handbook.* New York: Macmillan, 1987.

Lunsford, Andrea, and Robert Connors. *The St. Martin's Handbook.* New York: St. Martin's, 1989.

VI

How Affective Discourse
Constructs Its Public

All three essays in this section offer rhetorical analyses of texts that depend on emotion to shape their audience's attitudes and actions. The underlying argument of this section is that such appeals to pathos are neither uncommon nor necessarily illegitimate in public discourse. The ubiquity and power of pathos is revealed by the variety of the genres that these essays consider—political oratory, business communication, and narrative romance—and even by the forums of rhetoric that they represent—deliberative, forensic, and epideictic.

In the first essay, Jeffrey Walker adumbrates an Aristotelian concept of anger to analyze arguments by Cicero and Thomas Paine. He shows that both incite their audiences to action by forcing them to choose between an unresolved state of shame and a more satisfactory closure achieved through an angry response. Walker argues that Aristotle's concept of emotion is superior to Quintilian's in accounting for the content and structure of the texts and for establishing the legitimacy and effectiveness of the pathetic argument. Although most contemporary rhetoric and composition texts have unthinkingly followed Quintilian, Walker's analysis will encourage teachers and scholars to take a new look at pathos.

Aletha Hendrickson explores another emotion, fear, the result of intimidation as practiced by the consummate masters of the art, the Internal Revenue Service. The "success" of the IRS's tactics derives largely from its powerful rhetorical, political, and legal stance. In its notices, the IRS intentionally exploits its power in moves designed to inspire so much anxiety in taxpayers that they will pay whatever is asked without challenge. However, Hendrickson's analysis also points to awe-ful features of IRS notices that result from apparently inadvertent "user-hostile" document design. Other intimidating tactics may be face-saving maneuvers: the IRS often needs information from taxpayers to sort out discrepancies, but cannot publicly admit that it lacks accurate records or is overwhelmed by the complexities of its task.

Steven Katz offers a rhetorical analysis of Tracy Kidder's Pulitzer Prize-winning book, *The Soul of a New Machine,* showing how Kidder turns a documentary of the development of a new computer into a narrative romance. Narrative romance, as described by Northrop Frye and Joseph Campbell, allows readers to invoke familiar mythic schemas and cast engineers in the unexpected role of heroes. By inspiring readers to admire and identify with computer engineers, Kidder's book helps to resolve our society's ambivalence toward technological advances. In fact, Katz argues that the schema of narrative romance even functions within the culture of the computer engineers, as a way to create solidarity within the team and reinforce their adherence to their quest.

The texts analyzed in these essays each represent one of the three classical rhetorical forums. Clearly, Paine and Cicero engage in deliberative rhetoric; their aim is to move their hearers to action, in both cases to war. Theirs is the rhetoric of political assemblies, concerned with the future action of the state. In contrast, the IRS engages in a species of forensic rhetoric; it uses intimidation to convince taxpayers to accept a guilty verdict for apparent discrepancies in their tax returns. Although the IRS is quick to invoke the threat of legal penalties, its discourse is exploitive because it is not conducted in an actual forensic setting where innocence is presumed and arguments on both sides are invited in an effort to determine the truth. Finally, Kidder is obviously engaged in epideictic discourse; his intention in praising the builders of the new machine is to unite his readers in accepting technology as a locus for the celebration of shared values.

In addressing the issue of pathetic appeals, these essays inevitably raise questions about the morality of rhetoric—since most critics of rhetoric consider it unethical to induce decisions that are based on any but rational premises. Walker confronts this issue and discusses the problem explicitly in examining the assumption that rhetors often use emotion deliberately to compensate for weaknesses in the logical argument. He argues that such conclusions can be based on only *post hoc* analyses that cannot reconstruct the intentions or sincerity of any particular rhetor.

In contrast, Hendrickson demonstrates that the IRS is perfectly willing to sacrifice clarity and good relations for the sake of effective tax collection. The IRS makes intimidation a standard operating procedure; it neither knows nor cares in any individual case whether its facts are true or false. It merely wants compliance. Both essays raise questions about the relations between ends and means within a political structure, and both ultimately arrive at conclusions that are essentially pragmatic. Hendrickson decides finally that the dangers of an ineffectual IRS may well exceed the benefits of increased friendliness. (Of course, if people get angry enough about arbitrary methods of taxation, there is the potential for political revolt—as King George III found out.) Walker concludes that when political conditions demand immediate action, a purely philosophical analysis of the evidence is sometimes irrelevant and frequently impossible.

Even the use of romantic narrative in Kidder's book raises similar ethical questions. Kidder uses a culturally proven and positive schema to domesticate otherwise threatening and arcane advances in technology. Because Kidder employs a narrative form and because his purpose is to celebrate achievement rather than move readers to action, critics may be less likely to accuse him of inappropriate emotional appeals. Nevertheless, the book is an argument. Katz questions whether it is appropriate for Kidder to cast computer engineers as heroes when this mythification exploits emotion-laden cultural and religious icons to valorize the ideology of entrepreneurship. A commitment to this economic and political idealization, the American Dream, is taken in Kidder's book as a basic premise rather than as matter for debate, to be argued with both rational and emotional appeals. It seems overly fastidious, however, to call Kidder's methods unethical; in relying on his audience's shared values, he is simply being a good rhetorician drawing a cultural enthymeme.

Agreement on potentially controversial cultural values is tacitly assumed in all three essays. As Katz concedes, the mythos of the narrative romance is couched almost exclusively as a male experience. The same can be said of the oratory that Walker analyzes—both Cicero and Paine call on their audiences to escape the *unmanly* shame of continued insult by taking action to release their anger in effective revenge. Of course, this idealization of manliness is a cultural construct—a product of societies in ancient Rome and colonial America which enfranchised only males. The construct of manliness is neither self-evident nor inherent. From the distance of our present culture, we can see that this ideal is no longer unproblematic though it may still be widely shared—which may in part explain the success of Kidder's book. Furthermore, from our modern vantage point, we can see anger as a *human* response to frustration and powerlessness—not an essentially male one, any more than compassion is essentially female. Thus, as typically pragmatic rhetoricians, we can analyze texts and explore what makes them effective without sharing *all* the cultural constructs on which they are based.

As a rhetorician, like Walker and Hendrickson, Katz is pragmatic in his conclusions. He recognizes the seductive potential of narrative and proposes a broad humanistic education in rhetoric and culture as the antidote to gullibility. Thus the role of rhetorical analysis in the modern world is to bring the public to awareness of the *techne* that political rhetors, institutions, and apologists of all kinds practice. While such textual analyses necessarily look backwards, their lessons can be applied to future practice and debate. We will probably not find ourselves in situations identical to those described by Paine and Cicero, but emotional appeals abound in every form of political action and we need to understand how they work. Similarly, while we may not be able to prevent the IRS from intimidating taxpayers, we may know better how to respond to it if we understand how it works. And even when we read popular forms of literature, we need to recognize their essential rhetoricity. That, ultimately, is why we need rhetorical education.

❧ 17

Enthymemes of Anger in Cicero and Thomas Paine

Jeffrey Walker

"The peculiar task of the orator," says Quintilian, "arises when the minds of the judges require force to move them, and their thoughts actually have to be led away from contemplation of the truth" (*Institutio* VI.ii.5). And for this, he says, pathos is required. Quintilian then gives us what has long been and still is the conventional account of emotion in rhetoric: a fundamentally irrational, even fallacious form of persuasion—except, of course, that Quintilian actively recommends it—mediated by "images" and "emotive language." According to Quintilian, moreover, an orator cannot provoke emotion in an audience unless he himself feels it or at least can simulate (like an actor) the passion he wants to provoke: "Will he [the judge] be angry, if the orator who seeks to kindle his anger shows no sign of laboring under the emotion which he demands from his audience? Will he shed tears if the pleader's eyes are dry? It is utterly impossible" (VI.ii.27). We should note that Quintilian's theory falters, or becomes inconsistent, when he takes up humor: should the orator laugh at his own jokes? The answer, of course, is no (VI.iii.26). Despite such inconsistencies, however, Quintilian remains committed to the basic paradigm: the orator presents images and emotes—preferably *sincerely*—with the intention of *infecting* his audience with a kindred feeling.

From Quintilian we derive the commonplace, traditional picture of the orator with his quavering voice, crocodile tears, and graphic details (holding up the bloodstained tunic, offering a lurid narrative or description). It is the picture we get, famously, in Shakespeare's Antony. And to a large degree, despite the work of Chaim Perelman (of whom more later), it is a picture that contemporary rhetoric still lives with. Indeed, with very few exceptions, it is the only account of pathos we find represented in composition textbooks—if there is any account at all—and one that typically treats "the emotional appeal" with great distrust.[1] And even when we find arguments (in *College Composition and Communication* and elsewhere) seeking to make a case for pathos, as an "alternative" and important mode of thought, it frequently remains just that: an alternative, a nonlogical, nonrational, prerational, or "arational" way of knowing and responding to the world. As Erika Lindemann has put it, in *A Rhetoric for Writing Teachers,* "Our culture tends to place greater emphasis on cognitive modes of thought, on logic, reason, and 'literacy.' However, imagination and feeling, affective modes, also represent an important way of thinking" (57). By and large, then, whether we treat pathos as pathological or as a creative alternative, we tend to remain, with Lindemann, within a basically Quintilianic tradition.

This essay, however, is devoted to a different, richer, and less dichotomized tradition, the one Quintilian forgot, or obscured, in his belated effort to resuscitate the Ciceronian ideal. I want to look, that is, at Aristotelian pathos-theory—or more specifically the rhetoric of anger, which is Aristotle's paradigm emotion, as we see it exemplified in Cicero's *De Imperio Cnaeus Pompei* ("On the Command of Cnaeus Pompeius") and in Thomas Paine's *Common Sense.* Cicero was certainly aware of Aristotle, and the *De Imperio* can be seen as a practical and probably conscious application of Aristotelian theory, or even as a textbook demonstration of it, by an acknowledged master of pathetic argument. It is unlikely, on the other hand, that Paine was working consciously from Aristotelian principles; yet, as we will see, his very potent rhetoric does indeed work according to those principles and cannot be fully understood without them. Together, Paine and Cicero provide us with an occasion for reflecting on and ultimately for extending the Aristotelian account of pathos argument—an account that is generally forgotten, misunderstood, made vague, or erased in both postclassical and modern traditions, although it explicates the thinking heart of rhetoric and what Aristotle called the "body of persuasion" (*Rhetoric* I.i, 1354a).

According to the relevant passages in the *Rhetoric,* "anger" is a *pained* feeling of *desire* for a *conspicuous revenge* for a *conspicuous insult,* accompanied by a *belief* that revenge is possible and the *pleasurable* anticipation of getting even (I.xi, 1370a; II.ii, 1378a-b). As some recent philosophical expansions of this line of thought suggest, such a definition makes anger a complex intentional state, an invoked cognitive construct that rises *enthymemically* as the "conclusion" from a number of beliefs that serve as "premises," which may or may not appear to consciousness in overt propositional form (Fortenbaugh; Grimaldi; de Sousa; Solomon; Calhoun and Solomon; A. O. Rorty; Searle). The relevant premises in the case of anger, then, are the belief that one has been insulted and the belief that appropriate revenge is possible. If one cannot believe both these things, the particular form of pathos that results cannot be anger but must be a different state—humiliation, perhaps, or shame or fear, or something else again—depending on which other beliefs are present to the mind. And beneath the focal premises of anger (or of any other pathos-state), there must be an elaborate set of supporting concepts, shading off into deep, prereflective, and possibly prelinguistic supposition: tacit ideas of what constitutes an "insult," for example, what constitutes "revenge," what constitutes the behavior-pattern of "an angry person," and so forth.

The Aristotelian analysis does not deny the turbulent, physiological aspect of anger, or of emotion generally—hormones, pulse-rates, muscular tensions, motivational compulsions—that is, the primitive "animal" part of pathos, the part that may not be culturally or conceptually constituted and may not be strictly "rational." Aristotle, for example, talks in *On the Soul* about blood boiling around the angry person's heart, and the *Rhetoric* introduces pathos as a force that "warps" the thinking of an audience (Fortenbaugh 15, 21-22; *On the Soul* I.i, 403a-b; *Rhetoric* I.i, 1354a-b). But, as more recent analyses suggest, this primitive, physiological aspect of emotion is best construed as a *diffuse arousal-state,* a preparation for bodily action, mediated by the lower "mammalian" portions of the brain (the limbic system and hypothalamus) that appear to handle such basic motives as aggression, escape, eating, eros, and so forth. Still, of course, what triggers arousal must be an interpreted percept. Significantly, the physiological processes involved are not sufficient to discriminate particular *human* emotions; what gives the diffuse arousal-state of "primitive pathos" its character as *a particular emotion,* and which allows the "discharge" of its motive-energies in *a particular mode of action* or *a particular mode of attention,* is its constitution as a defined intentional state through the mobilization of a network of presuppositions—including beliefs overtly present (as formulated statements) to the conscious mind and "dark" cognitions that lie below the threshold of articulation. (See A. O. Rorty 9-36, 103-26, 127-51; Calhoun and Solomon 142-51, 327-42; and de Sousa.) Thus, the diffuse arousal-state for "fight/flight" may be differentiated into such conceptually (and culturally) constituted emotions as "anger," "hate," "derision," "disapproval," "suspicion," "shame," "fear," "terror," "anxiety," and so on. Indeed, the arousal-state may not become intelligible or actionable until it becomes defined as *one* of these specific kinds of emotion—that is, as one of these specific kinds of intentionality.[2] Moreover, if the aroused pathos-state cannot be given such specificity, if it cannot be channeled into definite attitudes or behavior, the result is likely to be mere distress. This is an important point, and one to which I will presently return.

For now, let us simply note that the Aristotelian account of anger defines it, like every other species of human emotion, as a logologically constituted version of the primitive, diffuse arousal-state *in* which it is embedded, and *to* which it gives the possibility of "discharge" in a particular mode of intentionality. And with these ideas in view, it may be useful to repeat the definition of "anger" itself: a *pained* feeling of *desire* for a *conspicuous revenge* for a *conspicuous insult,* accompanied by *belief* that revenge is possible and the *pleasurable* anticipation of getting even.

That Cicero was aware of Aristotle's enthymemic account of pathos—or at least a later Peripatetic version of that account—seems obvious and in any case is evident in the *Tusculan Disputations,* where he gives it a direct discussion (III.iv-xi): pathos is a "perturbation" of the psyche (*perturbationis*), and is provoked by some definite idea or set of ideas. Likewise, he follows Aristotle in defining anger (but in somewhat more colorful, Roman terms) as a "lustful" wish to "stamp the brand of uttermost pain" upon the person that has wronged you, or at least to see that person in misery (III.ix.19-20). But we need not depend on the somewhat gentlemanly philosophizing of the *Tusculan Disputations.* We can see this awareness also in Cicero's actual practice, and *De Imperio* is something of a textbook case.

I mean the term "textbook" fairly literally. As we know, the published texts of Cicero's orations are literary productions—revised, idealized versions of the speech that actually took place. Among the motives that Cicero gave for publishing, and those that are attributed to him, are pamphleteering (presenting a defense of a particular principle, sometimes to protect himself against the accusations of political enemies in later years), self-promotion (showing potential clients his rhetorical powers), "patriotic" literary ambition (achieving a written eloquence worthy of comparison with Demosthenes and Isocrates), and providing examples of rhetorical practice for ambitious younger orators (an idealized "perfect orator" in action). We know that the *De Imperio* was, in fact, a successful speech, and that Cicero was highly satisfied with it. In what follows, then, I take the published text of *De Imperio* as a reasonable facsimile of what actually took place—with the rough edges, lapses and misdirections smoothed away, and the moments of genius amplified—and also as a self-consciously produced "textbook case" exemplifying pathos-argument as Cicero understands it. (See Enos; Bonner; Hodge 10-11; and Petersson 88-96.)

For those not familiar with this oration, a little background will be helpful. This is Cicero's first speech before the Roman Assembly, his political debut, for he has just been elected to the office of *praetor,* the first step on the ladder to the ultimate office of *consul*. Mithridates, an Iranian king, has for years been encroaching on Rome's lucrative Asian provinces, despite a number of (partially successful) expeditions sent against him; the most recent expedition, in fact, has ended in disaster, with the massacre of a Roman army. A certain Manilius has now proposed that Pompeius (better known to us as Pompey) be put in charge of yet another expedition, and with broad powers at his disposal: Pompeius has just crowned an already spectacular soldiering career with a brilliant naval campaign against pirates in the Mediterranean, and there is widespread enthusiasm for his generalship. However, what Manilius proposes will effectively place Pompeius in supreme and sole command of the entire Roman military. In his earlier campaigns he has already been given command of the western armies and the navy, and this new one will put him in charge of all military forces in the east. The campaign against Mithridates, then, will give him unprecedented, virtually unlimited, essentially irresponsible and at least potentially unrestrainable power—the dictatorial sort of power that would eventually be seized by Caesar and Augustus—and so there are serious objections to the Manilian proposal, especially from the conservative, aristocratic, senatorial class, with its republican ideals. At this juncture, then, Cicero debuts, as a "new man" in the political world, a nonaristocrat, an up-and-coming lawyer. And he is speaking in support of the Manilian proposal. (See Petersson 176-90; Grant 34-35; and Hodge 10-11.)

Cicero begins the *narratio* by simply ignoring the focal issues raised by the conservatives, saving them for refutation in his *reprehensio*. Instead, he starts to sketch an enthymeme of anger (*De Imperio* II, 4-5): Mithridates and his Armenian ally, Tigranes, are "mighty kings" (*potentissimus regibus*) but motivated by "impunity" and "exasperation"; their injuries to Rome include not only lost revenue but also, and focally, insult to Roman life and property—villages burnt to the ground, provinces occupied, the kingdom of a Roman ally overrun. At the same time, Cicero gives his audience perception of *a possible means of punishment* in the person of the excellent Pompeius. But this is not enough for anger yet. Mithridates is, after all, a "mighty king," and Cicero reminds his audience of the recently failed expedition, whose commander had also had a brilliant previous career. And behind that recent failure lie the many previous years of failure with Mithridates. This history suggests implicitly that perhaps neither Pompeius nor anyone, however brilliant, may be sufficient to the job. It is by this element of doubt, the gap between perception of possibility and belief in probability, that Cicero keeps anger in check—keeps his audience from *believing in its anger*—and forces pathos down, even as he arouses it, into more ambivalent and distressful channels.

Cicero then divides the *confirmatio* into three considerations: "the nature of the war," "its magnitude," and "the choice of a commander." As Cicero expands upon "the nature of the war," he "calls upon" the Roman assembly

> to wipe out that stain from the first Mithridatic war, which is now so deep and so long upon the honor of the Roman people; for he that on a single day through all of Asia and in many states, by one message and one dispatch marked out our citizens for slaughter and butchery, has so far not only failed to pay any penalty commensurate with his crime, but has remained on his throne for twenty-two years since then—a king that is not content with lurking safely in Pontus or Cappadocia, but bursts from his hereditary kingdom and flaunts himself in your tributary states, for all of Asia to behold. (*De Imperio* III,7-8)

Repulsive, murderous, criminal Mithridates thumbs his nose at impotent Rome. This is a memorable passage and a key one. The perception of insult is intensified, but so is perception of what Cicero calls "that stain . . . upon the honor of the Roman people." Mithridates has paid no penalty, has suffered no punishment at Roman hands. There is, in other words, a warrant for shame, a point to which Cicero soon turns:

> Our forefathers fought frequent wars to protect our merchants or shipmasters against any mistreatment: what, then, should be your feelings when . . . thousands of Roman citizens have been put to death? Because their envoys had been . . . spoken to disrespectfully, our ancestors extinguished Corinth, the light of Greece: will you leave unpunished the king that imprisoned, scourged, and put to death by every kind of torture a Roman envoy of consular rank? . . . See to it, since your forefathers bequeathed to you so glorious an empire—their proud achievement—that you not acquire the lowly shame of being powerless to protect and maintain this gift. (V, 11-12)

At this point, then, Cicero has made present to his audience, and in memorable terms, the premises for two very different modes of pathos: anger, the sanctified urge to punitive revenge, which is held in check by the ideas of impotence and failure; and shame, which this very same perception of impotence, failure and "stained honor" seems to invoke. Anger is desirable, and even inherently pleasurable, but blocked; shame is painful and undesirable, yet fully available.

When Cicero turns to the "magnitude" of the campaign proposed by the Manilian law, his audience is kept in this distressed emotional dilemma, as the orator declares "my chief task lies in persuading you not to underestimate those facts for which you need to make most careful provision" (VIII, 20). What this persuasion amounts to is yet another (but expanded) history of the previous campaigns, including Mithridates' alliance with Tigranes, the mobilization of "barbarian" tribes against the Romans, and the recent annihilation of the Roman army. What the audience is treated to, in short, is an increasingly prominent sense of Mithridates' resourcefulness, power, and ruthlessness—which contributes to nothing but a further erosion of their confidence and magnification of their doubts. Mithridates seems beyond the reach of Roman power, or superior to it. The premises that would let pathos unequivocally be channeled into anger, rather than shame, remain in check. But only temporarily; Cicero turns to "the choice of a commander" in the final movement of the *confirmatio.*

This relatively lengthy movement, and indeed most of the rest of *De Imperio,* I must largely pass over. Suffice it to say, for present purposes, that Cicero reviews Pompeius' qualities, focussing, significantly, on the special gifts that would have saved the previous and otherwise brilliant expedition (such as, for example, Pompeius' "heaven-sent" good luck, or his ability to maintain discipline—after initial victories, the previous expedition fell to loot-gathering and eventually grew mutinous). What I wish to suggest, in brief, is that Cicero now provides his audience with a prominent and gradually expanding sense that *a means of punishment is indeed available;* the qualities that Cicero brings forward make it seem highly probable, in the light of everything else that he has said about the war, that Pompeius can indeed successfully liquidate Mithridates and his allies. (As, in fact, he did, when given the command.)

And here I want to introduce a notorious but useful Aristotelian concept, namely the concept of "catharsis" or release. By "catharsis," in this context, I mean only the "discharge" of diffuse emotional arousal in the form of a specific, *logologically constituted* emotion, with its own specific intentionality.[3] Using the term in this particular sense, we can say that Cicero's praise of Pompeius gives his listeners in the forum the premises they need for a "cathartic" release of the distressed, unsettled, bipolar pathos-state that he has kept them in, through the first two parts of the *confirmatio.* They now can let themselves go in anger, and contemplate, with the special pleasure of such contemplation, "stamping the brand of uttermost pain" on Mithridates. A great part of this pleasure lies, indeed, in the special "catharsis" of primitive (i.e., limbic) pathos-energies that anger provides, since it tends outward toward resolution in approvable, honorable, public action. Shame, in contrast, tends inward, and is actionable only through self-directed attitudes and social withdrawal. As Aristotle says, shame is "pain or disturbance at bad things which seem likely to involve us in discredit . . . [it is] a mental picture of disgrace, in which we shrink from the disgrace itself . . . the people before whom we feel shame are those whose opinion matters to us . . . we do not wish to be seen" (II.vi, 1383b,1384a, 1384b). It is, in short, a version of fear. For Cicero's audience, moreover, the disapproving gaze that is feared is not only their own but that of the ancestors themselves. To fail to avenge Roman honor is, in effect, to be eternally condemned to unworthiness.

There is a point here that most available accounts of pathos generally miss. The audience is being asked to approve the Manilian law, giving Pompeius supreme command, *in order to give itself the pleasure of being angry, and to avoid the pain of being shamed:* they are asked to choose a conclusion for the sake of an emotion, or an emotional possibility. The anger that Cicero calls on is simultaneously the product of one enthymemic process and the ground of another, as it becomes the driving reason for adopting the Manilian proposal. It is truly a force, as Aristotle says, that "warps" or channels deliberation according to the pressures of an aroused intentionality.

This becomes even more clear in the *reprehensio,* where Cicero finally turns to the focal issue raised by his opponents. Now the anger already released is turned against them—for what are they doing but standing in anger's honorable way and counseling the way to shame? What would happen, Cicero asks, if Rome were to follow their advice? (XVII-XVIII). And besides, as Cicero points out, it is futile for the objectors to cite ancestral precedents and principles against the Manilian proposal (as they have done), for the ancestors in fact broke principle and precedent on several occasions for the sake of expediency in war; further, the objectors themselves have agreed to precedent-breaking measures in the past (XIX-XX). In the end, Cicero turns the angry feelings of the audience against his opponents by suggesting that what he calls their "ungracious opposition" to Pompeius comes merely from personal, jealous ill-will, and at a time when "the common weal" is at stake (XIX, 56): they wish to slight Pompeius; their actions are an insult to a popular hero and to Rome; and so they belong, in the eyes of anger, with Mithridates and his helpers. With the forum thus roused and *wanting to be angry,* and with its anger turned against them, those who resist the Manilian proposal are finally commanded by the orator to "bow to the authority of the Roman people." After which, there is nothing left for Cicero to do but briefly sum up, decorously conclude, and leave the rostrum. Cicero wins. Pompeius is appointed, and the orator secures his place in politics.

Before we leave Cicero, there are two slightly digressive but important questions that ought to be confronted, even if they cannot be fully dealt with here. First, how much did Cicero's use of Aristotelian pathos-argument actually contribute to his success? The question may be moot, though classicists tend to suggest that Pompeius would have been given the command with or without Cicero's support; however, their evidence seems less than clear to me. In any case, we can still argue that Cicero's argument cast whatever support existed within a particular emotional framework, and that it advanced his own career—which *De Imperio* certainly did—by giving his audience a cathartically strong and emotionally satisfying identification with Cicero's own terms of approval and thus with Cicero himself. The other question asks how Cicero's pathos-argument is supposed to work for the Roman reader of the printed speech, several years after the event, when the text is meant to function as literary rather than political discourse. I will suggest only that, insofar as the text works to give the reader a cathartic identification with the orator's terms of approval, its literary function is much like its political one—and in some ways is even more complete, since the reader is able to progress directly, through imaginative participation, from contemplating the shame of Roman failure to a version of anger that already knows that Mithridates has been destroyed, and so can contemplate with an enriched kind of satisfaction the pains inflicted on him by the Manilian proposal. (Perhaps this is not anger anymore, but some derivative—such as vindictiveness.)

If *De Imperio* presents a textbook case of pathos-argument modeled consciously from the Aristotelian/Peripatetic account of anger, the same probably cannot be said for Paine's *Common Sense,* the pamphlet that catalyzed American opinion, in early 1776, in favor of declaring independence. (When *Common Sense* first appeared, on 10 January 1776 in Philadelphia, the issue was by no means settled, and, indeed, the dominant view was not in favor of independence, even though hostilities were already in progress.) Paine may, of course, have absorbed some version of Aristotelian pathos-theory from popularized expositions of eighteenth-century faculty psychology (see Aldridge, *Paine's Ideology* 62) or from the stilted, bellettristic Ciceronianism that was propagated through contemporary rhetorical education. In general, however, there is no reason to believe that he had, like Cicero, delved into Greek philosophy in order to develop a rich theoretical base for his own rhetorical practice. Nevertheless, *Common Sense* can be seen to work the rhetoric of anger in Aristotelian terms: the basic enthymemic *structure* of anger remains the same as in *De Imperio,* though the presuppositional *substance* on which it depends is notably different. Indeed, there is no other way in which the rhetoric of *Common Sense* can be fully understood.

Consider the oft-remarked problem of Paine's fourth and final section in *Common Sense* (in the first edition), which is titled "On the Present Ability of America, With Some Miscellaneous Reflexions." This section is markedly short of the kind of inspirational exhortation that appears in the preceding sections (particularly the third), as the pamphleteer turns mainly to dry-seeming matters of finance, complete with calculations on the cost of building a navy and a review of the available resources: "Hemp flourishes even to rankness, so that we need not want cordage . . . Saltpetre and gunpowder we are every day producing" *(Writings* 106), and so forth. For the modern reader, it is dull going indeed, and in consequence Paine's modern critics generally find this section a disappointment. As Isaac Kramnick, one of Paine's recent editors, puts it in his introduction to the text, "Paine moves few readers with his excursions into finance and commerce . . . It was not Tom Paine's common sense but his rage that turned hundreds of thousands of Americans to thoughts of independence in the winter of 1776" (43); Kramnick believes the text comes "to life once more" in the more overtly hortatory appendices Paine added to the second edition, which appeared on 14 February 1776, about a month after the first edition. A. Owen Aldridge seconds this opinion, suggesting that Paine added his appendices to bolster the anticlimactic "weakness" of his original conclusion (*Paine's Ideology* 82).

There is no doubt that Paine's additions made the text more effective than before, but this line of thought explains poorly the instantaneous and profound effect of the *first* edition. The impact of this edition, which sold out (1,000 copies) within two weeks, is widely attested (see Aldridge's *Man of Reason;* Hawke; Bailyn; and Smith). Here, for example, is George Washington, writing from Maryland on 13 February 1776, the day before Paine brought out his second edition: "If you know the author of *Common Sense* [the first edition had been published anonymously], tell him he has done wonders and worked miracles, made Tories Whigs, and washed Blackamores white. He has made a great number of converts here" (Smith 27). And as Kramnick notes (30), when Paine revealed himself as the author in his second edition, he acquired "instant fame": the first edition, clearly, had won this fame already. In any case, we hear of no complaints about Paine's supposedly boring fourth section from his contemporaries, though there were hard-core Tories and conservatives who sought to refute, with impassioned arguments, Paine's ideas on government and finance. And further, *contra* Kramnick, Paine does not actually speak in the voice of rage—which is, after all, a ranting voice indisposed to presenting the kind of elaborate argument Paine develops—and this is particularly true in the problematic fourth section. A key part of Paine's rhetoric, indeed, is that he speaks predominantly with the voice of what his age would recognize as "common sense," or natural reason. The rage, the anger, is not so much in the speaker as it is *in the reader;* or rather, it is caused to happen there. And the fourth section is what finally permits it to emerge.

Consider what precedes the fourth section of *Common Sense;* consider, that is, the first three sections. Paine's opening section, "Of the Origin and Design of Government in General, With Concise Remarks on the English Constitution" is, like Cicero's *narratio,* not directed toward the focal issue to which Paine will ultimately speak. Instead, it is preparatory to that issue and to the pathos that Paine will call for later. Paine advances the theses that kingship is a perversion of the "true design and end of government" and that "the crown is the overbearing part in the English constitution" (*Writings* 69, 74). Paine's account of the "true design and end of government" is developed through a Lockean/Rousseauvian, pseudo-mythic narrative of the social contract evolving in a state of undisturbed nature, among a small "colony" of equals "in some sequestered part of the earth" (70-71), as they devise a more or less pure popular democracy. Paine's mythic "colony" is, obviously, an ideal version of America, and at the same time it resonates with prevailing eighteenth-century notions of natural reason and natural law: as the pamphleteer says of his myth, "the simple voice of nature and reason will say, 'tis right" (71). Paine's reader in 1776 is thus given strong reason to agree that the English constitution, with its system of checks and balances (the Monarch, the House of Lords, and the House of Commons) is in reality "unnatural": *"how came the king by a power which the people . . . are always obliged to check? . . .* neither can any power, *which needs checking,* be from God . . . the plain truth is that *it is wholly owing to the constitution of the people, and not to the constitution of the government* that the crown is not as oppressive in England as in Turkey" (73, 74; Paine's emphasis).

What emotion is called for here? It is not yet anger, nor is it "rage." George III emerges as a virtual oriental despot—with all the luxury, excess, cruelty, and tyranny that oriental despotism implies for the eighteenth-century Western mind—as a perversion of nature and thus of God's intentions. Following Aristotle, let us call the emotion asked for here *indignation,* the perception and judgment of unworthiness, immorality, undeserved privilege, and power unrightfully possessed (*Rhetoric* II.ix, 1387a-b). Or, if indignation waxes strong enough, the emotion may be "hate": not the will-to-punish of "anger," but an evaluative stance which holds that "the offender" should not exist at all (II.iv, 1382a). All kings are despicable, and George III is a king.

Paine's second section, "Of Monarchy and Hereditary Succession," works initially to add a new dimension to the reader's indignation, as the argument turns to lengthy scriptural quotation (76-79) showing that "Monarchy is ranked in scripture as one of the sins of the Jews, for which a curse in reserve is denounced against them" by God (76). Who among Paine's readers in 1776 could disagree with evidence like that? As Paine says,

> These portions of scripture are direct and positive. They admit of no equivocal construction. That the Almighty hath here entered his protest against monarchical government is true, or the scripture is false. (79)

The implication here for America, the New Jerusalem, is fairly clear. To set up a king over yourself is to earn, like the ancient Israelites, "a curse in reserve"; to indignation, then, there is added a kind of anxious fear, the perception of imminent and possibly unavoidable harm directed at you by an overwhelming power (*Rhetoric* II.v, 1382a-1383a).

From here, however, Paine turns back to amplifying the reader's indignation/hate, by arguing that a hereditary king—the product of "an unwise, unjust, unnatural compact" (79)—is, among all people, the most unfit to rule. The "race of kings" has a dishonorable origin (the first kings are usurping criminals, and William the Conqueror was a "French bastard with an armed Banditti," 80), and their offspring tend to be mentally deficient, isolated from the world's real concerns, insolent because of their power, and, as seen in the English wars of succession, prone to violence and the sowing of civil discord (80-83). This returns Paine to his earlier conclusions on monarchy: "'Tis a form of government which the word of God bears testimony against, and blood will attend it" (83); the English constitution is "sickly" because "monarchy hath poisoned the republic" and "the crown hath engrossed the commons" (83). These conclusions lead to an outright expression of indignation: "Of more worth is one honest man to society, and in the sight of God, than all the crowned ruffians that ever lived" (84). The reader is asked to join this indignation, on the belief that it is the voice of natural common sense aligned with God's intentions; but on the other hand, the reader is also given grounds for apprehension in the divine "curse in reserve" and the bloodshed that "attends" hereditary kingship. Indeed, the reader of 1776 can see this judgment and bloodshed as manifest already, in the ongoing conflict with England. The reader's emotional state is becoming more complex and at the same time less settled.

All the elaborate preparation of Paine's first two sections, his mobilizing of presuppositional and emotive structures in the reader, comes to focus in the third section, "Thoughts on the Present State of American Affairs." In this section, *Common Sense* first makes direct engagement with what is in fact its focal issue—namely, whether the colonies should declare independence or seek reconciliation with England once the ongoing "rebellion" has accomplished its objectives (i.e., the amending of taxation and representation practices for the colonies). Paine opens by asking the reader to "divest himself of prejudice and prepossession, and suffer his reason and his feelings to determine for themselves: that he will put on, or rather will not put off, the true character of a man, and generously enlarge his views beyond the present day" (84). This means, in the succeeding paragraphs, that the reader must consider the unmanliness of not planning and acting for posterity, of taking measures that suffice only for the moment, as Paine simultaneously gestures toward the vistas of American destiny: "The Sun never shined on a cause of greater worth. . . . Now is the seed-time of Continental union" (84, 85). But these ideas of manliness/unmanliness and destiny are only preparatory to Paine's key move. The argument turns immediately to reflection on "the many material injuries which these Colonies sustain" (85) through their relationship with England. These include basic conflicts of interest (in which England will always sacrifice America to global strategy), but more focally they include the warfare being conducted by the "mother country" against its supposed child: "Even brutes do not devour their young, nor savages make war upon their families" (86). We now come to the crucial perception of *insult,* the focal premise required for anger—and indeed, it is an unmerited, outrageous insult, because (as the preceding two sections have made abundantly clear) it comes from the perverted will of an unnatural, ungodly, morally unfit, and insolent creature who has "engrossed" the government of England and the virtues of the English people. Note that without these premises in place, it would be possible for Paine's reader, and especially the reader not already committed to the cause of independence, to regard English aggression as the king's rightful and perhaps unavoidable exercise of authority towards rebellious subjects (who are, after all, breaking the law) and to regard the American injuries sustained as simply the "fortunes of war" or as the wages of incivil disobedience.

Paine's reader, like Cicero's hearer in the forum, is at this point in *Common Sense* exposed to a double emotion or an emotional dilemma, namely the choice between the shame of "unmanliness" and an anger that is allied with the will of God and nature. Both soon come to focus (I partially quote):

> Men of passive tempers look somewhat lightly over the offences of Great Britain, and, still hoping for the best, are apt to call out, *Come, come, we*

shall be friends again for all this. But examine the passions and feelings of mankind . . . and then tell me whether you can hereafter love, honour, and faithfully serve the power that hath carried fire and sword into your land? . . . Your future connection with Britain . . . will be forced and unnatural. . . . But if you say, you can still pass the violations over, then I ask, hath your house been burnt? Hath your property been destroyed before your face? Are your wife and children destitute of a bed to lie on, or bread to live on? Have you lost a parent or child by their hands, and you the wretched survivor? If you have not, then you are not a judge of those who have. But if you have. and can still shake hands with the murderer, then are you unworthy the name of husband, father, friend, or lover, and whatever may be your rank or title in life, you have the heart of a coward, and the spirit of a sycophant. (91)

Paine immediately adds the reminder that "This is not inflaming or exaggerating matters, but trying them by those feelings and affections which nature justifies" (91)—thus keeping for himself the tone not of shrill "rage" but of "common sense." The balance of section four, however, is devoted to amplifying the topos of this passage, namely that "as Milton wisely expresses, never can reconcilement grow where wounds of deadly hate have pierced so deep" (91). This is further buttressed with reflections on English government and the nature of the relation between crown and colony, tending mainly to the conclusion that "reconcilement" would expose the colonies not only to the usual harm that comes from being attached to a king, but also from the ill-will of a vengeful despot toward his formerly rebellious subjects. Reconciliation is thus impossible, and there is no honorable course available but to seek independence through force of arms.

These arguments intensify the reader's emotional dilemma. On one hand, the reader is asked to choose independence for the sake of a righteous anger that is aligned with divine judgment—*to choose independence in order to punish England's perverted crown for the "insults" and "injuries" brought against the colonies.* On the other hand, the reader is simultaneously presented with the shame of cowardice and "sycophancy" in choosing to seek or accept the appearances of reconciliation. As in *De Imperio,* anger is honorable and pleasant (perhaps even more emphatically so, since it is aligned with the divine will) and leads outward to virtuous if difficult action; at the same time shame is painful and actionable only in terms of self-directed attitudes (plus the fear of judgment, including this time God's judgment as well as the judgment of one's neighbors).

But which emotional outcome is more available? The reader in section three is left, like Cicero's hearer in the first two thirds of *De Imperio's confirmatio*, with the still unresolved question of whether the means of "punishment"—in this case, depriving George of his sovereignty in America, and inflicting violence and indignities upon his adherents and representatives—is actually available. Is it *probable* that the colonies can in fact obtain independence through armed resistance to the world's preeminent military power? As one contemporary noted, public opinion in the weeks before the publication of *Common Sense* "had shuddered at the tremendous obstacles with which independence was environed" (in Hawke 47-48); there was considerable and indeed reasonable fear. In sum, then, we now have a reader who *wants* to release himself in anger, but who still lacks a crucial premise for *believing in his anger,* and who is thus left facing the prospect of his cowardice and sycophancy, his failure, and his almost infinite shame. At the end, that is, of section three.

The function of section four, "Of the Present Ability of America, With Some Miscellaneous Reflexions," is evident in this context. The voice of "common sense" now returns, in tones of confident optimism and with facts and figures, to argue that America's population, resources, and finances are sufficient "to repel the force of all the world" (101), that England's vaunted navy is less formidable than it seems, and that the present moment is opportune for obtaining victory (whereas in future time the circumstances may be less propitious). Paine then follows this discussion with his "miscellaneous reflexions" on what sort of government the new nation ought to give itself—as if, in other words, independence were virtually a foregone conclusion, with the confident pamphleteer considering what to do *after* victory is obtained. While the ending of section three is hortatory and inspirational—"Freedom hath been hunted round the globe. . . . O! receive the fugitive, and prepare in time an asylum for mankind" (101)—section four (and thus the pamphlet in its first edition) ends by suggesting that the task is smaller than it seems:

> These proceedings may at first seem strange and difficult, but like all other steps which we have already passed over, will in a little time become familiar and agreeable: and until independence is declared, the Continent will feel itself like a man who continues putting off some unpleasant business from day to day, yet knows it must be done, hates to set about it, wishes it over, and is continually haunted with the thoughts of its necessity. (111)

The reader's righteous war of independence is now reduced to an "unpleasant business" that needs to be taken care of soon, and the sooner the better.

These reflections, and the generally matter-of-fact tone in which they are brought forward, may well strike the modern reader as an emotional letdown and as a weak conclusion to Paine's pamphlet. But for the reader of the first edition in January 1776, I think, the case is rather different. Paine's calm and optimistic closing section is a crucial catalyst for mobilizing anger in that reader and for persuading him to choose a war of independence for that anger's sake—for Paine offers in this section the necessary warrant for a "cathartic" release from the ambivalent, distressful pathos-state built up by section three, a release into the relief and pleasure of the justified will-to-punish. The modern reader may of course object that Paine's analysis of American "ability" is grounded on poor evidence and somewhat unimpressive logic (Kramnick 46). All this may be true (though the outcome proved Paine's general contention more or less correct), but we would be judging Paine's rhetoric from the wrong perspective. For the reader of 1776, the *need to be angry* rather than shamed is a stronger force than the need to critique Paine's calculations, and this stronger need is truly a force that, in Aristotle's terms, "warps" or channels deliberation. *The need for anger rather than shame creates a need to believe Paine's analysis, in order that the anger may be warranted:* the reader is powerfully disposed by pathos-pressures to agree and to see Paine's optimism as the attitude to take. It seems doubtful, in short, that Paine's many "converts" in January 1776 were much disposed to a finicky scholar's analysis of the evidence presented in section four.

Clearly, the Quintilianic/conventional account of pathos seems inadequate to *Common Sense* as well as to *De Imperio*. The text does not depend on the speaker's "emoting" nor even particularly on "imagery" for its primary emotional force—at least not "imagery" in the typical textbook sense of picturesque and "concrete" description/narrative—although, indeed, figured language is used at certain points to *intensify* the psychological prominence of anger's premises and to make them memorable. To a large degree, in fact, the description and narrative in Paine and Cicero often have the character more of *summary* or *reference* to known "facts" than luridly detailed accounts of violation and suffering. What generates anger in Paine's and Cicero's audiences, or is meant to, is an enthymemically structured logology grounded in a network of "dark" or deep presuppositions that is held in suspension, elaborately played out, and finally resolved as the speaker's argument unfolds. There is a point here we ought to note: the rhetoric of anger, or (by extension) of pathos generally, is not limited to local effects. With *Common Sense,* as with *De Imperio,* it functions globally.

Quintilian's account of pathos, arguably, is suited to the mostly ornamental, decadent art of declamation taught by the rhetoric schools of Imperial Rome. As S. F. Bonner says of that highly artificial genre, "It was . . . difficult to work up any genuine emotion for the stock characters of the declamations, or even for their historical personages . . . but it is not pathos, merely pseudo-pathos. Here is the poor starving father . . . helped out by apostrophe, chiasmus, triple repetition, and climax . . . [or] the hero who had lost his hands in battle and been unable to kill his wife taken in adultery . . . The last moments of a disinherited son, commending to his father a child by a courtesan, afford the opportunity of a touching death-bed scene" (*Roman Declamation* 62-63). The declamations were primarily dramatic performances, soliloquies, and their aesthetic value probably did depend considerably on the performer's histrionic powers—the audience desired a "moving" performance, a mimesis that would engage their sympathies, since the nominal issue of the speech was a nonissue and nothing but entertainment was at stake. Much the same can happen for a modern reader reading *Common Sense:* the text becomes a literary artifact and its author a "declaimer," and the reader is bored by the long-dead "practical" issues of section four but thrilled by the "passion" of sections one through three. Within such a context, then, we can see the motives of Quintilianic "pseudo-pathos"—and we can see, as well, how Quintilianic theory nearly loses sight of what is grasped in Aristotelian theory and in the rhetorical sagacity that informs the potent suasory practices of Paine and Cicero.

The great contemporary departure from the Quintilianic/conventional account of pathos has been Perelman's "new rhetoric," with its collapse of the weary antithesis between emotional and rational persuasion. In essence, Perelman redefines pathos as intensity of "adherence" to ideas—the degree to which we value an idea or desire its truth (or disvalue or reject it)—and makes emotion a function of the valuative elements semantically inherent in the terms employed by an argument. As Perelman argues, the "emotive meaning" of a concept is an "integral part" of its general meaning and "not just an adventitious addition that does not belong to the symbolic character of language" (*New Rhetoric* 140). For the Perelmanian account, then, emotion is neither fallacious reasoning nor irrational (or nonrational) reaction; it is inseparable from the substance of logology itself, as the "emotive meaning" or valuative "adherence" encoded in the terms of an argument are carried over to that argument's conclusion.

To this analysis Perelman adds the concept of "presence," or the *psychological prominence* of any particular concept foregrounded in the reader/listener's attention—a prominence caused by such familiar strategies (and here they turn up) as graphic narrative, description, tropes, and schemes. Thus we see, *contra* the conventional account, that such devices as "imagery" and "emotive language" serve more to *amplify* pathos than to cause it: the audience may feel a little anger or a lot; they may "adhere" to their anger with greater or lesser intensity, depending on how much "presence" is given to anger's constitutive premises. Further, if an audience has *already been persuaded* toward anger through the presentation of anger-making concepts, we can see that an orator's dramatistic, emotional display can intensify the listener's pathos in ways that are more complex than the conventional analysis typically allows. The orator's becoming angry can (if he seems sincere) signify adherence to the values that motivated anger in the audience and so give his ethos greater credibility—thereby intensifying audience/orator "identification" as they join together in a "catharsis" of angry intentionalities and redoubling the audience's ability to believe in its own emotion. Quintilian, in truth, understands this better than does the conventional account. As he says, "if we wish to give our words the appearance of sincerity, we must assimilate ourselves to the emotions of those who are genuinely . . . affected" (VI.ii.27).[4] Still, neither "imagery" nor emotional expression is strictly necessary in the Perelmanian analysis, and, in fact, both are considered unreliable means of generating presence. A better means, for Perelman, is the use of such schemes of amplification as repetition, or "dwelling on a subject"—schemes which can, depending on the requirements of the rhetorical situation, remain at a fairly abstract level of discussion (*New Rhetoric* 117-18, 144-45; *Realm* 35-37): that, indeed, is the major means of generating "presence" for the premises that warrant anger in much of *De Imperio* and *Common Sense*.

Perelman's revision of the conventional account is thus close to and compatible with the Aristotelian account of pathos enthymemes. At the same time, however, there is nothing in Perelman comparable to Book II of the *Rhetoric;* there is no Perelmanian "book" or chapter specifically on the rhetoric and logic of emotion. Pathos, redefined as "adherence," remains something of an undifferentiated quality, a fluid substance operating *inside of reason* and as part of reason but with no specific structure of its own. But, as the Aristotelian account suggests (in both its ancient and modern versions), pathos is something more than degrees of adherence—more than simply plus or minus signs attached to the nouns and verbs employed in argument (or positive and negative "charges," as in electricity). Pathos has a complex structure of its own. Or rather, each species of pathos has a complex, logologically constituted structure that can be described. Each structure is a topology, involving both formal and material topics: the "formal topics" and "material topics" of anger, for example, are the *insult* + *means of punishment* = *will-to-punish* scheme (the formal topic), and the various presuppositions defining "insult," "punishment," and so forth (the material topics). (See also Grimaldi's account of enthymemic topics in *Studies* 17, 69.) Each topology can be thought of, in rhetorical terms, as providing the structure for a type of argument—just as *a fortiori* arguments, sign arguments, and arguments from antithesis (for example) can be thought of as types of arguments or *species of enthymemes,* each with its own characteristic mode of operation. In the light of *De Imperio* and *Common Sense,* then, we may say that the Aristotelian account supplies the deficiencies of both the Quintilianic/conventional and Perelmanian accounts, giving to pathos an emotional specificity and force and a complex rationality that neither the old nor the new rhetoric fully addresses.

Let us reflect a little further, as this essay ends, on some implications of the Aristotelian account. Emotions, appetites, desires and enthymemes all belong, for Aristotle, to the "spirited" and prereflective part of the psyche, the *thymos,* to which he accords rationality in the form of an inferential power to swiftly intuit relationships between ideas—a power given to the mind more or less by nature, a power that all minds inherently possess.[5] It is for this reason that enthymemes are the "body of persuasion," the substance of the three *pisteis* of ethos, pathos and logos (see Grimaldi; Fortenbaugh; Miller and Bee). To the other and more conscious part of the psyche Aristotle assigns the power of *logismos,* that is, the power of deliberately articulated reasoning or "calculation," a power which requires specific training and which, in consequence, *not* all minds possess. It is by *logismos,* in other words, that the well-taught rhetor will consciously construct a line of reasoning and by the enthymemic power that a receptive mind will interpret that line of reasoning's conceptual force within a dense context of presuppositions—and then respond by mobilizing the pathos state or states that the perceived array of concepts warrants. What this implies, in the long run, is that attitudes like rational conviction, assent, and even the mere perception of logical coherence are themselves pathos-states mediated by the enthymemic, inferential powers of the psyche.[6] Thus *all enthymemes are enthymemes of pathos* in one form or another, depending on which constitutive concepts (logologies, topologies) happen to be mobilized. At this point, all rhetoric begins to be absorbed within the rhetoric of pathos, and syllogistic dialectic becomes the counterpart and secondary echo of enthymemic rhetoric, for a proof of any kind is proof only when the enthymemic power can see an enthymeme in it. What is left over to *logismos,* finally, seems to be little more than a dependent power of articulation—dependent because, without the inferential process of the enthymemic power, it cannot perceive, interpret, or judge itself.

Quintilian and the rhetoric of *De Imperio* and *Common Sense* still leave us with a question. Were Paine and Cicero cheating—did they lead their audiences "away from contemplation of the truth" and compel assent by intellectually or morally dubious means? We certainly can accuse Cicero, as he has been accused, of ignoring and eventually sweeping away what was, after all, a genuine issue, one that he himself would later take up in his heroic and doomed effort to preserve the republic from Caesar and what came after. And we can say of Paine, as it has been said, that his argument plays a little fast and loose with the facts, falls a little short of adequacy according to the canons of philosophic inference, and works on the reader's passions while pretending to persuade according to natural reason. Perhaps Paine and Cicero should have conducted themselves more like philosophers—although, of course, they almost certainly would have failed had they done so. And, of course, according to the Aristotelian analysis of pathos, both Paine and Cicero *were* persuading by means of natural reason; what other kind is there? Or we might take a more aggressive stance, and argue that Cicero chose the course of virtue, the best that his immediate occasion made available (see Petersson 186-87); and we might do the same for Paine. Perhaps it is good that Paine succeeded with his enthymeme of anger; perhaps it is good that Cicero succeeded too. But by what means, other than an enthymeme of pathos, are we going to decide? ❧

NOTES

[1]A random survey of my own shelf, which probably resembles yours, yields the following representative examples: the ever-venerable *Writing With A Purpose* approaches the "emotional appeal" in pseudo-Quintilianic style as "dramatic examples, presented in concrete images and connotative language," which have their uses but "should never replace more rational appeals" (144); Edward P. J. Corbett's *Classical Rhetoric for the Modern Student* likewise counsels rousing emotion by "describing a scene" and/or using "emotion-laden words" (101-103); Maxine Hairston's *Successful Writing,* on the other hand, says nothing at all about pathos, except perhaps indirectly through discussion of the connotative dimensions of euphemism, jargon, and sexist language; Rise Axelrod and Charles Cooper's recent and highly praised *St. Martin's Guide to Writing* approaches pathos directly only under the rubric of a "fallacy" they call the "sob story" (516); and Wayne Booth and Marshall Gregory's recent *Harper & Row Rhetoric* approaches pathos only under the rubric of "emotionally charged language" (233-35), which comes, in their presentation, between "connotation" and "slanted language" (which is a "fallacy"). Two notable exceptions to this contemporary Quintilianism are John T. Gage's *The Shape of Reason* and Gerard A. Hauser's *Introduction to Rhetorical Theory*—both of which are much closer to the position this essay will develop.

[2]A standard example, recurring in several discussions, is the parent gripped by fear until a "lost" child turns out to be not lost after all—and whose relief suddenly gives way to anger. The point is that the underlying, diffuse arousal-state has remained the same and is in fact continous while the different and seemingly discontinuous emotions/actions in which it manifests itself are the products of different sets of constituting beliefs/cognitions, which arise in the parent's mind at two different points in time.

[3]I am calling this an "Aristotelian" definition of catharsis, insofar as it belongs to an Aristotelian tradition of critical discourse that extends from the *Poetics* to the present; I am, however, emphatically not claiming that it is *the* definition Aristotle used, or meant to use, in the *Poetics,* nor do I wish to adjudicate among the many interpretations of the term that have been offered over the centuries. My definition of "catharsis" as "release" of

a diffuse arousal-state depends, I hope obviously, on twentieth-century reinterpretation of the ancient concept.

[4]The classic example of emotional display as a dimension of ethos, one consistent with what Quintilian is saying here, would be Cicero's Catilene orations—known as "The Invectives" in the Middle Ages—and especially the first oration. Still, as I have noted above, Quintilian's statement doesn't work well for humor, and it doesn't work well for an account of pathos in *De Imperio* and *Common Sense*.

[5]Aristotle makes this point with the, for us, unfortunate-sounding observation that *even women, children, and slaves* have this enthymemic intuition, in the receptive form of the ability to appreciate and respond to the reasoning presented to them by others, and, to some extent, to generate reasoning of their own (Fortenbaugh 57-61). The essential point, extricated for present purposes from Aristotle's class/gender/ethnic politics, is that *even those not specifically trained to do so* perform enthymemic reasoning because it is inherent to the nature of the human mind—but those with training do it better.

[6]This argument has been made, on non-Aristotelian grounds, by William James in "The Sentiment of Rationality" (*The Will to Believe* 63-110).

WORKS CITED

Aldridge, A. Owen. *Man of Reason: The Life of Thomas Paine*. New York: J.B. Lippincott, 1959.

———. *Thomas Paine's American Ideology*. New York: U Delaware P, 1984.

Aristotle. *On the Soul [De Anima]*. Tr. W.S. Hett. Cambridge: Harvard UP, 1957.

———. *The Rhetoric and the Poetics of Aristotle*. Tr. W. Rhys Roberts and Ingram Bywater. New York: Modern Library-Random, 1954.

Axelrod, Rise B., and Charles R. Cooper. *The St. Martin's Guide to Writing*. 2nd ed. New York: St. Martin's, 1988.

Bailyn, Bernard. "Common Sense." *Fundamental Testaments of the American Revolution*. Washington: Library of Congress, 1973.

Bonner, S. F. *Roman Declamation in the Late Republic and Early Empire*. Liverpool: UP of Liverpool, 1949.

——. "Roman Oratory." *Fifty Years (And Twelve) of Classical Scholarship*. Ed. M. Platnauer. Oxford: Blackwell, 1986. 416-64.

Booth, Wayne, and Marshall W. Gregory. *The Harper & Row Rhetoric*. New York: Harper, 1987.

Calhoun, Cheshire, and Robert C. Solomon, eds. *What Is An Emotion? Classic Readings in Philosophical Psychology*. New York: Oxford UP, 1984.

Cicero. *De Imperio Cnaeus Pompei [Pro Lege Manilia]*. Tr. H. Grose Hodge. Cambridge: Harvard UP, 1927.

——. *Tusculan Disputations*. Tr. J. E. King. Cambridge: Harvard UP, 1927.

Corbett, Edward P. J. *Classical Rhetoric for the Modern Student*. New York: Oxford UP, 1971.

de Sousa, Ronald. *The Rationality of Emotion*. Cambridge: MIT P, 1987.

Enos, Richard Leo. *The Literate Mode of Cicero's Legal Rhetoric*. Carbondale: Southern Illinois UP, 1988.

Fortenbaugh, W. W. *Aristotle on Emotion*. London: Duckworth, 1975.

Gage, John T. *The Shape of Reason: Argumentative Writing in College*. New York: Macmillan, 1987.

Grant, Michael, tr. *Selected Political Speeches of Cicero*. New York: Penguin, 1973.

Grimaldi, William M. A., S.J. *Aristotle, Rhetoric I: A Commentary*. New York: Fordham UP, 1980.

——. *Studies in the Philosophy of Aristotle's Rhetoric*. Weisbaden: Franz Steiner Verlag GMBH, 1972.

Hairston, Maxine C. *Successful Writing*. 2nd ed. New York: Norton, 1986.

Hauser, Gerard A. *Introduction to Rhetorical Theory*. New York: Harper, 1986.

Hawke, David Freeman. *Paine*. New York: Harper, 1974.

James, William. *The Will to Believe, and Other Essays in Popular Philosophy*. 1897. New York: Dover, 1956.

Lindemann, Erika. *A Rhetoric for Writing Teachers*. 2nd ed. Oxford: Oxford UP, 1987.

Miller, A. B., and J. D. Bee. "Enthymemes: Body and Soul." *Philosophy and Rhetoric* 5 (1972), 201-14.

Paine, Thomas. *Common Sense*. Ed. Isaac Kramnick. New York: Penguin, 1982.

———. *Common Sense. The Writings of Thomas Paine*. Ed. Moncure Daniel Conway. New York: Putnam's, 1894. Vol. 1.

Perelman, Chaim, and L. Olbrechts-Tyteca. *The New Rhetoric: A Treatise on Argumentation*. Tr. J. Wilkinson and P. Weaver. Notre Dame: Notre Dame UP, 1971.

———. *The Realm of Rhetoric*. Tr. W. Kluback. Notre Dame: Notre Dame UP, 1982.

Petersson, Torsten. *Cicero: A Biography*. New York: Biblio, 1963.

Quintilian. *Institutio Oratoria*. Tr. H. E. Butler. 4 vols. Cambridge: Harvard UP, 1920-22.

Rorty, Amélie O., ed. *Explaining Emotions*. Berkeley: U California P, 1980.

Searle, John R. *Intentionality: An Essay in the Philosophy of Mind*. Cambridge: Cambridge UP, 1983.

Smith, Frank. *Thomas Paine, Liberator*. New York: Stokes, 1938.

Solomon, Robert C. *The Passions*. Garden City: Anchor-Doubleday, 1976.

Trimmer, Joseph F., and James M. McCrimmon. *Writing With A Purpose*. 9th ed. Boston: Houghton, 1988.

❦ 18

Narration, Technical Communication, and Culture: *The Soul of a New Machine* as Narrative Romance

Steven B. Katz

In "Narration in Technical Communication," Ben and Marthalee Barton question the devaluation of narration in technical communication by researchers and teachers. The Bartons argue that narration is not only pervasive in scientific and technical writing but also important in rendering abstract concepts concrete and in presenting technical information in a form that is both easy and fast to read. In addition, they suggest that narration may play a vital role in bridging the cultural gap between specialist and lay audience and that it may be "a valuable alternative to rational discourse in reconciling conflicting perspectives in the public arena" (44). In fact, they suggest that narration is useful for resolving not only public disputes but cultural disparities and intra-organizational differences as well (45). Thus, they conclude, "we need research aimed at more conscious and informed exploitation of narration in technical communication, at the use of narration appropriate at a variety of levels throughout technical discourse in given contexts and with given goals" (45).

    The need for investigation into the role of narration in scientific and technical communication is also highlighted by two recent books that argue for the centrality and importance of narration in human understanding. In *Narrative Knowing and the Human Sciences,* Donald E. Polkinghorne opposes the narrative configuration of knowledge to formal demonstration in order to assert the fundamental role of narration in "the human sciences," especially psychology, which heretofore have adopted the research model of the natural sciences as their paradigm of knowledge. And in *Human Communication as Narration: Toward a Philosophy of Reason, Value, and Action,* Walter Fisher not only posits the narrative paradigm as the basic mode of human understanding and discourse, but also touches on its importance in scientific and technical communication. Fisher sees human beings as *homo narrans* and narration—the story of life—as the basic logic of human meaning and value that underlies *all* rational discourse including scientific and technical argumentation (48-49). "There is no genre, not even technical discourse," says Fisher, "that is not constituted by both logos and mythos" (85).

Thus, as the need for further investigation into the role of narration in scientific and technical communication becomes clear, so does the method of research that should be used: genre criticism. As Michael Halloran argues, research in "the rhetoric of science" (and by extension, technology) must be based on rhetorical analyses of specific instances of discourse that reveal the peculiar differences as well as the general similarities of scientific discourse. Otherwise, we risk missing the particulars of scientific and technical communication that are the most significant and illuminating (80-81). According to Karlyn Kohrs Campbell and Kathleen Hall Jamieson, genre analysis "reveals both the conventions and affinities that a work shares with others" and "the unique elements in the rhetorical act, the particular means by which a genre is individuated in a given case" (18).

In addition, however, rhetorical genre criticism as defined by Edwin Black focuses on the similarities and differences of rhetorical *forms* as responses to recurring social, historical, and psychological situations (rather than on the responses of specific audiences to individual texts). For Campbell and Jamieson, the recurrence of a form may arise from "comparable rhetorical situations, the influence of conventions on the responses of rhetors, out of universal and cultural archetypes ingrained in human consciousness, out of human needs, or out of a finite number of rhetorical options or commonplaces" (26-27). A comparison of forms as responses to social, historical, and psychological circumstances therefore allows us not only to go beyond the limitations of an audience bound in time and place but to cross the borders of subject matter, discipline, and culture as well. This is necessary in the study of narration, which by its nature is interdisciplinary and basic to all human knowledge.

In this essay, I would like to explore and extend our understanding of narration in scientific and technical communication by conducting a rhetorical analysis of Tracy Kidder's use of the genre of narrative romance in *The Soul of a New Machine*. Published in 1981, *The Soul of a New Machine* is a journalistic but often technical account of the building of a new computer by a team of engineers at Data General. Despite the technical subject matter of the book, the cultural predisposition to view engineers as narrow, dull, apathetic, and unfeeling (Florman 4), and the general fear of computers among the populace at the time, the book was hailed by reviewers, became a national best-seller, and won the 1982 Pulitzer Prize. Through a rhetorical genre analysis, I will demonstrate that Kidder employs narrative romance to portray the efforts of a group of corporate engineers to build a computer *as a mythic heroic quest*. He does so, of course, to appeal to the widest possible audience. In his review, Samuel Florman called Kidder our modern Dante ("Hardy Boys" 18), recognizing and celebrating the fact that Kidder had written a narrative romance of the engineer, though he did not use that term.

More importantly, I will argue that Kidder's use of narrative romance was a successful rhetorical response to a psychological and social need to resolve the cultural disparity between the American ambivalence toward computer technology and the reality of it by integrating that technology into the mythological fabric of America. A rhetorical genre analysis of the narrative pattern of *The Soul of a New Machine* therefore might elucidate the relationship among narration, technical writing, and culture—a relationship I believe is essential in understanding the role of narration as a form of public discourse in our highly scientific and technological society. This relationship also may point to the need to teach students of science and technology how to speak this form of public discourse, the language of our culture, just as we now teach them to speak the forms of professional discourse, the language of experts and managers. I will discuss this need further at the end of this essay.

In arguing for a rhetorical genre criticism based on a comparison of forms, Campbell and Jamieson (25-26) point to connections between the genres of narrative romance, rituals, and myths that underlie much of Western literature, religion, and culture. *The Soul of a New Machine* closely follows Northrop Frye's pattern of narrative romance. As we will see, this is neither merely coincidence nor poetic license; rather, narrative romance is a deeply ingrained way of seeing, experiencing, understanding, and structuring the world—even in the corporate world of computer engineers. Not only does Kidder as writer perceive the situation this way, but this is how the engineers themselves perceive and describe it as well.[1]

The element that distinguishes narrative romance from other forms of narrative, according to Frye, is the theme of the hero's quest, the adventure or journey through which prosperity and/or order is restored to a community in decline. In *The Soul of A New Machine*, the journey is the quest of a group of engineers at Data General Corporation to build a computer. Data General has fallen behind in new orders for its line of computers, and in the cut-throat computer industry is now threatened by the introduction of a new mini-computer by its arch rival, DEC. Data General is in imminent danger of decline, of falling behind its competitor, even of failing. So it is that Ed de Castro, who as president rules over the realm of Data General, calls on Tom West, the leader and knight errant of a team of engineers, to work on improving the addressing system of another model, ECLIPSE. West, however, undertakes the quest of building an entirely new machine that will be compatible with ECLIPSE, despite the fact that a new facility in North Carolina was being set up explicitly for that purpose.

Frye identifies four phases of narrative romance that are associated with, if not originally derived from, the cycle of the seasons (185-206). It is usually autumn when the hero departs and descends into the underworld, winter when the hero disappears in battle, spring when the hero reemerges, and summer when the hero returns and is reunited with society. In *The Soul of a New Machine*, the schedule for building this machine—like human activities and rituals based on the cycle of the seasons—seems to accord with the pattern of narrative romance (Fraser, *The New Golden Bough*); but the god these engineers will revive is a machine. It is fall when the heroes begin their quest to save the company by bringing the computer to life (*Soul* 49, 113), moving down into the mysterious basement of Data General to draw up designs of the computer architecture. It is during winter that engineers responsible for building the hardware—nicknamed "the Hardy Boys"—begin constructing the actual computer and that the "Microkids," engineers assigned to create the machine language for the software, begin writing the microcode.

But it is early spring when they miss their first deadlines in their battle with their technological dragon: the round-the-clock debugging and correcting of the computer. That summer, they are unable, in mythic terms, to ascend. It is late summer when the project finally nears completion. But the computer continues to fail its tests, to approach what the engineers refer to as "never-never land," or to "fall off the end of the world" (*Soul* 263). They are doomed to another year of trial and tribulation. They must go "back underground" (256). After a second year, the engineers succeed in building, debugging, and running the computer ahead of the North Carolina team. The machine lives; de Castro accepts the computer. It is announced to the world in late April, is marketed, and seems destined for success. The quest is completed and the company saved—temporarily at least. In the end, West is transferred upstairs and literally ascends to a prestigious marketing job that may take him to the Far East.

There are many other elements of narrative romance here as well. According to Frye, the world of narrative romance tends to be idealized: the story is usually set in nature, far out at sea, for example, or in a dark enchanted wood. In addition, the hero of narrative romance usually possesses a rapport with nature. He tends to be a "stylized figure," a "psychological archetype" (304). He possesses mystery, virtue, power. His origins are usually shrouded in secrecy, with rumors of a miraculous birth. Thus, in *The Soul of a New Machine* the computer engineer as hero is introduced in a prologue entitled "A Good Man In a Storm." That is, the story of the building of a computer begins as an adventure story out at sea. Place and time are at first undefined, the tone one of mystery. On board a sloop, in the middle of the storm, far from the security of any land, four adults huddle together. They are all professionals: a psychologist, a lawyer, a physician, a professor. They are all seasick. All except West. He builds computers!

Indeed, throughout *The Soul of a New Machine*, Kidder uses the adjectives and situations found in the popular romances of ghost stories, detective stories, spy stories, war stories, Westerns, science fiction, fantasy, and fairy tales to depict West in heroic, almost supernatural terms, rendering him memorable, mysterious, fearless, sometimes demonic, seemingly possessed—always the mythic man who sits in the saddle of the machine, controlling the reins of technology. This recasting of the character of the engineer into a hero is important, for according to Barton and Barton, in an age of growing disillusionment with science and technology, the lay audience generally configures the story of their achievements and events as a "tragic emplotment" rather than a "romantic emplotment" of optimism and success, a mode sanctioned by professional disciplines and characteristic of most scientific articles and technical reports (44). However, this is a late nineteenth-century phenomenon; until then, and only again more recently with the publication of *The Double Helix* and other books on space exploration and the new physics, it was not uncommon for scientific treatises to report and discuss at length difficulties and failures as well as theories and successes in narrative form (Coleman, "Science" 45).[2]

In *Anatomy of Criticism*, Frye argues that the "dislocation" of the linear rhythm of narrative—working backwards and forwards in time—tends to lend a story *as a whole* a sense of timelessness, for it creates the illusion of simultaneity, of history still present (267). In recounting the steps of the building of a computer, the lives of the engineers, the problems and breakthroughs they encounter in their quest, and their relationship with West, Kidder slips easily among past, present, and future. By dislocating the narrative, as well as beginning with an adventure scene at sea, Kidder places his narrative account of the building of a new machine in a mythic context, rendering it timeless, a romantic journey sure to appeal to lay as well as more technical readers.

Of course, in genre criticism it is not only the similarities but also the differences between forms that constitute genres that are meaningful and significant (Campbell and Jamieson). The difference between this romantic journey and those of the past, the one that makes this journey contemporary and distinctly American, is announced in the title of the first chapter: "How To Make A Lot of Money." In *The Soul of a New Machine*, the magical realm of this contemporary narrative romance is set in what Kidder calls "the ghost country of rural Massachusetts" (8). But this mythic land of opportunity is the capitalistic world of computer corporations. Recounting the wondrous rise of the computer companies and the suburban society that sprang from it along Route 495 in Massachusetts, Kidder says that the area, like Troy, "contains evidence of successive sackings"; referring to the names of the companies set on the edge of the woods as prophecies, Kidder remarks: "the new order they implied had already arrived" (*Soul* 8-9). Here, then, we see Kidder integrating the world of computer corporations into American history and culture at the same time that he renders it mysterious by mythologizing it through narrative romance.

Like a contemporary fairy tale, the headquarters of Data General is referred to as a fort. An archetype of our time, it is a high-tech castle, replete with "latticed towers," an American flag, and a computer that greets the visitor with "the bare bones of a story that will feed the dreams of any ambitious businessman," 10 years of successful annual reports (9-10). As Kidder describes these reports that scroll over a blinking screen, "the computer in the case was telling an old familiar story—the international materialistic fairy tale come true" (11). Indeed, recounting the origins of Data General, Kidder states that the legends have assumed the nature and status of myth (15). In this capitalistic romance, the engineer's successful quest will result in prosperity, the revival of the company's "ailing health," and their continuing "ascent" in Fortune 500 (30). A businessman refers to West's mission as a "great act of recovery" (27). The engineers nickname their computer EAGLE. It is a high-tech quest for the American Dream itself.

But Kidder has not merely written a corporate success story. To see how this is so, it will be useful to discuss the mythic pattern of narrative romance. In *The Hero With A Thousand Faces*, Joseph Campbell argues that myths and rituals guide people through the difficult process of psychological transformation, escort them across the thresholds of change in their unconscious as well as conscious patterns of existence, by supplying new symbols (10-11). This is an important cultural function of narrative romance, especially as it is applied to science and technology. For Campbell, the stages of the quest represent "rites of passage: *separation—initiation—return,*" and the hero's perilous journey into a mythical underworld and the series of trials he undergoes result in the discovery of creative energy necessary for psychological wholeness and spiritual salvation, as well as prosperity (30-46).

In the second chapter in *The Soul of a New Machine*, entitled "Wars," what Campbell terms "the call to adventure" (49-58) is the announcement of DEC's new mini-computer to rival Data General's. The mission, then: to build EAGLE. It is a distinctly American grail. But before undertaking the quest, the hero must seek special knowledge essential to continuing the journey. As Kidder reports, shrouded in secrecy, West travels to a mysterious city somewhere in America (30). Unchecked, West enters an unnamed company, easily locates DEC's new computer, waits unseen for the technicians to leave, quickly takes the computer apart, and like the brave knight in the perilous chapel of yore (Weston, *Ritual to Romance* 175-188), has all his questions answered.

In another preparatory stage called "Atonement With Father" (Campbell 126-149), idolatry and fear of the all-powerful father figure must be surpassed, the immature self transcended, and the hero finally reconciled with the father, thereby releasing pent-up psychic energy and realizing the full power and potential necessary for the quest. In *The Soul of a New Machine*, de Castro, president of Data General and "West's Mentor" (47), undoubtedly represents the threatening, all-powerful father figure. He had dashed other projects—and the engineers' hopes—before. Kidder reports that during the building of EAGLE, de Castro was referred to "in tones of amazement, admiration and fear. Eventually, some of the survivors of the team would refer to him, forthrightly, as God" (269). Coincidentally, perhaps, the computer that de Castro had cancelled before was named EGO; it is the hero's self that must be transcended before the quest can continue. As Kidder remarks, "Dreams of Ego died hard" (40).

Yet West is able to transcend his doubt and his anger at de Castro. In trusting de Castro's judgment despite and perhaps because of his frequent vagueness, West finds the wisdom and strength necessary to go beyond de Castro's orders without disobeying him. West wouldn't really be doing anything wrong, Kidder states, for "according to local legend" de Castro had done the same thing when he was employed as a young engineer at DEC, and in the process had broken away from DEC, created Data General, and risen to success on his own (47). "If they (West and team) succeeded," Kidder reports, "they would be heroes" (45). Here we also see the role of narration within the corporation, how the formation and telling of stories reconciles the differing views of organization and employee (Barton, "Narration" 45). The conflict here is between official policy and the immediate needs of the organization and the individuals who serve it. It is the narrative romance of the corporation—the story of the miraculous birth of the company with the boss as brave and rebellious hero—rather than official policy that gives West the guidance and reassurance he needs to break corporate policy for the betterment of the company. In fact, the legend serves as a kind of *ad hoc* policy and provides these engineers with myths to live by.[3]

It is during this "ego-shattering initiation" that the hero may discover the magical comfort, protection, and encouragement of a supernatural mother figure (Campbell 130-131). In *The Soul of a New Machine*, this role is fulfilled by Rosemarie Seale, secretary for West's group. She is, Kidder reports, "dedicated, helpful, protective of the project" (*Soul* 274). She cares for West as she watches the mission "consuming his flesh" (178) and "grieves" for him when others misunderstand (228). She is referred to by the engineers as the "'mother of the team'" (274).[4] Campbell also discusses the hero's helpers (*Hero* 69-77). As he points out, the helpers must be willing to sacrifice everything, including their lives if necessary, for the successful completion of the quest. Kidder reports that every member of West's team had to pass "a mysterious rite of initiation" before beginning the technological labor of building a new machine. "By signing up for a project you agreed to do whatever was necessary for success. You agreed to forsake, if necessary, family, hobbies, and friends" (*Soul* 63). As Alsing, known as West's lieutenant, says, "'It was kind of like recruiting for a suicide mission. You're gonna die, but you're gonna die in glory'" (66).

A major phase of the initiation-quest is the separation or departure of the hero from society (*Hero* 49-89). In *The Soul of a New Machine*, West isolates his team of engineers from the others and quietly separates them from Data General (*Soul* 48). Consonant with the pattern of romance, the narrative now moves into the basement of the company, a dark, mysterious, labyrinthine underworld, baffling to the uninitiated, where the heroes will undertake the quest to bring a machine to life. As West says, "'What goes on here is not part of the real world'" (50). But in Chapter 5, "Midnight Programmer," the journey down into the underworld is made both more palpable and symbolic through Adventure, a computer game. The computer creates an underground, labyrinthine world called Colossal Cave through which, by typing directions on the keyboard, the player journeys through a maze of twisting passageways and hidden chambers populated by dragons, dwarfs, pirates, snakes, and trolls, looking for treasure that is bestowed and sometimes taken away (40). In *The Soul of a New Machine*, the journey down into the computer underworld parallels the one in the corporate basement and is in fact explicitly identified with it.

For these computer engineers, playing this game is thus the necessary "Crossing of the First Threshold" (*Hero* 77). Campbell points out that this threshold is usually controlled by a guardian who can be both beneficial and destructive (77-89). In the magical realm of the electronic world, the guardian is—who else?—the computer itself. As Kidder states, "The computer seems to act as game board, rule keeper, and, when you foul up, as both assistant and adversary" (*Soul* 87). The computer, like the guardian Campbell describes, holds both "treasures" and "threats" (*Soul* 87). The danger here—in "The Belly of the Whale"—is that the hero, rather than defeating or appeasing the guardian of the threshold, is swallowed up and disappears into the unknown (*Hero* 90). Kidder describes playing Adventure for the first time: "The game is a harrowing of Hell. . . .

I had the feeling I was lost in a forest" (*Soul* 88). Played obsessively by the engineers before actual work on EAGLE begins, Adventure serves as a form of initiation, of preparation for the new quest. Even Kidder must learn to play it if he is to accompany the team and report their fabulous quest to the rest of the world. Later, Adventure will also serve as a method of debugging EAGLE and finally as the supreme test of the quest: EAGLE will have to play Adventure by itself through the night without failing.

If the successful quest to build and bring Eagle to life restores prosperity for the company, it results in psychological growth and spiritual wholeness for the engineers. Their minds are expanded by the computer (*Soul* 96); the computer also gives their life structure, meaning, and fulfillment (97; 273). And this is not merely a matter of job satisfaction. Through the building of a computer, the interface of man and machine, these engineers seek the kind of transcendence called "Apotheosis" (*Hero* 149-171). Speaking of learning assembler language, Alsing says: "'It was so great for me to learn that priestly language. I could talk to God, just like IBM'" (*Soul* 98). West also wanted to build something larger than himself (181). But the essential purpose of narrative romance, and narration generally, is the discovery of identity, whether personal, corporate, or cultural (Polkinghorne, *Narrative Knowing* 105-123). In this narrative romance of engineering, then, the building of a new machine is a quest for identity itself. Kidder states that the computer becomes a part of the engineers who designed and built it (*Soul* 202). As West himself says, "These guys don't realize how dependent they are on that thing to create their identities" (232). And as these engineers transcend their own lives through the romance of building a machine and find their identity in it, they also invest a part of themselves in the machine. Similarly, as the machine helps the engineers achieve a transcendent identity, it too becomes a little more human (273). If Campbell's hero has a thousand faces, for Alsing the computer "presents a face, a person to me—a person in a thousand different ways" (96).

In Chapters 8, 9, and 10—"La Machine," "The Wonderful Micromachines," and, with its echo of a detective story, "The Case of the Missing Nand Gate"—the story of the actual building of the machine is related, again in mythic as well as technical terms, in the phase that Campbell calls "The Road of Trials" (*Hero* 97-109). This stage is so intense that even when Kidder does briefly explore the private lives of the engineers, the narrative never really leaves the underworld of computer hardware or corporate basement. Like a supernatural being, the computer is omnipresent, a "bogeyman" (*Soul* 153). When the Eagle successfully navigates Adventure, what Campbell designates "The Ultimate Boon" (*Hero* 172-193) is achieved. But these heroes of technology must complete "The Crossing of the Return Threshold" *(Hero* 217-229), or as the engineers at Data General say, "get a machine out the door" (*Soul* 69). To do this, Campbell explains, the hero must completely give up his personal attachment to the world, give up his ambitions, his hopes, his limitations, his fears; he must no longer resist the death that will lead to his resurrection and the restoration of his community in a rebirth of wholeness and health. He must surrender to his destiny, become "an anonymity" (*Hero* 236-7).

As the project nears completion, West, his hair cut and his body shrouded in business suit, has changed in appearance; although, as he says, the rumors of his death "have been greatly exaggerated," he is described as wan, thin, tired (*Soul* 267). He has lost confidence in himself. He no longer seems to care. He is preparing, says Kidder, "for a large change" (280). Unknown by many of the newer, younger engineers who were hired at Data General during the project, scorned by some, hated by others, misunderstood by all, West, the hero, reappears from his "cave" (*Soul* 120). For a time he is what Campbell calls "Master of Both Worlds" (*Hero* 229-238). Then, West announces he is going "to that distant country, the upstairs of Westborough" (*Soul* 283) to take a job in marketing.

Having transcended his own ego, West literally as well as figuratively ascends. As Kidder puts it: "West had risen from the small death of leaving the team" (284). Having earned what Campbell calls the "Freedom To Live" (*Hero* 238-245), the heroes of this technological romance are also now finally "unbound from their machine" (*Soul* 248), "free to go" (285). Some do go on to other projects. But many of them quit, "scattering their flesh," says Campbell of heroes at this stage, "like the body of Osiris, for the renovation of the world" (*Hero* 93). So West says at the end of Chapter 16, "Dinosaurs," that although the summer romance is "all blown apart . . . the ethic's still in place," and that "spreading that around may be beneficial" (*Soul* 287). Alsing compares it to the end of a Western: "A classic American Story" (208).

However, although the engineers have completed the quest, saved the company, and brought prosperity to their corporate kingdom, upon "surfacing" they discover their company in disarray; "what they returned to seemed nothing like the hero's welcome they had expected" (285-6).

Marketing even changes the computer's name. The laborer is alienated from his labor. Despite the positive corporate position represented by the narrative throughout the book, *The Soul of a New Machine* ends, "Clearly the machine no longer belonged to its makers" (291). As Frye suggests, narrative romance contains a "genuinely 'proletarian' element" in that it is never satisfied with its own manifestation or the society that results from it; it is always seeking new dreams to live on, new goals to attain, further change in what has become the status quo (*Anatomy* 186).

Apposite to narrative romance, then, *The Soul of a New Machine* also seems to conclude with a proletarian element—a critique of the role of computers in the social-military-industrial complex (240-248)—as well as an account and explanation, and perhaps a rationalization, through the narrative of the resolution of ethical conflicts: the laborer is absorbed—and trapped—by his labor (272-276). We may wonder here whether the "proletarian element" in *The Soul of a New Machine* constitutes a Marxist critique of capitalism, whether Kidder is trying to present the production and marketing of computer technology as a Marxist trope to stand the quest theme ironically on its head, or whether he is merely showing how narrative romance provides these engineers with an overriding, mythic reason for the sacrifices they make as their machine is divested of its human value by those who own the means of production. This is an open question. But the narrative implication of this romance is that in contrast to the purity of motives and values exhibited by the engineers, it is management, and by extension corporate society at large, that are forever in need of spiritual redemption, forever in need of the engineer as hero, thus insuring the continuation of narrative romance itself.

However, Kidder's book is also an accurate journalistic account of the building of a new computer at Data General by a team of engineers led by Tom West. Thus, although we may attribute some of its elements of narrative romance to fortuitousness, serendipity, or just plain coincidence, the question whether Kidder is imposing this narrative structure on events depicted is a moot one. Kidder describes the way these computer engineers perceive and present themselves, the way they self-dramatize.[5] This is not to say that Kidder does not contribute to this narrative romance. He certainly does, throughout—in organization, descriptions, chapter titles, and choice of language itself. But in doing so he follows the lead of the engineers. Indeed, if, as Campbell and Jamieson state, "a genre is a complex of elements—a constellation of substantive, stylistic, and situational characteristics" (*Form* 17), it also is possible to see these generic elements of narrative romance in *The Soul of a New Machine* as *topoi* used both to discover and to inform the argument that building a machine is a romantic journey.

But the fact that this account of the building of the computer so closely parallels the pattern of the quest theme also argues for the ubiquity of narrative romance in our culture and of narration as a basic mode of comprehending technical problems and achievements. For science and technology too are ultimately rooted in what Fisher calls "narrative rationality" (*Human Communication* 48) and are thus infused with the mythological patterns of human experience (85).[6] So powerful and pervasive is the pattern of narrative romance that the engineers as well as Kidder perceive the experience of building a computer in terms of narration and romance. In this regard, we can understand *The Soul of a New Machine* as a piece of ethnographic research rendered as a narrative (as ethnographic research so often is). But it is the pervasiveness of narrative romance in our culture that makes *The Soul of a New Machine*, and narration in general, so rhetorically effective in communicating scientific and technological information to a lay audience. The popular elements of the quest through which Kidder presents his account of the building of a computer appeal to the widest possible audience.

And not only because they are popular. If "form is the creation of an appetite in the mind of the auditor, and the adequate satisfying of that appetite," as Kenneth Burke maintains (*Counter-Statement* 31), the form of narrative romance induces in readers a Burkean identification with the experience of being an engineer and building a computer. It creates the desire in readers and then allows them to participate in the successful completion of what has become a new adventure story. Thus, if the writer's audience is always a fiction, that fiction in turn constructs a role readers are to assume as they respond to the form of the text: that of the questing engineer. Not only does narrative romance appeal to the widest possible audience by virtue of its popularity, it also helps construct that audience through the affective appeal of its form. It does so on several levels.

At its most basic, affective level, the language of the text itself creates expectations in the reader that are continued, modified, fulfilled, denied (Iser, *Act* 111); for Wolfgang Iser, the transaction between reader and text is a process of anticipation and retrospection that ultimately involves a reorganization and expansion of readers' values, feelings, knowledge, and experience ("Reading" 57; *Act* 132). But narration also plays a fundamental role in identity formation itself. Polkinghorne argues that because a person's life is essentially perceived and understood as an ongoing narrative always consisting of "some version of the general cultural stock of stories about how life proceeds," these stories help unify personal experiences and events into a coherent narrative whole that is necessary for emotional satisfaction, stability, and psychological growth (*Narrative Knowing* 107). Thus, at a deep, psychological level, narrative romance appeals to the need of readers as well as engineers to make sense out of their lives through the narrative form of stories. Understood in this way, *The Soul of a New Machine* not only portrays the psychological and spiritual growth of engineers in mythic terms but also constructs its audience by allowing, even inducing, its readers to experience this same process of growth through the affective appeal of the narrative as argument.[7]

The Soul of a New Machine thereby reconciles cultural disparities, bridging the gaps among science, technology, and the humanities. And it does so not only on the level of research but also on that of symbolic action. In *The Soul of a New Machine*, Kidder can be seen to have responded rhetorically to the psychological, social, and cultural need to adapt to the changes wrought by the advent of the computer age, and perhaps he has helped ease us into that age. By fusing technology and myth through narrative romance, Kidder mythifies the engineer while demystifying the technology of the computer, now exciting, beautiful—and human. Kidder transforms the engineer into a popular hero of American culture and renders the computer an expression and embodiment of human creativity, psychological growth, and spiritual wholeness. Imbued with the souls of the engineers who create them, navigate them, conquer them, computers are made a more familiar part of our world. As Leo Marx might say, Kidder has brought another "machine in the garden." If that is the case, however, Kidder has also given us an example of audience adaptation by acculturation and the use of narration in technical communication to adjust cultural disparities.

What makes acculturation and reconciliation possible is that the genre of narrative romance cuts across distinctions among journalism, literature, and scientific or technical communication and embraces all discourse in the culture. Despite the fact that Kidder's book is "journalism" rather than technical writing *per se*, narrative romance, like genre criticism itself, transcends traditional disciplinary boundaries. As we have seen, rhetorical genre criticism can account for the similarities and differences in *types* of discourse as well as for rhetorical responses in different times and places. This is important, for certainly some of the resistance to narration in scientific and technical communication comes from the entrenched belief that narration is too "literary" and the failure to see the possibilities of narration as a general pattern of understanding and communication in science and technology as well as in literature, history, anthropology, and the human sciences. In fact, the genre of narrative romance, and narration in general, offers a possible basis for understanding the cultural and linguistic ground for the relation of science, technology, the social sciences, and the humanities not only at the level of theory and research but also teaching and rhetorical practice. The narrative paradigm is grounded not in epistemology but in the ontological level of social reality (Fisher, *Human Communication* 65).

There are many variations of the pattern of narrative romance, and other types of narration (Stout *Journey*). Some of these are used, consciously or subconsciously, in the news media to communicate scientific and technical information to a general audience.[8] In addition to Kidder's, a number of books written by scientists (Sagan *Cosmos*, Bronowski *The Ascent of Man*) as well as journalists and writers (Mailer *Of a Fire On the Moon*, Wolfe *The Right Stuff*) use narration, even narrative romance, to make scientific and technical theories, concepts, and achievements comprehensible, palatable, and even appealing to a lay audience.[9]

In fact, the recent proliferation of books about science and technology that are addressed to a general public indicates the need for narration in our highly scientific and technical yet democratic society and constitutes an argument for further research on the uses of narration in scientific and technical communication. Narratives like Kidder's obviously respond to a felt need to inform the general public about recent developments in science and technology and to address the cultural gap left by the specialization of disciplines and knowledge in the twentieth century so that average citizens can make informed decisions about issues that affect not only their personal lives but the life of the nation. For despite the proliferation of books about science and technology, scientists and technologists (and anyone in a professional discipline for that matter) able or willing to write for the general public are few, the exception rather than the rule.

Perhaps most importantly, then, the proliferation of narratives in science and technology also speaks to the need to further educate scientists and technologists themselves in the communication of information to lay audiences. This may be especially important in light of the frequent complaints of scientists concerning the accuracy of reporting by nonscientists. Kenneth Houp and Thomas Pearsall long ago determined that lay audiences like drama and thus that narration would be useful (*Reporting* 69). Others, like Annette Bradford and Merrill Whitburn, have developed techniques and strategies for teaching audience analysis and adaptation in technical writing classes, some of which entail narrative techniques ("Analysis"). In fact, *The Soul of a New Machine* uses many of these techniques—such as analogy, metaphor, anecdote, and various kinds of definitions—to "unpack" the computer hardware as well as to "translate" and render palpable the technical information that is contained like soft candy in the center of the narrative romance.

But as we have seen through a genre analysis of *The Soul of a New Machine*, narration can entail not only the use of rhetorical devices or a discourse form but also a knowledge of culture. Polkinghorne emphasizes this point when he states that the meaning of narratives is contained in a culture's history and myths, of which a general knowledge is required to participate in that culture (*Narrative Knowing* 6). In teaching students in science and technology how to communicate to various audiences, then, perhaps we should teach them not only the language of experts and managers but also the language of public discourse, including the patterns of narration that permeate and constitute our culture. This may be especially important given the relatively brief liberal arts education most specialists in science or technology receive. Such education should entail more research and upper level or graduate courses in the discourse of science and technology to examine how specialists in science and technology address different audiences in different genres. It should also include genres besides the purely institutional (such as technical instructions, descriptions, reports, memos, letters, etc.) in traditional undergraduate science and technical writing courses, especially the uses of narrative genres to communicate with lay, managerial, and technical audiences, to resolve intra- and inter-organizational policy disputes and conflicts of value, to mediate misunderstandings between organization and employee, and to adjust cultural disparities.

In this wider view of the social role of the technical communicator, narration—and thus rhetorical criticism—may have an important part in scientific and technical education. But the most important implication of this genre analysis for teaching, it seems to me, may be the Ciceronian ideal of language that this wider view necessitates: put simply, you cannot teach rhetoric without teaching wisdom and virtue—even in science and technology. If style is not only sentence length and structure but the expression of the human personality (Halloran and Whitburn, "Ciceronian Rhetoric" 67-68), narration is not only a mode of discourse but the expression of a culture and an ethos. Thus, cultural and ethical knowledge is necessary to understand and use narration fairly and well, as Kidder does in *The Soul of a New Machine*. For narration and narrative romance, like all powerful and affective forms of rhetoric, can constitute a dangerous and harmful seduction. And as Cicero says in *De Oratore*, putting language in the hands of someone without wisdom and virtue "is like putting weapons in the hands of a madman" (III. 45). This Ciceronian vision of the technical communicator able to write for the general public through narrative romance may help us reconsider the role of scientific and technical communication in a democratic society. It may inform how we teach it. And it may lead us to an even truer and more complete "humanistic rationale" for scientific and technical communication (Miller "Humanistic Rationale"), one that moves beyond questions of epistemology to the ontological unity of form and content, of culture and ethics. It may be an ideal worth striving for. ❦

NOTES

[1]Here I must apologize, however, for the male orientation and language of the mythic pattern of narrative romance that will be evident throughout this essay; it indicates not only the patriarchal bias of Western myth, but also the continuing underrepresentation of women in technical fields, particularly engineering. (For a provocative and controversial critique of male ascendancy in Western mythology, see Graves *The Greek Myths*.) Feminist critics will be interested to see how and to what extent women adopt this mythic pattern of male experience as they continue to enter the ranks of computer engineers in the corporate work force. (For a brief discussion of the role of one woman in this narrative romance, Rosemarie Seale, see note 4.)

[2]Bob Coleman cites the writing of Robert Boyle, articles in the *Philosophical Transactions* of the Royal Society, early American scientific publications including Ben Franklin's, articles in the American Philosophical Society's publication *Transactions*, and of course Darwin's *Origin of*

the Species as earlier examples of scientific narratives ("Science" 1, 45-47). (For a citation of some contemporary examples, see note 9.)

[3]Polkinghorne makes a similar point concerning the purpose of narratives within an organization: "The narrative—also called organizational myths, sagas, and legends—function to help members to interpret and signify the purpose of the organization and the role of its individual members. The group narrative provides information about norms and values, and it fulfills a number of functions within an association—reduction of tension, concealment of power plays, the mediation of contradictions between theory and practice and between group and individual needs, and building bridges between the past and the present" (*Narrative Knowing* 122).

[4]Significantly, Rosemarie Seale, "the mother of the team," also considers herself "a new, liberated woman" (*Soul* 274). Although she admits that "Engineering is a man's world" (39), she states: "We all had something different to prove and we were all trying to prove the same thing" (274). It seems that she too has bought into the mythic pattern of narrative romance.

[5]It is well known that computer engineers and programmers like science fiction and fantasy. That they are deeply affected by the quest theme can be seen not only in the kind and number of computer games (like Adventure) that they invent and play each year, but perhaps also in the metaphoric terms they give to computer keystrokes and functions: search, execute, hit, quit, halt, escape, destroy, command, etc.. (These may also give the average user a sense of control over the machine and thus be understood by management to make computers more "user-friendly" and marketable as well.)

[6]There are two ways of looking at the relationship between science and mythology. For Stephen Toulmin (*Return to Cosmology*), contemporary mythology grows out of the discoveries of postmodern science and tends to distort them; for Gerald Holton (*Thematic Origins of Scientific Thought*), scientific discoveries grow out of mythology—taken in its broader sense as cultural and aesthetic themata—as well as analytic and empirical hypotheses and tend to help justify them in a larger context. Since the study of narration gives ontological priority to social reality (Fisher, *Human Communication* 64-65), Holton's view of the relation between science and myth is obviously more in line with this approach.

[7]For Fisher, narrative rationality demonstrates that values rather than

argumentative forms, of which logical demonstration is but one, are the most persuasive element of discourse (48); thus, for Fisher it is "narrative rationality" itself that ultimately provides "warrants for accepting or adhering to the advice fostered by any form of communication that can be considered rhetorical" or, in Chaim Perelman's terms, that can "elicit or increase the adherence of the members of an audience to theses that are presented for their assent" (*Realm of Rhetoric* 9).

[8]In this regard, one has only to think of *Nova, National Geographic, Discovery, The Brain, Cosmos,* and other science programs to see how narration and even narrative romance figure in the presentation of scientific material. (Narrative romance also is used in the advocacy of space exploration itself. For example, as participant at the Symposium on Space Research and Exploration, University of Pittsburgh at Johnstown, 1-2 October 1986, I observed that a manned space flight to Mars was being presented and argued in the mythic terms of the Conestoga Wagon trains used by American pioneers to cross the wilderness and settle the West. Of course, narrative romance can also be seen in the very names given to satellites and shuttles: Pioneer, Voyager, Enterprise, Challenger.)

[9]A genre analysis of the journey theme in Carl Sagan's *Cosmos* would reveal the underlying theme of mythic exploration. Jacob Bronowski's *The Ascent of Man* is constructed as an evolutionary narrative. Other recent examples of scientific narration or exposition that uses narrative techniques might include Gary Zukav's *The Dancing Wu Li Masters,* Heinz Pagels' *Perfect Symmetry: The Search for the Beginning of Time,* or Stephen Hawking's *A Brief History of Time.*

WORKS CITED

Barton, Ben F. and Marthalee S. Barton. "Narration in Technical Communication." *Journal of Business And Technical Communication* 2 (1988): 36-48.

Black, Edwin. *Rhetorical Criticism: A Study in Method.* New York: Macmillan, 1965.

Bradford, Annette N., and Merrill D. Whitburn. "Analysis of the Same Subject in Diverse Periodicals: One Method for Teaching Audience Adaptation." *Technical Writing Teacher* 9 (1982): 58-63.

Bronowski, Jacob. *The Ascent of Man*. Boston: Little, 1973.

Burke, Kenneth. *Counter-Statement*. Berkeley: U of California P, 1968.

Campbell, Joseph. *The Hero With a Thousand Faces*. Princeton: Princeton UP, 1949.

Campbell, Karlyn Kohrs, and Kathleen Hall Jamieson. "Form and Genre in Rhetorical Criticism: An Introduction." *Form and Genre: Shaping Rhetorical Action*. Eds. Campbell and Jamieson. Falls Church, Virginia: Speech Communication Association, 1978.

Cicero, Marcus Tullius. *De Oratore*. Books I-II. Trans. E. W. Sutton and H. Rackham. 2 vols. Cambridge: Loeb, 1942.

——. *De Oratore*. Book III. Trans. H. Rackham. 2 vols. Cambridge: Loeb, 1942.

Coleman, Bob. "Science Writing: Too Good to Be True?" *New York Times Book Review* 27 September 1987, sec. 7: 1+.

Fisher, Walter R. *Human Communication as Narration: Toward a Philosophy of Reason, Value, and Action*. Columbia: U of South Carolina P, 1987.

Florman, Samuel C. *The Existential Pleasures of Engineering*. New York: St. Martin's, 1976

——. "The Hardy Boys and the Microkids Make a Computer." Rev. of *The Soul of a New Machine* by Tracy Kidder. *New York Times Book Review* 23 Aug. 1981, sec. 7: 1+.

Fraser, Sir James. *The New Golden Bough*. Ed. Theodor H. Gastor. New York: Criterion, 1959. Mentor, 1964.

Frye, Northrop. *Anatomy of Criticism*. Princeton: Princeton UP, 1957.

Graves, Robert. *The Greek Myths*. 2 vols. Middlesex, Eng.: Penguin, 1960.

Halloran, S. Michael. "The Birth of Molecular Biology: An Essay in the Rhetorical Criticism of Scientific Discourse." *Rhetoric Review* 3 (1984): 70-83.

——, and Merrill D. Whitburn. "Ciceronian Rhetoric and the Rise of Science: The Plain Style Reconsidered." *The Rhetorical Tradition and Modern Writing*. Ed. J. J. Murphy. New York: MLA. 58-72.

Hawking, Stephen W. *A Brief History of Time: From the Big Bang to Black Holes*. New York: Bantam, 1988.

Holton, Gerald. *Thematic Origins of Scientific Thought: Kepler to Einstein*. Cambridge: Harvard UP, 1973.

Houp, Kenneth W., and Thomas E. Pearsall. *Reporting Technical Information.* New York: Glenco, 1980.

Iser, Wolfgang. *The Act of Reading: A Theory of Aesthetic Response.* Baltimore: Johns Hopkins UP, 1978.

——. "The Reading Process: A Phenomenological Approach." *Reader-Response Criticism: From Formalism to Post-Structuralism.* Ed. Jane P. Tompkins. Baltimore: Johns Hopkins UP, 1980.

Kidder, Tracy. *The Soul of a New Machine.* 1981. New York: Avon, 1982.

Mailer, Norman. *Of a Fire On the Moon.* Boston: Little, 1969.

Marx, Leo. *The Machine in the Garden: Technology and the Pastoral Ideal in America.* New York: Oxford UP, 1964.

Miller, Carolyn R. "A Humanistic Rationale for Technical Writing." *College English* 40 (1979): 610-17.

Pagels, Heinz R. *Perfect Symmetry: The Search for the Beginning to Time.* New York: Simon, 1985.

Perelman, Chaim. *The Realm of Rhetoric.* Trans. William Kluback. Notre Dame: U of Notre Dame P, 1982.

Polkinghorne, Donald E. *Narrative Knowing and the Human Sciences.* Albany: State U of New York P, 1988.

Sagan, Carl. *Cosmos.* New York: Random, 1980.

Stout, Janis P. *The Journey Narrative in American Literature: Patterns and Departures.* Westport, Connecticut: Greenwood, 1983.

Toulmin, Stephen. *The Return of Cosmology: Postmodern Science and the Theology of Nature.* Berkeley: U of California P, 1982.

Watson, James D. *The Double Helix: A Personal Account of the Discovery of DNA.* New York: Atheneum, 1968. Mentor, 1969.

Weston, Jessie L. *From Ritual to Romance.* Cambridge: Cambridge UP, 1920. Anchor, 1957.

Wolfe, Tom. *The Right Stuff.* New York: Farrar, 1979.

Zukav, Gary. *The Dancing Wu Li Masters: An Overview of the New Physics.* New York: Morrow, 1979.

❦ 19

Putting the IRS on Notice: A Lesson in the Tactics of Intimidation

Aletha Hendrickson

Teachers of writing have varying attendance policies for their writing classes. An excerpt from my class policy handout that I distribute to upper division students on the first day of class advises them that we are embarking on a semester of serious writing effort:

> Attendance: Because your active participation in workshops and class discussions is an essential element in the course, I require and record attendance in all class meetings and conferences. . . .
>
> Because peer critiques (workshops) are a useful and critical part of your learning, students who fail to critique, fail to submit drafts to be critiqued, or fail to turn in a peer critique with an assignment risk a grade drop for the assignment involved.
>
> You are allowed 3 absences without penalty; 4-6 absences will decide a borderline final grade downwards. Students who are absent for 25% or more of classes held automatically fail the course. ("Class Policies" 1)[1]

After reading this policy statement, most students adjust their attitudes and gear themselves for the long haul, but a few whose main interests lie in extra–curricular activities desert my classes to shop for another section of Technical Writing with less stringent requirements. My mild attempt at intimidation seems to work: most students are encouraged to apply themselves to the collaborative writing experience, and casual students remove themselves to greener pastures.

Intimidation in an academic setting not only improves student attendance but also exposes them to an effective tool widely used in nonacademic settings, such as business collection letters, designed to pry open debtors' checkbooks. Businesses typically employ a series of collection letters whose tone rises on the scale of intimidation, as illustrated by excerpts from a series of three collection letters in *The Business Writer's Handbook*. The first level tries to collect while retaining customer goodwill and soliciting additional business:

> . . . Perhaps in the rush of business you've overlooked paying your account of $742, which is now 60 days overdue.
> . . . When you send in your check for your outstanding account, why not send us your next order and take advantage of these special prices? (100)

The second level also helps to convince the debtor to pay in a reasonable, but firmer tone:

> . . . we are sure that you will want to settle this balance now. If your balance is more than you can pay right now, we will be happy to work out satisfactory payment arrangements. (101)

And the third level tries to force payment in an insistent, urgent tone:

> Because you have not responded to any of our letters, we will be forced to turn your account over to our attorney for collection if we do not receive payment immediately. (102)

In this final effort, most authorities recommend turning the heat up by threatening to damage the debtor's credit rating:

> Your failure to pay the $378.40 now seven months past due on your account leaves us no choice but to report you to the Omaha Credit Bureau. (Lesikar 279)

In an effort to force debtors to pay past-due bills, some businesses have begun to incorporate a collection agency's name in "precollection efforts" ("Collection" 127), apparently to evoke authority that a company letterhead alone could not suggest. Some businesses carry the litigation threat even further; hence, I suggest that there is actually a fourth level of intimidating collection letter. Following a last ditch and unsuccessful effort on company letterhead, a message on an attorney's letterhead is sent on behalf of a company prior to litigation (or indeed, when court costs pre-clude actual litigation). An attorney's letterhead suggests authority that company letterhead does not. The reader may not take a business's threat to sue seriously, but an attorney's letterhead connotes the unpleasantness of litigation including courtrooms, defense costs, judgment for the debt plus court costs—which a recipient is loath to ignore:

> . . . [T]his office has been retained by [XYZ Shoe Company] to collect the outstanding balance of [$1,234.00] on your account from [date first billed].
>
> . . . [W]e will expect the balance in full within ten days from receipt of this notice. If not paid within the given time, suit will be filed for the amount due, plus court costs and attorney's fees.[2]

Figure 1 summarizes levels of collection letters with progressively more unfriendly purposes, manipulative methods, and threatening over-tones:

Figure 1. *Purposes, Methods, and Tone of Collection Letters*

COLLECTION LETTERS	PURPOSE	METHOD	TONE
Level 1	Convince debtor to pay while retaining customer and soliciting new business	Reminder (on company letterhead) of amount due and good credit record	Factual, courteous, friendly
Level 2	Convince debtor to pay	(On company letter-head) collect, invite customer explanation, appeal to fairness and good credit record, offer payment plan	Helpful, polite, firmer
Level 3	Force debtor to pay	(On company letter-head) hint of legal action	Polite, urgent, firm
Level 4	Force debtor to pay	(On attorney's letter-head)	Demanding, authoritative, threatening, intimidating

Collectors invariably manipulate two components of intimidation: the power or authority that the intimidator holds over the debtor as well as the debtor's perceptions and expectations (related to schemata, discussed below) that influence reader response. We will see that the authority and schemata inherent in class policies and collection letters are two keys that unlock a larger, more complex puzzle: the often confusing, yet generally effective Internal Revenue Service collection letter.

The Role of Authority in Intimidation

The illustrations from my class policies and from the business collection letters indicate increasing levels of intimidation. The personal pronouns that I use in my class policies and that the businesses and attorneys employ in collection letters suggest an authoritarian relationship between rhetor and reader. As a teacher on the first day of class, I must establish credibility as an authority figure, as a professional in my field. Thus, as in Level 2 collection letters, I must straddle a line between intimidating authority and understanding problem solver.

The "we/you" of the collection letters indicates a more complex authoritative relationship—one which in Richard Sennett's view involves "a bond between people who are unequal . . ." (*Authority* 10) and is "based on images of strength and weakness" (4). To Sennett, "[t]he word 'bond' has a double meaning. It is a connection, but it is also, as in 'bondage,' a constraint" (4). Because of training and experience, a teacher and student are unequal. Also unequal in a sense are a merchant and a customer—without the customer, the merchant cannot exist, so the customer is superior because of buying *power*. Once a transaction is underway, however, the relationship changes: the merchant as a supplier of goods or services enters into a mutually beneficial relationship with a consumer who would receive and pay for the goods and services. When the bill's due date passes, the relationship again becomes unequal. The customer tries to assume a superior position, receiving goods or services and giving nothing in return. Consequently, the supplier—now a creditor backed by the force of law—drives the consumer into a defensive debtor's position. In Sennett's terms, nonpaying consumers place themselves in bondage to the creditor, thus destroying the original connective bond.

Unlike the supplier/consumer or creditor/debtor's shifting relationship, the we/you of an IRS collection letter signifies an unchanging relationship between tax collector and taxpayer: Sennett's double bond coexists from the start. The connective bond begins when an individual earns enough taxable income to owe tax; the IRS is empowered by the U.S. Congress to collect. The taxpayer is thus "in bondage" to the IRS when enough taxable income is earned.

The Role of Schemata in Intimidation

Written class policies promote class attendance partly because of the *unwritten* assumption by students that their all–important grades are at stake. Legal letterhead facilitates collections because debtors know that litigation can be unpleasant, not to mention expensive. These tacit assumptions by the reader, often exploited by rhetors, demonstrate "'structures of expectation'" (Tannen 138; Brown and Yule 248) which "characterize the influence of schemata" on discourse production and interpretation (Brown and Yule 148, 250). Gillian Brown and George Yule observe that when people have schemata they are predisposed to interpret experience "in a fixed way" (247). That is why a *legal* schema with all its unpleasant connotations can be activated, as we have seen, by an attorney's letterhead. A more fearsome, complex schema is activated by IRS discourse, but it is a schema difficult to title because IRS notices invariably trigger all the costly hassles associated with computing and paying taxes, such as unfair and unclear tax laws; expensive and burdensome accounting procedures; dependence on costly tax and accounting specialists; drawn out federal tax court procedures; insistent demands for tax payment as well as usurious penalties and interest; and, finally, possible incarceration.

Schemata, then, help explain the intimidating tactics employed in Internal Revenue Service letters and notices as well as the intimidation felt by recipients of IRS communications. The potent combination of schemata plus authority accounts for the anxiety most people feel toward the IRS. Consequently, no example of writing in the workplace rattles the recipient more than an actual IRS Notice of Deficiency which warns a taxpayer that it intends to seize property because taxes, penalties, and/or interest have not been paid. Individuals as well as businesses receive these notices, typified by an 1985 IRS Notice of Deficiency sent to a Maryland excavating contractor (see Figure 2).[3]

The Effect, Intent, and Implications of the IRS Notice of Deficiency

We teach students that the writer's rhetorical situation influences a range of appropriate appeals to the audience. Although common in written dis-

Fig 2. *A 1985 IRS Notice of Deficiency*

	008823	828	5201	PXT	TWV

Department of the Treasury
Internal Revenue Service   W 429 891 048   If you have any questions, refer
                                                         to this information:
                                                         Date of This Notice: 11–24–85 658 8301
Past Due   Taxpayer Identifying Number: 52–456789 WX
Final Notice (Notice of Intention to Levy)   Form   Tax Year Ended   Document Locator Number

Read Carefully   940   12–31–84   45398–590–23874–3

XYZ EXCAVATING COMPANY   Call: 555–3410 LOCAL BALTIMORE
P. O. BOX 1000   or   555–5600 DIST. OF COL.
BALTIMORE, MD 21220   1–800–555–1040 OTHER MD.
                                                         Write: Chief, Taxpayer Assistance Section
                                                                 Internal Revenue Service Center
                                                                 PHILADELPHIA, PA 19255

If you write, be sure to attach the bottom part of this notice.

ALTHOUGH NOTICE AND DEMAND HAVE BEEN MADE FOR PAYMENT OF YOUR FEDERAL TAX LIABILITY SHOWN BELOW, WE HAVE NO RECORD OF RECEIVING THE AMOUNT DUE. THIS IS YOUR FINAL NOTICE BEFORE WE PROCEED WITH ENFORCEMENT ACTION. THE PURPOSE OF THIS NOTICE IS TO INFORM YOU OF OUR INTENTION TO LEVY UPON YOUR PROPERTY OR RIGHTS TO PROPERTY IN ACCORDANCE WITH SECTION 6331 OF THE INTERNAL REVENUE CODE.

TO PREVENT SUCH ACTION, SEND US, WITHIN 10 DAYS FROM THE DATE OF THIS NOTICE, YOUR CHECK OR MONEY ORDER FOR THE TOTAL AMOUNT DUE, PAYABLE TO THE INTERNAL REVENUE SERVICE. SHOW YOUR TAXPAYER IDENTIFYING NUMBER (SOCIAL SECURITY OR EMPLOYER IDENTIFICATION NUMBER) ON IT AND ENCLOSE THE BOTTOM PART OF THIS NOTICE TO ASSURE PROMPT AND ACCURATE CREDIT. AN ENVELOPE IS ENCLOSED FOR YOUR CONVENIENCE.

IF YOU HAVE RECENTLY PAID THE AMOUNT DUE BUT YOUR PAYMENT HAS NOT BEEN CREDITED TO YOUR ACCOUNT, OR IF YOU CANNOT PAY THIS AMOUNT IN FULL, CONTACT THE OFFICE SHOWN ABOVE WITHIN 10 DAYS FROM THE DATE OF THIS NOTICE. THE TELEPHONE NUMBER IS SHOWN ABOVE.

IF WE DO NOT RECEIVE YOUR PAYMENT OR IF YOU DO NOT CONTACT OUR OFFICE, ENFORCEMENT ACTION MAY BE TAKEN AT ANY TIME AFTER 10 DAYS FROM THE DATE OF THIS NOTICE WITHOUT ANY FUR-THER NOTICE TO YOU. A NOTICE OF FEDERAL TAX LIEN MAY BE FILED WHICH CONSTITUTES PUBLIC NOTICE TO YOUR CREDITORS THAT A TAX LIEN EXISTS AGAINST YOUR PROPERTY. SALARY OR WAGES DUE YOU MAY BE LEVIED UPON, AS PROVIDED BY SECTION 6331 OF THE INTERNAL REVENUE CODE, BY SERVING A NOTICE OF LEVY ON YOUR EMPLOYER. BANK ACCOUNTS, RECEIVABLES, COMMISSIONS, OR OTHER KINDS OF INCOME YOU HAVE ARE ALSO SUBJECT TO LEVY. PROPERTY OR RIGHTS TO PROPERTY, SUCH AS AUTOMOBILES, MAY ALSO BE SEIZED AND SOLD TO SATISFY YOUR TAX LIABILITY.

TAX FORM NUMBER   940
TAX PERIOD ENDED   12–31–84

BALANCE OF PRIOR ASSESSMENTS $684.43
LATE PAYMENT PENALTY $0.00
INTEREST   Reply within 10 days $58.58
                                  to avoid enforcement action
TOTAL AMOUNT DUE   and additional penalties. $743.01

ENCLOSURES:
ENVELOPE

course, intimidation as an appeal is more complex than the classic business–writing textbook examples of collection letters would indicate. In examining the IRS version of intimidating discourse, we will see three types of intimidation operating in a situation in which a bureaucracy faces the unpleasant task of collecting taxes that people would rather not pay. Some intimidation is *inevitable* and appropriate, given the mandate and power of a federal collection agency. Other intimidation seems to be *intentional*, aimed at throwing reluctant taxpayers off balance. Both inevitable and intentional intimidation are appropriately and effectively exploited by the IRS, enabling them to carry out their enforcement mandate. Inappropriate, however, is the *abusive* intimidation born perhaps of incompetence, if not downright arrogance, which was doomed to backfire. An outraged public has long demanded basic rights often ignored by a federal agency more intent on filling collection quotas than on enforcing tax and collection laws equitably.

Like teachers who must at first mildly intimidate a student audience, and like creditors who must compel debtors to pay their past-due bills, IRS agents must intimidate delinquent taxpayers. The IRS mandate is, after all, to exact taxes—from a resistant, often hostile public. The IRS's need to communicate clearly with its audience to facilitate tax collection raises five questions regarding the IRS Notice of Deficiency. First, why does the Notice send a mixed, if not downright confusing message to its readers; is the confusion inevitable or intentional? Second, even though the apparent purpose of the Notice is to get the business owner, Mr. Smith, to forward his tax, what are other purposes of the Notice? Third, what rhetorical situation spawns this ambiguous Notice of Deficiency? Fourth, why do business people avoid communication with the IRS? Finally, what lessons can writing teachers learn from the wanted and unwanted response the IRS Notice evokes from the small-business community? The answers to these questions will demonstrate the role of authority and schemata in IRS intimidation. We will also see the unexpected consequences of tactics of inevitable, intentional, and abusive intimidation. Additionally, we will learn that government writing is riddled with problems. IRS rhetors contend with the diffusion of responsibility, the multiplicity of constraints that arise from a peculiar and complex rhetorical situation—with profound implications for both rhetor and reader.

1. A Mixed Message from the IRS

Because of the IRS's considerable clout and reputation for ruthlessness, most readers are alerted to possible trouble as soon as the Notice arrives in an official IRS envelope (which calls up an IRS schema): if it doesn't contain a tax refund check, it usually means *big* trouble. When Mr. Smith received his IRS Notice (Figure 2), he was shocked and upset that the IRS claimed he owed $743.01, because his CPA had recently assured him that all tax obligations were met. We know that writers inevitably raise expectations in their readers throughout their discourse. Mr. Smith's expectations, however, were unfulfilled because he could find no *basis* in the Notice for the IRS's claim: was he accused of owing payroll tax, excise tax, unemployment tax, or personal income tax? The Notice indicated that the IRS would slap a lien on his property if he did not reply within 10 days; yet he received the Notice *after* the 10 days had expired. Thoroughly confused, he called—not the IRS as directed in the Notice—but his CPA, as he usually did when faced with an IRS communication. We will return to Mr. Smith and his IRS troubles after we examine why he and many other business owners fail to comprehend or to obey the directives of IRS notices.

Sources of Confusion

The overall message from the IRS is painfully clear: it *intends* to collect taxes. Analyzing the use of the noun "notice" (used 15 times in the Notice) demonstrates how the IRS intentionally uses intimidating language to extort obedience:[4]

> IF WE DO NOT RECEIVE YOUR PAYMENT OR IF YOU DO NOT CONTACT OUR OFFICE, ENFORCEMENT ACTION MAY BE TAKEN AT ANY TIME AFTER 10 DAYS FROM THE DATE OF THIS NOTICE WITHOUT ANY FURTHER NOTICE TO YOU. A NOTICE OF FEDERAL TAX LIEN MAY BE FILED WHICH CONSTITUTES PUBLIC NOTICE TO YOUR CREDITORS THAT A TAX LIEN EXISTS AGAINST YOUR PROPERTY.

"THIS NOTICE" reminds the reader he or she had better take notice. No "FURTHER NOTICE" convinces the reader that the IRS's patience is exhausted. The next appearance of "NOTICE" *denotes* federal court action and *connotes* personal loss of property. But "PUBLIC NOTICE" is the cruelest cut: small businesses, often undercapitalized, depend on creditors for services and goods. Notice of a federal tax lien alerts creditors that the business cannot meet ordinary costs of doing business. Some owners panic and pay, rather than face IRS hassle, loss of credit, and public humiliation.

Since IRS obviously means to carry out its mandate as tax collector through blatant intimidation, why have I claimed that the IRS Notice sends a mixed message and confounds reader expectation? Several sources of confusion befuddle the reader. To start with, although the amount of tax due plus interest is given at the bottom of the Notice, nowhere is the taxpayer advised exactly what kind of tax is due or when it was first due. Because the IRS levies diverse kinds of taxes, confusion abounds because the taxpayer is given no explicit context for the IRS claim. Certainly, "Taxpayer Form 940" at the top of the Notice may be an explicit cue to an unemployment tax return—to the IRS and to tax practitioners—but "940" might not be so informative to the business person who probably does not prepare his or her own tax returns. Hence, the usual reader reaction to the Notice is "Why do I owe this?"

A related source of confusion is that the IRS tells the reader at the top of the Notice, "If you have any questions, refer to this information": yet what follows are intimidating codes that make sense only to the IRS. The cumulative effect of these unknowns might be, "we are the IRS and we have your number." IRS's writer–based prose—apparently derived from its own schema—confuses its audience and results in audience consternation rather than audience compliance.

Another puzzlement is that the IRS does not directly accuse the reader of failing to pay the taxes: rather, the IRS states, "we have no record of receiving the amount due." But the reader may have paid the tax. The IRS assertion that it has no such record somehow implies that the taxpayer is at fault; it is up to the taxpayer to determine why IRS can find "no record." And, of course, the reader *cannot* find out why the IRS has no record; being asked to do the impossible further frustrates the taxpayer.

IRS's language and formatting—including the densely packed text, cluttered format, and telegram–like typography—tend to intimidate and to perplex the reader. The IRS's efforts to collect taxes seem geared to collection quotas rather than to audience accommodation. For example, to discover why he or she owes the tax, the reader needs a ruler to line up "Tax Form Number" (left) with "940" (right), and must also understand what "940" means (see Figure 3). Such apparent inattention to document design may be mere carelessness. Unfortunately, this format, which hinders comprehension of the true basis of the IRS's claim, has an impact on hundreds of thousands of taxpayers, thus thwarting the IRS's collection mandate.

Fig. 3. *Excerpt from the Notice of Deficiency*

TAX FORM NUMBER		940
TAX PERIOD ENDED		12–31–84
BALANCE OF PRIOR ASSESSMENTS		$684.43
LATE PAYMENT PENALTY		$0.00
INTEREST	Reply within 10 days	$58.58
	to avoid enforcement action	
TOTAL AMOUNT DUE	and additional penalties.	$743.01
ENCLOSURES:		
ENVELOPE		

Still another source of reader confusion involves an inconsistent message. The IRS invites the taxpayer to send the payment, to call, or to write. Yet even though enforcement action is imminent, the IRS fails to furnish the name of someone to contact. Instead, phone numbers in three different jurisdictions are given: for Baltimore, for the District of Columbia, and for "OTHER MD." If the reader chooses to write, he or she is directed to still another location, Philadelphia. And even though delivering the payment in person would be the quickest way to pay, the IRS furnishes no street address at which to deliver the money.

Many readers are also thrown off balance by the IRS's "helpful" gestures that send a mixed message. The last line of the Notice (omitted in Figure 2) contains this statement in small print: "To make sure IRS employees give courteous responses and correct information to taxpayers, a second employee sometimes listens in on telephone calls." It is small comfort to many taxpayers that IRS must monitor for courtesy and correctness, and some nervous taxpayers view being overheard by a second, unidentified IRS agent as threatening—two against one, as it were.

Another gesture which seems incongruous in a threatening Notice is the lack of a "LATE PAYMENT PENALTY." If the tax was to be paid for the tax year ended 12–31–84, the payment is clearly past due by the Notice's date (12–27–85). Since interest is charged, the reader would expect a late payment penalty as well.

Added to these confusions are options and hedges that undercut the IRS's threatening stance. Notice that Mr. Smith can prevent enforcement action by two responses: he can pay, or he can call or write. Considering IRS's threats, why are options other than making immediate payment offered? And why, in the most threatening fourth paragraph, are so many hedges employed alongside strong verbs and nouns: property *"may be"* next to *"seized and sold"*; "Enforcement action *may be taken . . ."*; and "A notice of federal tax lien *may be filed. . ."* ?

2. Another Purpose of the Notice

Considering the unspecified original due date and basis for the claim, the mixed messages, the options, and the hedges even in the strong enforcement paragraph, the purpose of the Notice cannot be solely to warn of imminent levy or to demand payment. I am arguing, therefore, that the primary purpose of this Notice of Deficiency is to prompt the reader to contact IRS, preferably by telephone. Why does the IRS not demand outright payment? Since previous Notices and demands have been issued, why should IRS extend further consideration? The answers to these questions lie in another point—that the IRS writes within a complex rhetorical situation.[5]

3. The Rhetorical Situation of the IRS Notice

The Exigence of the Notice

For the IRS to institute a lien upon Mr. Smith's property intimates nonpayment of taxes. But nonpayment is not necessarily the exigence that called this discourse into being. Instead, the exigence is that the IRS finds "no record of receiving the amount due." The reason may well be taxpayer nonpayment, but it could also be a payment incorrectly addressed or coded by the taxpayer, a payment not delivered by the Postal Service, or a payment incorrectly credited on IRS computers. The IRS must, therefore, offer options to payment and must qualify its threats. Thus, the IRS's slippery but truthful "we have no record" covers possible taxpayer or IRS error. The invitation to call is a plea for assistance in determining why the payment has not been "received." Since the taxpayer is presumed guilty, the IRS can demand *proof* of payment to clear its records—at the business owner's expense, naturally.

The Audience of the Notice

Another component of the rhetorical situation involves the IRS's public audience, including all who earn enough taxable income to owe taxes. Like businesses that try to save effort and money, the IRS employs impersonal boilerplate, sets of fixed text composed to address any taxpayer's situation. Taxpayers, however, tend to take IRS Notices *very* personally. Inevitably, poorly written and formatted IRS boilerplate correspondence fails a diverse audience and contributes to public attitudes that run the full range from utterly compliant to belligerently hostile—so hostile, in fact, that the IRS recently issued index cards to its agents, classifying aggressive taxpayers into four categories: anxious, defensive, angry, and violent ("Murder" 1). Small business owners in particular resent the IRS's onerous record-keeping requirements, which require a higher percentage of their income than larger businesses have to absorb. The IRS's presumption that the taxpayer is guilty forces honest business owners to maintain voluminous records just to prove innocence. As a result, IRS Notices address an already defensive audience. So to protect itself, the IRS incorporates options and hedges that weaken its intimidating stance but that also cover the possibilities of taxpayer innocence, not to mention IRS culpability.

The Constraints of the Rhetor

The last components of the IRS's rhetorical situation, and those that most affect its discourse, involve two bureaucratic and funding constraints. The first constraint involves Congress, which, in its struggle to levy taxes, passes laws that defy conversion into enforceable IRS regulations. Consequently, IRS is even today trying to write regulations to interpret laws passed *prior* to the 2,000–page 1986 Tax Reform Act—which was followed by the Revenue Act of 1987, which was in turn followed by the Technical Corrections Act of 1988—to correct the defects in the 1986 Tax Reform Act (Willens 46). The difficulties of interpreting hastily passed, ambiguous Congressional laws forces IRS to disavow its own telephone advice, to disavow written advice contained in its own tax publications, and to disavow applications of tax court rulings to any case other than the case in question.[6] Small business owners become dependent on the tax acumen of specialist CPAs and tax attorneys when they realize that IRS advice and tax court "precedents" cannot always be applied to their situations.

The second IRS constraint is bureaucracy complicated by lack of funding. Many talented CPAs and tax attorneys start their careers with the IRS, stay a few years, and leave for more lucrative careers—touting, of course, their intimate knowledge of IRS procedures and contacts. When contending with IRS on behalf of a taxpayer, these IRS–trained tax specialists are unconstrained by the layers of bureaucratic administration and procedure that so hamper the IRS. The IRS's notorious error rate, recently reported by the General Accounting Office as 50 percent in written

Fig. 4. *Software Advertisement*

Do You Trust the IRS?
-- Verify their notices / Catch their mistakes --
IRS-*InterestCalc* ®

- *Computer software developed and supported by a practicing tax attorney/CPA*
- *Calculates interest from 2/1/76, including 120% tax motivated rate, refunds, allocable partial payments*
- *Penalties and interest including Negligence, Fraud, Failure to File and Pay, Underpayment of Estimated Tax, and Substantial Understatements of Tax*
- *You update the interest rates yourself, quickly and easily*
- *Absolute, Unconditional 30 day Money Back Guarantee*

"Very easy to use, saves me a great deal of time . . ."
--M. Tony Bianchini, Santa Rosa, California.

Winning Strategies, Inc.
142 North-South Drive
Pittsburgh, PA 15237
(412) 931-1542

ORDER TODAY! $79.95

Yes, I don't trust the IRS! Rush me IRS-*InterestCalc*.
☐ Enclosed is $79.95, $2 postage, 6% sales tax if PA resident
☐ Bill me 30 days later.
NAME ____
COMPANY ____
ADDRESS ____
CITY ____ STATE ____ ZIP ____
IBM PC/XT/AT, 2.0 DOS, 384K RAM

responses (GAO 3), 21 percent in quickly answered telephone responses, and 44 percent in researched telephone responses to taxpayer inquiries (GAO 18), stems from the complex, ever–changing laws, constant professional turnover, poorly trained seasonal employees, and the demoralized clerical staff that plague the IRS. In fact, an ad geared to CPAs (see Figure 4) exploits the IRS's clerical errors, offering software designed to catch IRS mistakes on notices. "Do *you* trust the IRS?" it asks ("Winning" 51). IRS's error–prone environment spawns costly, erroneous Deficiency Notices.

In the face of bureaucratic problems, then, IRS discourse must not only intimidate the guilty into compliance but also compel the innocent taxpayer to furnish information so that the IRS can unsnarl its inadequate records—hence the IRS must incorporate options and hedges into its intimidating stance.

4. Avoiding Communication with the IRS

Because the taxpayer must prove innocence at his or her own expense, small-business owners, who can seldom afford in–house tax experts, dread the expense of communicating with the IRS. Consider the cost involved if a taxpayer is randomly selected by the IRS for the grand-daddy of all tax audits, the Taxpayer Compliance Measurement Program (TCMP), in which "[e]very single claim and deduction must be document-ed in person at the IRS, with complete detail," and in which the taxpayer must also "prove a negative: that no income was hidden" ("Ultimate" 4). TCMP is not administered to collect back taxes but to test the compliance system—unfortunately, at the expense of randomly selected taxpayers.

The IRS can also financially damage a small business by unjust levies; it recently relieved a small contractor's bank account of over $3,000. His CPA claims that "the levy was erroneously assessed due to an IRS clerical error; but it will take months for IRS to return the money."[7] Even if the IRS pays interest, can that compensate the contractor for being unable to access his funds for months, for his accountant's fees, or for his damaged reputation in the business community?

A different example of IRS-generated expense involved Nutcracker Electronics of Houston. The IRS informed the company that it was due a withholding tax refund of $1,700. A month later, the IRS stated without explanation that the refund was reduced to $200, and two months later, the IRS claimed the firm actually *owed* $270. The company's owner paid, saying, "Fear of being closed down prompted me to send the money without question" (Holzinger 39). No wonder a District of Columbia pho-tographer's reaction to IRS Notices is, "With IRS, first you pay, then you ask questions."[8]

To return to Mr. Smith and his IRS difficulties, you will recall that he did not obey the Notice's directives: he did not call or write the IRS; he called his CPA. Why would he incur this expense? Because he had previ-ously experienced the futility, frustration, and considerable cost of con-tending with the IRS's computers himself. Even though Mr. Smith and his CPA offered proof such as canceled checks that no further tax was owed, the unstoppable computers continued to crank out increasingly threaten-ing Notices, piling up interest upon interest. Worn down by unrelenting and unreasonable IRS demands, this contractor was tempted to go out of business. Other innocent business owners, who cannot afford the hefty hourly fees of tax specialists, succumb to IRS intimidation: they either pay or they go under. The CPA who handled Mr. Smith's notices wrote 17 letters and made innumerable calls before the matter was settled. According to the CPA involved, once the Notices ceased, Mr. Smith started receiving IRS *refund* checks which totaled over $700. It seems Mr. Smith had actually overpaid his taxes—a small consolation since the accounting fees exceeded his "refund." And, as another taxpayer who had been found innocent in a routine IRS inquiry observed, there was "[n]o 'Sorry about the inconvenience.' No 'Sorry about the time you had to waste or the chunk of money you had to pay. . . '" (Horowitz 37).

No wonder tax practitioners employ creative strategies to avoid unnecessary communication with the IRS. Some employ this strategy even when IRS mistakes seem to work in their favor. An excavating contractor received IRS refund checks (with no letter of explanation) totaling several thousands dollars to which he was *not* entitled. Rather than returning the checks, his CPA advised him to deposit them in a special account and to wait until the IRS realized the error and requested the funds.

5. Response Generated by the IRS Notice

Such evasive strategies triggered by IRS correspondence prove that the IRS's writing works: its intimidation gets results, ranging from loosening the purse strings of recalcitrant tax dodgers to scaring innocent citizens into overpaying taxes, from closing businesses to keeping tax specialists busy. As writer, the IRS assumes an authoritarian role—which assigns the reader to a defensive role; thus through inevitable, intentional, and abusive intimidation, the IRS is able to maintain an enviable collection record compared to that of private industry: it has collected 13 percent of business accounts and 43 percent of individual accounts that were deemed "uncollectible" ("IRS" 48). But the IRS's emphasis on pathetic and ethical appeals has also evoked *unwanted* response. The IRS's sometimes arrogant abuse of power has spurred unwanted reader response—the hotly contested (by the IRS) Taxpayer's Bill of Rights passed on Oct. 22, 1988.[9] Some provisions contained in the Bill address the abuses of the Notice. Among other guarantees, the taxpayer now has the right: to have 30 (instead of the previous 10) days' notice before the IRS can seize property, to know the *basis* for the IRS's claim, and to have the exact amount due spelled out in plain language. Most important, the bill seeks to shift "the burden of proof for the [IRS] to prove that their claim was substantially justified . . . " (5), thus mollifying the presumption of guilt that previously placed the costly responsibility on the taxpayer to prove innocence. The presumption of guilt, long disputed by taxpayers, contradicts the presumption of innocence cherished and usually protected by the American legal system. The IRS has been served with a *taxpayer's* "Notice of Deficiency," and writing teachers have an object lesson about intimidation drawn from a bureaucratic discourse community that pressed its text too far.

How do generally compliant citizens revolt without anarchy? Sennett outlines strategies that periodically disrupt authority without chaos, "to negotiate with [authority] and to see more clearly what . . . rulers can and cannot—should and should not—do" (168). The first of these strategies forces authority to make "explicit statements of who decided, why, when, and to what end" (181). In the Notice of Deficiency, the IRS "decided," and the "end" is the lawful collection of taxes, but I have demonstrated that the IRS fails to state explicitly the "why" (why is the tax owed?) and the "when" (when was it originally assessed?) of Mr. Smith's tax liability. The IRS failed to satisfy reader expectation. As a result, the Taxpayer's Bill of Rights will force IRS rhetors to learn something about audience awareness and accommodation. Moreover, the IRS's "almost unlimited power to harass delinquent [and not so delinquent] taxpayers" (McKenzie 50) will be neutralized somewhat. The IRS has already agreed to reimburse taxpayers for "bank charges resulting from erroneous levies placed on their bank accounts" ("New" 16).[10] The IRS is also under pressure to prohibit "collection quotas on agents" ("Memo" 46). And the IRS has agreed to lessen the intimidating tone of one of its Notices "so that it will get the message across, but come across as less threatening" ("Memo" 46).

Obviously, the IRS must assert its authority because of the Congressional mandate to enforce collection of unpopular taxes, because of pressure to close an enormous tax gap by 1992 ("Task" 66), because of its bureaucratic and funding constraints, and because of its general and often hostile audience. Nevertheless, the Taxpayer's Bill of Rights is meant to curb the kind of authoritarian abuse implicated in the sign on an IRS office door in Los Angeles: "Seizure Fever—Catch It" ("Congress" 3). The IRS obviously fought the bill because it undercuts its intimidating stance and thus could seriously weaken future tax collection efforts. According to the IRS Commissioner, revenue losses could be "significant—probably hundreds of millions of dollars" (Holzinger 39).

Early reaction to and consequences of the bill are already evident in the IRS's extraordinary attempt at taxpayer accommodation—in its "Application for Taxpayer Assistance Order to Relieve Hardship" form, issued in

1989 a few months after the bill was passed. To "stop the IRS from causing 'significant hardship' to the taxpayer in cases where it is administering the law improperly" ("IRS Emergencies" 1), the IRS was forced to offer an "emergency 911 form" to forestall unfair, imminent seizure. The number 911 is no accident; it calls up an *emergency/rescue* schema involving the emergency 911 telephone number that summons the police, rescue personnel, and firefighters in many communities. (Of course, beleaguered taxpayers might claim that hailing the IRS in a tax lien emergency is analogous to a hen calling the fox for help.)

Pedagogical Implications of Intimidation

We teachers of writing can use the IRS version of the rhetoric of intimidation as an example of the benefits (as in effective collections), the misuse (as in the IRS's aggressive tactics that backfired), and the consequences (as in the 911 form) of intimidating discourse. Despite inevitable grousing from citizens over paying taxes and IRS collection efforts, the community as a whole benefits when IRS seizes upon delinquents. My analysis of IRS discourse suggests that we must teach our students to analyze a rhetorical situation carefully, to tailor an appropriate message that, in Scott Consigny's terms, meets "the condition of *integrity* and the condition of *receptivity*," a message that is simultaneously faithful to the rhetor *and* truly responsive to realities of the situation (Consigny 180). Failure to do so can complicate an already complex rhetorical situation and can infuriate readers to revolt, as the IRS has discovered. We should also teach that intimidation can be a useful, powerful weapon in the arsenals of certain writings of authority—but a sensitive weapon that should be used with caution: it has a tendency to fire at both ends.[11] ❦

ACKNOWLEDGMENTS

I am indebted to CPAs, attorneys, and their clients for their comments and access to their IRS Notices of Deficiency. I am particularly grateful to Professors Linda Coleman, Jeanne Fahnestock, and Michael Marcuse for their suggestions.

NOTES

[1]Adapted from Keith A. Grant–Davie, "Course Policies and Procedures," Fall 1986.

[2]Excerpts are from a Maryland attorney's collection letter on letterhead dated July 11, 1988. The company's name and the amount owed have been altered.

[3]The text of the Notice is as received by "Mr. Smith" except that his name and address have been deleted and IRS reference numbers have been altered.

[4]"The intimidator could see the extorted obedience rendered irrevocably on the spot." John Stuart Mill, *Representative Government* (1865), cited in *The Compact Edition of the Oxford English Dictionary*, 1470.

[5]I found Lloyd F. Bitzer's discussion of exigence, audience, and constraints in "The Rhetorical Situation" invaluable in determining the rhetorical situation of the IRS and the reader (macro–analysis). The micro–analysis and findings were augmented by a modified form of analysis used in "Text Semantic Analysis of Reading Comprehension Texts," by Charles J. Fillmore and Paul Kay.

[6]A tax court opinion (*Sundermeier*, TC Memo 1987–50), reported in *The Practical Accountant*, May 1987, p. 14, asserts that "IRS is not bound by its own phone advice . . . . The IRS is bound by statutes, regulations, and case law—but not by telephone advice from its agents or information in its publications."

[7]Personal interview with a Washington-area CPA. July 14, 1988.

[8]Telephone interview with a Washington commercial photographer. July 14, 1988.

[9]The "Taxpayer's Bill of Rights" is part of the *Technical and Miscellaneous Revenue Act of 1988*. For a detailed explanation of the Bill, see *Explanation of Technical and Miscellaneous Revenue Act of 1988 including Taxpayer Bill of Rights*.

[10]The cost of filing IRS Form 8546 "Claim for Reimbursement of Bank Charges Incurred Due to Erroneous Service Levy" usually outweighs the cost of bank charges.

[11]IRS intimidation is but one of several kinds of intimidating discourse that can be profitably studied for positive and negative results. This study is part of an ongoing work, *The Rhetoric of Intimidation*.

WORKS CITED

Bitzer, Lloyd F. "The Rhetorical Situation." *Philosophy and Rhetoric* 1 (1968): 1–14.

Brown, Gillian, and George Yule. *Discourse Analysis.* 1983. Cambridge: Cambridge UP, 1986.

Brusaw, Charles T., Gerald J. Alred, and Walter E. Oliu. *The Business Writer's Handbook.* 3rd ed. New York: St. Martin's, 1987.

"Collection Agencies." *Journal of Accountancy* April 1988: 127.

"Congress Responds to 'Seizure Fever.'" *Practical Accountant Alert* [sample issue] 1987: 3.

Consigny, Scott. "Rhetoric and Its Situations." *Philosophy and Rhetoric* 7 (1974): 175–186.

Explanation of Technical and Miscellaneous Revenue Act of 1988 including Taxpayer Bill of Rights. Chicago: Commerce Clearing House, 1988.

Fillmore, Charles J., and Paul Kay. "Text Semantic Analysis of Reading Comprehension Texts." *Final Report to the National Institute of Education.* Berkeley: U of California Institute of Human Learning, 1983.

"For IRS Emergencies Dial (Form) '911,'" *Client's Monthly Alert* June 1989: 1.

General Accounting Office. "GAO Reports Relating to the IRS—1988 to Date." "Tax Administration: IRS' Service Centers Need to Improve Handling of Taxpayer Correspondence" GGD–88–101: 2–3; "Tax Administration: Accessibility, Timeliness, and Accuracy of IRS Telephone Assistance Program" GGD–88–13: 17–18. Gaithersburg: U.S. General Accounting Office, Aug. 22, 1988.

Grant–Davie, Keith A. "Class Policies and Procedures." Junior Writing course packet [U Maryland]. n.p., Fall 1986: 1.

Holzinger, Albert G. "Making the IRS Accountable." *The Nation's Business* December 1987: 38.

Horowitz, Rick. "A Friendly Audit." *The Sun Magazine* April 10, 1988: 37–38.

"IRS Collects on Many 'Uncollectible' Accounts." *The Practical Accountant* September 1987: 48.

Lesikar, Raymond V. *Business Communication: Theory and Application.* Homewood, Ill.: Irwin, 1968.

McKenzie, Robert E. "Strategies for Dealing with the IRS Collection Division." *The Practical Accountant* Feb. 1988: 47–58.

"Memo Reveals Agents Pressured to Meet Collection Targets." *The Practical Accountant* Sept. 1987: 46.

"Murder on the IRS Express?" *The Practical Accountant Alert* April 15, 1988: 1.

"New IRS Policy Rectifies Erroneous Bank Account Levies." *Journal of Accountancy* Aug. 1986: 16.

The Compact Edition of the Oxford English Dictionary. Oxford: Oxford UP, 1971. Vol. 1, 1470.

Pryor, David. "Redraft of S. 604 [Senate Bill], Taxpayer's Bill of Rights." n.p., 1988: 1–6.

Sennett, Richard. *Authority.* New York: Knopf, 1980.

Tannen, D. "What's in a Frame? Surface Evidence for Underlying Expectations." *New Directions in Discourse Processing.* R. O. Freedle, ed. Norwood: Ablex, 1979.

"Task Force Recommends Ways to Close Tax Gap." *Journal of Accountancy* July 1987: 66.

"Ultimate Audit." *LS Newsletter* [Linton, Shafer and Company P.A.] Winter 1988: 1–4.

Willens, Robert. "The Technical Corrections Act: What Corporations Should Know Now." *Journal of Accountancy* July 1988: 46–48.

Winning Strategies, Inc. "Do *You* Trust the IRS?" Advertisement for IRS–*Interst–Calc* software. *The Practical Accountant* March 1988: 51.

Index

McKeown, K. R., 264, 266, 268, 274

Meaning, 238, 241, 243, 248, 279; networks of, 301; overdetermination of, 248; reader's creation of, 252, 280, 292; revision of, 288; units of, 247-48

Memory, 179-81, 257, 259, 260, 268, 271, 273

Methodology, 205, 220, 234, 253, 298, 304, 314, 331, 339

Meyer, B., 280

Michaels, Sarah, 64

Mielke, Robert, 21

Miller, A. B., 378

Miller, Carolyn R., 316, 327, 328, 398

Miller, Richard, 319

Miller, Thomas, 309

Minority dialects, 66, 82

Mitchell, Ruth, 188

Models: developmental, 206; for professional writing 142-46; of audience, 260, 267, 269, 273, 274, 275; of the writing process, 178, 181, 261, 262, 264, 266, 274; Toulmin, 253

Modern Language Association, 297, 335; *Style Manual,* 333-35, 345-46, 347

Mohanty, Chandra Talpade, 19

Montrose, Louis A., 301, 307-8

Moore, William J., 206

Moral reasoning, 217-18

Morgan, Bob, 17, 18, 21

Morgan, K. I., 259, 274

Morris, Adelaide, 13

Morris, Elizabeth Woodridge, 26

Mulderig, Gerald, 26

Murray, D. M., 280

Muth, Denise, 216

Myers, Greg, 22

Narration, 382-400

Narrative, 244, 252; and orality-literacy theory, 52-53, 55-56; discourse, 72; schemata, 181; structure, 306; women's, 12-13

Narrative romance, 353-55, 382-400

Needham, Lawrence, 3-4, 5, 6

Newell, A., 195

New historicism, 297-98, 299-316

Newkirk, T., 279

Newton, Judith, 20

Nonacademic writing, 141, 299, 300, 304, 308, 309, 315, 318

Norman, Donald A., 179

Normann, Richard, 311

Novice: readers, 231, 233; writers, 181, 260, 261-62

Nystrand, M., 259

Odell, Lee, 141, 304, 309

Ohmann, R., 150, 151, 167

Olsen, T., 167

Olson, G. M., 281

Olson, P., 150, 151, 167

Ong, Walter, 44-46, 51-56, 58

Orality, 1; and cognition, 43-44, 50-51; assumptions about, 43-44, 56-58. *See also* Orality-literacy theory

Orality-literacy theory, 43; and intellectual evolution, 44-46; and psychology, 51, 54-55; critiques of, 44; versus ethnography, 49

Oratory, 353, 357-78, 360, 363, 365-66, 375

O'Reilley, Mary Rose, 21

Osborn, Susan, 16

Overing, Gillian R., 6, 8, 22, 167

Pagels, Heinz R., 400

Paine, Thomas, 353-56, 358, 366-73, 374, 376, 377

Paradis, James, 309, 319

Patent, Dorothy Hinshaw, 237

Pathos, 353-56, 357, 358-66, 368, 373-79, 417

Pearsall, Thomas E., 397

Pechter, Edward, 302

Pedagogy, 292, 300, 309, 313, 419; developmental/constructionist, 220; feminist, 1, 6-16, 18, 21; process, 127, 176, 233, 260-64, 274

Peer review, 125, 129, 197, 219, 232, 280

Perelman, Chaim, 358, 374-76, 400

Periphrasis, 233

Perkins, D. N., 130

Perl, Sondra, 177

Perry, William, 202, 204, 213